EARLY MUSIC HISTORY 24

STUDIES IN MEDIEVAL
AND
EARLY MODERN MUSIC

Edited by
IAIN FENLON
Fellow of King's College, Cambridge

CAMBRIDGE UNIVERSITY PRESS
Cambridge, New York, Melbourne, Madrid, Cape Town, Singapore, São Paulo, Delhi

Cambridge University Press
The Edinburgh Building, Cambridge CB2 8RU, UK

Published in the United States of America by Cambridge University Press, New York

www.cambridge.org
Information on this title: www.cambridge.org/9780521104494

© Cambridge University Press 2005

This publication is in copyright. Subject to statutory exception
and to the provisions of relevant collective licensing agreements,
no reproduction of any part may take place without the written
permission of Cambridge University Press.

First published 2005
This digitally printed version 2009

A catalogue record for this publication is available from the British Library

ISBN 978-0-521-86144-1 hardback
ISBN 978-0-521-10449-4 paperback

Subscriptions and further information
for *Early Music History* can be
found at www.journals.cambridge.org/jid_EMH

CONTENTS

	Page
TIMOTHY J. DICKEY (University of Iowa) Rethinking the Siena choirbook: a new date and implications for its musical contents	1
MARY E. FRANDSEN (University of Notre Dame) *Eunuchi conjugium*: the marriage of a castrato in early modern Germany	53
JAMES GRIER (University of Western Ontario) The musical autographs of Adémar de Chabannes (989–1034)	125
YOSSI MAUREY (University of Chicago) A courtly lover and an earthly knight turned soldiers of Christ in Machaut's motet 5	169
LAURIE STRAS (University of Southampton) 'Al gioco si conosce il galantuomo': artifice, humour and play in the *Enigmi musicali* of Don Lodovico Agostini	213

EDITORIAL BOARD

WULF ARLT, University of Basel
MARGARET BENT, All Souls College, Oxford
LORENZO BIANCONI, University of Bologna
BONNIE J. BLACKBURN, University of Oxford
JUAN-JOSÉ CARRERAS, University of Zaragoza
DAVID FALLOWS, University of Manchester
F. ALBERTO GALLO, University of Bologna
JAMES HAAR, University of North Carolina at Chapel Hill
KENNETH LEVY, Princeton University
LEWIS LOCKWOOD, Harvard University
PATRICK MACEY, Eastman School of Music
ANTHONY NEWCOMB, University of California at Berkeley
EDWARD ROESNER, New York University
H. COLIN SLIM, University of California at Irvine
REINHARD STROHM, University of Oxford
ANDREW WATHEY, Royal Holloway, University of London

Timothy J. Dickey

RETHINKING THE SIENA CHOIRBOOK: A NEW DATE AND IMPLICATIONS FOR ITS MUSICAL CONTENTS

A 1481 date for the manuscript Siena, Biblioteca Comunale degli Intronati, MS K. 1. 2 (hereafter **Si**), which contains almost ninety pieces of late fifteenth-century liturgical polyphony including works of Obrecht, Isaac and Mouton, has rested uneasily upon an argument from Sienese copying records.[1] A fresh codicological analysis of this important source, including evidence of matching 'twin' watermark pairs in datable Tuscan archival documents, has yielded a new date and a new narrative for its compilation. The main corpus, in fact, is decades later than the fragmentary appendix containing works of Dufay and Josquin. The redating presented here has manifold implications for some of the most important

> This study expands on a paper delivered at the Annual Meeting of the American Musicological Society, Columbus, Ohio, 3 November 2002, and earlier as part of the Duke University Music Department Lecture Series, 15 October 2002. My deepest thanks go to Jennifer Hambrick, Thomas Brothers, Alexander Silbiger and John Nádas for their patient assistance and stimulating comments during all stages of its preparation, to Bonnie J. Blackburn, Frank D'Accone and Jeffrey Dean for their commentary on earlier versions, and to Joshua Rifkin for his helpful comments during the course of the Fall 2003 Josquin seminar at the University of North Carolina at Chapel Hill. Watermark photographs are courtesy of the Biblioteca Comunale degli Intronati, Siena (Figures 1 and 2), and Foto Testi (Figures 2 and 5). All rights reserved.
> Manuscript sigla follow the *Census-Catalogue of Manuscript Sources of Polyphonic Music, 1400–1550*, 5 vols., compiled by the University of Illinois Musicological Archives for Renaissance Manuscript Studies (Renaissance Studies, 1; Stuttgart, 1979–88).
>
> [1] On this manuscript see principally L. Illari, *La biblioteca pubblica di Siena*, v (Siena, 1846), p. 71; A. Ziino, 'Appunti su una nuova fonte di musica polifonica intorno al 1500', *Nuova Rivista Musicale Italiana*, 10 (1976), pp. 437–41; F. D'Accone, 'A Late 15th-Century Sienese Sacred Repertory: Ms. K. 1. 2 of the Biblioteca Comunale, Siena', *Musica Disciplina*, 37 (1983), pp. 121–70. See also J. P. Karr, 'The Psalms of Siena Ms. K. 1. 2: Evidence of the Origins of Falsobordone' (Ph.D. diss., Univ. of Kentucky, 1997); T. Dickey, 'Reading the Siena Choirbook: A Re-Appraisal of the Dating, Musical Repertories, and Marian Performance Context of the Manuscript Siena, Biblioteca degli Intronati, MS K. 1. 2' (Ph.D. diss., Duke University, 2003). Frank D'Accone's views on the manuscript are elaborated further in his introduction to the published facsimile: Renaissance Music in Facsimile, 17, ed. F. D'Accone (New York, 1986), and in *The Civic Muse: Music and Musicians in Siena during the Middle Ages and the Renaissance* (Chicago, 1997), pp. 237–41.

1

composers of the late fifteenth century, and for peninsular patterns of musical transmission. A secure early date for the appendix copy of Josquin's *Missa L'ami baudichon*, for instance, enables a reassessment of that piece's transmission to sources as far away as Poland and Bohemia in the light of recent discoveries in Josquin's biography. My new date for Josquin's mass also confirms a case of Josquin emulation within another, anonymous mass in **Si**. The new dating further enables a reassessment of ModE M.1.13's authority as a source for one of Johannes Martini's masses, and the identification of a heretofore unknown local Sienese composer. Finally, the new narrative for the Siena choirbook may reveal Florence as a link in the transmission of repertory from Milan and Ferrara to Siena.

Despite the size (some 216 paper folios) and importance of the manuscript, however, the scholarly community has failed to agree on its date. The volume was first simply described as a *Liber Choralis – Sec. XVI* by Lorenzo Illari in the nineteenth century.[2] Agostino Ziino 'rediscovered' the manuscript in 1976, and a fortuitous chance brought Frank D'Accone's attention it shortly thereafter.[3] Both scholars briefly discussed one watermark with reference to Briquet's catalogue.[4] Ziino suggested within Briquet's broad guidelines that the main body of the manuscript might date *c*. 1495–1524, and that the three gatherings at the end of the manuscript would represent an earlier collection of polyphony. Though Ziino's instinctive reactions were both correct, neither has been taken up in any systematic manner. Frank D'Accone identified the main corpus of **Si** instead with two volumes of 'canto figurato di nota grossa' ('polyphonic music in large notes'), one each of masses and Vespers music; the two volumes appear in the Cathedral library's inventory lists during the 1480s.[5] He then linked these same inventory records

---

[2] Illari, *Biblioteca pubblica*.
[3] Ziino, 'Appunti'; D'Accone, 'Late 15th-Century'.
[4] Ziino cites similarities to Briquet's numbers 5922, 5920 and 5923, in 'Appunti', p. 437; see also D'Accone, 'Late 15th-Century', p. 122; D'Accone, *Civic Muse*, p. 237, n. 48. Ziino does not actually assert that what I have termed Scala 2 is the only watermark in the central part of the manuscript, only that it is found on 'the greater part' of its pages. Again, the subtleties of his observations have been ignored.
[5] Some confusion exists in the literature concerning the first archival reference to the two volumes. D'Accone in 'Late 15th-Century', pp. 124 and 127–8, refers to vol. 867 of the Archivio dell'Opera Metropolitana di Siena (hereafter AOMS) and dates it 1485; in *Civic Muse*, p. 236, he cites the same inventory, but uses the enumeration from Stefano Moscadelli's unpublished inventory (as vol. 1492) and amends the date to *c*. 1488. My own research in the

to 1481 payments made to one Matteo Ghai Francioso, 'per ... scripttura di libri di canto figurato' ('for the writing of books of polyphony').[6] Rob Wegman questioned D'Accone's date, as a 1481 copy in **Si** would force an early *terminus ante quem* for Obrecht's *Missa Beata viscera*.[7] D'Accone's cautious 1997 response noted the problematic nature of any dating by Briquet's catalogue alone, and reiterated his association of **Si**'s main corpus with the 1481 archival documents.[8]

In this study, I will present systematic watermark evidence that divides the manuscript into two distinct temporal layers, and will finally resolve the notices in Cathedral inventories and archival documents. The Appendix provides an overview of the manuscript's structure and indicates the boundaries between its two layers. Briefly, the codicological evidence shows that one layer of **Si** does in fact coincide with the 1481 copying records. This layer, however, only consists of three fragmentary gatherings now at the end of the volume; D'Accone had guessed copying dates for this layer of 1508 or 1521.[9] Incontrovertible paper evidence for a 1481 first-layer date now makes this section of **Si** one of the earliest sources for the pieces by Josquin, Basiron and Martini found on its pages. We must now reconsider the authority of the Sienese readings in these first-layer pieces, with special emphasis on Josquin's *Missa L'ami baudichon* and Martini's *Missa Dio te salvi Gotterello*.

The second layer, the current gatherings I–XXV, originally had been a single independent volume dating from *c.* 1490–1506. It most likely dates from the more specific period 1502–4. D'Accone had read this layer as a late binding together, some time after 1545, of a 1481 Vespers volume beginning *Dixit dominus* and a mass volume beginning *Asperges me*; his interpretation required the

---

Archivio di Stato di Siena (hereafter ASS) has uncovered an identical description of the two books in a completely different inventory dated 1482 (ASS, Opera Metropolitana 27, nos. 126–7).

[6] D'Accone, 'Late 15th-Century', pp. 124, 127–8; *Civic Muse*, pp. 235–6.
[7] R. Wegman, *Born for the Muses: The Life and Masses of Jacob Obrecht* (Oxford, 1994), p. 100, n. 12; Wegman also cites Jeffrey Dean's observation that the principal copyist of **Si**'s main corpus exhibits numerous Italian scribal characteristics, whereas Matteo Ghai was French.
[8] D'Accone, *Civic Muse*, p. 237, n. 48. See also J. Rifkin, 'Munich, Milan, and a Marian Motet: Dating Josquin's *Ave Maria . . . virgo serena*', *Journal of the American Musicological Society*, 56 (2003), pp. 239–350, at p. 251, n. 22 and p. 327, n. 189. I am grateful to Mr Rifkin for providing me with a copy of his paper prior to publication.
[9] D'Accone, 'Late 15th-Century', p. 142.

transposition of gathering XXV to its current position at the end of the layer.[10] Instead, we will see that the two principal scribes of **Si**'s second layer began and executed a single, coherent volume containing generically organised psalms, hymns, Magnificats, motets, and mass music. In addition to presenting a more reasonable date for the music of Isaac, Compère, Weerbeke, Mouton and Obrecht found within this layer, this new second-layer date gives tantalising clues to the lost sacred repertories of Florence.[11] The current binding of this layer with the remains of Ghai's 1481 first-layer work may date from the early sixteenth century; the evidence for both layers' dates must begin with an examination of the datable papers comprising them.

As noted above, both Ziino and D'Accone mentioned a single watermark found on the bulk of **Si**'s pages. Neither scholar, however, grappled with the presence of fully three watermarks within **Si**. These are reproduced in Figure 1: the first-layer papers at the end of the manuscript all use a ladder mark and its twin (which I designate *Scala* 1), while the second layer contains a later type of ladder paper (*Scala* 2) and one gathering of crown paper (*Corona*).[12] Together, these three watermarks yield foundational evidence for both the date and the local provenance of the two layers of **Si**.

Exact and datable concordances for the paper type of **Si**'s final gatherings that I have identified in Tuscan archives confirm the

---

[10] This hypothesis was necessitated by the physical description of the inventoried music books.

[11] Alejandro Planchart has attempted to reconstruct some of this repertory; 'Northern Repertories in Florence in the Fifteenth Century', in P. Gargiulo (ed.), *La musica a Firenze al tempo di Lorenzo il Magnifico* (Florence, 1993), pp. 101–12. His findings must be read, of course, in the light of later research into the provenance of VatS 14 and 51, which removes these sources from the Florentine orbit. See below, n. 101.

[12] Allan Stevenson coined the term 'twin' to account for the fact that rag-paper watermarks made by hand appear in pairs of related forms. This pairing results from the practice of early modern papermakers, who used two paper moulds (crafted as a pair) in alternation. A. Stevenson, 'Watermarks are Twins', *Studies in Bibliography*, 4 (1951–2), pp. 57–91; see also id., 'Paper as Bibliographic Evidence', *The Library*, 5th ser., 17/3 (Sept. 1962), pp. 197–212; id., *The Problem of the Missale Speciale* (London, 1967); S. Spector (ed.). *Essays in Paper Analysis* (Washington, DC, 1987). For recent applications of this kind of post-Briquet methodology to the dating of music manuscripts, see P. Wright, 'Johannes Wiser's Paper and the Copying of his Manuscripts', in id. (ed.), *I codici musicali Trentini: Nuove scoperte e nuovi orientamenti della ricerca (The Trent Codices: Trento 24 Sept. 1994)* (Trento, 1996), pp. 31–53; id., 'Paper Evidence and the Dating of Trent 91', *Music & Letters*, 76 (1995), pp. 487–508; id., 'Watermarks and Musicology: The Genesis of Johannes Wiser's Collection', *Early Music History*, 22 (2003), pp. 247–332. **Si**'s *Scala* 1 watermark somewhat resembles Briquet no. 5911.

Rethinking the Siena choirbook

FIRST LAYER (1481)
Scala 1 and twin:

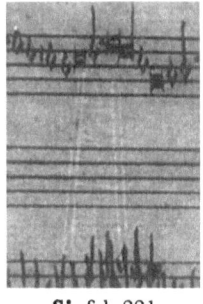

Si, fol. 221   **Si**, fol. 214

SECOND LAYER (*c.* 1490–1506; 1502–4?)
Scala 2 and twin:

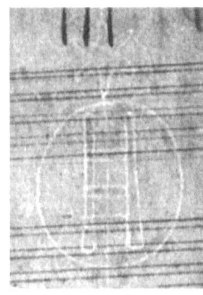 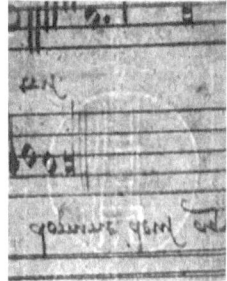

Si, fol. 144ᵛ   **Si**, fol. 159ᵛ

Corona and twin (1490s/1500s)

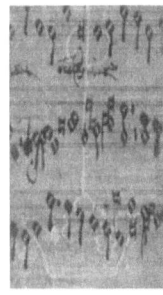 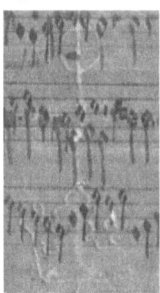

Si, fol. 204   **Si**, fol. 201ᵛ

Figure 1 The watermarks of **Si**

1481 date for the manuscript's first layer. Paper with the four-rung ladder (see Figure 1) was very popular with Sienese and Florentine institutional clients, and the archives preserve a large number of similar papers. Datable papers with watermarks of a four-rung ladder survive from 1475 to 1488 in *formato reale*, the size of **Si**'s paper; in medium-format paper, the span is from 1473 to 1492 (see the tabulation of all these surviving papers in Table 1). Small but significant variants between the ladder images – placement and tilt of rungs, behaviour of chain lines, etc. – allow the easy identification of concordant paper types. Both the principal mark of **Si**'s first layer and its twin have some telling idiosyncrasies: bent rungs, bulging posts and a hook in the centre chain line. The same pair of idiosyncratic watermarks appears on papers I have located in five datable Sienese archival sources; Table 1 indicates these five paper sources in boldface, and Figure 2 graphically illustrates one set of the matching watermarks. With one exception, the matching papers were all used in the last half of 1481 and the first two months of 1482. One of this pair of paper moulds (at the same temporal state) produced a single sheet in a later incunable. It is Siena, Biblioteca Comunale degli Intronati O.II.10 (IGI no. 7282): Paulus de Castro, *Lectura super sexto libro Codicis*.[13] It was printed in Siena by Enrico da Colonia e compagnia on 12 KL. aug. (21 July) 1484. This particular paper – a single bifolium (page x2) in Enrico's print run – was almost certainly not made in 1484, but rather was leftover stock from a previous paper purchase. The late date of this concordance thus does not detract from a 1481 paper date for the first layer of **Si**.[14]

A 1481 paper date for the first layer accords well with both its contents and the payment records D'Accone published. One 'Matteo Ghai francioso' copied two books of polyphony for Siena Cathedral around March and July of 1481.[15] The first layer of **Si** may today preserve the only surviving remnants of Ghai's work.[16] I will show later that Ghai's two volumes were soon bound together; an earlier foliation within **Si**'s first layer shows that its gatherings

---

[13] IGI is the *Indice generale degli incunaboli delle biblioteche d'Italia*, ed. Teresa Maria Guarnaschelli (Rome, 1943–).

[14] See A. Stevenson, 'Paper as Bibliographic Evidence', p. 202. He offers a similar example of a solitary sheet with a Pot watermark (made in 1598) which appears in the second quarto edition of *Hamlet* in 1604–5.

[15] D'Accone, 'Late 15th-Century', pp. 121–70. See also *Civic Muse*, pp. 237–41.

[16] The fragmentary remains of the first layer's three gatherings, and the large number of scribes whose work survives on their pages, make a specific identification of Ghai's hand very difficult. The most likely candidate, however, seems to be the elegant French hand that produced the Sienese copy of Basiron's *Missa de Franza* (current fols. 208–9).

Table 1 *Watermark concordances for Scala 1 in the Sienese archives*

Year	Large format	Small format
1473		Podestà papers by 1473 use small thin 4-rung
1475	ASS, Sped 524 (1/75)	
1476	ASS, Consiglio Generale 237 (1/76)	ASMF, Delib 5 (1/76)
1478		ASMF, E/U 13; 14 (1478–9)
1481		**ASS, Sped 525*** (late 1481) At least by 1481, Concistoro uses small 4-rung
1482	**ASS, CG 239 (1/82)** AOMS, D/C 718 (5/82?)	**ASS, Sped 527** (3/82) ASS, Sped 526 (5/82, different) **ASS, Bicch 337** (1/82) ASS, Sped 867 (5/82, different) 9/10/81: Balìa 26 begins using 4-rung
1483		**BCIS, O.II.10** (8/84, *terminus*)
1484		Gabella, Consiglio Generale use smaller 4-rung
1485	ASS, CG 240 (1/85)	ASS, Bicch 339 (1/85) (mixed with 3-rung)
1486		AOMS, Censi 160 (1486, aged forms)
1488		ASS, Sped 25 (3/88: 3-rung)
1492		Last forms in Concistoro, Podestà; first 3-rung, 3-rung with star

*Boldface = paper types concordant with **Si**
Sources:
AOMS = Archivio dell' Opera Metropolitana, Siena
ASMF = Archivio di Santa Maria del Fiore, Florence
ASS = Archivio di Stato, Siena
BCIS = Biblioteca Comunale degli Intronati, Siena
Sped = Ospedale Santa Maria della Scala, Siena

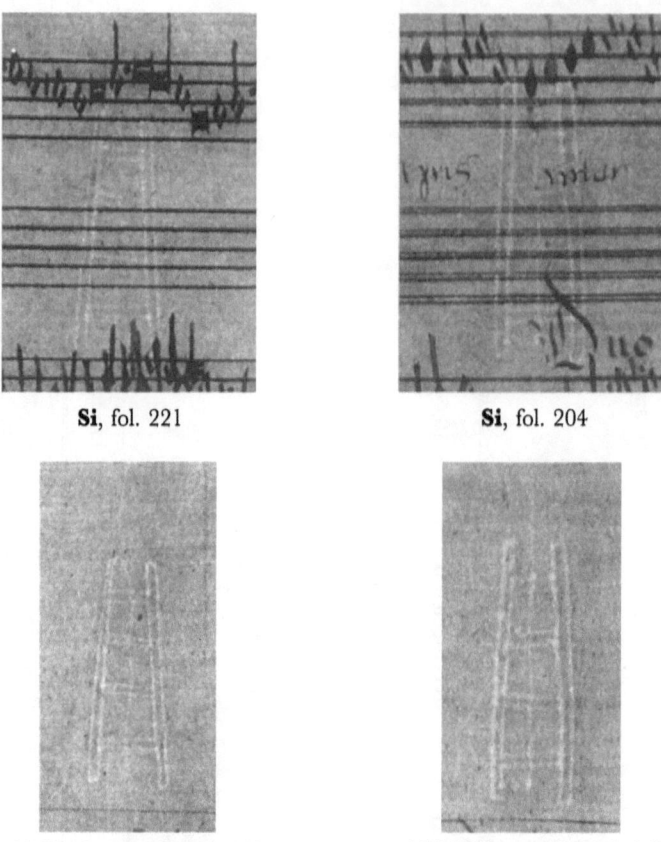

Figure 2 The *Scala* 1 watermark and concordances

indeed occupied different locations within a single large book. A 1481 date for the first layer also makes sense in the light of its earlier repertory, which includes masses of Martini, Basiron, Dufay and the *Missa L'ami baudichon*.[17]

---

[17] Beyond the added text underlay in an obviously later text hand, Joshua Rifkin has questioned whether both openings of Josquin's Gloria (fols. 212ᵛ–214) were copied by the same music hand; 'Munich, Milan', p. 327, n. 189. It is true that the *custodes* on the two openings adopt somewhat different forms, but I would argue that every other aspect of the notation – noteheads, c.o.p. ligatures, clefs, *coronae* and (pace Rikfin) text rubrics – are congruent throughout both openings. Rifkin himself demonstrates ('Munich, Milan', pp. 294–307) how the scribe of MunBS 3154 changed *custos* styles. There exists, furthermore, a more famous case where one scribe not only changed his *custodes* over time, but also allowed different forms to coexist in the same opening: 'Scribe B' of the Netherlands Court Complex seems to have

Rethinking the Siena Choirbook

The paper types in the rest of **Si**, on the other hand, indicate a second layer with a later date. Though I have found no exact match for the principal second-layer watermark and its twin, extant archival papers document patterns in the Tuscan use of related watermarks, as they did for the first-layer *Scala* 1 paper. These patterns enable us to date the second layer even in the absence of exact matches. The paper in the second layer almost certainly came from the same mill in the Tuscan town of Colle di Val d'Elsa which produced the *Scala* 1 paper for the first layer of **Si**. By the late fifteenth century, there were nearly twenty paper mills in Colle's lower districts, and the riverfront town held a virtual monopoly on paper supply to both Siena and Florence.[18]

Despite the wealth of paper evidence that Colle's paper-making industry has left in Tuscan archives, there has been little published documentation of Collegiane watermarks. Francesco Dini was able to document only two Collegiane watermarks. He noted that paper in possession of the brothers Lippo (owners of the two mills known as *Le due Botroni*) bore the signs of a hart and an anvil in the 1427

---

changed from a straight check-like *custos* to one ending in a loop, according to both Rifkin and Flynn Warmington; both scholars are cited by Fabrice Fitch in his Introduction to *Choirbook for Philip and Juana of Castile, c.1504–06: Brussel, Koninklijke Bibliotheek, MS. 9126*, ed. Fabrice Fitch (Peer, 2000), p. 7. Manuscripts copied by this scribe, even those in which one form of the *custos* dominates (BrusBR 9126 and VatC 234), show both forms concurrently.

Rifkin goes on to suggest that the Martini mass copied on the remaining openings of the same gathering in **Si** (fols. 214^v–221^v) are the work of his 'third' Josquin scribe. Rifkin's third scribe, however, only added text to Josquin's and Martini's masses; there is no reason to associate this scribe with the notation of the Martini mass. Rather, the minor (and apparently unprofessional) scribe of this text was most likely a Cathedral singer. Several other pieces in this section of the manuscript preserve accidental inflections and dots of division in triple-metre passages which most likely were performers' clarifications.

[18] C. Bastiononi, personal communication to the author, 19 September 2001. See also Bastiononi, *Impressum Senis: Storie di tipografia, incunaboli e librai* (Siena, 1988); id., 'Le cartiere di Colle Val d'Elsa e i loro segni nella prima metà del secolo XIV', in S. Cavaciocchi (ed.), *Produzione e commercio della carta e del libro secc. XIII–XVIII* (Prato, 1992), pp. 221–32; F. Dini, 'Le cartiere in Colle di Valdelsa', in *Carta e cartiere a Colle: Miscellanea di studi raccolti a cura del comitato scientifico per l'allestimento del Museo* (Florence, 1982; reprint of article of 30 March 1902 in *Bulletino Senese per la Storia Patria*), pp. 67–120; C. Magnani, 'Antiche cartiere toscane', *Pistoia: Periodico di informazione della Camera di Commercio, Industria, e Agricoltura di Pistoia*, 1 (1964), pp. 21–33; R. Sabbatini, 'La produzione della carta dal XIII al XVI secoli: Strutture, tecniche, maestri cartai', in *Tecnica e società nell'Italia dei secoli XII–XVI [Pistoia, 29–31 Ott. 1984]* (Pistoia, 1987), pp. 37–58. Oretta Muzzi has recently noted that the paper-making industry in Colle was still expanding into new mills as late as 1517; 'The Social Classes of Colle Valdelsa and the Formation of the Dominion (Fourteenth–Sixteenth Centuries)', in W. J. Connell and A. Zorzi (eds.), *Florentine Tuscany: Structures and Practices of Power* (Cambridge, 2000), pp. 264–92, at p. 268, n. 14. A museum dedicated to the Collegiane paper-making industry was launched in 1982, but never progressed beyond designation of a site within one of the old mills.

Timothy J. Dickey

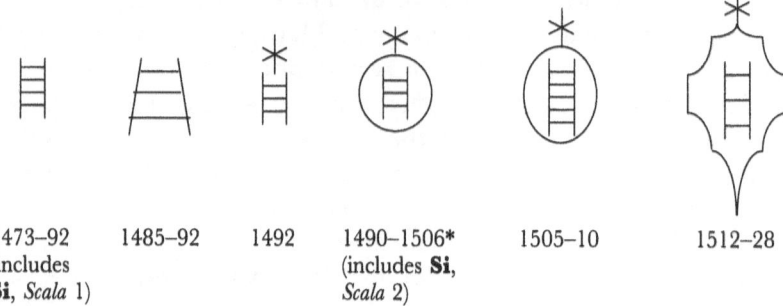

| 1473–92 (includes **Si**, *Scala* 1) | 1485–92 | 1492 | 1490–1506* (includes **Si**, *Scala* 2) | 1505–10 | 1512–28 |

*With gaps in surviving papers: 1493–4, 1496–9, 1502–4.

Figure 3 Development over time of the Ladder watermarks on large-format papers from Colle di Val d'Elsa

Catasto (tax inventory).[19] Both signs still appear in papers surviving from Siena and Florence at the end of the century. In the only significant expansion of Dini's study, Curzio Bastiononi documented a few more watermarks: the flower for the mill known as *Il Nespolo*, a G/P monogram for paper made by the two brothers Goro di Pesuccio and the popular ladder of four rungs (*Scala* 1).[20] The ladder was one of a series of Collegiane papers used in the first printing shop to operate in Siena, starting in 1484. My own intensive study of Tuscan paper indicates that a single mill would often use a single watermark image as a trademark, with gradual elaboration upon it over time.

Figure 3 traces a pertinent example of this development, with its implications for paper dates. The trademark Collegiane ladder watermarks – among them the *Scala* 1 of **Si**'s first layer – lose a rung over time, then add a star and a circle to become the type of *Scala* 2. Paper with this type of watermark first appears in a single gathering of a Sienese Cathedral account book; the paper must have been in production by 16 March 1490 [1489 old style], the date of the first entry copied onto the gathering (see the list of surviving *Scala* 2 papers in Table 2).[21] Related watermarks survive on paper with dates in the 1490s, around 1500 and then again around 1505.

[19] Dini, 'Le cartiere di Colle', pp. 101–2.
[20] Bastiononi, *Impressum Senis*, pp. 27–9.
[21] The source is fols. 496–527ᵛ of AOMS 718, *Debitori/Creditori 1482–1527*. Similarly, the *Scala* 2 type first appears on smaller-format paper on 20 March of the same year; the source is a piece of legal correspondence to the office of the Sienese Podestà, in ASS, Podestà 338. The

The watermark's development both before and after the *Scala* 2 stage solidifies its dating window. A three-rung ladder appears as early as 1485 and a three-rung ladder with star briefly in 1492; a later development of this trademark – five-rung ladder in a circle – survives from as early as 1505. This last appears uniquely as a *single* mould paired with a single aged mould of *Scala* 2. From this we may infer a phasing out of *Scala* 2 around 1505, as only one-half of an aged mould pair remains in use. The next complete development, a three-rung ladder in a filigreed shield with star, appears in 1512 and dominates the ladder paper types during the following couple of decades.

The date of **Si**'s second-layer paper thus clearly falls within a documentable window: 1490–1506. Since no surviving paper matches that of **Si**, I further propose that the date of **Si**'s *Scala* 2 paper falls within one of the gaps between surviving related papers. Three such gaps exist. The volumes for 1493 and 1494 are missing, for instance, from several Sienese archival series that use the mainstream Collegiane paper types: Biccherna registers and *Entrata/Uscita* volumes for the Sienese Hospital Santa Maria della Scala (see Table 2). The temporal gap in the archives coincides with an increase in transient chapel singers (who could have conveyed new repertory to Siena),[22] and the Cathedral's *Entrata/Uscita* volumes for 1494–1500, which might have held the copying records for a new volume of polyphony in these years, also do not survive. However, specific changes in the Collegiane paper-making moulds make it highly unlikely that **Si**'s *Scala* 2 paper dates from the archival gap 1493–4. The mould-smiths made several specific and comparatively large changes around 1493: the *Scala* 2 watermarks shift to the opposite side of the paper mould, the tiny stars nearly double in size and the circles become proportionally larger.[23] None of the marks surviving from around 1493 is congruent with the form and proportions of the mark in **Si**, and it is difficult to hypothesise a completely different pair of moulds inserted at this time.

Two further gaps in the surviving papers exist starting in 1496 and in 1502. Once again both paper records and music-copying

---

Sienese new year began on the 25th of March (the Feast of the Annunciation); I have adjusted all dates in the following to conform to modern style.
[22] D'Accone, *Civic Muse*, pp. 257–8.
[23] See Dickey, 'Reading', p. 22.

Table 2 Watermark concordances for Scala 2 in the Sienese archives

Year	Large format	Small format
1484		Undated appendix to Podestà 328; 4/84
1490	AOMS, D/C 715 (by 3/16/90) (single gathering) =ASS, Sped 876* (3/92)	First appearance in Podestà 338: 3/29/90
1492		
1493	ASS, Bicch 346 (1/92, gap follows)	Concistoro 760 begins form: 5/93 Podestà new form, 16 times, 1493–6 Concistoro 770, 774
1495	ASS, CG 241 (3/95)	
1496	=AOMS, D/C 718 (by early 1496) (two gatherings)	
1497		Podestà, 5 appearances, 1497–1500
1499		Concistoro 798
1500	ASS, Sped 880 (5/00)	AAS, Mensa 4265 (1500)
1501	ASMF, E/U 51 (7/01)	

Table 2 Continued

Year	Large format		Small format
1502			AAS, Cause 5622: 1502, single sheet
1503			Gabella 824: 1/03 =AOM S, E/U 460–2; 461: '03/04; '05/06
1504			Balìa 44 n.31: 1/04, single sheet
1505	ASS, Bicch 351 (1/05)	[AOMS, E/U 461: 5-rung in circle]	
1506	=? ASS, Sped 886 (5/06)		AOMS, E/U 462; 463: 1506–18
	ASMF, S. Giov. Censi 1 ('06, aged)	[ASF, Conv.102 79 5-rung, '07] [ASMF, E/U 67: 5-rung in circle, '10]	
		[Filigreed form in ASS, CG 241 '12; ASS, Conv. 1039 '26 AOMS, D/C 715 '28]	

* '=' indicates paper concordance with entry above
Sources:
AAS = Archivio Archivescovile di Siena
AOMS = Archivio dell' Opera Metropolitana, Siena
ASF = Archivio di Stato, Florence
ASMF = Archivio di Santa Maria del Fiore, Florence
ASS = Archivio di Stato, Siena

records from the wide temporal gap of 1496–9 are lacking. 1496, however, seems an unlikely date for a new book commission, as it falls in the political and economic instability that followed the French invasion of Italy (the effects were still quite fresh: Savonarola held power in Florence in 1494–7). Concessions by the radical Noveschi regime to the Popolari party in Siena only barely mitigated the political instability there, which also included a new military campaign against Florence in Montepulciano, Sienese involvement in the war between Florence and Venice, and the rising despotism of Pandolfo Petrucci that led to the July 1500 murder of his father-in-law.[24] Most Cathedral records from this time are lacking (itself a sign of disorganisation) and the choir may have retained only three adult singers during these years.[25] Performance of some music from **Si**'s second layer would thus be impossible during this period, as the music of this layer requires as many as five parts. In the absence of exact watermark matches, then, I argue that the gap between 1502 and 1504 remains the most likely date for the *Scala* 2 paper of **Si**'s second layer.

Furthermore, it is highly unlikely that any subsequent copying record could pertain to **Si**. After 1484, the next surviving record of Cathedral payment for the copying of polyphony lists L.30 paid to Frate Giovanni Pagliarini on 19 May 1509; the record specifies that he copied '7 Masses and other Psalms' on *fogli reali* paper for the Opera.[26] **Si** almost certainly cannot fit both the 1509 copying record and the vestigial foliation within the second-layer collection of masses.[27] Very soon before the 1509 record, furthermore, on 8

---

[24] For Siena in this period, see D. Hicks, 'The Rise of Pandolfo Petrucci' (Ph.D. diss., Columbia University, 1959); id., 'The Sienese Oligarchy and the Rise of Pandolfo Petrucci', in *La Toscana al tempo di Lorenzo il Magnifico: Politica, economia, cultura, arte [Convegno di Studi promosso dalle Università di Firenze, Pisa e Siena 5–8 Novembre 1992]*, 3 vols. (Pisa, 1996), iii, pp. 1051–72; G. Chinoni, 'La signoria breve di Pandolfo Petrucci', in *Storia di Siena*, i: *Dalle origini alla fine della Reppublica* (Siena, 1995), pp. 395–406; M. Gattoni, *Pandolfo Petrucci e la politica estera della Reppublica di Siena (1487–1512)* (Siena, 1997); P. Jackson, 'Political Ideas in Art, Literature and Practice: Siena and the Petrucci 1485–1524' (Ph.D. diss., Warburg Institute, University of London, forthcoming).

[25] The pertinent Cathedral records are missing, but the same three adult names and a handful of choirboys appear in both 1495 and 1500, when the records resume. D'Accone, *Civic Muse*, pp. 247–8 and 257–8.

[26] *Ibid.*, p. 285.

[27] The mass section of **Si** bears several instances of an earlier foliation, indicating that eighty folios (8–10 gatherings) once came before it (see the Appendix). The simplest explanation is that this collection of masses originally contained a total of thirteen to fifteen cycles, ending in the current Martini/Obrecht/Isaac/Anon. group, in which case the Pagliarini copying

Rethinking the Siena choirbook

December 1508, the Cathedral administration gave to its choirmaster Eustachio de Monte Regali one part of an immense lot of *Venetian* paper for the copying of polyphony.[28] It seems unlikely that having made this distribution, the Opera would purchase new reams of Collegiane paper five months later for the same purpose. Finally, the Cathedral choir had dwindled to near extinction by February 1507.[29] Thus the second layer of **Si** almost certainly does not represent either Eustachio's or Pagliarini's work.

As shown in the Appendix, the twenty-fifth gathering of this layer[30] abruptly changes watermark sign from *Scala* 2 to a large crown surmounted by an orb (*Corona*; see Figure 1 above).[31] This

record could not refer to **Si**. Two highly speculative computations could make **Si** congruent with the vestigial foliation. The principal scribe could have copied the current gatherings I–III, VI/VII/VIII, IX–XI ... XVIII ff.; with the unlikely reckoning of VII as a quaternion to which the central bifolium was later added, this amounts to eighty folios. It cannot, however, account for the loss of musical material (vv. 1–7 of a Magnificat) before the opening of gathering IX and before the opening of gathering XVIII (in this case a Kyrie and half a Christe). If Pagliarini copied no Magnificats, but motets instead, the following sequence could give the proper early foliation to the mass collection: I–III, VI/VII (as a quaternion), XIII (also reconstructed as a quaternion)–XIV, ... (two now-lost quaternions of masses), XVIII ff. This would in fact give seven masses to the copying of Scribe A. But neither account of Scribe A's work is convincing enough to support his identification with Pagliarini.

[28] D'Accone, *Civic Muse*, pp. 276–7 and 285. Eustachio, a composer of psalms and motets in his own right, was given an unspecified portion of eighty quinternions (800 folios) of Venetian paper acquired for music books. Ser Ambrogio de Battista copied music onto part of the same Venetian paper supply in 1507; I am grateful to Philippa Jackson for calling my attention to the second, unpublished record of Ser Ambrogio's work on music books.

[29] D'Accone, *Civic Muse*, pp. 248–9.

[30] The numbering of gatherings in my own reconstruction differs from D'Accone's published version. He hypothesises ('Late 15th-Century', p. 137) a now-missing ninth gathering, based on a gap in musical material. Whereas the musical gap is not in doubt, the current foliation of the manuscript includes a clear and unbroken enumeration of gatherings from 7 to 24, with the sole exception being number 17; I list this gathering as missing instead of 9. My gatherings IX–XVI thus correspond to D'Accone's 10–17. D'Accone (p. 140) speaks of this enumeration only beginning with fascicle 18, in support of his theory of an originally distinct mass volume; his hypothetical ninth gathering is perhaps an interpretation forced upon him by the oversight. Also, he labels fol. 198 as a separate fascicle, but in the manuscript's current binding this leaf is clearly bound to the previous gathering with repair strips. My own gatherings XXV–XVIII thus correspond to his 26–9.

[31] A single instance of the principal mark occurs on fol. 204; the twin (four instances) presents the only example in **Si** of a watermark in such a late state that an entire section of wire has broken off (see Figure 1). Briquet's nos. 4659 (Milan, *c.* 1473) and 4766–71 resemble this mark in concept, but clearly not in precise form. The presence of some *Corona* paper in Milan might demonstrate the attempts of Collegiane paper-makers to market their wares abroad, even in the face of competition from mills in Genoa and the Milanese Val di Toscolano. See F. Piardi, *La valle delle cartiere: Ambiente e segni di una storia industriale a Toscolano* (Brescia, 1984). On the travel of Italian paper, Laura Yvonne Kozachek has noted the presence of Italian paper types – including a four-rung ladder – among the papers in the Speciálník Codex; 'The Repertory

paper most likely was a gathering added to the end of the manuscript when the principal paper supply ran out. The crown was an extremely well-known Italian watermark from the end of the previous century. Several Crown papers – some in circles, though none surmounted by orbs – survive in Tuscan archival sources, especially from the 1490s and early 1500s. An outside possibility exists that this gathering preserves one of the elusive 'fascicle manuscripts' hypothesised for the transmission of fifteenth-century polyphony.[32] But though it contains different repertory and a new scribal hand, the paper is of the same size, condition and quality as the 1502–4 *Scala 2* paper that precedes it, and it bears an identical pricking and rastration. The most likely explanation, and the one supported by countless examples in Tuscan archival codices, is a remnant gathering added to the volume's end when the principal paper supply had been exhausted.

The paper evidence thus presents serious problems for Frank D'Accone's association of the 1481 Matteo Ghai copying record with the bulk of **Si**. D'Accone, without noting the change in paper types, argued that fols. 199–207^v were transposed to their current position in a rebinding, but originally began the 1481 mass volume. This arrangement would allow early Cathedral inventory descriptions of Ghai's books to represent the second layer of **Si**: one of the 1481 books began with an *Asperges me* setting, as does the current gathering XXV.[33] However, contemporary Sienese compilation practice without exception places remnant gatherings and gatherings of a different paper type at the end of manuscript volumes. The one *impossibility* is that this gathering once began a book: its vestigial

---

of the Speciálník Codex: Hradec Králové, Krasjké Muzeum Knihovna, MS II A 7' (Ph.D. diss., Harvard University, 1998), p. 34.

[32] The thesis of the fascicle manuscript was first proposed by C. Hamm, 'Manuscript Structure in the Dufay Era', *Acta Musicologica*, 34 (1962), pp. 166–84.

[33] The coeval polyphonic manuscript VatSP B80 similarly ends a mass collection with *Asperges me* and *Vidi aquam* settings, pointing to a possibly wider compilation practice in fifteenth-century Italy. Furthermore, the majority of polyphonic psalm repertories in Italian Vespers manuscripts open with *Dixit Dominus*, the first psalm in several common Vespers cycles. Thus neither of the 1481 copying records that D'Accone associated with **Si** allows a unique description of the manuscript. I have spoken elsewhere about the Sienese Vespers liturgy and a specific liturgical function for **Si**'s Marian motets; T. Dickey, 'A Specific Function for Marian Motets: The Evidence of the "Siena Choirbook" ', paper read at the Annual Meeting of the American Musicological Society, Seattle, 13 November 2004.

foliation 'k1, k2, ... k5' clearly indicates that it was the tenth gathering of some prior compilation.

Furthermore, the scribes' work upon the papers of **Si**'s second layer gives every indication that they planned and executed this layer as a single book project; the current state of the second layer closely preserves the original plan.[34] All twenty-five gatherings of the second layer underwent a remarkably stable preparation process. Someone carefully gathered bifolia directly from paper stock into the current fascicles and gave them all nearly identical pricking and rastration. Two-thirds of the second layer fascicles – including number XXV – are gathered with all their bifolia in the same alignment with respect to watermark orientation and mould/felt side. Twenty-four of the twenty-five gatherings use the exact same system of wheel-marked pricking (the single exception being a mirror image that reverses the system), and all twenty-five were ruled with the same two-stave rastrum. One principal scribe – Scribe A – began the second layer with a clear liturgical plan; he carefully copied a number of pieces into each of five generically distinguished sections: psalms, hymns, Magnificats, motets and masses. Two successive assistants expanded each genre section with new pieces. The first of these assistants – Scribe B – also began the first index and foliation (see Figure 4, which compares the Hand B rubric found on fol. 65^v with samples of the index and foliation). Both Scribe B's index and foliation encompass all five generic sections and prove their early unity in a single volume.[35]

Scribe B also copied music directly from early prints of Ottaviano Petrucci; his copies offer more circumstantial evidence for my second-layer date. In the second-layer motet section, Scribe B entered a copy of Weerbeke's *Virgo Maria, non est tibi similis* that is virtually identical to the copy in Petrucci's *Motetti A numero trentatre* of 1502; later in the second layer, he copied Compère's *O genetrix*

---

[34] See Dickey, 'Reading', 30–9.
[35] One early foliation continues from fol. 1 to fol. 136, through all five genre sections. It clearly matches the numeric script of Scribe B. A second foliation hand, which continues from fol. 137 through the end of **Si** (including the three fragmentary first-layer gatherings), also produced a second, more complete index on fols. iv^v–1^r. It is a much later hand, with no further concordances within **Si**. Interestingly, this later index/foliation hand added a foliation to another musical volume in the Biblioteca Comunale, the chant book SienBC I.I.7 (a Gradual assigned by Lusini to the Cathedral in the thirteenth century).

Timothy J. Dickey

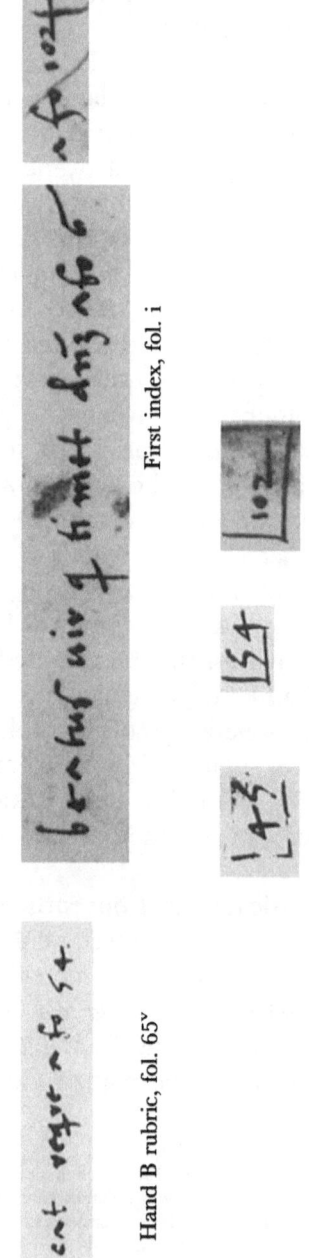

Figure 4 Comparison of **Sí**'s Scribe B hand with the Index/first foliation hand

gloriosa directly from the same print.[36] He also emended Scribe A's version of Mouton's *Sancti Dei omnes* by copying a missing passage – correct in all its numerous ligatures – from Petrucci's *Motetti C* of 1504. My paper date for the second layer and this scribe's work from Petrucci almost exactly coincide.

External evidence, finally, reinforces the dating of both layers and suggests their early cohabitation within the current binding of **Si**. The most specific clues appear in graffiti on the volume's rear pastedown sheet, which is now attached to the binding of both layers. The graffiti suggest a 1511–12 terminus for the binding of both layers. Under the 'date' 150ii, two separate hands have entered nearly identical lists of singers (two names are missing from the second list). Each of the adult singers – those for whom the priestly title 'Ser' precedes the name – may be identified with a Cathedral singer in the first decades of the sixteenth century (Table 3 lists the names and their dates of service at Siena Cathedral).[37] The only documented overlaps for this group in Siena occur in 1509 and 1511–12. One of the other names appears somewhat later, in the middle of the 1510s, perhaps indicating a choirboy paid briefly for singing once his voice broke. The combination of the 'date' and the singers' lists points to the year 1511 for the graffiti; it thus seems likely that the sheet, and the current binding of both layers, was in place by that date.[38]

---

[36] *Virgo Maria* is nearly identical to the copy in Petrucci's first motet book. Both sources of *Virgo Maria* share the only accidental found in the piece; no ligatures appear in either version, nor are there any pitch or rhythmic variants, however small. **Si**'s Scribe B does not introduce any minor color. The only change this scribe made to Petrucci's musical text fulfilled performance requirements: **Si**'s copy gives a more complete text underlay. One further concordance for this motet, heretofore unnoted in the literature, appears in FlorBN Panc. 27; its reading is again very close, but contains a small number of rhythmic variants from the closely linked readings in **Si** and Petrucci.

In the case of Compère's *O genetrix*, the scribe did take some tiny liberties with Petrucci's musical text, amounting to four minor variants of rhythmic duration; he also added a chordal *Deo gratias* as a prolongation of the final chord. Between these two pieces, Scribe B copied (or composed) the extremely odd motet, a unicum, *Petrus et Johannes*, on which see Dickey, 'Reading', 202–4.

[37] D'Accone, *Civic Muse*, tables on pp. 257–8 and 325–30. One other striking difference between the two lists is a fascinating Tuscanisation of the word 'cantore' to 'hantore' in every instance on the second list.

[38] The date 150ii signifying 1511 is found elsewhere, for example the account book Archivio di Stato di Firenze, fondo Corporazioni Soppressi dal Governo Francese 102 App. (Santa Maria Novella), 22, fol. 103^v.

Table 3 *The pastedown sheet lists of singers*

Si singers' list	Cathedral singer	Payments recorded	Remarks
Ano domini 150ii		1509; 1512–20	
Ser pietro cantore	Pietro di Domenico		
S. lonardo cantore	Lonardo di Cristofano	1500–19	
S. angnolo cantore	Agnolo di Piero	1500–19	
S. vieri cantore	Ulivieri di Jacomo	1509–21; 1527–55	not on second list
S. madalo cantore	Maddalo di Lorenzo d'Arezzo	1503–20	
S. giovăfrancesco cantore	Giovanfrancesco di Antonio	1511–12	
Anibale cantore			choirboys?
Domitio cantore			
Pietrătognio cantore	[Piero Antonio di Galgano?]	[1515]	
Nencino cantore			
Pierange cantore			not on second list

Evidence in surviving Cathedral inventories further supports both a 1481 first-layer date and an early sixteenth-century date for the second layer. The inventories also provide clues leading to a coherent early history of both layers. The 1481 volumes begun by Matteo Ghai and the later second layer both apparently received heavy performance use, and were removed from circulation in due course. Cathedral inventories list Matteo Ghai's volumes of *canto figurato* – the remains of which which I identify as **Si**'s first layer – as early as 1482.[39] The two books bear adjacent shelf numbers and were the most recent additions to the Cathedral library; the end of the inventory describes these two books as

Uno libro di canto figurato di nota grossa, per li Vesperi, legato e covertato di cuoio pavonazzo con coppe grandi e canti d'ottone, comincia Dixit Dominus Domino meo. Fece fare messer Alberto, S. 126

Uno libro di canto figurato per le messe, di nota grossa, legato e covertato di cuoio pavonazzo con coppe grandi e canti d'ottone, cominicia Asperges me. Fece fare messer Alberto S. 127

A book of polyphony in large notes, for Vespers, bound and covered with purple leather, with large studs and corners of brass, beginning *Dixit Dominus Domino meo*. Messer Alberto had it made, S. 126

A book of polyphony in large notes, for the Mass, bound and covered with purple leather, with large studs and corners of brass, beginning *Asperges me*. Messer Alberto had it made S. 127

[39] See above, n. 5.

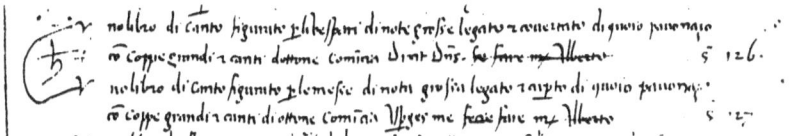

Figure 5 Inventory description (post-1506) of the two Matteo Ghai volumes, with marginal indications of their binding and removal from service. Source: AOMS 868 (*Inventarii, 1517?–1590*, fasc. 1), fol. 7

A verbatim description of both books appears in the two subsequent inventory lists (*c.* 1488 and post-1506).[40] Check marks in the margins indicate that scribes also used these lists periodically to verify the presence of both books.

Such marginal record keeping in the two subsequent inventories allows the tracking of Ghai's volumes into the 1500s. Marginal slashes in the *c.* 1488 inventory reflect three or four complete inventory checks against the copied list, with Ghai's two volumes present for each. When it comes to the list compiled just after 1506, however, a scribe has drawn a 'U' to connect the two entries at the very first check, signifying that the volumes numbered 126 and 127 had been united (see Figure 5). More importantly, the librarian reassigned the shelf number of the second book at the end of this very inventory. This must mean that the first layer of **Si** was bound as a single volume by *c.* 1506.[41] The Cathedral also apparently removed that single volume from service shortly thereafter; an inventory scribe marked it in the margin with an 'h', crossing it for good measure (both marks are visible in Figure 5). Both the symbol and the cross to its right indicate missing items; no items so marked in the inventory are copied into the subsequent (1525) list of

---

[40] The subsequent inventories, respectively, are AOMS 867 (*Inventarii, 1420–post c.1488*, fasc. 11, fols. 4ᵛ–6); AOMS 868 (*Inventarii, 1517?–1590*, fasc. 1, fols. 7–9ᵛ). D'Accone suggests 1517 for the date of the first inventory in AOMS 868 (*Civic Muse*, 236), though this would appear to be mistaken; Moscadelli dates this inventory to just after 1506, the year in which Pandolfo Petrucci seized the office of Cathedral overseer from Alberto Aringhieri and removed Duccio's *Maestà* from the high altar. It was quite common for the Cathedral Opera to begin a new inventory of its possessions immediately following a change of regime.

[41] The new book number 127 is described as 'Uno messale Grande et bello in carta pecora lettera formata miniato a oro con arme di Maestro thome vescovo di pientia comincia ad te levavi' ('A large and beautiful Missal in parchment, with formed letters, illuminated in gold with the arms of Master Thomas, Bishop of Pienza, beginning *Ad te levavi*'). The previous owner was Tomasso Piccolomini del Testa, second bishop of Pienza (r. 12 November 1470–19 January 1484).

Cathedral holdings. Matteo Ghai's two volumes, well before 1525, had for all practical purposes ceased to exist.

The new book of polyphony, **Si**'s second layer, probably replaced Ghai's work at this time. But the second layer itself might have enjoyed a relatively brief period of service: my reading of the next five Cathedral inventory lists identifies the complete bound contents of **Si**'s two layers with a 'libro vechio vechio' being used for teaching purposes only by 1524, and a 'libro anticho con messe antichissime' in 1527. Three inventory lists of Cathedral possessions (1525, 1527 and 1536) and the separate holdings lists of the Scuola del Canto Fermo and Scuola del Canto Figurato (1524 and 1546) include a number of printed and manuscript music books kept in the room of the choirmaster.[42] Several provide details of each book's contents and description. The history of specific volumes thus may be traced with little difficulty through all five of these inventories (I have harmonised the inventory descriptions in Table 4). Two old volumes of masses on *foglio mezano* paper most likely represent the work of the copyists active between 1507 and 1509.[43] A trio of large-format volumes containing motets, masses and Vespers music specify new music ('motetti nuovi'), and probably pertain to the next group of music copying records, in 1524 and 1527.[44] The only explanation supported by this group of inventories is that before 1524 **Si**'s second layer was bound together with Ghai's fragments (as I suggested above with the 1511 pastedown sheet *terminus*). The single volume that is now **Si** disappears from Cathedral records after this point.

Both layers of **Si**, however, now take on overtones of local Sienese politics. **Si**'s first layer was commissioned just after a regime change in the city. The Duke of Calabria, with his Aragonese army, had resided in Siena from 23 June to 7 August 1480, and was probably attended by his chaplains.[45] The new regime was dominated by the Sienese Noveschi party and retained close ties to Aragonese Naples.

---

[42] See D'Accone, *Civic Muse*, Table 6.2, pp. 299–300, for his transcription of these five inventories. The first leader of the Sienese Cathedral choir whose duties included music teaching was Eustachio de Monte Regali, starting in 1508. *Civic Muse*, pp. 276–82.

[43] They are Ser Ambrogio di Battista, Eustachio de Monte Regali and Frate Giovanni Pagliarini. See D'Accone, *Civic Muse*, p. 285, and above, n. 28.

[44] *Ibid.*, pp. 285 and 297–8.

[45] On Duke Alfonso's personal chapel, Allan Atlas has collated some notices of individual singers, in *Music at the Aragonese Court of Naples* (Cambridge, 1985), pp. 45, 48.

Rethinking the Siena choirbook

Table 4 Descriptions of polyphonic music books in five Sienese Cathedral Inventories

Type of book	1524	1525	1527	1536	1547	Remarks
1 ancient manuscript:	uno libro vechio vechio	—	Uno libro anticho, covertato di verde, scripttovi mexe antiquixime	—	—	Ghai's 1481 volumes; probably the entirety of Si
3 large MS volumes:	uno libro grande di Mangnifichato e inni, in penna	Uno libro di hymni psalmi et magnifiche chovertato di chioamo rosse	3 libri grandi, uno di mexe, uno di Magnifiche e inni, uno di motetti nuovi	as 1525	Uno libro di Salmi e magnificat, in tavole, di foglio reale	copied Turri 1524; Golppini 1527 ?
	uno libro grande di motetti, in penna	Uno libro de motetti chovertato di . . . rosse		missing	Uno libro di motetti, di foglio reale . . .	
	uno libro grande di messe, in penna	Uno libro di messe . . . verde con . . .		as 1525	Uno libro di messe, scritto a mano, figurato, . . . di foglio reale	
2 old MS volumes:	due libri mezani di messe, in penna, vechi	Uno libro di messe covertato . . . pavonazo	2 libri vechi, uno covertato di pavonazo suvi mexe antiche,	as 1525	(?? one volume in mezano of magnificats/ hymns ??)	copied Eustachio 1508 ?
		Uno libro di messe covertato . . . rosso con . . .	l'altro covertato di roxo con mexe antiche	as 1525	Uno libro di messe, scritto a mano, a meza choverta di rosso	Paglarini 1509 ?

Table 4 *Continued*

Type of book	1524	1525	1527	1536	1547	Remarks
1 printed mass collection:	uno libro mezano di messe in istampa, figurato	Uno libro di messa in stampa ...	Uno libro con 15 mexe in stanpa, leghato in tavole	as 1525	Uno libro di XV messe, di vari autori, in tavole	D'Accone: Antico 1516
small processionals:	10 libretti da processioni	—	8 libri da portare a la procixione ...	—	VIII libri delle processioni, picholi ...	
quarto mass books:	5 libretti picholi, leghati in 4 vilumi	Quattro libri di messa in quarto foglio ...	—	as 1525	—	
octavo motet books:	4 libretti picholini da pocissioni [*sic*]	Quattro libri di mottetti chon due messa ... ottavo foglio...	—	as 1525	—	
volume of 10 masses:				—	Uno libro di X messe, in tavole	1535 record of purchase (D'Accone: Moderne 1532)
3 mass collections: Morales, Carpentras				—	Uno libro di messe Morales, in istanpa	

Table 4 *Continued*

Type of book	1524	1525	1527	1536	1547	Remarks
2 groups of five-voiced motet books:				—	Uno libro di messe in istanpa, dalla Magna Uno libro di 5 messe di Carpentras, in tavole Uno corpo di libri di mottetti della divinità, a cinque Un altro corpo di mottetti di Ghonberto, a cinque (Uno altro libro, in tavole ??)	1546 record of purchase, 2 motet volumes

Sources: See n. 40.

It may have desired to place its personal stamp upon the highest civic worship, in emulation of the Duke.[46] The music surviving in **Si**'s first layer apparently presents a completely new approach for the Sienese: systematic polyphony for both the Mass and Vespers, including international repertory by Philippe Basiron, Johannes Martini and Josquin des Prez. Its copyist was a professional French scribe, late of the papal chapel. Yet the music also betrays local connections, in its specific reading of the Josquin mass (discussed below), and in its inclusion of music by the local composer Simone da Siena.

The new date of 1502–4 for the second layer of **Si** places it in an entirely different political context. Though Alberto Aringhieri still maintained his grip on the Cathedral administration, Pandolfo Petrucci (known as *Il Magnifico* as Lorenzo de' Medici had been in Florence) was open master of the town from 1500. And the story of the second layer preserves indications of the Sienese political nexus of 1500–5. On the one hand, **Si**'s second layer is a testament to continuity with the 1480s of the first layer. The contract for its paper went to the same mill in Colle di Val d'Elsa that had supplied the Cathedral's paper for decades. The scribes probably adopted the same pragmatic liturgical organisation that Matteo Ghai had used in the first layer, and may have recopied some of the same music. A similar mingling of local and international repertories characterises the music of both.

On the other hand, the new book of **Si**'s second layer also signifies certain undercurrents of political change. Whereas Rome was a principal source for the transmission of the first-layer repertory, the mass collection of the second layer travelled to Siena from Sforza Milan (see below). Milan, though historically an ally of Siena, was specifically at this time the home of Pandolfo Petrucci's long-time patron Ludovico Sforza, 'il Moro', who was attempting to

---

[46] Atlas has already noted a close relationship between the Neapolitan chapel and musical life in Medicean Florence; 'Aragonese Naples and Medicean Florence: Musical Interrelationships and Influence in the Late Fifteenth Century', in Gargiulo (ed.), *La musica a Firenze*, pp. 15–45. D'Accone cites the contemporary writer Raffaele Brandolini on Lorenzo's musical emulation of Naples, *Civic Muse*, p. 222. On the political ties between the new Sienese regime and Aragonese Naples, see A. Isaacs, 'Cardinali e "Spalagrembi": Sulla vita politica a Siena fra il 1480 e il 1487', in *La Toscana al tempo di Lorenzo il Magnifico*, iii, pp. 1013–50, at pp. 1014–19.

exercise greater influence in Tuscany.[47] Political ties could foster the transmission of music, and emulation of the Milanese repertory could do Pandolfo no harm. The Milanese transmission link thus also exudes the odour of politics. On a more personal side, it perfectly served Pandolfo's purposes to allow a new revision of the Cathedral's worship; it would act as one more sign of the new age of Sienese potency he intended to inaugurate.[48] **Si**'s second-layer motet cycle even made possible a uniquely splendid celebration of the city's worship during the feasts of the Blessed Virgin.

Yet this latter facet of the book might have led to its suppression by the end of the decade. Shortly after assuming the post of Cathedral overseer, Pandolfo Petrucci replaced Duccio's *Maestà* on the Cathedral's high altar with a simpler bronze tabernacle. Likewise, it seems, he replaced the volume now surviving as **Si**'s second layer with new polyphonic collections copied in 1507, 1508 and 1509, choirbooks copied on Venetian paper by the *maestri di cappella* Giovanni Pagliarini and Eustachio de Monte Regali, both hired by Petrucci. Thus both the commissioning and the decommissioning of **Si** were acts intimately bound up in the influence of politics.

At the time of their original compilation, though, each layer of **Si** gave to the Sienese Cathedral singers repertory that was very current. The 1481 date for the first layer makes the Siena choirbook quite possibly the earliest surviving source for both the Basiron *Missa de Franza* and Josquin's *Missa L'ami baudichon*. In the case of Johannes Martini's *Missa Dio te salvi Gotterello*, compilation of both surviving sources (**Si**'s first layer and ModE M.1.13) began in the same year: 1481. For this piece, the Sienese reading now makes a claim to authority. Scholars have generally considered the Ferrarese manuscript ModE M.1.13 the most authoritative source for Martini's music, especially in the light of Lewis Lockwood's argument that Martini himself oversaw its compilation.[49] Murray Steib

---

[47] For the Milanese influence on Pandolfo, see D. Hicks, 'The Sienese Oligarchy and the Rise of Pandolfo Petrucci, 1487–97', in *La Toscana al tempo*, iii, pp. 1051–72, at pp. 1051, 1069.
[48] See Gattoni, *Pandolfo Petrucci*.
[49] L. Lockwood, *Music in Renaissance Ferrara: The Creation of a Musical Center in the Fifteenth Century* (Cambridge, Mass., 1984), pp. 171–2. See also M. Steib, preface to Johannes Martini, *Masses I*, ed. E. Moohan and M. Steib (Recent Researches in the Music of the Middle Ages and Early Renaissance, 34; Madison, 1999), p. xvii.

notes that three Masses in ModE M.1.13 seem to preserve readings that suggest direct revisions (presumably by Martini) of earlier versions.[50] Steib finds **Si**, on the other hand, so 'full of errors' that he may practically discount its readings.[51] The Sienese version of the *Missa Dio te salvi Gotterello* does present some clear errors, but in several places contains a reading clearly stronger than that found in ModE M.1.13. This situation weakens the supposed authority of the Ferrarese source as well as the notion of Martini's editorial participation.

Of the admittedly large number of variants between the two sources for Martini's mass, the majority give no indication of compositional precedence. The Sienese copyist, for instance, shows a somewhat greater tendency towards coloration to signify a hemiola within triple-metre passages, while ModE M.1.13 more often uses dots of division. The Sienese version of the mass more frequently ornaments its cadential suspensions with anticipations and under-third figures; it often adds minim passing notes to fill descending intervals. In addition to these variants of orthography and embellishment, **Si** contains more explicit accidentals (ten, of which only one is shared with ModE M.1.13). The text underlay is generally more complete in **Si**, though mostly it is the work of a second scribe; Scribe J only entered the incipits to most movements.[52] The texting scribe (perhaps a singer) did make one serious error in underlay. Presented with an incipit of 'Sanctus' but no 'Agnus Dei', he began texting 'Agnus Dei' underneath the music for Martini's Pleni sunt coeli. This resulted in several sections of untexted music left over at the end of the mass. The error of this second scribe, however, neither strengthens nor weakens the Sienese source's authority.

Several specific variants, on the other hand, testify that **Si**'s musical text is older. ModE M.1.13 frequently gives a reading that indicates scribal intervention to correct or to revise an earlier version. Pointedly, none of these revisions necessitates the hand of

---

[50] *Ibid.* The masses are Martini's *Missa cucu*, Faugues's *Missa L'homme armé* and the anonymous *Missa O rosa bella II*. In the case of Martini's *Missa Ma bouche rit*, Steib suggests that a later reworking (also by Martini?) travelled to MilD 3 and VerBC 761.

[51] *Ibid.*, p. xviii.

[52] As with the Josquin *Missa L'ami baudichon*, the minor Scribe V filled in text. For a detailed analysis of the seventeen scribal hands found in **Si**, see Dickey, 'Reading', pp. 40–55.

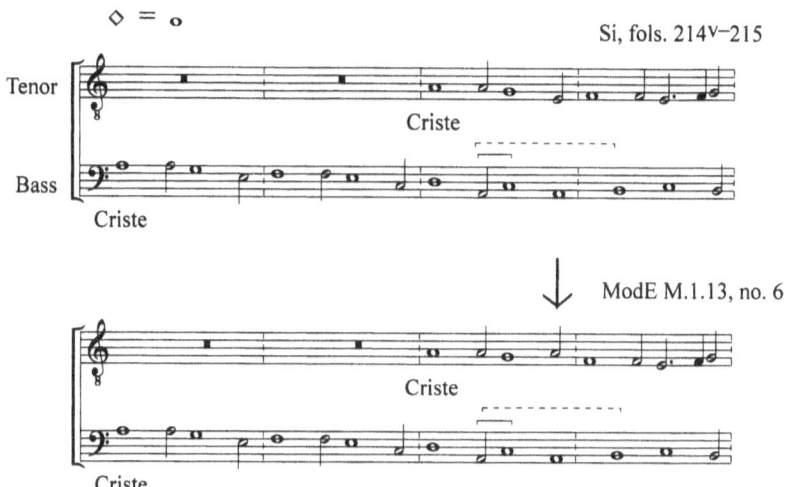

Example 1   Johannes Martini, *Missa Dio te salvi Gotterello*,
Tenor and Bassus of the Christe opening, **Si** and ModE M.1.13 versions

the composer. Two important cadences in the Sienese copy of the Credo ('et homo factus est' and the final Amen) use an archaic Bassus octave leap; the version in ModE M.1.13 'modernises' both cadences.[53] In a variant passage early in the Credo, **Si** marks a mensuration change to ₵ to clarify the agogic accents and cantus firmus placement.[54] Imitative motifs throughout the Sienese version follow the rhythm of the cantus firmus (♩ ♩ ♩ ♩ ♩ ♩) more strictly, while the Ferrarese version often strays from it. With a short text such as Sanctus, the ModE M.1.13 version achieves a smoother underlay. Yet **Si**'s stricter, more consistent imitation of the cantus firmus – especially at the beginning of movements – indicates its priority.

In some cases, the Ferrarese edition corrects a contrapuntal 'flaw' found in **Si**. A passage in the Christe containing parallel fifths in the Sienese reading is emended to fifth–octave in ModE M.1.13 – at the expense of altering the cantus firmus line (see Example 1). The

---

[53] The Ferrarese reading of this Martini mass does retain three other instances of the octave-leap cadence – at 'filius patris', at 'descendit de coelis' and at the conclusion of the second Agnus Dei.

[54] The passage occupies bars 20–9 in Steib's edition; his critical notes do not include this variant at all. ₵ mensuration is relatively rare in Martini's masses, the only other example being in the *Missa Ma bouche rit*, also found in ModE M.1.13. The musical substance of this Bassus line, however, requires a triple grouping. Each of the other four movements of the mass, furthermore, establishes a pattern of early and rapid changes from duple to triple metre.

Example 2 Martini, *Missa Dio te salvi Gotterello*, Kyrie I opening, **Si** and ModE M.1.13 versions

Sienese reading of Kyrie I is even more telling (Example 2). **Si** begins the movement with clear four-voiced imitation of the cantus firmus incipit. The Bassus in this version enters on a dissonant pitch against a suspension. ModE M.1.13 overwrites the dissonance with a looser paraphrase in the Discantus and free counterpoint in the Contratenor and Bassus.[55] The same harshly dissonant gesture, however, could be a stylistic fingerprint for Martini; it appears elsewhere in his music, three other times in this mass alone.[56] A

---

[55] The Bassus dissonance in **Si** does resolve properly, and I would argue it arises from a higher compositional priority (imitation of the cantus firmus). Murray Steib has characterised Martini's writing as 'more dissonant than those of his contemporaries'; Introduction to Martini, *Masses I*, p. xiii.

[56] The other locations in the *Missa Dio te salvi* are Kyrie bar 9, dissonant Tenor 4th against the Contratenor suspension; Credo bar 31, dissonant Discantus and Contra entry at the 9th and 11th against the Bassus suspension; Sanctus bar 17, dissonant Discantus entry (at the 7th and

similar recomposition takes place in the ModE M.1.13 version of Kyrie II and Agnus Dei I, causing each to hew less closely to the cantus firmus. Each of these variants supports the hypothesis that **Si** preserves an earlier reading.[57]

For Basiron's *Missa de Franza*, Rome emerges as a key transmission link.[58] The Sienese copy may again boast authoritative readings, despite the fragmentary nature of its preservation: two of four voices for the Osanna and Benedictus, followed by the Agnus Dei. We might reasonably expect, of course, authoritative readings of the 'French' mass to have been copied by the Frenchman Matteo Ghai. A comparison of the passages shared by the four sources for this mass (roughly 5 per cent of the mass's notation) reveals a straightforward filial relationship among those sources, with a vital connection between **Si** and VatS 35. Such a stemmatic link comes as no surprise, however. With the redating of **Si**'s first layer to 1481, its copy of Basiron's mass and the Roman copy in VatS 35 stand in close temporal proximity, in addition to their geographical proximity and their connection via the major north–south pilgrims' road, the Via Francigena.[59]

Central readings and Roman transmission also characterise **Si**'s copy of the *Missa L'ami baudichon* attributed in later sources to Josquin des Prez.[60] The anonymous Sienese copy of the Gloria

---

11th) against the Contratenor and Tenor double suspension. In addition, it happens five times in the *Missa Dominicalis* (Credo bars 9, 16, 193, 298, 306), twice in the *Missa Orsus, orsus* (Credo bar 31, Sanctus bar 10) and once in the *Missa Ma bouche rit* (Sanctus bar 97).

[57] Joshua Rifkin has suggested that the opposite is true: that the Sienese version is a revision of Martini's mass as it appears in ModE M.1.13, and an attempt to 'modernise' it by adding imitation; 'Munich, Milan', p. 327, n. 189. I doubt, however, that any Sienese revisions would *introduce* new dissonances to the music, such as the Bassus Kyrie entry. In addition, several other movements already open with three- or four-voiced imitation, clearly suggesting Martini's intention to use imitation of the cantus firmus more consistently.

[58] On this mass, see G. Gore, 'The Music of Philippe Basiron (Philippon?)' (Ph.D. diss., West Virginia University, 1978). Further biographical information is in P. Higgins, 'Tracing the Careers of Late Medieval Musicians: The Case of Philippe Basiron of Bourges', *Acta Musicologica*, 62 (1990), pp. 1–28. In addition to **Si**, versions of this mass survive in Petrucci's *Missarum diversum auctorum* (RISM 1509¹), in VatS 35 and in the Speciálník Codex (HradKM 7). Gore used Petrucci as the primary source for his edition, as he considered VatS 35 difficult to read and unaccountably thought that Speciálník only contained Basiron's Kyrie. He was unaware of **Si**.

[59] VatS 35 was compiled between *c.* 1487 and 1490, with some later additions *c.* 1492. See C. Reynolds, 'The Music Chapel of San Pietro in Vaticano in the Later Fifteenth Century' (Ph.D. diss., Princeton University, 1982), pp. 87–8 and 95–6.

[60] An edition is in *Josquin Desprez: Werken*, ed. A. Smijers, Deel 2, afl. 20, no. 9 (Leipzig, 1940), pp. 67–92.

provides new insight into the mass's date and early transmission, though unfortunately it can lend no direct support to Josquin's authorship.[61] The 1481 date for the first layer of **Si** is surprisingly early for the mass; it is especially surprising in the light of Josquin's revised biography, which makes of him a much younger man in 1481 than was once thought.[62] Even if the Sienese copy represents an addition to the first layer, as argued by Joshua Rifkin, it begins a gathering; I would hardly date this copy later than 1484, the date of payments for music copying to Pieter Bourdon.[63] By the end of June 1485, moreover, the Sienese Cathedral had lost four of its five adult singers, a loss in personnel only made worse by a citywide outbreak of the plague in the following year.[64]

The Sienese version of this mass could now date from a mere six to nine years after the earliest notice of Josquin's career;[65] it ranks among the earliest sources for any music attributed to him.[66] Without an attribution in **Si**, this early reading unfortunately cannot directly support Josquin's authorship. A lack of attribution, though, to such a young French composer in an attribution-poor Italian

---

[61] Questions of *Missa L'ami baudichon*'s attribution have been raised by Rob Wegman, 'Who Was Josquin?', in R. Sherr (ed.), *The Josquin Companion* (Oxford, 2000), pp. 21–50, at pp. 31–3, and J. Rifkin, 'A Singer Named Josquin', paper read at the Duke University Symposium on the music of Josquin Desprez, 20 February 1999.

[62] For the biographical revisions, see most pertinently L. Matthews and P. Merkley, 'Iodochus de Picardia and Jossequin Lebloitte *dit* Desprez: The Names of the Singer(s)', *Journal of Musicology*, 16 (1998), pp. 200–26; P. Merkley and L. Merkley, *Music and Patronage in the Sforza Court* (Turnhout, 1999), pp. 197–215 and 425–43; R. Sherr, 'Chronology of Josquin's Life and Career', in id. (ed.), *Josquin Companion*, pp. 11–20.

[63] See above, n. 17.

[64] See D'Accone, *Civic Muse*, pp. 246–7, and the discussion of correlations between Sienese politics and musical events in Dickey, 'Reading', pp. 229–51.

[65] Paul Merkley presented a case for extending Josquin's service to King René d'Anjou backwards into 1475 in 'Josquin Desprez, Singer in the Court of René d'Anjou', paper read at the Annual Meeting of the American Musicological Society, Toronto, 4 November 2000; also id., 'The Desprez(s), the Almoner, and the Cathedral of Aix', paper read at the Annual Meeting of the American Musicological Society, Seattle, 13 November 2004.

[66] The most prominent other manuscript which could contend for this honour is RomeC 2856, with a 1480 date argued by Lockwood, *Music in Renaissance Ferrara*, pp. 225–6; but see the prominent reservations expressed by D. Fallows, 'Josquin and Milan', *Plainsong and Medieval Music*, 5 (1996), pp. 69–80, at p. 73. Fallows identifies three other sources from the early 1480s with possible (though questionable) Josquin attributions, and observes that Josquin's music only begins to 'take serious place' in Florentine and Roman sources from the 1490s. One motet – *Domine non secundum peccata* – is ascribed to him in VatSP B80 (*c.* 1475), though the piece is probably a later addition to the manuscript. Otherwise, the earliest manuscript attributions to him are two chansons in FlorR 2794 (of French provenance, before 1488) and the copy of *Domine, non secundum* attributed to him in VatS 35. See Rifkin, 'Munich, Milan', pp. 313–33, for further arguments against an early date for RomeC 2856, and in favour of *Ave Maria . . . virgo serena* as once again the earliest surviving piece of Josquin's music.

source from 1481 makes perfect – if historically regrettable – sense. Despite the obscurity of its composer, the mass must have travelled rapidly onto the Italian peninsula. It reached Siena by 1481 and then, perhaps via Innsbruck, arrived in Leipzig and points east by the mid-1480s. Unfortunately, **Si** transmits only the Gloria, leaving the stemmatic relationship between it and many of the eastern European sources (which preserve the only Credo) impossible to prove.[67]

The Sienese copy of Josquin's mass nevertheless fits into a coherent transmission narrative. Stemmatically, **Si** appears most closely related to the linked pair of sources VerBC 761 and VienNB 11778; the Speciálník Codex, BerlS 40021 and LeipU 1494 share a similarly close relationship to this pair of sources in the Credo.[68] If sections of VerBC 761 were copied in Rome, as argued by Adalbert Roth, that would suggest the early presence of the *Missa L'ami baudichon* in Rome.[69] From Rome, as in the case of Basiron's mass, the journey to Siena poses no difficulty: either the mass was copied during a stop in Siena by a musician travelling the Via Francigena,[70] or a musician such as Matteo Ghai brought it to Tuscany after a Roman sojourn. Ghai sang in the papal chapel from 1475 to 1478 before coming to Siena, and Alberto Aringhieri

---

[67] The group of eastern sources includes: BerlS 40021 (c. 1485–1500, Credo amen only), LeipU1494 (c. 1490–1504, Credo amen only), ZwickR 119/1 (first half of the sixteenth century, Kyrie, Gloria and fragment of Credo), HradKM 7 (c. 1480–95, Credo only with a spurious attribution to Tinctoris) and PozU 7022 (late fifteenth-century fragments). On these sources, see principally M. Just, *Der Mensuralkodex Mus. ms. 40021 der Staatsbibliothek Preußischer Kulturbesitz Berlin* (Tutzing, 1975); Kozachek, 'The Repertory of the Speciálník Codex'; M. Perz, 'The Lvov Fragments: A Source for Works by Dufay, Josquin, Petrus de Domarto, and Petrus de Grudencz in 15th-Century Poland', *Tijdschrift voor Nederlandse Muziekgeschiedenis*, 36 (1986), pp. 26–51.

[68] Among the principal variants which link **Si** closely to this pair of sources are the reading at *Gratias agimus tibi*, the Bassus switch to '2' mensuration at the end of the Gloria and the canonic disposition of the cantus firmus voice.

[69] Adalbert Roth found the same paper and the same copyist for parts of VatS 35 and all of the fascicle of VatS 51 that contains Obrecht's *Missa Salve diva parens*, then further related this copy to the same Obrecht mass in VerBC 761, concluding that the copying took place in Rome. Roth, *Studien zum frühen Repertoire der Päpstlichen Kapelle unter dem Pontifikat Sixtus IV (1471–1484): Die Chorbücher 14 und 51 des Fondo Cappella Sistina der Biblioteca Apostolica Vaticana* (Vatican City, 1991), pp. 267–8. See also *New Obrecht Edition*, xi, ed. C. Maas (Utrecht, 1990), p. xix. I am grateful to Joshua Rifkin for calling my attention to the arguments for Roman copying in this manuscript.

[70] Such as those Frank D'Accone has enumerated in *Civic Muse*, p. 254.

personally sent to Rome in August of 1481 for singers to fill his roster for the Sienese Assumption Day liturgy.[71]

Like **Si**, none of the five stemmatically related sources gives an attribution to Josquin. The careful scribe of VerBC 761, especially, would have been likely to transmit an attribution if he had it: he did retain all the canons in the Tenor voice, both notational and textual (including the 'mute' canon of *Et incarnatus*). The attribution to Josquin thus depends on Petrucci 1505 and the clearly derivative readings in VatS 23, and these two sources are the lone representatives of a second stemmatic tradition. However, with the evidence from **Si**'s first-layer date that the *Missa L'ami baudichon* was travelling in Italy by c. 1480, before Josquin was known to be there, the omission of a 'no-name' attribution (in a source, as mentioned, that almost completely eschews composer attributions) comes as no surprise. Furthermore, two later witnesses – Petrus Alamire and the theorist Giovanni Spataro – both considered the mass to be by Josquin. Spataro refers to 'Josquin's *Missa L'ami baudichon*' in a 1532 letter to Pietro Aaron (though he may not necessarily be an independent witness this late in the century); Alamire earlier gave his tacit attribution by including the *Missa L'ami baudichon* in VienNB 11778, a manuscript containing only Josquin masses.[72]

Si's new *terminus ante quem* for the mass's composition does locate it within the time of Josquin's service to his French patron René d'Anjou (and possibly Louis XI); it also represents an early period of his compositional life, as David Fallows recently concluded on stylistic grounds.[73] Paul Merkley, furthermore, has discovered documentary evidence of a teacher named 'Baudichon' who taught

---

[71] Reynolds, 'The Music Chapel', pp. 168–9; D'Accone, *Civic Muse*, pp. 228–9.

[72] For the Spataro letter, see *A Correspondence of Renaissance Musicians*, ed. B. Blackburn, E. Lowinsky and C. Miller (Oxford, 1991), pp. 590–1. I may add that the Tinctoris attribution in Speciálník (which arrives several generations down the stemma from the Italian sources) seems completely without basis, and was probably a scribal intervention. It may, however, provide support for the hypothesis that Tinctoris travelled to Hungary to visit Beatrice of Aragon around 1493. On Tinctoris, see R. Woodley, 'Iohannes Tinctoris: A Review of the Documentary Evidence', *Journal of the American Musicological Society*, 34 (1981), pp. 217–48, and Atlas, *Music at the Aragonese Court*. Note also Peter Király's recent suggestion that Josquin may have visited the Hungarian court of Matthias Corvinus in the 1480s; 'Un séjour de Josquin des Prés à la cour de Hongrie?', *Revue de Musicologie*, 78 (1992), pp. 145–50. On the Alamire choirbook collections of Josquin's masses, see David Fallows, 'Approaching a New Chronology for Josquin: An Interim Report', *Schweitzer Jahrbuch für Musikwissenschaft*, NS 19 (1999), pp. 131–50.

[73] Fallows, 'Approaching'. For Josquin's service to René D'Anjou, see Merkley and Merkley, *Music and Patronage*, p. 428; Sherr, 'Chronology', p. 12. For Josquin's service to Louis XI, the

music to a number of 1460s choirboys in Condé, quite possibly including the young Jossequin Lebloitte.[74] Well-known resemblances in the *Missa L'ami baudichon* to the technique of Dufay and Busnoys – head-motifs, closely imitative duos and widely spanned melodic lines – support all three conclusions.[75] Finally, there exists a hypothetically direct link between the court of René d'Anjou and Siena. The composer Pietrequin Bonnel sang at the Sienese Cathedral at the same time Matteo Ghai was being paid for music copying; if Bonnel may be identified with the 'Pierre Donnel' in service to René d'Anjou as late as 1479, the identification provides a direct link from Josquin des Prez to 1481 Siena.[76]

The stylistic evidence is futher reinforced by other examples of Josquin's music travelling together with other early pieces of French provenance. Sections of the Speciálník Codex contain a remarkable concentration of pieces with both French and north Italian ties, including early music by Josquin. The transmission of all these pieces seems to take place via northern Italy.[77] One fascicle in Speciálník, copied by a single scribe on the same Italian (possibly Collegiane) Ladder paper, contains Josquin's *Ave Maria*, a small group of other motets (including the work of Agricola) and the Basiron mass that is also found in **Si**'s first layer. The very same scribe and paper type overlap in a second gathering containing

---

argument has been made by P. Macey, 'Josquin's *Misericordias Domini* and Louis XI', *Early Music*, 10 (1991), pp. 163–78.

[74] Merkley, 'The Desprez(s)'.

[75] The Dufay connection is well represented in the literature on the *Missa L'ami baudichon*; see most recently Bonnie J. Blackburn, 'Masses Based on Popular Songs and Solmization Syllables', in Sherr (ed.), *Josquin Companion*, pp. 51–89, at p. 71.

[76] D'Accone noted Pietrequin's work in Florence (1490), and later in the chapel of Anne of Brittany; 'The Singers of San Giovanni in Florence in the 15th Century', *Journal of the American Musicological Society*, 14 (1961), pp. 307–58, at pp. 342–3. Y. Esquieu published the 'Donnel' records in 'La musique à la cour provençale du roi René', *Provence Historique*, 31 (1981), pp. 299–312; Joshua Rifkin first connected the two singers, in 'Pietrequin [Pierre] Bonnel', *The New Grove Dictionary of Music and Musicians*, ed. Stanley Sadie (London, 1980), xiv, p. 743. Unfortunately, Paul Merkley argues against the identity of Donnel and Pietrequin in 'The Desprez(s)'.

[77] Laura Kozachek has argued that the main routes for Western music travelling to Prague would all run through Italy: via Nuremberg (an established trade route), via Innsbruck (with its ties to Milan), or via Hungary. She specifically views the latter route – Italy to Hungary to Prague – as most likely, carefully explicating the Hungarian ruler Matthias Corvinus's relations with Bohemia; his ties to Naples are well known. Kozacheck, 'Repertory', pp. 173–4 and *passim*. At least three Western musicians are known to have spent some time in the Hungarian court during the period of Speciálník's compilation: Johannes Stokem (*maestro di cappella* for Matthias Corvinus c. 1483 to 1487), Barbireau (visited in 1490) and the Italian Pietrobono (visited in 1488).

Obrecht's *Missa Je ne seray*, Ghiselin's *O gloriosa domina* and another Josquin motet. A later group of gatherings (XI, X and XII) contains the work of a different but related scribal hand, all on Italian Anchor paper. This group includes a gathering with a Busnoys chanson contrafact, the Credo *L'ami baudichon*, a well-travelled Weerbeke mass and a motet of Brumel.

All these details support my transmission narrative for *L'ami baudichon*. The mass, with other pieces of French provenance, came to Siena in the hands of musicians travelling the Via Francigena to and from Rome. Many pieces of the same vintage travelled very soon thereafter from northern Italy to eastern Europe; several survive on Italian paper in Speciálník. Concordances in BerlS 40021, MunBS 3154, WarU 2016 and LeipU 1494 further document the eastern travels of this repertory from Italy.

The early presence of this mass in Siena – and the specific form of its notation – also illuminates a previously unnoticed case of Josquin emulation within **Si**'s second-layer masses. The anonymous *Missa De tous biens plaine* unique to **Si**'s second layer (fols. 168ᵛ–181) displays a virtuosic cantus firmus technique, featuring a transposing ostinato on the cantus firmus.[78] The transposing ostinato is extremely rare in contemporary mass settings, with infrequent examples only in the first 'Naples' *L'homme armé* mass, in Isaac, Compère, de Orto and Obrecht, as well as in Josquin – the Hercules mass and the *Missa L'ami baudichon*.[79] Indeed, the only movement of Josquin's Mass that survives in **Si** – the Gloria – begins by transposing its three-note cantus firmus motto ($e'd'c'$) into a different hexachord ($b\flat a\, g$), a gesture found twice in the anonymous mass.

Other details of the Tenor's notation in the anonymous mass closely resemble **Si**'s first-layer copy of the *Missa L'ami baudichon*, details which are lacking in Petrucci and in the Capella Sistina copy

---

[78] The cantus firmus manipulations in this mass include migration, polyphonic borrowing, mensural transformation, ostinato and a 'crab' canon. For an edition of the mass and a general discussion, see T. Bookhout, 'Transcription of *Missa de tous biens playne*, anonymous, circa 1480' (DMA thesis, Arizona State University, 1995); a more recent edition also appears in Dickey, 'Reading', pp. 405–27. On the model chanson, see Hayne van Ghizeghem, *Opera Omnia*, ed. B. Hudson (Corpus Mensurabilis Musicae, 74; n.p., American Institute of Musicology, 1977), pp. xxxix–xli; C. Gil, 'De tous biens plaine: Un tema favorito en el cancionero de la Catedral de Segovia', *Nassare*, 8/1 (1992), pp. 71–154.

[79] See S. Schlagel, 'The Sequential Ostinato in the Music of Josquin and his Circle' (MA thesis, University of North Carolina at Chapel Hill, 1991), for a list and an analysis of a distinct subset of late fifteenth-century pieces employing a transposing ostinato in sequential patterns.

Rethinking the Siena choirbook

of the mass.[80] Kyrie I of the anonymous mass and the Sienese copy of the Qui sedes from the *Missa L'ami baudichon* (see Figure 6) share the use of repeat signs just before the final cadence and the dual mensuration signs C over ₵. The anonymous mass makes its most daring gesture at the Et resurrexit: a mensuration canon on its transposing ostinato, employing the same compact notation. The Et resurrexit is missing from the Sienese copy of *L'ami baudichon*, but it is precisely the section in which Josquin deploys his transposing ostinato. Finally, the 'Cum sancto spiritu' of the *De tous biens plaine* mass not only opens with two ostinato statements; its final notes directly echo the fermata-marked chords that close the Gloria of *L'ami baudichon*.

A first-layer date of 1481, finally, allows me to make a tentative identification of the only attribution surviving from this layer: 'Simonis', who is very likely a local Sienese musician. The name appears above an otherwise unknown *Asperges me* in the first layer (fols. 210ᵛ–212).[81] Its musical style supports a 1470s composition date: it is characterised by an alternating pair of fundamentally chant-derived Discantus and Tenor voices, largely homophonic textures, meandering harmonies and often clumsy dissonance treatment. D'Accone advanced the suggestion that Simonis might refer to the Ferrarese singer 'Maestro Simon', who was active in 1516 in Loreto and perhaps in Bologna in 1518.[82] There is a better candidate closer at hand, however. The Milanese ducal secretary Cicco Simonetta owned a 'liber . . . cancionum Simonis de Sena' (a 'book of songs by Simon of Siena'), according to a 1476 inventory of his Pavian library.[83] Simon of Siena, composer of at least one complete book of songs before 1476, must be the Simon whose music survives in the Siena choirbook. This notice also documents the early operation of a musical transmission link between Siena and Milan.

---

[80] Both VerBC 761 and VienNB 11778 retain details of the notational canons, but these two sources post-date the Sienese copy by roughly two and four decades, respectively.
[81] An edition appears in Dickey, 'Reading', pp. 436–9.
[82] D'Accone, *Civic Muse*, p. 237, n. 47. He cites E. Alfieri, *La Cappella Musicale di Loreto* (Bologna, 1970), who on pp. 49–52 published a document concerning one 'Maestro Simon' who was the *maestro di cappella* at Loreto Cathedral in 1516. This Simon even acquired for Loreto 'un libro di 15 Messe in canto figurato' ('a book of fifteen polyphonic masses', probably Antico's 1516 print) in that year. Alfieri then attempts to link this Simon with a 'Symon ferrariensis' to whom two motets are credited in a Bolognese manuscript from 1518.
[83] Published by Merkley and Merkley, *Music and Patronage*, p. 269.

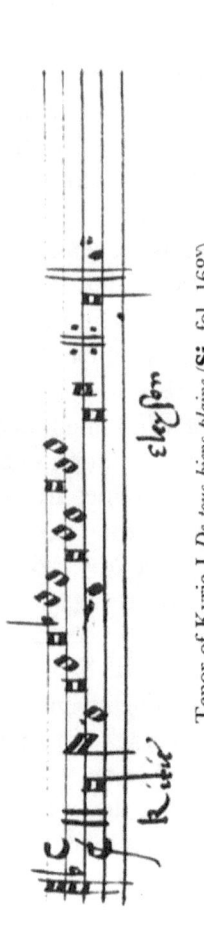

Tenor of Kyrie I *De tous biens plaine* (**Si**, fol. 168ᵛ)

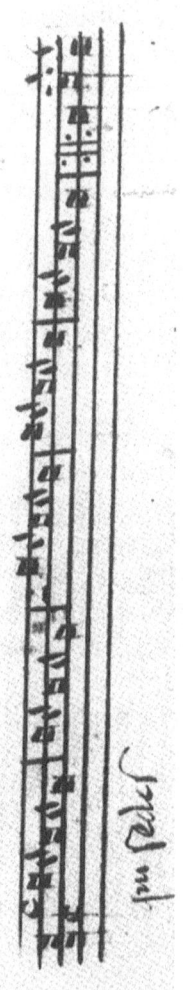

Tenor of Qui sedes *L'ami baudichon* (**Si**, fol. 213ᵛ)

Tenor of Et resurrexit *De tous biens plaine* (**Si**, fol. 175ᵛ)

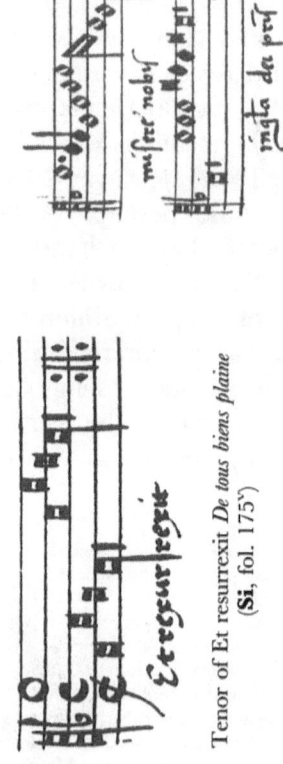

Tenor of Cum sancto spiritu *De tous biens plaine* (**Si**, fol. 172ᵛ)

Figure 6 Comparison of notation of anonymous *Missa De tous biens plaine* with Josquin des Prez, Gloria *L'ami baudichon* (Sienese version)

This nexus of relationships brings us to the music of the second layer. Within the relatively complete generic sections of this layer, surprising evidence exists that masses and motets were travelling along separate paths through Italy. On the one hand, the principal scribe of **Si** copied a group of five masses into the manuscript which all share two overarching characteristics. First, all five display an international character either in musical style or in wide international transmission. Martini's *Missa Coda di pavon* combines Italian sources and northern ties in its instrumental model, the *Pfobenschwanz*. Isaac's *Missa Quant j'ay au cueur* appears in two distinct manuscript traditions, one Italian and the other northern. The anonymous *Missa Carminum* (**Si**, fols. 148ᵛ–155ᵛ) mingles Germanic and Italian stylistic elements in its composition, being a mass clearly founded upon the Germanic practice of multiple cantus firmus settings yet containing some elements of the Milanese Missa brevis tradition.[84] The anonymous *De tous biens plaine* mass betrays knowledge of specifically Sienese readings, as shown above. It also reveals familiarity with the large tradition of northern masses on this chanson and with the style of, for instance, Compère's two large (French) cantus firmus masses.[85] Obrecht's *Missa Beata viscera* is transmitted in two sources only, MunBS 3154 and **Si**; the two show different traditions, though they are close in their readings. Both sources are now reasonably equidistant both in time and geography from the composer, and a later date for the Sienese copy no longer poses any threat to Obrecht's biography.[86]

Second, and more importantly, each of the five masses in its Sienese reading stands within central transmission patterns for the first decade of the sixteenth century. The three masses concordant

---

[84] On the *Misse carminum*, see most recently R. Strohm, *The Rise of European Music 1380–1500* (Cambridge, 1994), p. 531; R. Schmalz, in 'Selected Fifteenth-Century Polyphonic Mass Ordinaries Based in Pre-existent German Material' (Ph.D. diss., University of Pittsburgh, 1971), may have been the first to identify the *Missa carminum* 'tradition'. Adelyn Peck Leverett has uncovered a similar example of mingled national styles in the Trent Codices, in 'An Early Missa brevis in Trent Codex 91', in J. Kmetz (ed.), *Music in the German Renaissance: Sources, Styles, Contexts* (Cambridge, 1994), pp. 152–72. For an edition of this Mass, see Dickey, 'Reading', pp. 387–404. Rob Wegman had suggested Obrecht as a possible composer for the anonymous mass, in *Born for the Muses*, p. 166, n. 9. I have argued elsewhere, however, that Johannes Martini is a much stronger candidate; 'Reading', pp. 153–70.

[85] For *De tous biens plaine*, see H. Meconi, 'Art-Song Reworkings: An Overview', *Journal of the Royal Musical Association*, 119 (1994), pp. 1–42, at pp. 28–9, and Hayne, *Opera Omnia*.

[86] The date of the Sienese copy had been disputed by Wegman, in *Born for the Muses*, p. 100, n. 12.

with other sources present mainstream Italian readings; often they show ties to Milan and the recently copied Gaffurius codices.[87] For Martini's *Missa Coda di pavon*, for instance, both **Si** and MilD 2 lack a complete section – the Confiteor – found only in ModE M.1.13; a further conjunctive variant (Credo, bars 89–90) more closely links **Si** to the Milanese reading.[88] **Si** also stands next to MilD 2 in the stemma for Isaac's *Missa Quant j'ay au cueur*. A link between **Si** and MunBS 3154 via Milan for Obrecht's *Missa Beata viscera*, though speculative, is nevertheless strongly implied.[89] All five masses make sense in a source from the first decade of the century.

When it came to motets, however, the same Scribe A tapped into much less central streams of transmission. He had access, in fact, to a large number of musical curiosities. The first fragmentary motet in **Si**, *Obsecro te sancta Maria* (fol. 105^v), sets a popular Marian prayer in fifteenth-century books of hours.[90] The motet has a previously unnoticed concordance in the motet section of VerBC 758 (fols. 22^v–24).[91] The Sienese motet repertory also includes four complete settings of the *Ave Maria*. Each of them tropes the angelic greeting with different texts, probably indicating a cycle of motets for the liturgical year.[92] Finally, an anonymous setting of *Petrus et Johannes* copied by the second principal scribe (fols. 121^v–123)

---

[87] D'Accone first suggested a Milanese transmission link, in *Civic Muse*, p. 237, n. 48.

[88] An edition is in Martini, *Masses II*, ed. E. Moohan and M. Steib (Recent Researches in the Music of the Middle Ages and Early Renaissance, 35; Madison, 1999), pp. 42–73.

[89] Both sources for the Obrecht mass are very close in their readings; Thomas Noblitt calls them 'near descendants of the composer's original or of the archetype', *New Obrecht Edition*, ii (Utrecht, 1984), p. xiii. The transmission route between Innsbruck of MunBS 3154 and Milan of the Gaffurius Codices (MilD 1–3) is well established; two other masses by Obrecht appear in the Milanese choirbooks. From the Sienese side, all of the other four second-layer masses show ties to Milan. The anonymous *Missa De tous biens plaine* was copied continuously with the Obrecht mass; this same chanson served as model for two other masses in the Gaffurius Codices. The anonymous *Missa carminum* borrows the Milanese *Missa brevis* style, represented by numerous pieces in the same Codices. And both the Martini *Missa Coda di pavon* and Isaac's *Missa Quant j'ay au cueur* betray a close stemmatic relationship to the versions of those masses in MilD 2. Little speaks against a Milanese transmission of Obrecht's mass.

[90] See R. Wieck, *Time Sanctified: The Book of Hours in Medieval Art and Life* (New York, 1988), pp. 94–6. He notes that this Marian prayer, with the *O intemerata*, is often found following the Gospel lessons, and immediately before the Hours of the Virgin.

[91] The apparent reason for its obscurity is that both Frank D'Accone, in 'Late 15th-Century', p. 161, and Masakata Kanazawa, in 'Two Vesper Repertories from Verona, ca. 1500', *Rivista Italiana di Musicologia*, 10 (1975), pp. 153–79, at p. 174, identified the motet by the incorrect incipit *Sancta Maria mater dei*. The piece (see Dickey, 'Reading', pp. 366–70 for an edition) begins with an extended duet for Contratenor and Bassus, setting the actual incipit *Obsecro te*.

[92] See Dickey, 'Specific Function'.

preserves the only example I have seen of a single motet encompassing a complete cycle of Vespers propers (Josquin's *O admirabile* cycle serialises a group of antiphons in successive motets).[93] Chant-based sections within this Sienese motet present three antiphons for Vespers of the feast of SS Peter and Paul in sequence, followed by the Magnificat antiphon for St Peter's Chains and an unknown devotional prayer to St Peter.

The motets copied by Scribe A with other surviving concordances reveal similar curiosities. These three motets – Gaspar van Weerbeke's *O virginum praeclara*, Compère's *Ave Maria* and the *Sancti Dei omnes* attributed to Mouton – all found their way into the Milanese Gaffurius Codices.[94] For all three, however, the Sienese readings deviate significantly from the Milanese, and from every other source. Scribe A's copy of Gaspar's *O virginum praeclara*, for instance, shows numerous points of divergence from MilD 1, the only other source. In the space of a mere seventy-six breves, the two sources contain an astounding forty-eight variants, several of them drastic.[95] The weight of these variants indicates a definite break in the Milanese transmission link that seems to be present for the masses.

Scribe A's contribution to **Si** continues with a highly anomalous reading of Compère's *Ave Maria*. As Jennifer Bloxam has noted, only **Si** omits a complete section of music: the lauda-like *Beata es Maria* at the end of the motet.[96] The Mariocentric Sienese would hardly have

---

[93] For an edition, see Dickey, 'Reading', pp. 382–5.

[94] For editions of the three motets, see Gaspar van Weerbeke, *Collected Works*, ed. G. Croll (Corpus Mensurabilis Musicae, 106/3; Neuhausen-Stuttgart, 1993), pp. 14–16; Loyset Compère, *Opera Omnia*, ed. L. Finscher (Corpus Mensurabilis Musicae, 15/4; [Rome], 1958), pp. 8–10; Jean Mouton, *Motets à 4 et 5 voix*, ed. H. Expert (Maîtres Anciens de la Musique Française, 5; Paris, 1898; repr. New York, 1975).

[95] **Si** redistributes the pitches of a Contratenor line (bars 48–50), completely omits two pitches (bar 51, CT; 70, T), and uses a different mensuration (3/2 instead of coloration) for the concluding triple-metre section. The Sienese version of the motet also prolongs the final chord in all voices, though this was an emendation by a later scribe. In addition, **Si** and MilD 1 diverge six further times over pitch, sixteen times over rhythm, four times over cadential ornaments, nine times over ligation (when **Si** only uses five ligatures), three times over accidentals (they only agree once) and nine times over minor color.

[96] J. Bloxam, 'La Contenance Italienne: The Motets on *Beata es, Maria* by Compère, Obrecht, and Brumel', *Early Music History*, 11 (1992), pp. 39–89, at pp. 71–2. Bloxam argues for the piece's composition during Compère's Milanese period, with revisions before the composer left Italy. She bases this on her observation that Obrecht apparently knew the version of the motet with lauda in 1486 in Ferrara. Joshua Rifkin, in 'Munich, Milan', p. 310, n. 149, notes that the first part of her argument stems from D'Accone's old date for **Si**, and counters with a hypothesis based on the grouping of the motet's earliest sources between *c.* 1495 and 1500.

cut off a passage lauding the Virgin Assumptive, leading us to the conclusion that their exemplar lacked the passage. But from whence did that exemplar come to Siena? The final passage was part of the *Ave Maria* in both Rome and Milan in the 1490s; this same version travelled to Venice, Leipzig, Bohemia and Toledo by the turn of the century.[97] Whether the complete piece was composed in 1470s Italy or 1490s France, the version that travelled to Siena lacked a complete section. The passage could have been excised, which seems unlikely; it could also antedate the sources that include it. These sources, however, often represent the same lines of Roman and Milanese transmission from which the Sienese scribes received mass music. Again, the transmission link appears to have been broken.

A similar break obtains for Mouton's *Sancti Dei omnes* (fols. 116ᵛ–120). My stemma for this motet suggests a reasonably clear circuit through mostly Italian sources around the turn of the century: Verona, Milan, Savoy and then Rome.[98] The Sienese scribe, however, again copied from an exemplar that completely lacked an entire passage: the homophonic *O Christe audi nos* that opens the *secunda pars*.[99] I have found no evidence for the omission of Christ from the All Saints' liturgy in Siena. Furthermore, the Sienese Scribe B later emended this inexplicable omission. He copied the missing homophonic passage into the margins, using, it seems, the complete version in Petrucci.[100] From wherever the Sienese received their motet exemplars, they either lacked or ignored updated readings of both pieces. These readings should

---

[97] The relevant sources and their dates from the *Census-Catalogue* are: VatS 15 (*c*. 1495–1500), MilD 3 (*c*. 1490–1500), Petrucci 1502, VerBC 758 (*c*. 1500), BerlS 40021 (*c*. 1497–1500), WarU 2016 (*c*. 1495–1500) and SegC s.s. (*c*. 1502). The 1492 date of MilD 3 proposed by Matthews and Merkley would provide the earliest possible *terminus ante quem* for the *Beata es Maria* addition; 'Gaffurius, Leonardo, and Ludovico: Patronage and Clientage in Milanese Music during the Reign of *Il Moro*', paper read at the Annual Meeting of the American Musicological Society, Pittsburgh, Pa., 6 November 1992; see the objections to this date raised by B. Blackburn in *Josquin Companion*, p. 68, n. 38 and J. Rifkin, 'Munich, Milan', p. 253, n. 29, and Merkley and Merkley's response in *Music and Patronage*, pp. 323–30.

[98] The sources and their dates from the *Census-Catalogue* are: VerBC 758 (*c*. 1500), MilD 3 (*c*. 1490–1500), LonR 1070 (*c*. 1505–17; for this date and Savoyard provenance of the manuscript see L. Urkevich, 'Anne Boleyn, a Music Book, and the Northern Renaissance Courts: Music Manuscript 1070 of the Royal College of Music, London' (Ph.D diss., University of Maryland, 1996)), Petrucci 1504 and VatS 42 (*c*. 1508–9).

[99] Bars II/1–7 in the edition by Henri Expert.

[100] Petrucci printed the motet in *Motetti C* of 1504. Though the passage is brief, the Sienese version – and only this version – agrees in every particular with Petrucci's ligatures.

have been available along the same lines of transmission from which the masses arrived. If the Sienese scribes of the second layer had two transmission routes – the first for the masses through Milan – where did the second path lie? Likely candidates include neighbouring Florence and earlier Sienese sources.[101] **Si**, in fact, provides some circumstantial evidence relating the music of the rival Tuscan cities. Anthony Cummings first noted the presence of two Ninot le Petit motets, *Si oblitus fuero* and *Psallite noe*, as a pair in both **Si** and FlorBN II.I.232.[102] A fourth scribe, working after Scribe A and his assistants, entered this pair of motets into blank pages of **Si**; it took place perhaps after the binding of **Si** around 1511, and certainly before the 'vechio vechio' inventory description of 1524.[103] The Sienese reading of this pair is clearly dependent upon Petrucci; both motets use the rare mensuration sign ♀ that Bonnie Blackburn has identified as a sign of Petrucci's editor, and only these two sources contain Petrucci's peculiar correction of a notational error.[104] Though the Florentine reading does not completely follow **Si**, the Sienese pair are in the same order as in the closely contemporary Florentine source, and they show a marked visual similarity to FlorBN II.I.232 and other Florentine sacred sources; perhaps the

---

[101] See Planchart, 'Northern Repertories'. His findings, as noted above, must be read in the light of the relocation of VatS 14 and 51 to Ferrara by Anna Maria Talamo, in *Codices codicorum: Miniature e disegni nei codici della Capella Sistina* (Rome, 1997), pp. 23–39. Earlier work on the provenance of the two manuscripts was presented by F. Warmington, 'The Winds of Fortune: A New View of the Provenance and Date of the Cappella Sistina Manuscripts 14 and 51', paper read at the Annual Meeting of the American Musicological Society, Chicago, 1991; see also Roth, *Studien*; id., 'Napoli o Firenze? Dove sono stati compilati i manoscritti CS 14 e CS 51?', in Gargiulo (ed.), *La musica a Firenze*, pp. 69–100.

[102] A. Cummings, 'A Florentine Sacred Repertory from the Medici Restoration', *Acta Musicologica*, 55 (1983), pp. 267–322, at p. 314. FlorBN II.I.232 dates from *c.* 1516 to 1521. An edition of the motets is in Ninot le Petit, *Opera Omnia*, ed. B. Hudson (Corpus Mensurabilis Musicae, 87; n.p., 1979), pp. 84–107.

[103] The two travel as a pair as well in VatS 42 (*c.* 1504–7), where they are not adjacent, and in *Motetti C* (1504). In the Florentine source, they are preceded by a third Ninot motet; as the pair in **Si** ends incompletely at a gathering break, the Sienese version could have originally contained all three.

[104] Thomas Noblitt first noted the error and Petrucci's correction in 'Textual Criticism of Selected Works Published by Petrucci', in L. Finscher (ed.), *Formen und Probleme der Überlieferung mehrstimmiger Musik im Zeitalter Josquins Desprez* (Quellenstudien zur Musik der Renaissance, 1; Munich, 1981), pp. 201–42, at p. 227, n. 27. See also B. Blackburn, 'The Sign of Petrucci's Editor', paper read at the international conference 'Venezia 1501: Petrucci e la Stampa Musicale', Venice, 12 October 2001 (forthcoming in the conference proceedings). I am grateful to Dr Blackburn for sending me a copy of her paper prior to publication.

scribe worked concurrently in Florence.[105] The Florentine manuscript also contains two motets by Eustachio de Monte Regali, who served as Sienese *maestro di cappella* in the first decade of the century.

Frank D'Accone has documented numerous occasions throughout the fifteenth and sixteenth centuries when musicians travelled between Florence and Siena.[106] The sharing of musicians opened a conduit for musical transmission that could operate even when the two were nominally at war. A transmission link between **Si** and FlorBN II.I.232 would date from the 1510s. My forthcoming study of musical transmission between the two cities, including a new source, will extend the link back into the previous century. Thus, it is possible that a great deal of the second layer of **Si** (possibly including the anomalies) was shared between Siena and Florence. The redating of the Siena choirbook opens many new vistas for scholarly enquiry into both the local and the international repertories playing across Italy in the fifteenth and early sixteenth centuries.

University of Iowa

---

[105] The style of Scribe D's ornamental capitals and voice designations echoes several volumes of polyphony compiled for the Florentine Duomo, such as Florence, Archivio Musicale dell'Opera di Santa Maria del Fiore, Ms. mus. 11; facs. edn., ed. F. D'Accone (Renaissance Music in Facsimile, 3; New York, 1986). Several similar volumes have been dated to the mid-sixteenth-century by their repertory and by dates inscribed on banderoles within their initial capitals.

[106] Some examples discussed by D'Accone are in *Civic Muse*, pp. 205, 228, 243, 471, 526, 548, 551.

Rethinking the Siena choirbook

APPENDIX

Inventory and Contents of SienBC K.1.2

Fascicle: gathering number, with the type of gathering (quaternion, quinternion, etc.) in subscript; gathering signatures, in the upper right-hand corner, are indicated in parentheses.

Folio: current foliation of the manuscript. Scribe B foliated through f. 13[6]; a second hand later added foliation from 137 to 224.

Alternate foliation: alternate vestigial foliations.

Watermark: Scala 2 (three-rung ladder in circle), *Corona* (crown surmounted by an orb), *Scala* 1 (four-rung ladder).

Hand: seventeen scribes, enumerated in the order of their appearance, first the major scribes, those whose work included at least one complete polyphonic piece (scribes A–D in the second layer and F–K in the first layer), followed by the scribes whose contribution was limited to minor additions within each layer, scribes P–T and U–W.

Number: each complete and partial piece in **Si** is numbered editorially.

Ascription: composers identified from other sources are given in square brackets.

Title: titles have been standardized. A downward arrow indicates continuous copying between fascicles.

The Second Layer (c. 1502–1504)

Fascicle	Folio	Alternate foliation	Watermark	Hand	No.	Ascription	Title
	(leaf)						index
	i–ii						(blank)
	ii^v			B			
	iii			↓			
I$_5$	1		Scala 1				
	1^v–3			A	1	[anon.:]	Dixit Dominus [Ps. 109]
	3^v–5				2		Confitebor [Ps. 110]
	5^v–7				3		Beatus vir [Ps. 111]
	7^v–9				4		Laudate pueri [Ps. 112]
	9^v–10^v				5		Credidi [Ps. 115]
II$_4$	12						Dixit Dominus
	12^v–13				6		Laudate pueri [Ps. 112]
	13^v–15				7		Laetatus sum [Ps. 121]
	15^v–17				8		Nisi Dominus [Ps. 126]
	17^v–18				9		Lauda Jerusalem [Ps. 147]
	18^v–19^v			↓	10		
III$_5$ (3)	20						In exitu Israel [Ps. 113]
	20^v–24				11		De profundis [Ps. 129]
	24^v–26				12		Memento Domine [Ps. 131]
	26^v–29			B	13		Pange lingua
	29^v			↓	14		
IV$_4$ (4)	30						Dixit Dominus
	30^v–32				15		Confitebor
	32^v–34				16		Laudate Dominum [Ps. 116]
	34^v–35				17		Credidi
	35^v–36				18		

Rethinking the Siena choirbook

	Folios		No.		Title
		(P)	18b		(Credidi alt.)
			19		Dixit Dominus
V₄ (5)	36ᵛ–37		20		Beatus vir
	37ᵛ	→ C	21		Memento Domine
	38–39	(Q)	22		(alt. Memento)
	39ᵛ–41				(blank)
	41ᵛ–44				(blank)
	44ᵛ–45	A	23		Veni Creator
	45ᵛ		24		Pange lingua
VI₅ (6)	46		25		Jesu nostra/Amor
	46ᵛ–47		26		Lucis creator optime
	47ᵛ–48		27		Nardi Maria picisti
	48ᵛ–49		28		Deus tuorum militum
	49ᵛ–50		29		Tibi Christe
	50ᵛ–51		30		Exultet celum laudibus
	51ᵛ–52	→	31		Sanctorum meritis
	52ᵛ–53				(blank)
	53ᵛ–54				(blank)
	54ᵛ–55	C/B	32		Christe redemptor/Conserva
	55ᵛ	B	33		Conditor alme siderum
	56	→ D	34		Christe redemptor/ex
VII₅ (7)	56ᵛ–57	B	35a/b		Conditor alme siderum
	57ᵛ–58		35c		→
	58ᵛ–59		36		Domine probasti me [Ps. 138.I]
	59ᵛ–60		37		Confitebor [Ps. 138.II]
	60ᵛ–61		38		O lux beata trinitas
	61ᵛ–63				
	63ᵛ–65				
	65ᵛ				

Continued over

The Second Layer (c. 1502–1504) Continued

Fascicle	Folio	Alternate foliation	Watermark	Hand	No.	Ascription	Title
VIII$_{[4]}$ (8) lacks 2nd bifol.	66			A	39		Magnificat ottavi toni
	66^v–70						
	70^v			B	40		O lux beata trinitas
	71	54		→			→
	71^v			A			[textless fragment]
IX$_4$ (9)	72–73				41		Magnificat ottavi toni
	73^v–78				42		Magnificat quinti toni
	78^v–79^v				43		Magnificat primi toni
X$_5$ (10)	80				44		
	83^v–87				45		Magnificat primi toni
	87^v–89				46		Magnificat [primi toni?]
	89^v						(blank)
XI$_4$ (11)	90						(blank)
	90^v–96				47		Magnificat primi toni
	96^v–97			B	48		Ad cenam agni
	97^v			→	49		Magnificat primi toni
XII$_4$ (12)	98–100				50		Magnificat ottavi toni
	100^v			(R)			→
	101			(Q/B)			
	101^v			B			
	102			→			
	102^v–103				51		Asperges me
	103^v–10[4]				52		[textless fragment]
	10[4]^v			E	53		Ad cenam agni

Rethinking the Siena choirbook

Gathering	Folio	Composer	Title	Section
XIII[5?] (13) now 3 bifolia	105		[Anon.] Obsecro te sancta maria (2vv.)	A
	105ᵛ		Ave Maria ... quomodo fiet istud (2vv.)	
	108			
	108ᵛ–110	[Weerbeke]	O virginum praeclara	
	110ᵛ	[Compère]	Ave Maria ... Kyrie (2vv.)	
	112		(2.p. Sancte Michael, 2vv.)	
	112ᵛ–113	[Anon.]	Sub tuum presidium	
	113ᵛ	[Anon.]	Ave Maria ... mortis nostrae	
XIV₅ (14)	114			
	114ᵛ–116	[Anon.]	Ave Maria ... ut in valle	A/B
	116ᵛ–117	[Mouton]	Sancti Dei omnes	A
	117ᵛ–118		(Christe audi nos addition)	B
	118ᵛ–120	[Weerbeke]	Virgo Maria, non est tibi similis	
	120ᵛ–121	[Anon.]	Petrus et Johannes	
	121ᵛ–123		(blank)	
	123ᵛ		(blank)	
XV[4?] bifolium only	12?		Verbum caro factum est (2vv.)	
	12?ᵛ		(blank)	
	130		Verbum caro factum est	A
	130ᵛ			B
XVI[4] (16) lacks final fol.	131	[Martini]	Missa Coda di pavon	
	131ᵛ–13[6]	'Agricola secundi toni'	Magnificat	
	13[6]ᵛ			

Continued over

The Second Layer (c. 1502–1504) *Continued*

Fascicle	Folio	Alternate foliation	Watermark	Hand	No.	Ascription	Title
[XVII]							
XVIII₅ (18)	137–147ᵛ			A	68	[Isaac]	Missa Quant jai au cueur
XIX₄ (19)	148	142: '85'					→
	148ᵛ–155ᵛ				69	[Anon.]	Missa carminum
	149–152:	'94–95'					→
	156						(blank)
XX₅ (20)	156ᵛ–165ᵛ	159: '1 …'			70	[Obrecht]	Missa Beata viscera
XXI₅	166–168						→
	168ᵛ–175ᵛ				71	[Anon.]	Missa De tous biens plaine
XXII₅ (22)	176–181						→
	181ᵛ–182			B			(blank)
	182ᵛ–184				72	[Compère]	O genetrix gloriosa
	184ᵛ–185						(blank)
	185ᵛ				73	[Compère]	Missa brevis (Gloria)
XXIII₍₂₎	186–186ᵛ	193					→
	187–187ᵛ				74	[Martini]	Missa Orsus, orsus (Credo)

Rethinking the Siena choirbook

XXIV₅₊₁ (24)	188			
	188ᵛ		75	Exultet celum
	189		76	Deus tuorum militum
	189ᵛ–190	(P)	77	Deus tuorum militum
	190ᵛ–191		78	Iste confessor
	191ᵛ–192	D	79	Sanctorum meritis
	192ᵛ–196		80	Si oblitus fuero [Nino le Petit]
	196ᵛ–197ᵛ	(S)	81	Psallite noe [Nino]
	198	B	82	[textless, 2vv.]
	198ᵛ		83	Sumens à 3 [textless]
XXV [5] (25) lacks final fol.	199	k1		(blank)
	199ᵛ–201	T	84	Asperges me
	200–202: 'k2–k4'			
	201ᵛ–202	A	85	Asperges me
	202ᵛ–203		86	(blank)
	203ᵛ–205		87a/b	Vidi aquam
	205ᵛ		87c	Verbum caro factum est
	206ᵛ			
	207ᵛ			(blank)

Corona

The First Layer (1481)

Fascicle	Folio	Alternate foliation	Watermark	Hand	No.	Ascription	Title
XXVI[4] outer 2 bifolia	208–209	279–280	Scala 2	F	88	[Basiron]	Missa De Franza (Osanna–Agnus Dei)
	209ᵛ						(blank)
	210	285		(U)	89		[textless fragment]
	210ᵛ–211	211: '286'		G	90	'Simonis' [Simone da Siena]	Asperges me
	211ᵛ						(blank)
XXVII₅212	287–296					(blank)	
	212ᵛ–214			H/V	91	[Josquin]	Missa L'ami baudichon (Gloria)
	214ᵛ–221			J/V	92	[Martini]	Missa Dio te salvi gotterello
	221ᵛ						[textless fragment, 2vv.]
XXVIII[P] 1 fol./1 bifol.	222	94		K	93	[Dufay]	Missa Se la face ay pale (Benedictus, Osanna)
	222ᵛ						(blank)
	223	98					(Patrem, 2vv.)
	223ᵛ						(Et iterum, 2vv.)
	224	99					(blank)
	224ᵛ			(W)			[textless fragment]

MARY E. FRANDSEN

EUNUCHI CONJUGIUM: THE MARRIAGE OF A CASTRATO IN EARLY MODERN GERMANY

Although the castrato played a central role in seventeenth- and early eighteenth-century musical life, he occupied a position at the margins of early modern society. As a consequence of the surgical alteration of his body and the superior musical training that he received as compensation for his 'acquiescence' in that act, he found himself navigating a path through a bifurcated world. For him, the surgery had both public and private consequences: while society would publicly celebrate his vocal virtuosity, it would also circumscribe his private activities, and withhold from him the right to marry, or to enjoy an intimate relationship with a woman. As he soon realised, the realities of his special status meant that many of those who would revel in his phenomenal vocal abilities would also ridicule him as effeminate and as a sexual misfit, and would accuse him, ironically, of possessing a voracious sexual appetite that rendered him a threat to women. When he travelled north to work in German-speaking societies, particularly those in which the Lutheran confession held sway, that simple migratory act instantly compounded the number of those qualities that contributed to his 'Otherness': while in his homeland his standing as an emasculate and a musician already set him apart from others, in Lutheran regions, his status as a foreigner, an adherent of an outlawed (and highly suspect) confession, and a member of a privileged group that

The research and writing of this study were made possible in large part through a Summer Stipend from the National Endowment for the Humanities and a Fellowship from the American Council of Learned Societies. Some of the material discussed here was presented at the Sixty-Ninth Annual Meeting of the American Musicological Society in Houston, Texas, November 2003. I wish to thank Howard Louthan for his helpful comments on an earlier draft of this essay, and Paula Higgins for many profitable discussions on the subject. I also thank David Bachrach and Margaret Garnett for providing translations of the Latin texts, and Mathias Thierbach for assisting with several German translations. Finally, I thank Bonnie Blackburn for her editorial suggestions, which have improved this article, and Leofranc Holford-Strevens for his invaluable assistance with a number of translation issues.

53

moved in the rarefied atmosphere of the local court all served to intensify his marginality. Difference, it would seem, governed every aspect of his life, from his upbringing and early socialisation to his vocal range and physical appearance. As a result, he represents an extraordinarily complex specimen of the early modern man, the meaning of whose existence can be decoded only with difficulty.

But despite the many obstacles that this acquired difference placed in his path, the castrato nevertheless succeeded in developing strategies for survival, and managed to carve out a place or places for himself in public circles as well as in the private realm. Most of the time he seems to have accepted the fundamental dichotomy – that is, simultaneous centrality and marginality – defining his condition, and learnt somehow to deal with its inherent contradictions. Thus he normally sought to take up residence only in those spaces into which he had been welcomed, primarily the musical spaces of the stage, the church, and the court. At times, however, he occupied one of the few other spaces open to him at court and in civic life.[1] When not performing or serving in one of these capacities, however, the castrato generally retired from view; the relative scarcity of information about his private existence suggests that he typically lived a quiet life. In such ways the castrato and his 'otherness' could be accommodated both publicly and privately, so that he did not pose any more of a threat to accepted norms than he already did as a result of his indeterminate sexuality. But very occasionally, in an attempt to resolve the ambiguities caused by his status as musical insider/sexual outsider, the castrato rejected his fixed position at the margins of society and tried to force himself into the centre, and sought to claim for himself a place normally reserved for the uncastrated man: a place in the marriage bed. In so doing, he threatened to subvert established codes of order regarding intimate relationships, many of which had been recognised for centuries.

---

[1] Castrati are known to have served as courtiers of lower rank, as court agents and low-level diplomats, and occasionally as public officials; see, for example, M. Fürstenau, *Zur Geschichte der Musik und des Theaters am Hofe zu Dresden*, 2 vols. in 1 (Dresden, 1861–2; repr. Leipzig, 1971), i, pp. 11–16, 260–2; J. Rosselli, 'The Castrati as a Professional Group and a Social Phenomenon, 1550–1850', *Acta Musicologica*, 60 (1988), pp. 143–79, at pp. 169–73; and R. Freitas, '*Un atto d'ingegno*: A Castrato in the Seventeenth Century' (Ph.D. diss., Yale University, 1998).

Eunuchi Conjugium

One of the most remarkable and well-documented instances of such an effort by a castrato occurred in seventeenth-century Dresden, and involved the castrato Bartolomeo Sorlisi, a singer in the electoral Hofkapelle there. In 1667, after a prolonged and at times trying engagement, Sorlisi succeeded in marrying a young woman named Dorothea Lichtwer, the stepdaughter of a lawyer who practised in that city.[2] Sorlisi, it would seem, was a rather plucky individual of great resolve. After falling in love with Dorothea, he managed to ingratiate himself with her mother and stepfather to the extent that he was able to persuade them to draw up and sign a betrothal agreement. He subsequently acquired permission from local church authorities to marry Dorothea, in part by asserting that he possessed the capacity to 'render the marital debt'. As might well be imagined, the decision and subsequent nuptials unleashed a firestorm of criticism from some members of the Lutheran theological establishment. But contemporary theologians did not speak with one voice on the matter; instead, a surprising number wrote in support of the unusual union, which was ultimately allowed to stand. And both before the wedding and throughout the long battle with church authorities that ensued afterwards, Sorlisi received considerable support from an individual whose trust he had gradually garnered: his German father-in-law, the lawyer Moritz Junghanns. Sorlisi's fascinating story, with all of its twists and turns, chronicles the experience of a castrato *cum* private citizen in seventeenth-century Germany. Not only does this microhistory illuminate the personal relationships that one castrato developed with the members of a *bürgerlich* Lutheran family, it also details the far-reaching consequences of his decision to push one of those relationships far beyond traditionally accepted limits.

Owing to the highly controversial nature of the Sorlisi–Lichtwer relationship, news of it spread quickly throughout all Saxony, and

[2] Dorothea was a member of a prominent Dresden family with strong connections to the court. Her father, Augustin Lichtwer (1594–1646), served in the 1620s as court organist to the Dowager Electress Hedwig in Lichtenburg (Saxony) as well as at the court of Duke Friedrich III of Schleswig-Holstein-Gottorf until he was called to Dresden in 1625 by Elector Johann Georg I (r. 1611–56) to serve as Saxon 'Renterei- und Steuersekretär'. Several of Dorothea's elder half-brothers also held court appointments, as did the husbands of two of her half-sisters. See P. Zimmermann, 'Chronik der Familie Lichtwer von 1520 bis 1800', *Familienforschung in Mitteldeutschland*, 42 (2001), pp. 165–75, at 167–8.

made the couple the target of much gossip and debate. Even the deaths of those immediately involved could do little to quell the storm – only fifteen years after Sorlisi's death, many of the theological opinions were published, together with his petition, in a collection aptly entitled *Eunuchi conjugium*.[3] This collection, which went through numerous editions, continued to provoke debates on the matter among members of the contemporary theological and lay communities well into the eighteenth century. The marriage, and the scandal that enveloped it, became part of the Saxon historical landscape, and received passing mention in numerous eighteenth- and nineteenth-century publications, particularly earlier histories of the electorate and the electoral court.[4] It continues to surface in contemporary scholarship on the castrato, where the treatment is often similarly cursory.[5] But given its singularity, as well as its

---

[3] H. Delphinus (pseud.) (ed.), *Eunuchi conjugium: Die Capaunen-Heirath, Hoc est Scripta et judicia varia de conjugio inter eunuchum et virginem juvenculam Anno M. DC. LXVI. contracto, T. T. A. quibusdam supremis theologorum collegiis petita, postea hinc inde collecta ab Hieronymo Delphino, C.P.* (Halle, 1718); this represents the third of nine editions; the preface is dated 1685. (The 1718 edition is available on microfilm in the Harold Jantz Collection of German Baroque Literature, no. 2885.) Many of the documents included in this publication also survive in manuscript in the Sächsisches Hauptstaatsarchiv (hereafter Sächs. HStA) in Dresden; these concordances are noted below. The Sächs. HStA also holds additional related materials, in Loc. 7445/18, *Die Vereheligung des Churfürstl. Geheimen Cämmeriers, Bartholomaei de Sorlisi, mit Dorotheen Elisabethen Lichtwerin bel. ao. 1667*. In addition, a previously unknown set of papers survives in the Universitätsarchiv Greifswald (hereafter UAG), Theologische Fakultät Nr. 3 (unfoliated). I would like to thank Greifswald University Archivist Dr Dirk Alvermann for his help in locating the latter set of documents.

[4] These include: 'Mr Bruckner', *Décisions du droit matrimonial*, published by J. Basnage, Sieur de Beauval (1653–1723) in *Histoire des ouvrages des sçavans*, Feb. 1706, cited in C. Ancillon, *Traité des eunuques* (Berlin, 1707), ed. D. Fernandez, Latin trans. by J. Raabe (Paris, 1978), p. 213; Ancillon also mentions the Sorlisi case on p. 219; J. C. Hasche, *Diplomatische Geschichte Dresdens von seiner Entstehung bis auf unsere Tage*, pt. 3 (Dresden, 1817), p. 233; C. W. Böttiger, *Geschichte des Kurstaats und Königreiches Sachsen* (Hamburg, 1831), p. 167; E. Vehse, *Geschichte der deutschen Höfe seit der Reformation*, pt. 5: Saxony: *Geschichte der Höfe des Hauses Sachsen* (Hamburg, 1854), vol. 4 (vol. 31 in overall series), p. 60; M. B. Lindau, *Geschichte der königliche Haupt- und Residenzstadt Dresden*, 2nd edn (Dresden, 1885; first published Dresden, 1859–63), pp. 492–3; Fürstenau, *Zur Geschichte der Musik und des Theaters*, i, p. 14; B. Auerbach, *La diplomatie française et la cour de Saxe (1648–1680)* (Paris, 1887), p. 414; T. Distel, 'Aus kursächsischen Ehesachen (1667, 1729 und 1746)', *Deutsche Zeitschrift für Kirchenrecht*, 6 (1896), pp. 233–8.

[5] Taken chronologically, these include: F. Haböck, *Die Kastraten und ihre Gesangskunst* (Berlin and Leipzig, 1927), pp. 302–9; A. Heriot, *The Castrati in Opera* (London, 1956), p. 57; Rosselli, 'The Castrati as a Professional Group', p. 176; P. Barbier, *The World of the Castrati: The History of an Extraordinary Operatic Phenomenon*, trans. M. Crosland (London, 1996), p. 142; Rosselli, *Singers of Italian Opera: The History of a Profession* (Cambridge, 1992), p. 52; H. Ortkemper, *Engel wider Willen: Die Welt der Kastraten. Eine andere Operngeschichte* (Munich, 1995), pp. 192–202. Only Haböck and Ortkemper have treated the case at any length; both include a number of quotations from *Eunuchi conjugium*.

Eunuchi Conjugium

potential to inform modern scholarship on the castrato, this marriage event and all that surrounded it merit a much closer look. Although it does not seem to have cleared the path for other similar unions, Sorlisi's successful bid for permission to marry did expose vulnerabilities in the stronghold of views regarding intimate relationships and the reasons for marriage. For ultimately, Sorlisi's story foregrounded a conundrum that had perplexed Western society for centuries: what conjugal rights could be claimed by the ungenerative yet virile man?

Given that Sorlisi sought to avail himself of a right traditionally withheld from castrates, questions about his sexual capacity immediately rose to the surface, and dominated much of the discussion of the case. In themselves, these discussions shed interesting light on this much-debated subject, and present challenges to some of the views held today. But the details of Sorlisi's protracted but ultimately successful struggle to win the hand of Dorothea also raise fundamental questions about several of the more elusive facets of the castrato's persona, particularly his sense of self and capacity for emotion. In contrast to the stereotyped view of the castrato as effeminate held by many of his contemporaries, Sorlisi seems to have been determined to see and represent himself as an utterly 'masculine' man, one who not only participated in many of the public activities closely bound up with early modern concepts of masculinity, but also in those private behaviours that had been identified with manhood from time immemorial. Yet he also revealed a more tender side, and showed himself to have been unafraid to express true affection. His desire to marry may suggest that he (not surprisingly) was unable to reconcile himself entirely to the implications of his physical condition, or, alternatively, that he did not view his condition as limiting. Although a wild rhetoric that sought to portray him as a dangerous creature with uncontrollable carnal desires threatened to dominate the discourse from the moment his courtship of Dorothea began, the quieter message of his yearning for close society grew continually stronger, and refused to yield place. In the end, although his story speaks to many topics, the most enduring lesson it teaches may be quite elemental, for it underscores the importance of love and acceptance to the human condition.

Mary E. Frandsen

Sorlisi, a soprano castrato, was probably born in Milan in 1631 or 1632.[6] While no information regarding his musical training has surfaced, his first northern musical appointment seems to have been at the electoral Bavarian court in Munich, where he may have arrived as early as 1646.[7] Sorlisi's association with the Dresden court began in 1651, when he was one of four Italian musicians that the Saxon electoral prince, Johann Georg II (1613–80), attempted to lure away from the Bavarian court through the offices of the castrati Bandino Bandini and Giovanni Andrea Bontempi – an attempt that raised the ire of the Bavarian electress Maria Anna.[8] Sorlisi remained in Munich for seven more years; in 1657, he sang in Johann Caspar Kerll's *Orontes*.[9] In 1658, now as elector, Johann Georg II (r. 1656–80) appointed him to his Hofkapelle; three years later, he elevated the singer to the rank of privy chamberlain (*Geheime Kammerdiener*).[10] Sorlisi continued to climb the ladder of success in Dresden; in November 1665, he and another castrato, Domenico Melani, were ennobled by the emperor, doubtless at the request of Johann Georg, who announced the honour that had been bestowed on the singers on

---

[6] Moritz Junghanns, Sorlisi's father-in-law, indicated that the castrato hailed from Milan (UAG, Theologische Fakultät Nr. 3, letter of Junghanns to the Greifswald faculty); see n. 155 below. He died in Dresden at age 40 on 3 March 1672 (Sächsische Landes- und Universitätsbibliothek (hereafter SLUB) Msc. Dresd. Q 255, *Alter und Neuer Schreib-Calender auf das Schalt-Jahr ... M.DC.LXII* (unfoliated), entry for Sunday, 3 March 1672: 'Frühe halb 8. Uhr ist in Dreßden der Churf. Amts Haubtmann zu Dippoldiswalda Hr. Bartholomeo de Sorlisÿ verstorben, im 40. Jahr seines alters'). According to the singer's will, his mother later lived in Pavia, which Horst Leuchtmann suggested was his birthplace; see T. Distel, 'Einiges über den Kastraten Sorlisi', *Monatshefte für Musikgeschichte*, 28 (1896), pp. 87–8, and Leuchtmann, 'Die Maximilianische Hofkapelle', in *Um Glauben und Reich: Kurfürst Maximilian I. Beiträge zur bayerischen Geschichte und Kunst 1573–1657*, 2 vols. (Munich and Zurich, 1980), i, pp. 364–75, at p. 371.
[7] According to Leuchtmann, Sorlisi (Sorlisio) was a singer at the Bavarian court from 1646 ('Die Maximilianische Hofkapelle', p. 371). Robert Eitner indicated that his service began in 1651 (*Bio-bibliographisches Quellen-Lexikon der Musiker und Musikgelehrten* (Leipzig, 1900–4), ix, p. 211), while Sandberger located a contract for him in the Bavarian court archives dated 27 July 1652; see *Ausgewählte Werke des kurfürstlich bayerischen Hofkapellmeisters Johann Kaspar Kerll (1627–1693)*, ed. A. Sandberger, pt. 1 (Denkmäler der Tonkunst in Bayern, 2. Jahrgang, 2; Leipzig, 1901), p. xix.
[8] Sächs. HStA Loc. 8561/5, *Correspondenz Churf. Johann Georg II. A-E.*, no. 15 (... *mit Maria Anna, Churfürstin von Bayern, Tochter Kaiser Ferdinand II*), fols. 236ʳ–237ʳ.
[9] Sandberger, *Ausgewählte Werke ... Kerll*, p. xxviii.
[10] SLUB Msc. Dresd. Q 238, *Calendar Churfürst Johann Georgens der Andern. Die Jahre 1657. 58. 59. 60. und 61.* (unfoliated), entry for 28 May 1661: 'Wurde auch von Sr Churf. Durchlt. der Italiener Bartholomeus Sorlisius als geheimer Cammer Diener verpflichtet.'

Eunuchi Conjugium

24 January 1666.[11] Not long thereafter, both were elevated to the rank of *geheimer Kämmerer*, the lowest of the three ranks of aristocratic chamberlains.[12] Some time in 1670, Johann Georg named both Melani and Sorlisi to the ever-expanding complement of court *Kammerjunker*,[13] along with the appointment to this significantly higher rank came positions in the *Hofordnung* and numerous privileges, such as the right to participate with the other courtiers in court festivities.[14] Johann Georg also appointed both castrati to the post of district magistrate (*Amtshauptmann*) in the Saxon town of Dippoldiswalda, south of Dresden, from which both were able to draw additional income; Sorlisi was awarded the post in 1670, and Melani in 1678.[15]

Throughout his career in Dresden, Sorlisi enjoyed the favour of Elector Johann Georg II, who evidently suggested to the singer that he buy property in Saxony and retire there after his days of service

---

[11] Sächs. HStA Loc. 8681 Nr. 6, fol. 232ʳ, entry for 24 January 1666; see also Fürstenau, *Zur Geschichte der Musik und des Theaters*, i, p. 11. The patent of nobility was dated 23 November 1665; see Karl Friedrich von Frank, *Standeserhebungen und Gnadenakte für das Deutsche Reich und die Österreichische Erblande bis 1806* (Schloss Senftenegg, 1967), iii, p. 223; v, p. 23.

[12] J. C. Adelung (1732–1806), 'electoral Saxon court councillor and chief librarian', gives the three ranks as *Kammerherr*, *Kammerjunker* and *Kammer-page*; see *Grammatisch-kritisches Wörterbuch der Hochdeutschen Mundart, mit beständiger Vergleichung der übrigen Mundarten, besonders aber der Oberdeutschen*, ed. F. X. Schönberger (Vienna, 1811), at http://mdz.bib-bvb.de:80/digbib/lexika/ adelung. However, the term *Kammerpage* is never used at this time in Dresden, and *Kämmerer* seems to have been the equivalent, given its position in the later *Hofordnungen*. Sorlisi is still described as 'geheimbte Cammerdiener' in July 1665 (SLUB Msc. Dresd. K 80, *Diarium Anno Christi M.DC.LXV.*, fol. 43ᵛ, entry for 29 July 1665), but both men are described as 'geheimer Cämmerirer' in July 1667 (Sächs HStA Loc. 8681 Nr. 7, *ChurFürst: Sächssl: Hoff-Diaria de Anno 1667 usq. 1671*, fol. 2ᵛ, entry for 31 July 1667).

[13] Adelung defines a *Kammerjunker* as 'a young man of high birth who has been appointed to the service of a royal person in his rooms, and who stands midway between the *Kammerherren* and the *Kammer-Pagen*; an aristocratic chamber valet of the second rank' ('ein junger Edelmann, welcher zur Bedienung einer fürstlichen Person in ihren Zimmern bestimmt ist, und zwischen den Kammerherren und Kammer-Pagen in der Mitte stehet; ein adeliger Kammerbedienter vom zweyten Range'); see *Grammatisch-kritisches Wörterbuch der Hochdeutschen Mundart*, on-line edition.

[14] On 1 January 1671, the *Hofordnung* of 1666 was revised, at which time the names of Melani and Sorlisi were added to the category of *Kammerjunker*, Melani as no. 138, and Sorlisi, 'Ambts Hauptmann zu Dippoldiswalda', as no. 165 (the numbers refer to their respective positions within the entire *Hofordnung*); Sächs. HStA Loc. 8685/3, *Hofordnungen 1661–1716* (unfoliated).

[15] According to Fürstenau, Johann Georg appointed Sorlisi to the post on 1 June 1670, with a salary of 200 tl, and Melani followed his colleague (but not directly) in the post on 18 May 1678 (*Zur Geschichte der Musik und des Theaters*, i, pp. 13, 15). Melani's commission as *Amtshauptmann* appears in Sächs. HStA Loc. 8685/11, *Intimationes aus dem Hoff-Marschall Amte, Ao 1667 sqqv.*, fol. 99. For a description of the responsibilities and duties of an Amtshauptmann during this era, see H. Haug, 'Die Ämter-, Kammerguts- und Rentkammer-Rechnungen des Hauptstaatsarchivs zu Dresden', *Neues Archiv für sächsische Geschichte und Altertumskunde*, 20 (1899), pp. 72–104, at pp. 84–5.

at the court had come to an end.¹⁶ Thus, at some point in 1661 or 1662, the castrato set out to find a suitable property to purchase. He soon began to suspect that he was being dealt with less than honestly, however, and secured the services of one Moritz Junghanns, J.D., a lawyer in Dresden affiliated with the electoral court.¹⁷ Junghanns travelled with the castrato to view several properties, one of which, a *Ritter-Guth* (a feudal estate or manor) in Schmiedeberg, a town south of Dresden, Sorlisi decided to purchase. According to Junghanns, Sorlisi paid 10,000 gulden in cash for the property – a sum equal to ten times his annual salary as a singer in the Hofkapelle.¹⁸ After the legal transactions had been completed, however, Sorlisi continued to visit the Junghanns household, and gradually fell in love with Junghanns's then 16-year-old stepdaughter, Dorothea Elisabeth Lichtwer. Eventually he asked for her parents' consent to marry her, 'a request that struck [them] as not a little odd, and also seemed very peculiar'.¹⁹ Junghanns and his wife, citing the writings of Benedict Carpzov (1595–1666), a Lutheran scholar of ecclesiastical law,²⁰ strongly cautioned Dorothea that such a marriage would not be allowed, and 'with the greatest earnestness, admonished her to abandon her plan,

---

[16] Unless otherwise noted, the information in the narrative that begins at this point as well as the quotations derive from Moritz Junghanns's letter of April 1668 to the theology faculty at the University of Greifswald, UAG, Theologische Fakultät Nr. 3. As is discussed below, in the spring of 1668 Junghanns wrote to the theology faculties at the universities of Jena, Greifswald and Königsberg, and requested their opinion on two questions.

[17] Junghanns signed himself the 'Chur-SächB. Renth-Cammer-*Procurator* und deroselben *Advocatus ordinarius*', in which office he presumably provided legal counsel in matters related to the court treasury (*Rentkammer*). Ortkemper states that Sorlisi purchased the property in 1665 (*Engel wider Willen*, p. 194), but by that time Sorlisi had already become engaged to Dorothea (May 1664), and the betrothal took place some time after the purchase.

[18] For Sorlisi's salary, see G. Spagnoli, *Letters and Documents of Heinrich Schütz, 1656–1672: An Annotated Translation* (Ann Arbor, 1990), p. 91. It is possible that he received some or all of these funds from Elector Johann Georg II.

[19] 'Welcheß anbringen Unß nicht wenig befrembdet, besondern auch sehr wunderlich vorgekommen.'

[20] Junghanns cites Carpzov's work as *Beat. Carpzov. Jurisprod. Consistorial. lib 2. tit. 1. n. 2. et seqq*; this is the latter's *Jurisprudentia ecclesiastica seu consistorialis*, first published in Hannover in 1649. Carpzov's main argument against the marriage of eunuchs, which he draws from Johann Gerhard's *Loci theologici*, Book 7: *De conjugio, coelibatu et similibus argumentis*, ch. 25, §235 (discussed below), appears in Book 2, title 1, definition 16 (*Jurisprudentia ecclesiastica* (Leipzig, 1708), ii, pp. 26–7). Gerhard bases his argument on the ninety-eighth Novel of Leo the Wise, a portion of which is quoted by Carpzov, and concludes that since the principal goal of marriage is procreation, and eunuchs cannot procreate (although they may be capable of copulation), they should not be allowed to marry.

Eunuchi Conjugium

and to change her mind'.[21] It is impossible to determine from Junghanns's letter just what he and his wife understood to be the realities of marriage to a castrato, and what information they imparted to Dorothea on the subject – did they simply explain that no children would issue forth from such a union, or did they tell her that a sexual relationship with Sorlisi would be impossible? Despite her parents' protestations, however, Dorothea had become equally smitten with the wealthy and prominent singer, and was quite unwilling to part with him. According to Junghanns, 'thereupon she (as an otherwise sensible young woman, better educated in Scripture than the average) immediately declared that she could not give him up, and that if she could not have this man, it would be impossible for her to love another'.[22]

Sorlisi proved to be a persistent suitor, and continued both to visit Dorothea on nearly a daily basis, and to press his case with her parents. As time passed, the Junghanns's resolve began to weaken, and finally, on 1 May 1664, they entered into a betrothal agreement with the castrato.[23] This remarkable document may well be the only one of its kind in existence. For this reason, and because the act of its signing set in motion such an extraordinary sequence of events, the text is worth quoting in full:[24]

Be it known by these presents that on behalf of these two people, namely Mr Bartolomeo Sorlisi, well-appointed Privy Chamberlain to His Electoral Highness of Saxony, and Miss Dorothea Elisabeth Lichtwer, this has been transacted on this day, Namely, the aforementioned Mr Sorlisi has brought up and put forward to us, as the maiden's natural mother and her stepfather, to wit how he for some time had borne an honourable and sincere affection for the aforementioned Miss Lichtwer, and therefore also sought the opportunity to become acquainted with her, and when he had succeeded in doing so, he revealed to her his intentions of love, that is to say that he wished to wed and marry her; soon thereafter, she promised her love to him in return, and with affectionate words also promised to continue therein until death. But to keep such entirely secret from us, the parents, as well as from our friends, would not have

---

[21] 'darbeÿ mit höchsten ernst ermahnet von ihren vorhaben abzustehen, und ihren Sinn zu ändern'.
[22] 'Darauff hatt Sie sich (alß eine sonst verständige und in Heil. Schrifft über die masen wohl belesene Weibes persohn) alsobalden erkläret, daß Sie von Ihme nicht laßen könte, und wenn Sie diesen nicht haben solte, were es in ihrem gemüthe unmöglich, einen andern lieb zu gewinnen.'
[23] UAG, Theologische Fakultät Nr. 3 (copy in Junghanns's hand included with his letter to the faculty). It was usual at this time for such an agreement to be concluded between the father or guardian of the bride-to-be and the future bridegroom; see Barbara Becker-Cantarino, *Der lange Weg zur Mündigkeit: Frau und Literatur (1500–1800)* (Stuttgart, 1987), pp. 49–50.
[24] The German text appears as Doc. 1 in the Appendix.

been gentlemanly of him. So, a few days later, he disclosed everything to us, and also sought our consent and good will. As such an intention certainly struck us as not a little strange, we also took the maiden in hand immediately afterwards and questioned her about it, and then both of us objected clearly and at length to both parties, and explained that this marriage could not take place, or ever be allowed. However, they both remained determined not to part from one another, unless death should separate them; in particular, however, the daughter let herself be heard with thoughtful words that she would not be dissuaded from it, and that one should not imagine that she would marry any other besides this Mr Sorlisi all her life long. Subsequently, after many intervening circumstances, we thus considered the fact that these two people intended to remain with one another unceasingly in mutual love, and we not only informed our other friends of such, but we finally, out of altogether exigent necessity, and because there was no other means to be devised, came to this conclusion, that we, along with other of our friends, would finally betrothe our daughter to him in such a manner, but with these express reservations and attached conditions: (1) Mr Sorlisi shall prove definitively in the eyes of the law, but especially before the ecclesiastical judges, whether he may be allowed to marry this person. In addition to this, (2) if the marriage should ever be permitted, he will allow her to remain for ever in the Lutheran religion, and will in no way give her cause to [convert to] his doctrine, neither through unpleasantness nor in other ways, and then finally, (3) he will provide for her in such a manner upon his death that she shall not suffer want and need until her death. Above all, before the marriage takes place, the marriage agreement shall be worked out and executed, and pledges concerning this shall be handed over. Since the aforementioned Mr Sorlisi has now acquiesced in all of this, so are we for our part also satisfied with it, and will in no way renounce what was promised to be performed. To that end we prepared this wholly in duplicate, and it was signed in their own hand by those in attendance as well as by the principal interested parties and by us, and was sealed. Executed in Dresden on 1 May 1664.

> Bartolomaeo Sorlisi
> George Lebe
> Johann George Baumgarten.
> Anna Dorothea Junghannßen
> M. Junghannß D(octor).

As a lawyer, Junghanns was doubtless responsible for drawing up the agreement, and thus it cannot be mere fortuity that the document makes no specific reference to Sorlisi's status as a castrato, but simply alludes to this all-important fact in the recounting of Dorothea's parents' opposition to the marriage, and in the first of the three stipulations. In this respect, the agreement is probably modelled upon those for confessionally mixed marriages, which would presumably have included all three stipulations.[25] But not only does Junghanns omit any and all references to Sorlisi's

---

[25] On marriage contracts and their provisions, see Dagmar Freist, 'One Body, Two Confessions: Mixed Marriages in Germany', in U. Rublack (ed.), *Gender in Early Modern German History* (Cambridge, 2002), pp. 275–304, and Becker-Cantarino, *Der lange Weg zur Mündigkeit*, pp. 49–50.

eunuchism, he makes a quite striking effort to craft an image of Sorlisi that conforms to early modern 'codes of masculinity': his affection for Dorothea is 'honourable and sincere', he is 'gentlemanly', that is, he acknowledges and adheres to accepted codes of social conduct, and finally, he sought her parents' 'consent and good will'.[26] Despite his use of even-handed, legalistic language, however, Junghanns was nonetheless unable to avoid revealing the angst experienced by parents faced with this exceptional turn of events, for their wishes were clearly at odds with those of Dorothea. Despite their parental desire for her happiness, and their apparent respect and fondness for Sorlisi, they had grave concerns about the implications of this marriage for her, and probably for the family as well, for such a match was bound to bring much unwelcome scrutiny and attention to their doorstep. But at the same time, they also recognised that the love professed by the couple was genuine, and worthy of consideration.[27] Under considerable pressure from the couple, the Junghanns finally devised what appeared to be a workable solution: they would accede to the couple's wishes by preparing a betrothal agreement and lending their consent to the marriage, but would impose three conditions on the match, one of which they must have felt certain Sorlisi could never satisfy. Surely no Lutheran cleric would ever permit a castrato to marry, and thus eventually Sorlisi's inability to gain official sanction for his intention would render the entire agreement null and void. But in this they vastly underestimated both Sorlisi's and Dorothea's determination, and the degree to which disagreement reigned among Lutheran theologians with respect to the goals and objectives of marriage.

With the signing of this agreement in May 1664, Sorlisi won his first victory in a battle that would rage on for at least four more

---

[26] Ulinka Rublack has written that 'early modern German men were confronted with several codes of masculinity. The dominant one instructed that their honour depended on fearlessness and combativeness as well as the withdrawn (*einbezogenes*) behaviour befitting a bourgeois *Biedermann* – a term which became common currency during the sixteenth century denoting respectability and honesty.' See 'Meanings of Gender in Early Modern German History', in ead. (ed.), *Gender in Early Modern German History*, pp. 1–18, at p. 6. On the question of consent for marriages at this time, see M. R. Sommerville, *Sex and Subjection: Attitudes to Women in Early-Modern Society* (London, 1995), pp. 178–93.

[27] In its stress on mutual love as the main condition for the marriage this agreement may be unusual; according to Dagmar Freist, the motives that lay behind mixed marriages (mixed with respect to confession) were more often socio-economic; 'love marriages seem rarer; they are certainly less well-documented'; see her 'One Body, Two Confessions', p. 277.

years. As the first stipulation made by the Junghanns was unquestionably the most crucial, Sorlisi next paid a visit to the current senior court preacher, Jacob Weller (1602–6 July 1664), to whom, as a member of the Hofkapelle, he needed no introduction. This visit seems to have been instrumental in furnishing Sorlisi with a plan of action. In their meeting, Sorlisi revealed his connubial intentions to Weller, and enquired as to how he should proceed. Junghanns does not reveal the preacher's reaction to Sorlisi's announcement, but does report that Weller first reminded Sorlisi that two impediments stood in his way, the ninety-eighth Novel (new constitution) of Emperor Leo the Wise,[28] and the 1587 papal brief of Sixtus V, *Cum frequenter*,[29] which explicitly forbade the marriage of eunuchs.[30] In response to Weller's invocation of the latter document, Sorlisi replied that he would procure an indult (*Indulgentz*), or special dispensation, from his bishop – in his eyes, it seems, the papal prohibition was nothing to worry about.[31] Sorlisi's response may

[28] Cited by Junghanns as *Novell. Imperat. Leon. 98. Constitut. ad Stylian.* The 98th Novel of Byzantine Emperor Leo the Wise (Leo VI, r. 886–911) can be found in *Les Novelles de Léon VI le Sage*, trans. P. Noailles and A. Dain (Paris, 1944), pp. 320–7. The text was available in numerous editions in both Greek and Latin in the sixteenth and seventeenth centuries (see *ibid.*, pp. li–lv).

[29] Cited by Junghanns as *Syxti V. Papae, ad Episcopum Novariens. Sedis Apostolicae in Regnis Hispaniarum Nuncium Bulla*; Junghanns indicates that the brief is to be found in the '*Bullario magno in lit. M.* beym *verbo Matrimonium*'. This brief of Sixtus V, *Cum frequenter*, bears the date 27 June 1587; the source consulted for this study was the *Magnum bullarium Romanum, a Beato Leone Magno usque ad S. D. N. Benedictum XIII opus absolutissimum*, ... Editio novissima (Luxembourg, 1727), ii, p. 634. Although the document appears in collections of papal bulls, canonists explain that it is more properly described as a brief; see A. McGrath, OFM, *A Controversy Concerning Male Impotence* (Analecta Gregoriana, 247; Rome, 1988), pp. 15–16.

[30] Readers may wonder why in Saxony, a Lutheran state in which the public practice of Catholicism was forbidden and canon law had no standing, a Lutheran pastor would invoke Catholic legislation in the form of a papal brief. Although Lutherans did not recognize canon law as the law of the church, Lutheran theologians and ecclesiastical jurists did regularly cite various of its provisions (those deemed theologically 'sound') in support of their own arguments; see, for example, the monumental *Loci theologici* of Johann Gerhard (cited below). In this particular case, Weller probably reminded Sorlisi of the papal brief because of the latter's Catholicism, knowing that Sorlisi fell under its jurisdiction regardless of his place of residence. As will be seen below, a number of the theologians who considered this case introduced the Sistine brief, some to buttress their argument against Sorlisi's marriage, and others (who viewed it critically) to support their argument in favour of the marriage.

[31] 'Darauff hatt er geanttworttet, daß er von seinem Bischoff schon *indulgentz* erlangen wolte.' As Sorlisi lived in a Lutheran state where the public exercise of Catholicism was forbidden, except in parts of the eastern province of Lusatia, the bishop to which he refers was either in Bohemia or at the Cathedral of Bautzen (Upper Lusatia), which had been a *Simultankirche* (a church shared by Catholics and Lutherans) since the Reformation. Although both Upper and Lower Lusatia (*Ober-* and *Niederlausitz*) were incorporated into Saxony during the Thirty Years War, the cathedral and several religious houses there were allowed to remain Catholic. See

Eunuchi Conjugium

well have been a simple reflection of his own hubris and his willingness to manipulate the current confessional situation, given that he lived in a Lutheran land and thus technically stood beyond the reach of canon law, but it may also suggest that despite *Cum frequenter*, the marriage of castrati continued to occur more commonly than is currently believed. Sorlisi then asked Weller if he had any other objections, at which point the pastor gave a lengthy disquisition on the subject, and concluded by informing Sorlisi that he knew of no passage in the Holy Scriptures that expressly prohibited such a union. But what the cleric went on to say was probably equally if not more important to Sorlisi, for it opened a window of opportunity to the castrato: Weller also pointed out that God had instituted marriage not only to ensure the perpetuation of the human race, but also to provide humans with mutual help (*mutuum adjutorium*) in life. He thus advised Sorlisi to prepare his case as a question, present it to a consistory, and secure a ruling from that body.[32]

Armed with this encouraging news, Sorlisi went back to Junghanns and recounted the substance of his conversation with Weller. His report plainly alarmed Junghanns and his wife, who immediately sought to impede the matter, as they felt sure that Sorlisi could not fulfil the first of the conditions, that the daughter would come to a better 'understanding [of the situation]', and that both parties would 'change their minds and notions'.[33] But the Junghanns'

S. Seifert, *Niedergang und Wiederaufstieg der katholischen Kirche in Sachsen 1517–1773* (Leipzig, 1964), pp. 91–104.

[32] In Lutheran Saxony at this time, a consistory was a church court with jurisdiction over a particular region. Consistories sat in Leipzig and Wittenberg, and the High Consistory (*Ober Consistorium*) sat in Dresden. The consistories of Leipzig and Wittenberg each included four members – two laymen, one of whom served as president, and two clerics, one of whom was usually the local superintendent or supervising minister. In addition, the High Consistory, which had authority over the other two bodies, normally comprised either five or six members – an aristocratic layman as president, two jurists and either two or three clerics; when he so desired, the elector could add his senior court preacher to the High Consistory as the sixth member. The composition and duties of the consistories were established in the 1580 *Kirchen-Ordnung* of Elector August I of Saxony; see *Die evangelischen Kirchenordnungen des XVI. Jahrhunderts*, ed. E. Sehling, i: *Sachsen und Thüringen, nebst angrenzenden Gebieten* (Leipzig, 1902), pp. 401–10. For a general discussion of Lutheran church councils and consistories, see M. E. Wiesner-Hanks, *Christianity and Sexuality in the Early Modern World: Regulating Desire, Reforming Practice* (Christianity and Society in the Modern World; London and New York, 2000), pp. 60–100.

[33] 'Alß er mir und meinem Weibe nun dieses hinwiederumb *referiret*, haben wir die sache auffgehalten, wie wir nur gekund, in meynung, daß Er eines theilß die schwere *condition* nicht *adimplir*en, Sie die Jungfrau auch zu beßern vorstande gelangen, und beyderseits ihre Sinne und gedancken endern solten.' Italics represent text in roman script in the original.

attempts to dissuade Dorothea from marrying her intended remained ineffectual, as Junghanns himself admitted. Not only had 'a great mutual love grown daily' between the two, but, unbeknownst to his future in-laws, Sorlisi had not been an idle suitor, but had 'caused to be drawn up a very detailed question, had advanced the *rationes dubitandi et decidendi*, as well as the manner in which he was opposed by us [the family], and had obtained a hearing in the Leipzig Consistory', and had eventually received a judgement in support of the marriage.[34] Although Sorlisi seems to have been quite forthcoming in his dealings with Junghanns from the outset, at this point he apparently resorted to secrecy, perhaps for fear that Junghanns and others might attempt either to prevent him from applying to the consistory, or to prejudice that body before he had had a chance to present his case.

According to the published version of the *Urthels-* (i.e., *Urteils-*) *Frage* that Sorlisi presented to the Leipzig consistory, the petition was dated 25 August 1666, and the consistory rendered its decision in October of the same year.[35] Sorlisi submitted his lengthy petition under the pseudonym 'Johannes Gericke, *Jur. Cand.* und *Practicus*' of Stargard (now Szczeciński), a town formerly in Pomerania that now lies in north-west Poland.[36] No manuscript copy of Sorlisi's petition has yet been located; neither does it appear among the supporting materials sent to Greifswald by Junghanns, for, as the lawyer explained with evident embarrassment in his letter to the

---

[34] 'hatt auch der von *Sorlisi* gantz unvermercket eine sehr weitläuffige Frage auffsetzen, die *rationes dubitandi et decidendi*, auch welcher gestalt von Unß Ihme *contradicir*en worden, hinan rücken, und im *Consistorio* zu Leipzig sich *informir*en laßen, auch entlichen einen spruch *pro matrimonio* erhalten'.

[35] In the 1718 print of *Eunuchi conjugium*, the first decision of the Leipzig consistory (pp. 14–15) bears the date *Mense Octobr. 1663*; in the 1697 print (p. 14), it bears the date *Mense Octobr. 1693*. Junghanns, however, provided a handwritten copy of the same decision to the Greifswald faculty; in his set of documents the decree is dated '*Mens. Octobr. Anno 1666*' (UAG, Theologische Fakultät Nr. 3, Extract no. 2). In the second decision handed down by the Leipzig consistory in May 1668, the body makes reference to Sorlisi's 'Urthels-Frage', which it claims to have received in 'Wein-Monat' (October) 1667 (*Eunuchi conjugium* (1718), pp. 94–5; (1697), pp. 90–1). Both dates in the printed sources are erroneous, as the former antedates Sorlisi's petition (and the betrothal agreement), and the latter post-dates the entire episode by nearly thirty years.

[36] Delphinus, *Eunuchi conjugium*, pp. 1–13 ('Urthels-Frage an das *Consistorium* zu Leipzig'). It remains inexplicable why the Leipzig consistory agreed to rule on this case, which would seem to have fallen under the jurisdiction of the Pomeranian consistory in Greifswald. This in itself may suggest that, despite Lange's protestations to the contrary (see pp. 99–100 and n. 140 below), the body was aware of the true identity of the petitioner.

Eunuchi Conjugium

theologians there, 'it was not something that was suitable to be sent by post, owing to its great impropriety'.[37] In his *Frage*, Sorlisi perpetrated a grand deception on the consistory, for he cloaked himself in the garb of a northern European knight-errant, and invented a scenario involving the desire of 'Titius', a fictitious Swedish aristocrat, to marry 'Lucretia', an aristocratic Pomeranian woman, despite injuries sustained in battle that had rendered him incapable of fathering children.[38] And in his description of these injuries, as Junghanns had no doubt observed, Sorlisi was careful to leave little to the imagination:[39]

> Some years ago, in the well-known fierce battle on the Isle of Fyn between their Royal Majesties of Denmark and Sweden, a Swedish aristocrat of distinguished lineage whom we shall call Titius was hit on both thighs and in his genital organs by a very dangerous canister shot. As a result, he lost the greater portion of the scrotum, as well as one complete testicle, and his other testicle was crushed, so that subsequently in treatment it was completely destroyed, and had to be removed. As a result of this misfortune, Titius became utterly incapable of and unfit for the perpetuation of the human race. Owing to the discretion of the doctor and field surgeon, this misfortune remained a secret; no one in the entire army knew any more than that Titius had been wounded on the thigh. Nevertheless, he did not wish to return to the army, but instead bought a house and settled in Hither Pomerania. There, despite the accident, he could at times nevertheless perceive the erection of the virile member, and he found himself not entirely incapable of sexual congress, especially as his virile member had been a little less damaged in the foreskin and the glans. Moreover, being weary of the solitary life, particularly on his remote estate, he resolved to marry Lucretia, an aristocratic woman of Pomerania.[40]

---

[37] 'und ob ich wohle gerne die Frage zugleich mit übermachen wollen, so hatte es doch wegen großer unbequemligkeit durch die post sich nicht wohl fügen wollen'.

[38] Sorlisi's choice of fictional names here is worth comment. According to a linguist at Random House, 'Titius' is the equivalent of the modern 'John Doe' or 'Joe Bloggs', and is used (along with Gaius and Seius) as a fictional name for a male in early Roman legal proceedings (http://www.randomhouse.com/words/ under 'John Doe', accessed 17 December 2004); the name is used in this manner by Ancillon (*Traité des eunuques*, p. 235), and the custom continues in Italy today (I thank Giulio Ongaro for this information). But while the name 'Titius' might at first seem rather innocuous, it actually recalls 'Titus', which also means 'penis' (thanks to Leofranc Holford-Strevens for this reference). The name 'Lucretia' is also fraught with sexual significance, but a close look at Livy's account of the rape of Lucretia provides no real clue to the reasons behind Sorlisi's choice; he may simply have selected the name for its associations with virtue and chastity.

[39] The use of High German interspersed with frequent Latin quotations, the assembling of theological and other canonistic sources, and the general erudition of the petition make clear that Sorlisi had employed either a sympathetic theologian or an ecclesiastical jurist to assist him in its formulation. As the identity of this 'ghostwriter' cannot yet be ascertained, the petition will be ascribed to Sorlisi alone in this discussion, for it was drawn up on his behalf and surely with his help, and doubtless incorporated many of his own ideas and opinions.

[40] Delphinus, *Eunuchi conjugium*, pp. 1–2; the German text appears as Doc. 2 in the Appendix. This passage is quoted in part by Ortkemper, who misattributes a significant portion of the document to the Leipzig consistory (*Engel wider Willen*, pp. 192–4).

Mary E. Frandsen

The stipulation in the betrothal agreement that he gain permission to marry forced Sorlisi to suffer a humiliation that non-castrated men were not asked to endure: not only was he compelled to plead for that which other men could claim as a right, he was obliged to describe both his genitalia and his sexual capacity in frank detail to a panel of unseen judges who would decide his marital fate. Forced into this eventuality by Dorothea's family, however, Sorlisi dealt with the situation with aplomb, and in his description of his injuries and resulting condition would seem to proclaim himself an adherent of the 'new science' of the later seventeenth century, for he does not resort to metaphor, but describes his body and its functions with the analytical precision of an anatomist.[41] But it is not only his frankness that is impressive here, but also his strategy. First, by casting himself as a Swedish – and thus presumably Lutheran – nobleman[42] who had been rendered infertile (but not impotent!) through an accident of war, rather than through a deliberate act to which he had ostensibly consented, Sorlisi clearly sought to oblige the consistory to consider his case just as they would that of any other Lutheran male who had been rendered sterile by an accident or through natural causes.[43] Second, his fictitious account also places him squarely among the ranks of those castrated post-pubertally, in whom sexual function was understood to continue. Given that a number of writers, mostly his own churchmen, believed that a man castrated prepubertally lacked any and all sexual capacity, Sorlisi's 'Swedish soldier' gambit probably was intended to dispel any notion that his claims were disputable.[44] Both

---

[41] On the 'new scientists" rejection of metaphor and their adoption of a more 'masculine', clinical approach to the description of the body, a change which fundamentally altered the nature of scientific discourse, see J. Sawday, *The Body Emblazoned: Dissection and the Human Body in Renaissance Culture* (London and New York, 1995), pp. 230–70.

[42] Sorlisi's casting of Titius as an aristocrat also reflects his own societal rank (see above).

[43] Here the fictionalisation of the event of Titius's castration as a battle wound to the loins may well reflect the input of Sorlisi's German ghostwriter, for the story strongly recalls an event in Wolfram von Eschenbach's *Parzival*, in which King Anfortas, 'guardian of the Holy Grail, is described as having been wounded in the scrotum through a battle injury, after being encouraged in a foolhardy display of courage, ironically, by his love for a woman'. See Mathew S. Kuefler, 'Castration and Eunuchism in the Middle Ages', in V. L. Bullough and J. A. Brundage (eds.), *Handbook of Medieval Sexuality* (New York and London, 1999), pp. 279–306, at p. 290. Kuefler points out that the tradition of 'wounded loins' can be traced back to such authors as Chrétien de Troyes.

[44] See McGrath, *A Controversy Concerning Male Impotence*, pp. 29–31, 40, 67, 70–2, 76, and I. Gordon, SJ, 'Adnotationes quaedam de valore matrimonii virorum qui ex toto secti sunt a tempore Gratiani usque ad breve "Cum frequenter"', *Periodica de re morali canonica liturgica*, 66

strategies, of course, effectively masked his identity as a castrato.[45] His representation of this event may also suggest that he regarded his castration as an 'accident' in which he had no complicity. If his strategy succeeded, none of the members of the consistory would have reason to deny his petition based on the prohibition enshrined in the papal brief *Cum frequenter*, or to argue that a man who was 'knowingly and willingly' castrated does not enjoy the same right to marriage and sexual activity as do those who managed to escape the surgeon's knife.[46]

For the modern reader, Sorlisi's description of Titius's injuries would seem to be a clear indication that he had undergone a bilateral orchidectomy – the removal of the testes – at some time in his youth.[47] While his description might suggest that he suffered a

(1966), pp. 171–247, at pp. 189–90. From these sources it is not clear if this view persisted into the seventeenth century; McGrath states it as an indisputable fact, but provides few citations from historical sources (p. 29). One writer who did express this view was the canonist Andrea Alciato (1492–1550): 'Castrati qui penitus non arrigunt, sive quia naturaliter sine testibus progeniti sunt, quia ante pubertatem omnino excisi'; *Digestorum titulos aliquot commentaria*, as cited in McGrath, *A Controversy*, p. 26.

[45] In this manner Sorlisi also avoided the question of his Catholicism, which in itself required that he receive permission from the consistory and the elector to marry a Lutheran; see Freist, 'One Body, Two Confessions', pp. 275–6, 295–7.
[46] As court preacher Martin Geier would argue; see n. 117 below.
[47] It is not clear whether this procedure was the one most commonly employed. The most frequently cited 'authority' on the subject of the procedure itself is Charles Ancillon (1659–1715), a Huguenot refugee whose *Traité des eunuques* first appeared in Berlin in 1707; it is unclear, however, whether he was actually acquainted with any castrati. The English translation of Ancillon's treatise, *Eunuchism Display'd*, published in London in 1718 (three years after his death), does include a supplement of castrato singers including Nicolini, but this supplement does not appear in the 1707 edition and was added by the English translator, as pointed out by Fernandez in the preface to the *Traité*, p. 24. Ancillon discusses four types of eunuchs: (1) those who are 'born that way', (2) those who have undergone complete castration, (3) those whose testes have been badly bruised (or crushed), so that they disappear; the veins 'that carried their nourishment' having either been cut out or severed, such that the organs wither and dry up or become flaccid, and (4) those whose organs are intact but dysfunctional ('La premiere [Classe] est de ceux qui sont nez tels.... La seconde est de ceux ausquels, soit malgré eux, soit de leur consentement et par leur propre fait, on a retranché tout ce qui fait l'homme et sa virilité.... La troisiéme Classe est de ceux auxquels on froisse tellement les Cremastéres qu'ils disparoissent, et qu'il semble qu'ils soient evanouis: La veine qui leur portoit l'aliment étant retranchée, ils se flétrissent, ils se sechent et se réduisent à rien ... Cette troisiéme sorte d'Eunuques sont ceux qu'on appelle en Droit *Thlibia*. Ceux qu'on nomme *Thlasia*, sont à peu près de la même qualité, toute la différence qu'il y a, c'est qu'on se contente de leur couper les veines qui servent à fortifier les parties viriles, de sorte qu'elles restent bien à la vérité, mais si flasques et si flêtres qu'elles ne sont d'aucun usage.... La quatriéme Classe, enfin, est de ceux qu'on appelle *spadons*, qui sont nez si mal conformez, ou d'un tempérement si froid, ou qui le sont devenus par quelque incommodité, qu'ils sont incapables de contribuer à la genération'; *ibid.*, pp. 63–5). Contrary to the view of several scholars, in the original French version, Ancillon neither includes what is now commonly taken to be the most common procedure, the surgical removal of the testes, nor makes mention of the severing of

somewhat botched castration, which left him with one shriveled testicle, it is more likely that he tinkered a bit with his description of his anatomical reality in order to disguise his identity as a castrato, for this opening gambit represents the first stage of an elaborate deception aimed at securing an unbiased decision from the consistory. His claims concerning his sexual capacity are also of considerable interest, for he asserts that he could both experience an erection and engage in intercourse – in other words, that he could also sustain an erection.[48] While Sorlisi's claims may have been exaggerated, or even fabricated, they raise interesting questions none the less. One does wonder, however, if his assertion was based on personal experience, or upon a rather naive presumption that the simple fact of this perceived erectability automatically placed him among the ranks of those capable of copulation. Whatever the case, his claims suggest that, while many in society might see him as sexually passive, effeminate, more woman-like, lacking in 'vital heat', and thus as somewhat less male than a non-castrated man, Sorlisi did not regard himself as so very different from his unaltered contemporaries.[49] In the light of Roger Freitas's research on the sexuality of the castrato, and his location of castrati, together with boys, in the middle of a vertical sexual spectrum, beneath active, non-castrated men but above more passive women,[50] it is significant

the 'spermatic ducts', a procedure that would result in vasectomy, and would not cause the organs to atrophy; see Rosselli, 'The Castrati as a Professional Group', p. 151; Katherine Bergeron, 'The Castrato as History', *Cambridge Opera Journal*, 8 (1996), pp. 167–84, at p. 170; Freitas, '*Un atto d'ingegno*', p. 188, and id., 'The Eroticism of Emasculation: Confronting the Baroque Body of the Castrato', *Journal of Musicology*, 20 (2003), pp. 196–249, at p. 226, n. 80. The procedure of vasectomy was known in the sixteenth century, if not earlier: Miguel de Palacios (Michael de Palatio) (fl. 1557–79, d. 1585?) describes 'vasectomia', and states that the testes are spared but retain no potential to generate, and the procedure was also discussed by Andrea Alciato; see Gordon, 'Adnotationes quaedam de valore matrimonii virorum', p. 189, and McGrath, *A Controversy Concerning Male Impotence*, p. 29.

[48] This question has been much debated; for the most recent and detailed study on the sexual capacity of the castrato, see Freitas, '*Un atto d'ingegno*', pp. 190–6, and 'The Eroticism of Emasculation', p. 223–33, esp. p. 233, where he reaches the conclusion that 'the most capable could probably have had erections and something like an orgasm; others may have had lesser abilities'.

[49] See Freitas, '*Un atto d'ingegno*', pp. 159–60, and 'The Eroticism of Emasculation', 203–6.

[50] Freitas borrows the one-sex hierarchical model famously propounded by T. Laqueur in *Making Sex: Body and Gender from the Greeks to Freud* (Cambridge, Mass., 1990), pp. 1–148. According to Laqueur, the model was valid from the time of Aristotle until the late seventeenth century. Laqueur does not include eunuchs in the hierarchy, and Freitas expands the model by placing castrati, largely through analogy with boys (seen at the time as their sexual equivalent), in the middle ('*Un atto d'ingegno*', pp. 155–66; 'The Eroticism of Emasculation', 203–6).

Eunuchi Conjugium

that Sorlisi sees himself assuming the active role – the male role (as seen at this time) – in sexual intercourse: *he* can satisfy *Lucretia* – *she* is the one whose sexual requirements must be met.[51] Thus there is no indication here that he sees himself occupying anything but the highest position on the vertical axis constructed by Thomas Laqueur and Freitas.[52] Sorlisi refers neither to his own sexual desire, nor to his own need for satisfaction; he introduces the facts of his sexual capacity here solely in the context of the needs of 'Lucretia'. But his decision to lead with this aspect of his argument, to which he will return, is also worth considering. Given the centuries-old censure of eunuchs as sexually rapacious, and the clear effeminising associations of this characterisation (given that a 'beast-like [sexual] appetite' was 'associated with the feminine'),[53] it is odd that Sorlisi would begin with an attestation of his sexual capacity that would seem to threaten to effeminise him.[54] Certainly he could have chosen to argue that he possessed absolutely no sexual capacity, and was desirous of marriage solely for reasons of love and companionship; the materials that he introduces below demonstrate that he could have mustered substantial support for that approach. But the contemporary circumstances virtually compelled him to deal first with the question of his sexual capacity, for, as he reveals below, some had levelled the charge that he could not satisfy his future

---

[51] See the discussion in Freitas, '*Un atto d'ingegno*', pp. 173–81.
[52] Although Laqueur's 'one-sex theory' has found wide acceptance, it is not without its detractors, particularly among scholars of the early modern era. See, for example, the review by K. Park and R. A. Nye, 'Destiny is Anatomy', *The New Republic*, 18 February 1991, pp. 53–7, the essay of M. Wiesner, 'Disembodied Theory? Discourses of Sex in Early Modern Germany', in Rublack (ed.), *Gender in Early Modern German History*, pp. 152–73, at pp. 156–7, and most recently, the essay of Michael Stolberg, 'A Woman Down to her Bones: The Anatomy of Sexual Difference in the Sixteenth and Early Seventeenth Centuries', *Isis*, 94 (2003), pp. 274–99. In his study, Freitas adduces much contemporary evidence to demonstrate that many regarded the castrato as 'other', and associated him more closely with women and boys than with men. Questions of the historical validity of the hierarchical model aside, Freitas's development of a construct that allows the assignment of a specific social place to the castrato would seem to have much to speak for it as a way in which to understand how 'contemporaries . . . understood the sexual life of a castrated man' ('*Un atto d'ingegno*', p. 155).
[53] Sawday, *The Body Emblazoned*, p. 219. Most of the literature that treats questions of sexuality in the medieval and early modern eras includes at least some discussion of this theme; for a more detailed treatment, see N. Tuana, *The Less Noble Sex: Scientific, Religious, and Philosophical Conceptions of Woman's Nature* (Bloomington, Ind., 1993), J. E. Salisbury, 'Gendered Sexuality', in Bullough and Brundage (eds.), *Handbook of Medieval Sexuality*, pp. 81–102, at pp. 84–6, and Wiesner-Hanks, *Christianity and Sexuality in the Early Modern World*, p. 43.
[54] The characterisation of eunuchs as sexually unappeasable informs many of the writings cited by various authors in *Eunuchi conjugium*, beginning with Aristotle.

wife sexually, and that by marrying her, he would place her in danger of committing fornication or adultery, as she (owing to her own 'uncontrollable' desires) was bound to seek her satisfaction elsewhere.

Sorlisi's version of subsequent events agrees for the most part with that of Junghanns. According to the petition, he proceeded to get to know Lucretia and her parents, and impressed both her and her family with his 'courtesy and modesty'. Her parents took a special liking to him, while Lucretia fell in love with him. But according to the petition, other relatives of the young woman strenuously objected to a marriage between the two, particularly because Titius was a foreigner whose father had been ennobled by Queen Christina of Sweden. In the course of events, Titius had visited the same doctor who had treated some of Lucretia's relatives, and had disclosed his condition in confidence to this man. The doctor, however, 'in order to do a good turn to the relatives of the young woman, had acted against his duty and his conscience, and had perjuriously and wantonly revealed to them [the particulars of Titius's physical condition]'.[55] This information proved particularly useful to Lucretia's relatives, who made the information public throughout the entire region. Not only did the rumour gain strength, and force Titius into many dangerous duels (both on foot and on horseback), it eventually reached Lucretia's mother (her father had since died), and finally Lucretia as well. Realising this, Titius, 'due to his upright and honourable nature', revealed everything to mother and daughter, and asked the former for her final decision on the marriage. Lucretia's mother was somewhat taken aback by Titius's revelations, and at first wanted to withdraw her support for the proposed marriage, since Titius, according to his own admission, could not father any children. The young woman, on the other hand, remained steadfast in her love for Titius despite his disclosures, and declared of her own volition that his inability to beget children was immaterial to her; she would never be separated from him, and would sooner give up her life than her resolve to marry him. Upon hearing her daughter's declaration, Lucretia's

---

[55] *Eunuchi conjugium*, p. 2: 'hat er wider seine Pflicht und Gewissen/ bloß der Jungfrau Anverwandten einen Liebes=dienst zu erweisen/ solches denenselben meineydiger und leichtfertiger Weise offenbahret'.

Eunuchi Conjugium

mother changed her mind, and decided to allow the marriage. She again granted Titius free access to her daughter, whose love for him continued to grow. Titius and Lucretia subsequently promised themselves to one another, at first in secret, but later publicly, before her mother, her mother's lawyer, and several others. At this point, the two were ready to proceed to the wedding. Their friends, however, again protested vigorously, and threatened to bring the matter before the ecclesiastical authorities, to establish, through the expert opinion of the doctor, that Titius was unable to father children, and also to question under oath the field surgeon who had treated him, all with the intention of preventing this marriage, because some felt that it could not be allowed by the authorities.[56]

At the same time that Sorlisi carefully crafted this fictionalised account to parallel closely the real-life situation, he also seems to have sought to present the most virile image of himself possible by employing the topos of the military man engaged in the ultra-masculine pursuit of soldiering, one who fights duels both on horseback and on foot in defence of his lady love.[57] In the former, Sorlisi the courtier would seem to take a page from the *Libro del Cortegiano* (1528) of Castiglione, where the author warns that a courtier must not appear too womanly, and that he could 'counter the charge of effeminacy' by being 'a perfect horseman for everie saddle', among other things.[58] Like Sorlisi, Titius is a foreigner and

---

[56] Summarised from Sorlisi's petition, Delphinus, *Eunuchi conjugium*, pp. 2–3. This last portion of Sorlisi's account does not appear in Junghanns's letter.

[57] Sorlisi's status as an Italian Catholic and a castrato complicates any discussion of 'masculinity' here, as contemporary German concepts of masculinity may well be irrelevant in his case. He was raised in Catholic Italy, and first came under the influence of his father's value system, but from the age of 9? 12? 14? he was 'raised' in a conservatory, together with other young castrati and other singers, where his teacher assumed the role of father. On the education and socialisation of castrati, see Freitas, '*Un atto d'ingegno*', pp. 14–24; Rosselli, 'The Castrati as a Professional Group', pp. 158–62; and P. Barbier, 'Über die Männlichkeit der Kastraten', in M. Dinges (ed.), *Hausväter, Priester, Kastraten: Zur Konstruktion von Männlichkeit in Spätmittelalter und früher Neuzeit* (Göttingen, 1998), pp. 123–52, at pp. 138–9. Thus his socialisation took a dramatically different course than that of others of his age, particularly German Lutheran men, who were taught to aspire to the role of 'Hausvater'; see H. Wunder, 'What Made a Man a Man? Sixteenth- and Seventeenth-Century Findings', in Rublack (ed.), *Gender in Early Modern German History*, pp. 21–48, at pp. 23–33.

[58] As quoted in Sawday, *The Body Emblazoned*, p. 204 (from the 1561 English translation of Sir Thomas Hoby). Many authors have noted the association of masculinity with horsemanship during the early modern era; see, for example, Wunder, 'What Made a Man a Man?', p. 29. See also J. Low, *Manhood and the Duel: Masculinity in Early Modern Drama and Culture* (New York, 2003).

an aristocrat of recent lineage – here it is his father who was ennobled – who purchased a country estate and sought an aristocratic wife with whom to settle down in marital bliss. While the members of the Junghanns–Lichtwer clan could lay no claims to membership in the aristocracy, they certainly belonged to the upper stratum of *bürgerlich* society in Dresden, particularly given the court connections of both the lawyer Junghanns and his brother-in-law, one of the elector's tax councillors.[59] Like Sorlisi, Titius set his sights on a woman, secured her affections, and then won the favour of her parents (here her mother) through his *courtoisie* and modesty. Upon learning of his lack of reproductive powers, here through information leaked by an unethical physician, the woman's mother, now a widow, at first recoiled at the idea of a marriage between such a man and her daughter. Like the Junghanns, however, Lucretia's mother abandoned her objections upon seeing her daughter's determined love for the man, and the two became betrothed. But the chronologies of Junghanns and Sorlisi do deviate in at least one respect; according to Junghanns, he and his wife (surely 'the relatives' in Sorlisi's account) did their best to discourage Dorothea from marrying Sorlisi after the betrothal, while in Sorlisi's version, this conflict occurred before the two became engaged. Nevertheless, the parallels between the two accounts are so numerous as to leave no doubt that Sorlisi attempted to reconstruct the situation as closely as possible, without revealing his true identity.

Once he had established the facts of the case for the members of the ecclesiastical jury, Sorlisi launched into arguments for and against the marriage – the *rationes dubitandi et decidendi* referenced by Junghanns in his letter to the Greifswald faculty. At this point it becomes even more evident that he must have found a sympathetic party to help him prepare his argument and to serve as ghostwriter, for it seems doubtful that the castrato alone could have composed the petition in the elevated German found in the document, or that he could have assembled the array of sources brought to bear here, which are drawn from canon and imperial law, as well as from the writings of a multitude of Lutheran and Catholic theologians, both

---

[59] Junghanns never identifies his brother-in-law by name, but refers to him simply as the *Steuer-Rath;* he may be the George Metzner mentioned in Junghanns's letter to Pastor Kühn, which appears below.

Eunuchi Conjugium

medieval and modern. Sorlisi opens his *rationes* in the disputational style with a rather clever rhetorical manoeuvre, and first presents six arguments *contra nuptias* as a sort of counter-*propositio* against (rather than for) which he will then argue. These objections, which he attributes to Lucretia's friends, probably include some of the actual points raised by the Junghanns; significantly, they also form the central arguments made against the marriage by many of the theologians who later rendered opinions on the case:

1. Such a marriage is contrary to the primary object of marriage, the perpetuation of the human race, for which Titius is manifestly unfit, and as a consequence is not to be allowed to marry.[60]
2. The marriage would scandalise and trivialise the priestly blessing that concludes the marriage ceremony, 'be fruitful and multiply'.[61]
3. For Lucretia, this marriage could not fulfil the second reason for marriage, namely the avoidance of fornication and the quelling of sexual desire, and therefore would cast her into the danger of fornication and adultery.[62]
4. Such a marriage would leave the impression that it was allowed simply to satisfy Titius's lust.[63]
5. Such a marriage would seem to be forbidden by canon law, which is especially observed in the Roman Empire, even in the lands of the Lutheran estates, in matrimonial matters, for it is there ordained that:

> Whoever is incapable of copulation is also incapable of contracting a marriage, *cap. [2]. X. de frig. & malef. & ibi Gl.* Furthermore, a natural impediment to copulation that cannot be overcome by the physician's art shall be an impediment to marriage, *cap. 3. X. C. eodem Gloss. & Dd. ad Can. Hi qui. caus. 33. q. 7.*

[60] Delphinus, *Eunuchi conjugium*, p. 3: 'Weil solch *Matrimonium fini primario Conjugii* zuwider: Denn der heilige Ehestand/ zur Fortpflanzung des menschlichen Geschlechts/ eingesetzt/ zu welcher denn *Titius manifesto* untüchtig/ und *per consequens* zum heiligen Ehestand nicht zuzulassen.'
[61] *Ibid.*: 'Wie denn auch zum 2. die *benedictio sacerdotalis: crescite & multiplicamini: non nisi per lusum & jocum*, zum Aergerniß und Verkleinerung dieses heiligen Wercks *adhiberet* werden würde'.
[62] *Ibid.*: 'Dieses *conjugium* auch 3. den *finem secundarium matrimonii*, nehmlich *evitandae fornicationis, et extinguendae ustionis* an Seiten der *Lucretiae* nicht erreichen könte/ also sich die *Lucretia* in *periculum fornicationis & adulterii praecipitire.*'
[63] *Ibid.*, p. 4: '4. Es das Ansehen gewinnen würde/ als wenn dem *Titio*, bloß zu Erfüllung seiner Geilheit/ diese Ehe verstattet würde.'

Mary E. Frandsen

Whoever lacks both testicles shall not contract a marriage because whether a marriage is contracted for the sake of children or to avoid fornication, he lacks the means for either case, *Gl. ad d. cap. 3. X. de frig. & malef.* (etc.).[64]

6. Such a marriage is also forbidden by secular law.[65]

But even in offering these six charges, all of which he would strive to refute, Sorlisi the strategist is busy at work: missing entirely from these citations is the much more recent brief of Pope Sixtus V, *Cum frequenter*, issued in 1587, which, as Weller had reminded him, expressly prohibited the marriage of eunuchs.[66] As offended as he may have been by the brief, which is accusatory in nature and filled with invective, Sorlisi must have been well aware that as a castrated Catholic, he fell directly under its jurisdiction – or would have, under normal circumstances. Of course, his Swedish soldier stratagem allowed him to avoid discussion of the papal brief altogether. Even if his opponents had introduced it as a reason to prevent the marriage, Sorlisi did not feel obligated to mention it in his petition, as he was not arguing his case as a castrato. But he must also have realised that its plainly prejudicial argument, which resorts to the

---

[64] *Ibid.*: 'Solches *Conjugium* in Päbstlichen Rechten/ so in *matrimonialibus per Romanum Imperium*, auch in der Evangelischen Stände Ländern *potissimum attendi*ret werden/ verbothen zu seyn scheine/ indem daselbst verordnet: *Quod impotens ad copulam sit impotens ad contrahendum matrimonium cap. [2]. X. de frig. & malef. & ibi Gl. Et naturale impedimentum ad coitum, irreparabile arte Medicorum, matrimonium impediat, cap. 3. X. C. eodem Gloss. & Dd. ad Can. Hi qui. caus. 33. a. 7. Quod carens utroque testiculo non contrahat, quia cum omne matrimonium contrahatur aut causa prolis, aut causa vitandae fornicationis, & in secto utraque causa deficiat, Gl. ad d. cap. 3. X. de frig. & malef. Ibique Abbas antiqu. Innocentius: Johann. Andreas: Antonius Butrius. p. Anchoravus* [recte Anchoranus] *Panoramit. Hostiensis in Summ. Tit. de frig. & malef. vers. quae impotentia: Cenedus col. 33. Joh. Baptist. Vivianus in ration. L. 4. Jur. Pont. aliique communiter.*' The second passage ('*Quod carens . . .*') derives from a gloss on the third chapter of the decretal *De frigidis et maleficiatis, et impotentia coeundi* (X. 4, 15, 3) by Vincentius Hispanus (d. after 1234). All the scholars listed as writing in support of this view are canonists; see Gordon, 'Adnotationes quaedam de valore matrimonii virorum', pp. 211–25.

[65] Delphinus, *Eunuchi conjugium*, p. 4: 'Sey auch solches *Conjugium* in weltlichen Rechten verbothen.' Here cited are *L. si serva. 39. §. Si Spadoni. 1. ff. de jure dotium* [Digest 23. 3. 39. 1] and *Novell. Leon. [98]. etc.* The number of the Novel of Leo VI is erroneously given here as 68 rather than 98, which deals with the question of the marriage of eunuchs.

[66] Sixtus's brief is potentially illuminating with respect to the sexual capacity of castrati, for it seems to indicate that these men, despite their surgical emasculation, are nevertheless capable of orgasm – while they 'cannot emit true semen', they may 'pour out a certain humour that is somewhat similar to semen, but which is not at all suited to procreation or to the cause of matrimony' ('Cum frequenter in istis regionibus Eunuchi quidam et Spadones, qui utroque teste carent, et ideo certum ac manifestum est, eos verum semen emittere non posse, quia impura carnis tentigine, atque immundis complexibus cum mulieribus se commiscent, et humorem forsan quemdam semini, licet ad generationem, et ad matrimonii causam minime aptum effundunt'; as found in *Magnum bullarium Romanum*, ii, p. 634). At the time, 'verum semen' was taken to be that 'elaborated' in the testes, and full of procreative potential; see McGrath, *A Controversy Concerning Male Impotence*, pp. 31–41.

Eunuchi Conjugium

same sort of sexual stereotyping of the castrato that had characterised writings on eunuchs for centuries, would have given his opponents a powerful weapon to use against him. Despite the fact that it could be viewed as irrelevant in this situation, given that Sorlisi was seeking permission to be married to a Lutheran woman, presumably by a Lutheran pastor in a Lutheran church, the proscription in the brief might easily have caused the members of the Leipzig consistory to regard it as reason enough to reject his petition out of hand and thereby avoid a potentially messy case. Hence Sorlisi avoided all mention of the document, and opted instead to cite only that portion of canon law that did not erect as insurmountable a barrier before him.

Faced with the strong arguments propounded by those who opposed the marriage, Sorlisi was compelled to make an equally convincing case *pro nuptiis*. Thus, after briefly enumerating the six objections raised by Lucretia's friends, without further comment, he advanced nearly three times as many arguments in favour of the proposed union.[67] Here he (with the help of his ghostwriter) displays considerable erudition, and adduces corroborative evidence from numerous sources.[68] To begin, he builds his framing argument upon the strong piece of evidence furnished to him by Jacob Weller: since no express prohibition of the marriage of eunuchs was to be found in the Scriptures, such a marriage could be allowed by the authorities.[69] Leaving nothing to chance, however, Sorlisi cites the works of a number of writers to buttress this assertion.[70] He then begins to argue his case, which rested upon a single, fundamental truth: throughout history, both church and secular authorities have allowed those who love one another, but who suffer from impotence or infertility, to marry and/or to remain married. But as a castrato, he was keenly aware of the fact that whenever one of his kind entered into an intimate relationship with a woman, those in

[67] These arguments appear on pp. 5–11 of *Eunuchi conjugium*.
[68] Although well supported with corroborating citations, Sorlisi's arguments themselves lack a certain degree of complexity, and may well derive from the singer himself.
[69] Delphinus, *Eunuchi conjugium*, p. 4: 'Weil solche Ehe nirgends in heiliger Schrifft *expresse* verbothen/ dahero von dem *Episcopo* oder derjenigen Obrigkeit/ so die *Jura Episcopalis* zuständig/ solche wohl zugelassen werden könne.'
[70] These include Aristotle (his *Ethics*, bk. 5, ch. 10); Diego de Covarrubias y Leyva (Didacus Covarruvias a Leyva, 1512–77); Dietrich Reinking (1590–1664), *Tractatus de regimine seculari et ecclesiastico* (Marburg, 1632); Hugo Grotius (1583–1645), *De imperio summarum potestatum circa sacra*; and Charles Annibal Fabrot (1580–1659).

Mary E. Frandsen

positions of authority quickly resorted to characterisations of such unions as vile, lascivious, depraved, illicit, abnormal, and self-serving on the part of the castrato. In order to demonstrate the inherent injustice of such characterisations, which denied that the castrato possessed any capacity to form emotional attachments, Sorlisi founds his central argument on the mutual love that he shares with Dorothea, and hammers away at the illogic of those who would use the 'procreation argument' to impugn the motives of the infertile who sought to marry:[71]

> (2) Although God established marriage primarily for the reason of procreation, among other reasons, so that the human race should be perpetuated and preserved, it does not follow that it is against God's order or will, or against reasonable natural law, if a couple who cannot reach this goal for one reason or another, nevertheless proceed together into marriage, and vow to spend the rest of their lives together in true love, as helpmates. . . . (3) As the aforementioned two betrothed people have no hope of producing children, but, as will be shown, seek to join together out of another, Christian intention, and promise and vow the inseparable association of life with one another, and thus employ the means of holy matrimony, who would assert that such an undertaking is against divine and natural law, which consists of ordering and inhibiting, and establishes the limits of human potential?[72]

Again and again in his argument, Sorlisi invokes the phrase 'against divine and natural law' – so often, in fact, that it suggests that these words had come to serve as a mantra for those friends and relatives of Dorothea who opposed the marriage, and that he found them particularly galling. For, as he reveals in this petition, Sorlisi views

[71] Here Sorlisi the Catholic would seem to take his lead from the post-Tridentine Roman Catechism of 1566, which ranked companionship and mutual help over procreation and the avoidance of fornication as the primary reasons for marriage. Among the three blessings of marriage, however, the 1566 Catechism lists first 'offspring', then 'fidelity' and 'sacrament'; see *Catechism of the Council of Trent*, trans. J. A. McHugh and C. J. Cullan (New York, 1923), pp. 343–5, 350–1. The significance of the shift in emphasis (from procreation to companionship) is discussed by Wiesner-Hanks, *Christianity and Sexuality in the Early Modern World*, p. 113.

[72] Delphinus, *Eunuchi conjugium*, pp. 5–6: 'Und ob 2. nicht ohne/ daß der heilige Ehestand von GOtt unter andern zu dem Ende fürnehmlich eingesetzet/ daß Kinder gezeuget/ und dergestalt das menschliche Geschlecht fortgepflantzet und erhalten werde/ so will doch daraus nicht eben folgen/ daß solches alsobald wider GOttes Ordnung und Willen/ oder die vernünfftigen natürlichen Rechte/ wenn Personen/ so wegen eines dergleichen Zufalls solchen Zweck oder End=Ursache nich erlangen können/ sich nichts destoweniger zusammen in Ehestand begeben/ und die Zeit ihres Lebens/ als Gehülffen/ in treuer Liebe zuzubringen *vovirem*. . . . (3) Wie nun die beyden obgedachten verlobten Personen/ zwar nicht in Hoffnung/ Kinder zu zeugen/ dennoch aber/ wie folgends ausgeführet werden soll/ aus einer andern und Christlichen *Intention* sich zusammen fügen, *individuam vitae societatem* einanden versprechen, und geloben/ und sich hierbey des Mittels der heiligen *Copulation* gebrauchen/ wer wolte *asseriren*/ daß solch Werck *contra jura divina & naturalia, quae in praecipiendo aut inhibendo consistunt, et potentiae humanae limites constituunt*.'

Eunuchi Conjugium

himself as a man with the same needs and desires as other men – a 'natural' man – despite his sexual impairment, and feels that he has every right to seek satisfaction for these needs and desires. Thus he argues strenuously that there are other reasons for marriage besides procreation, and emphasises the importance of the 'subsidiary' benefits (if not goals) of marriage – mutual aid, companionship, comfort in sickness – which the reigning view of marriage as a sheerly reproductive enterprise would seem to disregard entirely:

(4) The intention of Titius and Lucretia in this undertaking is that, as they love each other from the heart, so they will continue in their love towards one another throughout their lives, they will live with one another in true affection and marital intimacy, will stand by one another in need and death, and will care for and wait upon each other in sickness and other misfortunes, as is characteristic of and due to other true and Christian married people. Since according to the common wisdom, 'there can be many ends for a single thing'; therefore it also cannot be denied that at times, other goals besides the procreation of offspring enter into marriage, for certainly mutual cohabitation and society of life are no less for the purpose of matrimony, yea are almost to be held as primary ends, in that God, after the creation of the human race, and in the establishment of holy matrimony in Genesis 2, pronounced these words first of all: 'It is not good that man should be alone. We shall make a helper for him so that he will not be alone, and so that he will have a companion in life with whom he can live and keep company familiarly in perpetual love and trust.' And who would deny that one finds this help, this aid, in the many duties of life, rather than solely in procreation and the education of children?[73]

In these rather poignant expressions of mutual love and human need, the duelling, almost obsessively 'masculine' man who opened the petition would seem to have vanished, and to have been replaced by a man of feeling and sensitivity. So stark is the contrast that one wonders if the male image that Sorlisi worked to create at the outset was merely for the benefit of the consistory, and did not accurately reflect his true self-image. But he may well have seen no conflict in the two images, and no need for reconciliation – perhaps for him, one need not deny one's softer, more emotional side in order to 'be a man'.

Sorlisi here takes firm exception to the privileging of procreation as the primary reason for marriage, a view that remained standard among seventeenth-century theologians and social philosophers.[74] Many of these writers, however, also acknowledged both the avoidance of fornication and companionship as supplementary goals of

---

[73] Delphinus, *Eunuchi conjugium*, pp. 6–7; the original text appears as Doc. 3 in the Appendix.
[74] See Sommerville, *Sex and Subjection*, pp. 114–16, and the theological opinions below.

marriage, and some, under the influence of Aristotle and Augustine, stressed the importance of cooperation and companionship for a successful union.[75] But the concept of 'mutual help', which Sorlisi so frequently invokes in his petition, was often construed during this era as relating only to the bearing and rearing of children, just as Sorlisi indicates. Two of his own co-religionists, Cardinals Tommaso de Vio Cajetan (1469–1534) and Roberto Bellarmino (1542–1621), went so far as to deny any purpose to woman's existence save reproduction.[76] As Margaret Sommerville has pointed out, 'unless discussing housework, virtually no one suggested that women had anything of importance to offer mankind except the ability to produce and raise a family. To the end of the seventeenth century and beyond, various theorists portrayed women's primary function, purpose, and use as providing children.'[77] But it would seem that Sorlisi, a man incapable of fathering children, saw a woman's role very differently, and accorded her far more dignity as a human being than did these contemporary writers; in his petition, he liberates Dorothea from this subordinate state, and elevates her to the status of true companion. Here, for once, was a man arguing that procreation was *not* a woman's sole purpose in life, but that her companionship, as well as her caring and nurturing qualities, were all of value to him. In fact, it was these very qualities that made her so desirable.

In Sorlisi's view, his situation is no different from that of those who are allowed to marry despite having passed their childbearing years. As so many who would later consider this case would do, Sorlisi cites first the biblical example of King David, who, when he was old and entirely 'effœtus, frigidus et impotens', took the young Shunamite woman Abishag as his wife for the sole reason that she

---

[75] *Ibid.*, pp. 129–30; these same views, and the establishment of three reasons or goals for marriage, also permeate the writings of the Lutheran theologians who considered the Sorlisi–Lichtwer case (see below).

[76] Sommerville, *Sex and Subjection*, p. 115.

[77] *Ibid.*, p. 116. Although Sommerville examined a wide range of writings from the early modern period, her survey of German sources is almost exclusively limited to sixteenth-century writings; of the four seventeenth-century authors cited, Samuel Pufendorf appears most frequently. The important writings on marriage of Johann Gerhard, Johann Conrad Dannhauer and Benedict Carpzov are unfortunately overlooked. An examination of these writings would have revealed that these Lutheran theologians, like those who considered this case (see below), did not take such an extreme view; while most saw procreation as the primary aim and purpose of marriage, none raised this as the woman's sole reason for existence.

Eunuchi Conjugium

could keep him warm; according to the account in 1 Kings, he did not come to know her in the biblical sense.[78] But then Sorlisi cited a much more recent incident with relevance to his petition, and pointed out that 'this past June in Hamburg, in St Catherine's church, a 76-year-old shoemaker's widow by the name of Trina Bolter married a shoemaker's apprentice who was about 20 years old, and the command "be fruitful and multiply" was very ceremoniously pronounced over them'.[79] In his commentary on the blessing, Sorlisi not only answered the objection raised by Dorothea's friends (no. 2 above), but also strongly intimated that, rather than enjoin these newly-weds from engaging in 'fruitless' sexual relations, the minister had actually sanctioned such activity.[80] Sorlisi then went on to point out that in many marriages, age, injury, or unidentified causes conspire to render a couple incapable of procreation, and added that such marriages are neither forbidden nor dissolved; in fact, as he points out, both canon and secular law provide that when two people marry in full knowledge of the fact that one among them is incapable of procreation, they cannot be granted a divorce if they then presently seek a separation, even if the marriage has not yet been consummated.[81] 'If now such *Conjunctio* is *contra jura divina & naturalia*', he asked, 'how could it be tolerated simply for the reason that both sides knew of it beforehand? Surely it would be illogical to reach such a conclusion.'[82] Although never stated as such, his underlying argument seems to rest on the fact that

---

[78] Delphinus, *Eunuchi conjugium*, p. 7. The account appears in 1 Kings 1: 1–4.
[79] *Ibid.*, p. 8: 'gestalt im abgewichenen Monat *Junio* jüngsthin zu Hamburg in der Kirchen zu St. Catharinen/ eine Frau von 76. Jahren/ Namens Trina Bolters/ eine Schuhmachers Wittwe/ einem Schuh-Knechte/ von ungefehr 20. Jahren/ öffentlich anvertrauet/ und das *crescite & multiplicamini* gar herrlich über sie ausgesprochen worden'.
[80] According to Ulinka Rublack, however, the marriages of younger men to post-menopausal women 'breached accepted roles, as there was no "commitment to reproduction and patrimony" '; see 'Meanings of Gender in Early Modern German History', 8. Given the inheritance laws in effect during this era, this was one way a widow could retain control of her husband's business.
[81] Delphinus, *Eunuchi conjugium*, p. 9. Here Sorlisi cites [1] *Cap. consultationi X. de frig. & Malefic. & ibi Dd. omnes cum Gloss.*, [2] *Bidenbach in promptuario connub. append. c. 7. qu. 6* (=Felix Bidenbach (1564–1612), *Promptuarium connubiale*) and [3] *Carpz. Jurispr. Eccl. Lib. 2. Tit. XI. def. 202* (=Carpzov, *Jurisprudentia ecclesiastica*, cited above). Carpzov argues that although he has stated that a marriage may be dissolved owing to impotence (in bk. 2, title 11, definitions 200–1), he wishes to make two exceptions to this rule, the first of which is that stated by Sorlisi: 'Si aliquis vel aliqua scienter nuptias cum impotente contraxisset' (source: *cap. consultationi. 4. extr. de frigid. & maleficiat.*).
[82] Delphinus, *Eunuchi conjugium*, p. 9: 'Wenn nun solche *Conjunctio contra jura divina & naturalia*, wie könte solche bloß auß der Ursache/ weil beyderseits von dem *vitio corporis & impotentia*

fertility is beyond one's control, and that people who love one another and wish to marry should not suffer punishment for something they are powerless to change.

In his petition, Sorlisi also seeks to establish that, contrary to what had been alleged, both the medieval canonists and some theologians of the local confession actually permitted marriages such as the one he has proposed to be contracted and to abide, if such were the wish of both parties. But in offering this as supporting evidence in his own case, he introduces a conflict with the assertions that he has made above, for this discussion clearly implies that he and Dorothea intend to live together in a celibate state. Sorlisi made no effort to resolve this particular conflict, which may indicate that he was unsure which argument was the stronger of the two. Here he draws his arguments from glosses and commentaries on the decretal *De frigidis et maleficiatis, et impotentia coeundi*, and first quotes a commentary that indicates that 'it is permitted for some labouring under the burden of impotence or other bodily defect to contract a marriage with another who knows of the defect or impotence', and that, 'in similar cases, the Roman church was accustomed to judge that those whom they could not have as wives, they might have as sisters'.[83] And, he argues, while the doctors of canon law have ruled that impotence certainly represents a hindrance to marriage, as indicated in the fifth point against the marriage (given above), these same canonists also restricted the ability of the parties involved in such a marriage to dissolve it, once contracted.[84]

To this reasoning Sorlisi then adds the teachings of Lutheran theologians on the subject, and first cites petitions submitted to the theology faculty of the University of Wittenberg in 1596 and 1599 concerning cases in which the 'frigid and impotent' were married to women; in both cases, the faculty held in their favour.[85] With reference to this case, Sorlisi next directed the consistory's attention

Wissenschaft gehabt/ geduldet werden/ es würde warlich keine *ratio juris* zureichen/ solches *conclusum* zu erhalten.'

[83] Ibid.: '*Quod personae impotenti vel vitio corporis laborandi, conjugium cum alia, cui de vitio aut impotentia constat, matrimonium contrahere permitti possit. Cum Romana Ecclesia consueverit in consimilibus judicare, ut quas tanquam uxores habere non possint, habeant ut sorores.*' The source for these quotations is given as *cap. consultationi & cap. laudabilem X. de frig. & malef.* The decretal appears in the *Decretales* of Gregory IX, X 4. 15; see *Corpus juris canonici*, ed. E. Friedberg (repr. Graz, 1959), pt. 2, cols. 704–8.

[84] Ibid.

[85] Ibid., p. 10.

to the writings of the most eminent Lutheran theologian of the previous generation, Johann Gerhard (1582–1637). In his monumental *Loci theologici* (1610–22), Gerhard had wrestled with the very question that formed Sorlisi's petition to the consistory: 'An eunuchis ac spadonibus matrimonium permittendum?'[86] Most of Gerhard's argument on such marriages, the validity of which he clearly questioned, is based on the ninety-eighth Novel of Emperor Leo VI, which he quotes at length. But by citing the Wittenberg cases, Gerhard seems also to have opened the window for those in Sorlisi's situation, for from this the singer concluded that the theologian did not 'categorically and roundly reject the marriage of eunuchs and castrati',[87] and cited Eichsfeld's interpretation of Gerhard as proof: 'It should not be easily permitted for women to marry eunuchs. It is necessary to warn women of this type that they not sin in these regrettable non-marriages and cast themselves into the danger of fornication.'[88]

At the conclusion of these, his major arguments, Sorlisi added a few items that he felt were also worthy of the consistory's consideration. Here he stressed that Titius and Lucretia had already publicly entered into an engagement, and that Lucretia and her family were fully aware of and accepting of the fact that she would not be able to have children. He then returned once again to the matter of his sexual capacity, to which he had not made direct reference since his opening narrative, and made an unequivocal statement about his ability to satisfy his wife: 'Titius is not entirely incapable of the venereal exercise, but has often declared to prove that he still experiences the erection of the penis, can engage in sexual intercourse, can also give satisfaction to a woman, and can quell and extinguish her desire, inasmuch as he should be be allowed to do

---

[86] J. Gerhard, *Loci theologici*, Book 7: *De conjugio, Coelibatu et similibus argumentis*, ch. 25, §235 (Johann Gerhard, *Loci theologici*, ... *Opus praeclarissimum* ... *editionibus ann. 1657 et 1776 collatis* ..., vol. 7 (Berlin, 1869), pp. 140–2).

[87] Delphinus, *Eunuchi conjugium*, p. 10: 'denn auch unsere Herren *Theologi* nirgends denen *Eunuchis und Spadonibus Conjugium categoricie & rotunde* abgeschlagen'.

[88] *Ibid.*, p. 10: '*Mulieribus non facile permittendum, ut Eunuchis nubant, et praestare mulieres ejusmodi graviter admonere, ne in paenitendas et innuptas illas nuptias et scortationis periculum se praecipitent.*' As his source, Sorlisi cites Johann August Eichsfeld, *Orthodoxia casuali, sect. 3. c. 13. Th. 32*. The original passage appears in Gerhard's *Loci theologici, lib. 7., Artic. de Conjug. num. 235* (as cited by Sorlisi) as follows: 'Sed praestat ejusmodi mulieres graviter monere, ne in poenitendas et innuptas illas nuptias, adeoque in scortationis periculum sese praecipitent.'

so.'[89] In addition, he pointed out, since the two had already taken vows (at their betrothal), to separate them now would cause them to suffer guilty consciences. Sorlisi also warned that the two might be inclined to cultivate their love and desire in secret, or in a forbidden manner, and that Titius himself 'might strive towards lustful roaming'. Thus, in order to elect the lesser of two evils, as it were, the marriage should be allowed.[90]

Only after building his case carefully, thesis by thesis, did Sorlisi return to the six objections raised by Dorothea's friends. These he now dealt with in short order, without much commentary or corroborating evidence, as he had already addressed most of these points in his preceding arguments. Perhaps the most interesting point in these responses appears in no. 6, on the question of secular law and the marriage of eunuchs, for it includes a portent of things to come:

And moreover, as concerns *L. Si serva. 39. § Si spadoni. 1. ff. de jure dotium*: (1) Marriage to a *spado* is not prohibited in this law but, at the same time, the civil law is effectively in favour of the prolificity for which the Roman State is always most zealous. (2) Rather, this marriage is permitted in this law by the phrase, 'if she shall have married'. (3) In matters of matrimony, let the most widespread canon law restrict civil law.

As to the *Novellae Constitutiones* of Leo VI, because (1) according to Jacques Godefroy in his *Manuale iuris*, and others, these [constitutions] have never been observed in the Western Empire, let alone in the German Empire; and (2) because the canon law, rather, should be observed in this case. (3) In any case, one hopes to receive a dispensation concerning the external ecclesiastical power from the royal Swedish government.[91]

If the Leipzig consistory actually believed 'Titius' to be a Lutheran, this final bit of argumentation must have struck them as a bit odd.

---

[89] Delphinus, *Eunuchi conjugium*, p. 11: 'Der *Titius* zu dem *Exercitio venereo* nicht gäntzlich untüchtig/ sondern daß er annoch *erectionem penis* empfienge/ den *congressum* halten/ auch einem Weibes=Bilde *Satisfaction* thun/ und ihre Brunst stillen und *extingui*ren könne/ sich/ daferne es ihm zugelassen würde/ zu erweisen offt erkläret.'

[90] Ibid.: 'Oder 17. der *Titius* sich auf *Vagas libidines* befleißigen. Dannenhero gleichsam *ex duobus malis minimum* zu erwählen/ und dieses *Conjugium* zu verstatten.' (This is Sorlisi's point no. 17.)

[91] Ibid., p. 12: 'ad 6. *Et quidem L. Si Serva. 39. §. Si Spadoni. 1. ff. de jure dotium*; (1) *Quod in illa lege non prohibeatur matrimonium cum Spadone, sed saltem ei effectus juris civilis in favorem polypediae, cujus Respublica. Romana studiosissima semper, ademti.* (2) *Quin potius permissum hoc matrimonium in lege hac, verbis: si nupserit,* (3) *in matrimonialibus jura canonica civilibus derogent, per vulgatissima.*

Quoad Leonis Novellam Constitutionem, quod (1) *secundum Jacobum Godofredum in manual. Histor. Jur. aliosque constitutiones hae Imperio occidentali nunquam fuerint observatae, nedum in Imperio Germanico;* (2) *quod dotius* [recte potius] *in hac causa attendendum Jus canonicum.* (3) Man auf allen Fall bey der Königlichen Schwedischen Regierung/ was die *potestatem Ecclesiasticam externam* belanget/ *dispensationem* zu erhalten verhoffet.' The Genevan jurist Jacques Godefroy (1578–1652) published his *Manuale iuris* in 1645.

Eunuchi Conjugium

Although in his preceding argument, Sorlisi did attempt to use canon law to establish a precedent for his proposed marriage, he presented that discussion as one of many pieces of evidence, as if to suggest to the Lutheran clerics, 'even canon law permits such marriages'. But here he signalled his intention to ask the 'royal Swedish government', that is, the Elector of Saxony, to decree that canon law (or the Catholic Church generally) had no authority in his case – an action which, as *summus episcopus* of the Lutheran church in Saxony, Johann Georg was empowered to take. But in invoking the spectre of this 'external ecclesiastical power', Sorlisi, perhaps unwittingly, revealed Titius to be an individual actually subject to canon law, one who stood in need of such a 'dispensation'.

In October 1666, just two months after receiving Sorlisi's hypothetical 'Frage', the Leipzig consistory issued a concise response.[92] Not only did the consistory decide in Sorlisi's (i.e., Gericke's) favour, they also presented him with a ringing endorsement of the marriage:

As both principal parties were aware of the fact [of Titius's infertility], and nevertheless remain constant in their wish to marry, the mother of the bride has agreed to it, the engagement has continued, and the other friends had nothing to say, and as marriage was established by God for the honourable and lawful perpetuation of the human race, but at the same time He delivered the woman to the man as a helper, and moreover it has nowhere been commanded that a man who cannot have children should for this reason not wed or take a wife, and especially when it does not come about through deceit, and the woman understands this ahead of time, and in her feeding, tending, and caring shall seek no helper, to say nothing of the fact that in this man is not to be found such impotence and impossibility that hinders marital relations, *generationis actum*, as the schoolmasters say, but only that which hinders *generationis effectum*, the fruit of marriage, and similarly of the other conditions and grounds that are well advanced by you; thus the ecclesiastical court can in no way justly dissolve this betrothal and engagement, which were considered and handled with all assiduousness and good intention, against the public wills of the principal persons, nor less still deny to them the priestly union and marriage ceremony, but instead the same shall fittingly continue on their further

---

[92] UAG, Theologische Fakultät Nr. 3, Addendum no. 2, and Delphinus, *Eunuchi conjugium*, pp. 14–15; in the latter, the decree is incorrectly dated *Mense Octobr: 1663* (Sorlisi's question is dated 1666). As Sorlisi submitted his 'Frage' under the pseudonym of Johannes Gericke, an intermediary must have been involved in the delivery of the document as well as in the reception of the decision, as the consistory presumably did not send its decision directly to Sorlisi. With respect to this question, it is quite interesting to note that Junghanns had an acquaintance, Nicolaus Lüterius, who lived in Pomerania; according to the covering letter that accompanies Junghanns's materials for the Greifswald faculty, the lawyer sent them first to Lüterius, who forwarded them to the university faculty from 'Alten Stettien' (UAG, Theologische Fakultät Nr. 3, covering letter).

85

appropriate quest, by rights. Authentically sealed with our seal in the month of October 1666.[93]

In their decision, the members of the Leipzig consistory articulated a broader view of the purpose of marriage than solely that of procreation, and acknowledged that sexual relations per se represent an essential part of marriage, even when such activity cannot produce children. In his invention of a fictional protagonist castrated by pure accident in the service of the realm, rather than 'knowingly and willingly' by a backstreet surgeon, Sorlisi had made a brilliant calculation, for Titius's misfortune seems to have aroused the sympathy of the consistory, and caused the members to be wary of setting a precedent that might be used to ban or dissolve childless marriages in the future. As the consistory pointed out, God never forbade a man who cannot have children to marry. In their reluctance to separate the couple against their wills, the consistory also seems to have held a more modern view of individual freedom than did some of the other principals in the case, who appear to have been unable to grant humanity to the two individuals involved.

As he was now armed with a favourable decision from church authorities, Sorlisi was anxious to get married, but Dorothea's parents were in no hurry. And although Sorlisi's petition and the consistorial judgment were handled confidentially, the matter itself had not remained a secret. Junghanns later reported to the Greifswald faculty that by this time (1666), the case had been *in ore omnium* for five years. The fact that Sorlisi and Dorothea sought to marry had become well known not only in Dresden, but also throughout nearly all of Saxony, and the validity of such a marriage had been much discussed by theologians and lay people alike. In fact, two Leipzig theologians had contributed thoughts on the matter, and had countered the arguments of those opposed to the marriage.[94] In the words of one of these anonymous theologians,

As the marriage of a youth to a 70-year-old woman is good, so is the marriage of a virgin to an impotent man. But the marriage of a youth to a 70-year-old woman is good and blameless according to the practice of the church. It is likewise with the marriage of a virgin and an impotent man. Moreover, whatever marriage involves the first and most holy element of divine intention (namely mutual aid) is legitimate. But this is the

[93] UAG, Theologische Fakultät Nr. 3, Addendum no. 2; the German text appears as Doc. 4 in the Appendix. The language of the decision is virtually identical to that found in Delphinus, *Eunuchi conjugium*, pp. 14–15.
[94] As reported by Junghanns in his letter to the Greifswald faculty.

Eunuchi Conjugium

case not only with the marriage of the youth to the 70-year-old woman but likewise with the marriage to the impotent man.[95]

Apparently the degree of notoriety that the case had gained caused Junghanns's brother-in-law (the electoral *Steuer-Rat*) to suggest to him that it was time to seek the advice of the family's pastor and confessor, the rather ironically named Revd Daniel Schneider, the preacher at the Dresden Kreuzkirche.[96] Junghanns and his brother-in-law thus went to see the pastor, 'revealed everything to him, and did not conceal the least little thing'.[97] Finally, Junghanns's brother-in-law (who was also one of Schneider's parishioners) asked the minister if he had any objections to the marriage, and whether he would perform the ceremony. Schneider responded that while he had no actual objections to the marriage, he feared that the consequences of the union for Dorothea's health would be grave, as

> it would soon make one or the other of these two people ill and exhausted, for in her the semen would be irritated, but (as the doctors say) not elicited. Whereupon putrefaction of the womb would follow, and after this great heaviness of the womb, and then dropsy would quite probably follow as well, and might well finish her off.[98]

Schneider's answer is quite revealing with respect to contemporary perceptions of the sexual capacity of the castrato, for he expresses no doubt that Sorlisi can perform sexually. And, although Sorlisi had not made such a claim in his petition, Schneider also presumes that the castrato possesses the ability to emit semen. That a Lutheran minister in Saxony held such a belief is quite striking; its source may have been the Sistine brief, or perhaps Junghanns himself, for the

---

[95] UAG, Theologische Fakultät Nr. 3, addendum no. 6 of Junghanns's letter to the faculty: 'Quam bonum est conjugium juvenis et septuagenariae, tam bonum etiam est conjugium virginis atque spadonis. Atqui conjugium juvenis et septuagenariae ex praxi Ecclesiae est bonum et inculpabile. E. etiam conjugium virginis ac spadonis. Porro: Quocunque conjugium utitur primo ac sanctissimo divinitus instituto fine (sc. Adjutorio mutuo) illud est legitimum. Atqui conjugium non tantum juvenis et septuagenariae sed et aeque virginis ac spadonis utitur.'

[96] Junghanns describes Schneider as the local city preacher (*hiesigen Stadtprediger*) and senior minister (*ministeris seniorn*) in Dresden. Acccording to Johann Andreas Gleich, Schneider was *diaconus* at the Kreuzkirche in 1664, and delivered the funeral oration before the burial of Jacob Weller in the Sophienkirche in July of that year; see Gleich, *Annales ecclesiastici* (Dresden and Leipzig, 1730), pt. 2, p. 259. At this time in the Lutheran church, a deacon was an ordained minister who served in a city church with a clerical staff of several members.

[97] 'da Ihme dann von unß alles entdecket, und nicht das geringste verschwiegen worden ist'.

[98] 'es würde eines das andere von diesen beÿden leuthen bald ungesund machen und auffreiben, denn bey Ihr würde das *semen irriti*ret, aber (wie die *Medici* redeten) nicht *elici*ret werden: Alßdenn würden bey Ihr *putridines in matrice* entstehen, worauff große Mutterbeschwerung, auch wohl gahr die waßersucht folgen, und Ihr den Rest geben dörffe.'

lawyer may have indicated to the pastor that such was the case, given his acknowledged 'no holds barred' approach to this crucial conversation.[99]

Schneider's comments would also seem to reflect his acceptance of the Galenic 'two-seed' model of reproduction, in which both the male and the female produce seed, that of the male being the more potent.[100] Thus in his view, given Sorlisi's inability to contribute this essential life-giving spark, sex with him would cause Dorothea to become quite ill, and might just signal her demise. Like the others who would contribute to this case, Schneider makes no reference to 'vital heat', although this concept may underlie his understanding of sexuality and reproduction. Yet his statement still bears a striking correspondence to what Thomas Laqueur has discussed as the medical consequences for the 'cold woman' (one whose vital heat was abnormally low); she was 'thought more likely to suffer retention of the seed or of surplus blood, amenorrhea, which in turn might have a variety of clinical sequels: depression, heaviness of limb, barrenness, green sickness, hysteria'.[101] Schneider's words might also be read as adding a new twist to the ancient topos of sexual 'pollution'. Often associated with menstrual blood, which threatens to 'pollute' the man who comes into contact with it, or with the semen emitted nocturnally that sullies the ritually pure cleric, here the concept is extended to include male fluids that lack the life-giving spark, and as a result act as a corrupting agent in the woman.[102] Rather inexplicably, given his overwhelmingly negative views on the implications of the sexual aspect of this future relationship, Schneider then added that he would gladly perform the wedding ceremony, on the condition that he receive an electoral order (*Befehl*) to do so.[103] Apparently the couple had already begun

---

[99] In fact, it seems unlikely that Junghanns would not have had a frank talk with Sorlisi, in order to determine just what his stepdaughter would encounter with respect to the sexual aspect of their marriage.

[100] See Laqueur, *Making Sex*, pp. 28–41, and N. Siraisi, *Medieval and Early Renaissance Medicine: An Introduction to Knowledge and Practice* (Chicago and London, 1990), pp. 81, 110–11.

[101] Laqueur, *Making Sex*, p. 107.

[102] See Salisbury, 'Gendered Sexuality', pp. 89–90, and D. Cannon, *Fallen Bodies: Pollution, Sexuality, and Demonology in the Middle Ages* (Philadelphia, 1999), pp. 2–7, 14–27. Cannon indicates that the 'potent metaphors of female pollution were used to feminise and discredit those perceived as spiritually suspect' (p. 6); this may be Schneider's intent here as well.

[103] Here the term 'Befehl' refers to a decree permitting the pastor to marry the couple without fear of prosecution, rather than to a command or order – an order of protection, as it were.

Eunuchi Conjugium

to exert great pressure on Dorothea's parents, for Junghanns next confessed his fear to his pastor that, should the wedding be prevented, the couple would slip over the Bohemian border to be married by a Catholic priest.

Junghanns then reported the substance of his conversation with Schneider to Sorlisi, who immediately paid another visit to the court preacher, this time to seek the special order for the marriage requested by Schneider. Since his last visit, however, the more reasonable previous occupant of that office had died, and had been replaced by Martin Geier (1614–80), who was a friend neither of Catholics nor of Italian music and musicians.[104] In the unyielding Geier, Sorlisi would meet his nemesis, a man who would agitate for the dissolution of his marriage long after it had finally been consummated. Geier refused to grant Sorlisi's request for the special order, and declared that he could not allow such a marriage in Dresden, for it would represent a precedent-setting case that would absolutely not be permitted by the High Consistory (*Ober Consistorium*), of which he was a member. But rather than order Sorlisi to submit a new petition to the High Consistory, which had the prerogative to rule on marital matters, Geier rather inexplicably advised the singer that the question would have to be resolved by the 'supreme bishop' (*Oberst Bischoff*) of the Lutheran church in Saxony, Elector Johann Georg II. Geier's surrender of the High Consistory's authority in this matter is surprising, for once such questions were turned over to the elector, he was free to issue a decree on the matter, and, unlike the decisions of various theological faculties, his decision had the force of law.

At this point, as Junghanns later reported to the Greifswald faculty, Sorlisi realised that neither Schneider nor Geier had

---

Such a document was subsequently issued to the pastor who performed the ceremony (see below).

[104] Jacob Weller died in July 1646; Geier was sworn in as the Ober Hofprediger on 30 December 1664, and preached his inaugural sermon in the Dresden court chapel on 1 Janaury 1665 (SLUB K 80, fol. 5^{r-v}). Prior to his appointment in Dresden, he had served as Superintendent in Leipzig and pastor of the Thomaskirche, and a member of that city's consistory (Gleich, *Annales ecclesiastici*, pp. 336–46). See also J. Hahn, 'Zeitgeschehen im Spiegel der lutherisch-orthodoxen Predigt nach dem Dreißigjährigen Krieg – dargestellt am Beispiel des kursächsischen Oberhofpredigers Martin Geier' (Ph.D. diss., University of Leipzig 1990), pp. 22–8. Geier used the occasion of Schütz's funeral to present a diatribe against Italian music and musicians; see R. A. Leaver (ed.), *Music in the Service of the Church: The Funeral Sermon for Heinrich Schütz* (St. Louis, Mo., 1984).

explicitly opposed the marriage, but that on the contrary, Schneider had given his approval, and Geier, in referring the case to the elector, had tacitly signalled his acquiescence as well. Thus, although no doubt weary of climbing over the barriers erected before him by Lutheran clerics, the determined suitor then went to Johann Georg II and explained the matter yet again (at this point, however, the elector cannot have been unfamiliar with the details). Since there was no negative judgement standing between him and his betrothed, Sorlisi requested that Johann Georg grant him permission to marry, and explained to his patron that everything now rested on his 'most gracious Resolution'. On 14 January 1667, Johann Georg granted his favourite's wish, and, unbeknownst to the Dresden High Consistory, issued a *Befehl* bestowing upon Pastor Matthias Kühn of Sadisdorf, a town near Schmiedeberg, the permission to marry the couple in a private ceremony to be held in Sorlisi's residence, following a reading of the order.[105] Recognising the risks that this would pose to the minister, Johann Georg also promised to protect and indemnify the Lutheran pastor.[106] On Sunday, 27 January 1667, Sorlisi sang a leading role in the inaugural performance of Ziani's *Il Teseo* in the new Komödienhaus, a performance undoubtedly attended by Dorothea.[107] Although the cast list does not survive, Sorlisi and Melani apparently sang the leading roles, and for their performances received an encomium in the form of a sonnet from Giovanni Andrea Bontempi, a fellow castrato at the Dresden court.[108] Two days later, on Tuesday, 29 January, the long-awaited nuptials finally took place at Sorlisi's estate, 'in the presence of the parents, sister, closest friends, and other people, who were very well fed afterwards'.[109] Perhaps some

---

[105] Sächs. HStA Loc. 7445/18, fol. 5ʳ; the Dresden consistory included a copy of the decree as an exhibit in their letter of protest to the elector (see below), as did Junghanns in his letter to the Greifswald faculty. The German text of the decree appears as Doc. 5 in the Appendix.

[106] The exact language reads: 'Höchstgedachte Churfürstl. Durchl. wollen ermelten Pfarr, aller verantworttung halber, dißfals gnädigsten Schutz leisten, undt schadtlos halten.' ('His most highly regarded Electoral Highness will in this case, taking full responsibility, afford the aforementioned pastor his most gracious protection, and will indemnify him.') Ortkemper reports that Kühn received two cords of wood annually for life as compensation (*Engel wider Willen*, p. 195).

[107] Fürstenau, *Zur Geschichte der Musik und des Theaters*, i, p. 226.

[108] *Ibid.*

[109] Sächs. HStA Loc. 7445/18, fol. 5ᵛ: 'Daß die Trawung in beÿseÿn der Eltern, Schwester, Nähesten Freunde undt auch anderer Personen, geschehen, undt were darauf gar *repetir*lich gespeiset worden', drawn from a copy of Junghanns' report of 3 February 1667 to Pastor

of these 'other people' were members of the Dresden Hofkapelle who made the journey to Schmiedeberg to witness this extraordinary event; if so, the ceremony may have been enhanced by performances of the music of Kapellmeister Giuseppe Peranda (*c.* 1625–75) by Sorlisi's virtuoso colleagues.

Seven days after the nuptials in Schmiedeberg, the foresighted Junghanns wrote to Pastor Kühn with a number of instructions, including the manner in which the pastor should respond if questioned by church authorities. The tone of the letter suggests that Kühn felt less than comfortable with the central role that he had played in the recent event, and feared that this deed would not redound to his advantage. Junghanns thus tried to allay the minister's fears, and reminded him that his actions were sanctioned by none less than the elector himself. But Junghanns was also keen to make certain that the marriage was registered, and lent the church's official *imprimatur* without delay:

> Most honourable, most estimable, most learned and above all most gracious Pastor, I report to you that we here think it would be a good idea if you would report the recent marriage to the Superintendent in Pirna, and enclose for him a copy of your most gracious *Befehl*; you can simply report that you certainly would have liked to have delayed the ceremony, but that I, Mr George Metzner, and the Administrator insisted on the wording [of the decree], that the marriage should take place immediately after the reading of the most gracious decree, and that His Electoral Highness afforded you protection, and will indemnify you; *Item*: His Electoral Highness is the Supreme Bishop, and has the power to decree as he will; *Item*: You will not bring disgrace upon yourself; you can also report that the wedding took place in the presence of the parents, sister, and closest friends, as well as other people, and that they were very well fed afterwards. Such must be done quickly, otherwise you may be called before the High Consistory. However, when they see your *Befehl*, the matter will soon be put to rest. You should send the report back with bearers; I will have it copied for you here. Counsel will soon be taken of your cassock.[110] Farewell.
>
> Moritz Junghannß Dr.[111]

Kühn, included as the third attachment to the letter of 13 February 1667 of the Dresden High Consistory to Johann Georg. The wedding date appears in the 13 February letter of the Dresden High Consistory, Sächs. HStA Loc. 7445/18, fol. 2ʳ. See also Delphinus, *Eunuchi conjugium*, p. 40.

[110] That is, steps will be taken to see your career in the church does not suffer. My thanks to Leofranc Holford-Strevens for the translation and explanation.

[111] Sächs. HStA Loc. 7445/18, fols. 5ᵛ, 8ʳ: Statement of Dr Moritz Junghanns, written to Pastor Kühn, 3 February 1667; the text appears as Addendum no. 3 to the 13 February 1667 letter of the Dresden High Consistory to Johann Georg II. The German text appears as Doc. 6 in the Appendix. The town of Pirna lies about 20 km south-east of Dresden on the Elbe River; the Superintendent (a supervising minister) in Pirna probably had jurisdiction over both Sadisdorf and Schmiedeberg. Ortkemper quotes the entry of the marriage that appears in the records of the *Gemeinde Sadisdorf* (Sadisdorf parish): 'Es ist auch zu Hause getraut worden den

Junghanns's comment that the minister would have preferred to delay the marriage may well be an allusion to the provisions of the Saxon *Kirchen-Agenda*, which stipulated that all marriages were to be announced in church for three successive Sundays prior to the date the ceremony was scheduled to take place; Junghanns had prevented Kühn from following normal church procedure in this respect, as he had insisted that the ceremony proceed immediately upon the reading of the elector's *Befehl*.[112]

As he had taken precautions to see that everything was done according to the letter of the law, Junghanns seems to have been quite confident that the marriage of his stepdaughter and new son-in-law rested on solid legal ground, and that any dust raised by the event would soon settle. Unhappily for him and his newly expanded family, however, nothing could have been further from the truth. Almost immediately, rumours concerning the wedding made their way back to the Dresden High Consistory, which contacted Pastor Kühn. The pastor confirmed their suspicions, and also revealed that he had, of his own volition, altered the text of the marriage ceremony as given in the Saxon *Kirchen-Agenda* by means of omissions, substitutions and glosses.[113] Concerned about the scandal (*Ärgernis*) that this marriage was likely to cause, the members of the High Consistory wasted no time in making their objections to the marriage known to Johann Georg.[114] In a letter dated 15 February 1667, they expressed their deepest regret that the elector had failed

---

29. Januarii Herr Bartholomeo de Sorlisi und die Jungfrau Dorothea Elisabeth geborene Lichtwer' (*Engel wider Willen*, p. 195).

[112] *AGENDA, das ist/ Kirchen=Ordnung/ Wie sich die Pfarrherren und Seelsorger in ihren Aembtern und Diensten verhalten sollen. Für die Diener der Kirchen In Hertzog Heinrich zu Sachsen/ V. G. H. Fürstenthum gestellet. Jetzo auffs neue aus Chur=Fürst AUGUSTI Kirchen=Ordnung gebessert/ Auch mit etlichen Collecten der Superintendenten vermehret* (Leipzig, 1702), p. 31. The *Agenda* was first published in 1539, and reprinted repeatedly with very few changes.

[113] The text of the Lutheran marriage ceremony, as given in the *Kirchen-Agenda*, is very brief. After each party has answered in the affirmative to the questions 'do you take this man?' and 'do you take this woman?', and the rings have been exchanged, the pastor pronounces the couple man and wife. As the service continues to the Admonition ('Vermahnung'), however, there are a number of references to children, including the command to 'be fruitful and multiply'; these Kühn probably altered or omitted (*Kirchen-Agenda*, pp. 32–44). As the entire wedding text lacks any and all references to Lutheranism or 'pure doctrine' (*reine Lehre*), Kühn's modifications were probably unrelated to confessional issues.

[114] Sächs. HStA Loc. 7445/18, fols. 2^r–4^r, Dresden High Consistory (*Ober Consistorium*) (signatories Carl von Friesen, president, Superintendent Christopher Buleus, Martin Geier and Botth. Berringer) to Johann Georg II, 13 February 1667. The summary in this paragraph is based on this letter.

Eunuchi Conjugium

to consult them before making a decision in such an 'awkward case' ('verfänglichen *casu*'), and also expressed their fear of the 'detrimental consequences that this recent manner of proceeding' (*'modus procedendi'*) might have for the elector's reputation. The members of the consistory made it clear to Johann Georg that they had grave doubts concerning the validity of the marriage, and they also cast aspersions on the 'misrepresentational *Informat*' – presumably Sorlisi's petition – upon which the decision was based, for they claimed that the document was 'established entirely on presuppositions other than appear in the present case'.[115] In questioning Kühn they had learned of the changes to the approved marriage text, and thus asked the elector to issue an order that both 'acceding parties' ('*excedi*rende Partheÿen') be rigorously examined, in order that the clergy might not be 'confounded by this example' ('durch dieses *exempel* nicht irregemacht'). They also lodged a protest over the fact that they had been prevented from carrying out their official responsibilities as defined by the Saxon *Kirchenordnung* of 1580. But as the power to declare the marriage null and void rested not with them, but with civil authorities, they appealed to the elector to allow them to formulate a question more truly reflective of the situation and to solicit opinions on this question from one or two theological faculties, and they asked Johann Georg to defer to the decision of these faculties in making his final determination concerning the validity of the marriage.[116] As formulated for the elector's examination, the 'Frage' (question) openly betrays the sentiments of its authors, who are quick to ascribe intentionality to the young boy who had suffered surgical mutilation:[117]

---

[115] *Ibid.*, fol. 3ʳ: 'zumahl das vorgeschützte *Informat*, darauf man sich etwan zu gründen vermeinet haben mag, ... gar auf andere *praesupposita*, als beÿ gegenwertigen *casu* erscheinen, eingerichtet'.

[116] On the right of civil authorities to grant divorces in Lutheran areas, see W. Elert, 'Zur Geschichte des evangelischen Ehescheidungsrechtes', in *Ein Lehrer der Kirche: Kirchlich-theologische Aufsätze und Vorträge von Werner Elert* (Berlin and Hamburg, 1967), pp. 151–66, at p. 152.

[117] In the passage quoted below, Geier's use of the phrase 'knowingly and willingly castrated' represents a careful calculation, as a number of Lutheran theologians writing on the subject of divorce opined that in cases of impotence that arose unexpectedly (*impotentia superveniens*), if the impotence was brought about by one's own fault (*selbstverschuldet*), the marriage could be annulled. If it arose through natural causes, however, it was to be considered an illness, and thus did not provide grounds for divorce. See Elert, 'Zur Geschichte des evangelischen Ehescheidungsrechtes', pp. 159–63.

Mary E. Frandsen

Question:
Can a man who was knowingly and willingly castrated in his youth, and who is everywhere held and known to be a castrato, and who still remains devoted to the Catholic Church, against that church's own decrees enter into a lasting marriage with a young woman from an Evangelical Lutheran congregation, even if she already knowingly and willingly agrees and has her mother's consent, without detriment to the divine order of holy matrimony, without scandalising the righteous, and without having negative repercussions in the corrupt? And, as such persons are already married, should such be held as a proper marriage, and be further tolerated?

The *rationes dubitandi* and *decidendi* concerning the same shall be advanced, according to divine and ecclesiastical law.[118]

Oblivious to the machinations of Geier, the newly-weds embarked upon their life together. Given Sorlisi's duties at court, the newly married couple must have commuted regularly between his estate in Schmiedeberg and his home in Dresden, which may still have been in a flat in one Dr Höÿmann's house on the Pirnaische Gasse, where Sorlisi shared his 'Logierung und *Quartier*' (lodging and quarters) with Melani.[119] Not long after his wedding, on 4 and 10 March, Sorlisi's musical presence was demanded in Dresden, where he performed in repeat performances of *Il Teseo*; the latter performance was 'improved with some machines and inventions'.[120] Apparently many at court had eagerly anticipated hearing Sorlisi's voice *post conjugium*. According to Henri de Chassan, the French ambassador in Dresden, Sorlisi's voice suffered no ill effects

---

[118] Sächs. HStA Loc. 7445/18, fol. 6ʳ, included as addendum no. 2 in the 13 February 1667 letter of the Dresden consistory to Johann Georg: 'Frage: Ob eine Manns Persohn, so 1. in ihrer jugend wißent- und williglich *castrir*et worden, auch 2. allenthalben *pro castrato* gehalten wird undt bekand ist, Vndt 3. annoch der Päbstischen Kirche zugethan verbleibet, 4. wider derselbigen Kirche selbsteigene *decreta*, 5. könne ein junges mensch aus einer Evangelischen Lutherischen gemeine, ob sie schon wißent- undt williglich mit ihrer mutter darein williget, 6. unbeschädigt götlicher ordnung des heiligen ehestandes, 7. ohn großes ärgernüs der rechtgläubigen, vndt 8. ohne übele nachklang bei den widerwertigen, 9. beständig heirathen? Vndt 10. da solche Personen albereit *copulir*et worden, ob solches für eine rechte ehe zu halten, vndt ferner zu dulden sei? Hierüber sollen *rationes dubitandi* vndt *decidendi* angeführet werden, göttlichen vndt Kirchen rechten gemäß.'

[119] Sächs. HStA OHMA O IV Nr. 21, *Alter und Neuer Schreib-Kalender* . . . *M.DC.LXVII* (unfoliated), entry for 22 October 1667: 'Dienstags den 22. Es hat der neübestellte Cornet . . . Jochim Dietrich von Jüdstadt, einen Cornet-Schmauß oder Panquet in des Doctors Höÿmanns Hause uf der Pirnischen Gassen, aldar die beyde Italiäner Dominico und Bartholomeo Ihre Logierung und *Quartier* haben, angestellet.'

[120] Sächs. HStA OHMA O IV Nr. 21, entries for 4 and 10 March 1667; also reported in OHMA O IV Nr. 20, *Alter und Neuer Sonderbahrer Schreibe-Calender Auff das Jahr* . . . *M.DC.LXVII* (unfoliated), entries for 4 and 10 March 1667. See also Fürstenau, *Zur Geschichte der Musik und des Theaters*, i, p. 227.

Eunuchi Conjugium

as the result of his marriage; rather, to the surprise of all, it had retained all of its 'virginal purity', 'despite copulation'.[121] The newly-weds could hardly rejoice in Sorlisi's public musical triumphs, however, for events in their private life had already begun to demonstrate that their long struggle had not yet ended. Within several months of the wedding, after it had become clear that the couple would not separate despite the attempts of some to convince them to do so, Pastor Schneider sentenced Dorothea to effective excommunication (*kleiner Bann* or *excommunicatio minor*):[122] he refused to hear Dorothea's confession, pronounce absolution over her and admit her to the Holy Communion table.[123] Suddenly, and apparently without warning, Dorothea found herself cast out of the community of believers by her own father-confessor, despite the fact, as Junghanns emphasised in his letter to the Greifswald faculty, that the minister had expressed no opposition to the marriage when visited by Junghanns and his brother-in-law. At this point, one begins to sense the gravity of the implications of this marriage for Dorothea. One can only imagine the degree of public humiliation that she suffered, first as the subject of gossip and rumour for many years, and then at the hands of her own pastor. One wonders if Schneider communicated his decision concerning the sacrament to Dorothea in writing, as stipulated by the Saxon *Kirchenordnung*, or if he flaunted the rules and publicly humiliated her by ordering her out of the confessional late one Saturday afternoon after vespers in the Kreuzkirche.[124] Perhaps both pastor and penitent came bursting out of their respective booths, to the shock and surprise of all those waiting in line for confession.

---

[121] Auerbach, *La diplomatie française et la cour de Saxe*, p. 414: 'Or, au grand ébahissement de tous, dont Chassan se fit l'écho, le signor Bartolomeo continua à chanter l'opéra et conserva la pureté virginale de sa voix "nonobstant", écrivit le Résident [Chassan] en un style un peu cru, "nonobstant la copulation".'

[122] The Bill of Anathema did formally exist in the Lutheran church, but was rarely used; effective excommunication was far more common.

[123] UAG, Theologische Fakultät Nr. 3, Junghanns to the faculty at Greifswald; Junghanns indicates that at the time of his writing in April 1668, his stepdaughter has been denied Communion for over a year. Junghanns's letter to the Greifswald faculty reveals that Schneider believed that the marriage of Sorlisi and Dorothea did not exist in God's eyes, and that they thus were living in a state of mortal sin ('Es kan nicht sen, die Ehe bestehet vor Gott nicht, die leuthe geriethen in einen Todtsünde, wie mann es anietzt sagen will, mahnet Sie davon abe, so hette man sich darnach gerichtet').

[124] Confession and absolution took place after Saturday vespers in the Lutheran church at this time. On the excommunicatory process prescribed in the Saxon *Kirchenordnung*, see *Die evangelischen Kirchenordnungen des XVI. Jahrhunderts*, ed. Sehling, i, pp. 431–2.

Not all of the clergy in town saw the situation in the same light, however; Superintendent Buleus remonstrated against Schneider's decision in an *Assertio* in which he argued that 'this marriage could by no means be dissolved, but on the contrary, could be tolerated and endured'.[125] Schneider, however, remained resolute in his position.[126] Junghanns, infuriated by Schneider's complete turnaround, exchanged written charges and recriminations with the pastor on at least two occasions.[127] In his letters, the lawyer apparently claimed that the minister had actually encouraged the marriage, for during their meeting, when Junghanns had expressed his fear that the two might slip off to Bohemia to be married by a Catholic priest, Schneider had retorted that they could do that 'in God's name', as the Lutherans and Catholics had no differences concerning the marriage ceremony itself.[128] For his part, Schneider felt that the accusation was unfair and ungentlemanly, and pointed out that there was a significant difference between answering 'that you could do', when someone has already decided upon a course of action, and actually advising that individual to do the same.[129] Schneider would neither admit that he had misled Junghanns and his brother-in-law nor readmit Dorothea to the table; ultimately, Junghanns would be forced to seek redress for his stepdaughter and her husband from higher authority.

After learning of the objections of the Dresden High Consistory in February, Elector Johann Georg II did not issue an immediate response, but remained silent on the matter for a full six months. During the following summer of 1667, while travelling about Saxony inspecting his territories, he paused on 27–8 August for a

---

[125] 'wie nemlich diese Ehe keines weges getrennet, besondern vielmehr *toleriret* und erduldet werden könte'; from Junghanns's letter to the Greifswald faculty, UAG, Theologische Facultät Nr. 3. A portion of Buleus's *Assertio* appears as Addendum no. 8 to Junghanns's letter; the entire document appears in Delphinus, *Eunuchi conjugium*, as the *Assertio D. Bulaei*, pp. 96–111.

[126] It remains unclear why Buleus, who was Schneider's direct supervisor, did not or could not order Schneider to reverse his decision.

[127] In his letter to the Greifswald faculty, Junghanns included excerpts from letters that he had received from Schneider dated 5 September 1667 and 14 January 1668 (UAG, Theologische Facultät Nr. 3).

[128] 'Worauff Er mir denn geanttworttet, das könten Sie in Gottes Nahmen thun, und gab darbey die *rationem decidendi* also: *Differir*en wir doch mit den *Catholicen in actu copulationis* gantz nicht.'

[129] As indicated by the 'Extract aus H. M. Daniel Schneiders an H. D. M. Junghannßen Schreiben *sub dato* den 5. *Septembr*. 1667', which appears as Addendum no. 5 to Junghanns's letter to the Greifswald faculty (UAG, Theologische Fakultät Nr. 3).

Eunuchi Conjugium

brief visit in Wittenberg, the birthplace of the Reformation.[130] Significantly, Wittenberg was also the home of the 'urevangelische Universität' and its renowned theological faculty.[131] Johann Georg's decision to issue his decree concerning the fate of the Sorlisi–Lichtwer marriage from this city cannot have been mere fortuity, for the Wittenberg imprimatur lent substantial weight to the decision, and implied the approval of the theology faculty there; indeed, the passing references to theologians in the decree itself suggest that Johann Georg had used his visit to consult the members of that faculty, which included General Superintendent Abraham Calov. On Wednesday, 28 August 1667, Johann Georg finally promulgated his reply to the High Consistory, in the form of a legally binding decree.[132] His response cannot have pleased Geier and the other members of the tribunal, for he declared that he would allow the marriage to stand, and that Sorlisi and his spouse were to be left 'unassailed and undisturbed by one and all'.[133] Johann Georg artfully placed the blame for the situation squarely at the feet of the High Consistory, the members of which, he said, had brought the matter to his attention far too late for him to have given due consideration to their views, for by the time he received their petition, 'the matter was already so far developed that we, on the most obedient supplications of the parties, both advanced by them and supplied by others, ... let ourselves be moved to look most graciously upon this marriage'.[134] In his opinion, to dissolve the

---

[130] Sächs. HStA Loc. 8681 Nr. 7, fol. 32ᵛ, entries for Tuesday, 27 August, and Wednesday, 28 August 1667. Johann Georg's retinue that summer included musicians; the court diaries reveal that Sorlisi won a hunting prize in Freiberg on 15 August, and there is little doubt that he accompanied Johann Georg to Wittenberg two weeks later (*ibid.*, fols. 28ᵛ–29ʳ, and OHMA O IV Nr. 21 (unfoliated), entries for Thursday, 15 August 1667).
[131] The university was founded in 1502 by Elector Friedrich der Weise, the protector of Luther and one of Johann Georg's ancestors; in 1525, Friedrich's brother and successor Johann der Beständige brought about the Reformation in Ernestinian Saxony, and established Wittenberg University as his state university ('Landesuniversität'); see H. Holborn, *A History of Modern Germany: The Reformation* (Princeton, 1959; repr. 1982, pp. 106, 124–40, 154–67), and G. Naumann, *Sächsische Geschichte in Daten* (Berlin and Leipzig, 1991), p. 93.
[132] Delphinus, *Eunuchi conjugium*, pp. 15–17 ('*Decretum Electorale*'). The decree also appears in its entirety as Addendum No. 4 of Junghanns's letter to the Greifswald faculty, where the text is identical to the published version.
[133] Delphinus, *Eunuchi conjugium*, p. 17: 'Er deshalber so wohl/ als seine Verheyrathete/ von männiglichen unangefochten und unbekümmert gelassen werden sollen.' This directive may have been directed at Martin Geier specifically.
[134] Delphinus, *Eunuchi conjugium*, p. 16, Decree of Johann Georg II, 28 August 1667: 'Nachdem es aber bereit damahls in der Sache so weit gediehen gewesen/ daß wir/ auf unterthänigstes

marriage at this point, after the two had dwelt together for months as husband and wife, would cause an even greater scandal, and would present more problems than simply tolerating the unusual union. In what would turn out to be a rather prescient observation, he also pointed out that theologians were not in total agreement on the matter, and that their disagreement left room for debate. He also argued that, once performed, other marriages considered equally impermissible were allowed to stand. Near the end of the decree, however, Johann Georg revealed himself to be less than completely comfortable with his decision, for he warned that no one, including those members of his cohort of castrati, would be allowed to cite this case as a precedent in the future, for such a marriage would not be allowed again. Finally, he directed that Sorlisi and his wife should immediately offer something 'for pious causes' ('zu milden Sachen').

The Dresden consistory received the elector's decree within a few days, and on 10 September 1667, pursuant to the instructions of the elector expressed in the document, Superintendent Buleus informed Sorlisi and Dorothea of Johann Georg's decision, and wished the couple 'happiness and blessings'.[135] Upon hearing of his patron's suggestion that something should be done *in loco dispensationis*, Sorlisi promptly declared that he would build a Lutheran church, and would endow a Lutheran pastorate in perpetuity.[136] With this, according to Junghanns, all thought that the matter had been settled, but the couple's problems soon began anew, for they now found themselves under attack by those who claimed that the two could not live together in good conscience, and who clamoured for a *Rescission* (divorce or annulment). But as Junghanns approvingly reported to the Greifswald faculty, the newly-weds were deeply in love and sexually satisfied with one another, and thus would not hear of divorce:

The fact is that these two people truly love each other with their entire hearts and care for one another devotedly; in addition, both parties have made it known that they would rather let their lives be taken than let one be separated from the other. Neither

Suppliciren des Ansuchen der Partheyen/ so wohl von ihnen angeführten/ als auch andern eingeholten/ . . . dieses matrimonium gnädigst nachzusehen.'

[135] Delphinus, *Eunuchi conjugium*, p. 41: 'und darbey diesen beyden Glück und Seegen gewündschet'.

[136] According to Ortkemper, Sorlisi began to build a church and to endow a pastorate in Johnsbach, a town near Schmiedeberg (*Engel wider Willen*, pp. 198–9).

Eunuchi Conjugium

has any complaint whatsoever to bring about the other, but on the contrary, both are extremely content with one another *in all things* (Junghanns's emphasis).[137]

On 6 December 1667, two months after the promulgation of the elector's decree, Geier wrote again to Johann Georg.[138] Undeterred by his patron's public decision, Geier continued to press his case with the elector, and to urge him to change his ruling on the marriage. According to his letter, he had not let the matter drop after signing (and probably writing) the Dresden High Consistory's February letter to the elector, but had approached Johann Georg several times in the interim; on the most recent occasion, the elector had referred him to his privy council. By December, however, nearly after a year after the controversial wedding had taken place, Geier had acquired new ammunition for his arsenal, with which he stood ready to repel any and all contrary opinions. As requested by the Dresden High Consistory, the theological faculties of the Lutheran universities of Giessen and Strassburg had both rendered opinions on the matter, and Geier now presented both to Johann Georg for his consideration.[139] Together with these decisions, the preacher also included an excerpt from a letter he had received from the late Samuel Lange, former Superintendent of Leipzig and member of the consistory that had considered Sorlisi's petition. Apparently, contrary to Junghanns's assertions, the members of the Leipzig consistory had not been aware that the petitioner in the case under review was a castrato, and the realisation of this fact had caused considerable consternation among their ranks:

We certainly never ordered that our decision be applied to a eunuch. It is rather the case that if we had suspected anything about a eunuch, we would not have judged any differently in this case than the late Dannhauer [citation follows] had done in a similar matter. I will provide a full and clear account of his thinking in the case about the

---

[137] 'Nun ist es aber an deme, daß diese beyde leuthe von rechten gantzen hertzen einander treulich lieben und redlich meÿnen, auch beiderseitß sich vernehmen laßen, daß Sie sich lieber das leben nehmen, alß eines von dem andern sich scheiden laßen wolten, führen darbey über einander gantz keine clage, besondern seynd vielmehr *in allen dingen* mit einander gahr sehr wohl zufrieden.' Junghanns wrote all of the German text of this letter, save these three words, in German script; the words 'in allen dingen' appear in a larger, roman script.

[138] Sächs. HStA Loc. 7445/18, fol. 9ʳ⁻ᵛ.

[139] Delphinus, *Eunuchi conjugium*, pp. 17–37; manuscript copies of both decisions survive in Sächs. HStA Loc. 7445/18, fols. 13ʳ–16ʳ, 18ʳ–22ʳ. The Strassburg faculty may not have been entirely impartial in this case, for Geier had spent time there in Dannhauer's circle in the early 1630s; see Gleich, *Annales ecclesiastici*, pp. 315–16. Gleich mentions no particular connections between Geier and the theology faculty in Giessen.

99

eunuch. We never approved this case regarding the eunuch and we never shall approve it.[140]

With the decisions of the Strassburg and Giessen faculties, it becomes clear that the views of Lutheran theologians on the ends (or goals) of marriage, and the number and order of these ends, were not absolutely consistent – a fact that ultimately would work to Sorlisi's distinct advantage. In its opinion, for example, the Strassburg faculty focuses solely on impotence (particularly that of eunuchs) as an impediment to marriage, and does not invoke any of the commonly cited goals to which the marital estate aspires. The Giessen faculty, on the other hand, mentions just two ends, procreation – to which it believes all other ends are subordinate – and the quelling of sexual desire; with respect to the third end, mutual help, which figures so prominently in Sorlisi's petition, this faculty argued that any benefits to be derived from mutual help are completely outweighed by the sexual dangers posed by such a marriage.[141] Both faculties buttressed their arguments with citations from the writings of Lutheran theologians, and from the works of a number of canonists and other writers who had addressed the question of the marriage of eunuchs, including some who wrote during the castrato era, such as Juan Gutiérrez, Tómas Sánchez, Francisco de Toledo, Martín Azpilcueta (alias the doctor Navarrus, a friend and confidant of Sixtus V) and Pope Sixtus V himself.[142] Owing primarily to the known inability of the husband in this case to father children, neither the Strassburg nor the Giessen faculty would recognise the marriage as valid, for it stood in contravention of the scriptural dictum 'be fruitful and multiply' (*crescite et multiplicamini*), which was understood at the time to define procreation as the principal purpose for marriage.[143] But like Sixtus V, neither faculty regarded Sorlisi's infertile status as something benign; instead, it turned the sex act into the 'violent, deadly and scurrilous

---

[140] Sächs. HStA Loc. 7445/18, fol. 17ʳ, Samuel Lange to Martin Geier, 19 September 1667 (excerpt copied by Geier): 'Nos sane nunquam jussimus nostram sententiam ad Eunuchum applicari, sed potius, si de eunucho quicquam olfecissimus, non aliam certe sententiam tulissemus, quam illam, quam in simili casu tulit B. Dannhau[er] t. 1. conscien. p. [8]13. & 767: ejus n. menti in casu di eunucho plane et plene subscribo. Factum illud Eunuchi nunquam proba[v]imus, neque imposterum probaturi sumus.'

[141] Delphinus, *Eunuchi conjugium*, pp. 18, 21, 28–9.

[142] See *ibid.*, pp. 19–22, 33–4; the views of all are surveyed in McGrath, *A Controversy Concerning Male Impotence*, pp. 58–104.

[143] Delphinus, *Eunuchi conjugium*, pp. 18–19, 31, 34.

defilement of a maiden'.[144] The marriage of a eunuch simply made a mockery of the institution, and desecrated the marriage bed: 'Then, in place of a marital union established by God, nothing is practised except a wanton arrangement which is scurilous, lascivious, and the most foul abuse of woman. This is clearly intended to disrupt a precious and honourable union and to put in its place something that is ignominious and to expose it to extreme vileness.'[145]

But the Giessen decision also resonates with invective concerning the sexual appetite of the eunuch. While both faculties do concede that the satisfaction of sexual desire is a legitimate, if secondary, goal of marriage, the Giessen faculty argues with particular force that this has no bearing on this case, since (in their view) the eunuch is physically unable to satisfy the woman; furthermore, sexual congress with the eunuch is 'without perfection', for it lacks the 'emission of true semen'.[146] But the Giessen faculty goes on to describe the eunuch's insatiable desire for sexual activity in order to stigmatise him as a dangerous creature, one to be avoided by women:

That such eunuchs, from whom the testes alone have been removed, are more fiercely and ardently inflamed by lust, and are extremely impatient to be brought to sexual intercourse, because they cannot be emptied and relieved of that from which their craving arises – namely, semen – they extinguish the heat of lust by force, until exhaustion dissipates such madness.[147]

Consequently, such a marriage condemns the woman to suffer the 'perpetual flame of desire', and places her in danger of committing fornication, as the eunuch can arouse her desire but not satisfy it,

---

[144] *Ibid.*, p. 29 (Giessen): 'Minime omnium vero huic fini de procreanda prole juxta divinam institutionem satisfacere potest illa Eunuchiana, violenta, mortua et scurrilis juvenculae constupratio.' In his brief *Cum frequenter*, Sixtus V had excoriated eunuchs and *spadones* who he claimed 'frequently join themselves with women with foul lecherousness of the flesh and impure embraces' ('quia impura carnis tentigine, atque immundis complexibus cum mulieribus se commiscent').

[145] *Ibid.*, p. 22 (Giessen): 'Tum loco congressus maritalis a Deo instituti exercetur non nisi scurrilis, lascivus et procax contractus ac foeminae abusus turpissimus: Quod est pretiosum et honoratum Conjugium plane deturpare, ignominiosum reddere et extremo dedecori exponere.' See also *ibid.*, p. 37 (Strassburg), for similar views.

[146] *Ibid.*, p. 26: 'Eunuchus vero utitur foemina non ad gignendum, nec ad ardorem extinguendum'; p. 24: 'Congressus ergo illorum sicut est sine perfectione & emissione veri seminis.' This point may have been drawn from the Sistine brief.

[147] *Ibid.*, p. 24: 'Eunuchos tales, quibus soli abscissi sint testes, acrius & ardentius inflammari libidine, & ad concubitum impatientissime ferri, & quia non illo, unde pruritus exurgit, semine scil. evacuari, & alleviari possunt, vi extinguere libidinis aestum, donec hujusce rabiem fatigatio solvat.'

and she will be forced to seek her satisfaction elsewhere.[148] Such a view of course trades on the age-old notion of women as sexually insatiable. Junghanns and his wife also receive the censure of these faculties, as does Johann Georg, for the Giessen faculty takes pains to admonish both the parents and the 'Christian magistrate' who allowed the marriage to take place in the first place, and the Strassburg faculty condemns the 'inexcusable rashness' of Dorothea's parents, and calls upon Johann Georg, as a 'pious and prudent Magistrate', to punish the wrongdoers:[149] 'Therefore we believe that the rashness of the parents should be punished and curbed by a heavy penalty, because they exposed their daughter to such great danger, and offended [their] other pious relatives with the scandal, and did not value more the holy order of God.'[150] To conclude, the Giessen faculty declares the marriage null and void owing to Sorlisi's 'perpetual precondition of impotence, which is both incurable and irreparable'; their characterisation of the relationship between the newly-weds, however, is far different from that of Junghanns:

> When there is a union of this type, which is against the institution, opposed to nature, shameful, brings ignominy to holy marriage and is a complete abuse, it is always conducted with violent, obscene, lustful and unrestrained passion. So, just as was demonstrated above, the magistrate is not able to salve his conscience nor to remove this scandal from the midst of the church otherwise than by abolishing and disrupting this nefarious cohabitation.[151]

---

[148] *Ibid.*, p. 25: 'Unde talis juvencula nupta Eunucho, sicut se perpetuis ustionum flammis objicit, ita in praesentissimum fornicationis detestandae periculum praecipitem se agit Sir[ach] 23, 22. Eunuchi & Spadones quidam quibus testiculi exsecti, congredi cum uxore possunt, tamen commistio illa, tantum abest, ut saltem libidinem extinguat, nedum liberi inde gignantur, ut pruritum potius in foemina accendat: Quare non permittendum mulieri, ut Eunucho nubat, ait D. Carpz[ov] in Juris Prudentia Consistor. l. 2. [*sic*, numbers transposed] Defin. XVI. n. I.' (On this passage in Carpzov, see above, n. 20)

[149] *Ibid.*, p. 30: 'Pius autem prudensque Magistratus poenam determinabit.'

[150] *Ibid.*, p. 37: 'Existimamus etiam temeritatem parentum gravi poena coercendam et reprimendam, quod filiam tanto exposuerint periculo, et scandalo offenderint pios alios parentes, Deique sanctam ordinationem non majoris aestimaverint.'

[151] *Ibid.*, p. 31: 'Cum autem in praesenti casu Eunuchus impotentia legitime et naturaliter congrediendi et antecedente et perpetua seu insanabili et irreparabili laboravit et laboret, omnino matrimonium cum juvencula numquam jure ratum fuit, sed irritum et nullum. Cumque exinde congressus institutioni adversus, naturae inimicus, probrosus, et in sanctum matrimonium ignominiosus, et penitus abusivus, semper et cum vehementi ustione, obsceno et libidinoso atque effroeni propudio exerceatur, prout superius demonstratum fuit, omnino Magistratus conscientiam suam aliter salvare, et scandalum ex Eccclesia e medio tolli non potest, quam omnimoda hujus nefariae cohabitationis absolutione et dissipatione.'

Eunuchi Conjugium

By February 1668, Dorothea had been denied the sacraments for many months, and clerics in Dresden continued clamouring for the dissolution of the marriage. In fact, the 'Sorlisi Matter' had caused a schism between members of the local clergy: Superintendent Buleus himself had offered to admit Dorothea to confession, yet Pastor Schneider and various deacons defied Buleus and expressly denied her communion both before the elector's decree as well as afterwards.[152] Junghanns, seeing the dilemma in which Dorothea now found herself, and probably still smarting himself from the harsh criticism meted out to him and his wife not only by the theologians in Strassburg and Giessen, but also by Geier, who contended that their consent was motivated 'by the love of the riches and fame which this man possesses, as well as by the vain hope of rising with his own [family]',[153] now saw it as his parental duty to step in and come to the aid of his stepdaughter and her husband. Hence, in the late winter and spring of 1668, he sought opinions from three additional Lutheran theological faculties, those at the universities of Jena, Königsberg (now Kaliningrad) and Greifswald, as well as another from the Leipzig consistory.[154] His efforts not only reveal his anger and frustration at the situation in which members of his family now found themselves, but also attest to his acceptance of Sorlisi as his son-in-law. Had Junghanns and his wife remained opposed to the marriage, they could have made an effort to force the dissolution of the marriage by appealing against the decision of the Leipzig consistory to the Dresden High Consistory, and could have used the Strassburg and Giessen opinions to buttress their case. Rather than do that, however, Junghanns lent his full support and legal acumen to the case of his son-in-law and stepdaughter. Even allowing for a certain amount of bias on his part, his description of Sorlisi in his letter to the Greifswald faculty is still a touching testament to the affection and respect that he held for the man who

---

[152] Junghanns's letter to Greifswald faculty; see also Delphinus, *Eunuchi conjugium*, pp. 41–2.
[153] 'Consenserunt Parentes, sed non Justis de causis ... Fecerunt id inducti amore opum & gloriae, quas noster possidet, ut & vana spe cum suis assurgendi' (Delphinus, *Eunuchi conjugium*, p. 112); Geier made this accusation in his *Examen*, a lengthy rebuttal of the *Assertio* of Superintendent Buleus, who wrote in support of the marriage (*ibid.*, pp. 96–111; the entire *Examen* appears *ibid.*, pp. 111–35).
[154] Junghanns wrote to the faculty in Jena on 14 February 1668, to Königsberg before Easter (which fell on 22 March), to Greifswald on 18 April, and to the Leipzig consistory in April or May (the answer is dated May 1668); see Delphinus, *Eunuchi conjugium*, pp. 38, 48, 90, 94.

had broken down so many societal barriers to become a member of his family:

> His Electoral Highness of Saxony here has a Privy Chamberlain, who, as to his condition, is a eunuch, by the name of Bartolomeo de' Sorlisi, an Italian born in Milan, who, because of his great modesty and courtesy, and also owing to his unflagging, industrious service, lives in such a manner in the Elector's grace that he is up until this very hour loved and honoured, not only by the entire court, but also by the entire community, in that he refuses his service to no single person, whether cleric or layperson (regardless of the fact that he is of the Roman Catholic religion).[155]

Four years have now passed since Junghanns drafted the betrothal agreement, and during that time, Sorlisi has only risen in his estimation. But Junghanns also seems to have been well aware of the stereotyped views of the castrato as a sexually obsessed, self-serving libertine, and thus sought to challenge these from the outset by carefully painting Sorlisi as an honourable man who was highly regarded by all who knew him. Unlike his son-in-law, who took great pains to identify himself with all that was traditionally associated with the masculine before revealing his capacity for tenderness, Junghanns took a different approach, and celebrated Sorlisi's civility and integrity – the qualities that made a man in his eyes. In this respect, his characterisation of Sorlisi reflects a view of manhood in early modern Germany recently identified by Ulinka Rublack, who describes it as 'a more exuberant vision of a common good which was maintained through emotional openness and generosity and which required men to acknowledge feelings such as empathy, despair and care, and which was distant from the notion of a self-sufficient self'.[156]

In his letters to the three faculties, Junghanns related the entire saga from the very beginning, mentioned the principals by name, and did not suppress the fact of his son-in-law's lack of reproductive power and its non-accidental cause. After relating the facts of the case, Junghanns submitted two questions for the theologians'

---

[155] UAG, Theologische Facultät Nr. 3 (Junghanns's letter to the Greifswald faculty): 'Es haben Ihre Churfl. Durchl. zu Sachß. allhier einen Geheimen Cammerirer, so seines zustandes halber ein *Eunuchus* ist, Nahmens *Bartholomaeus de Sorlisi, natione* ein *Italiener*, von Meÿland bürtig, welcher wegen seiner großen bescheidenheit und höffligkeit, auch unverdroßener fleißiger Auffwarttung halber, dergestalt in Churfürstl. Gnaden lebt, das Er nicht allein vom gantzen hofe, gesondern auch von der gantzen landschafft, indeme Er keinen eintzigen Menschen, so wohl in Geistl. alß weltlichen Stande seine dienste nicht versaget (ungeachtet Er der Römischen Catholischen *Religion* zugethan ist) biß auff diese stunde gelibet und geehret worden.'

[156] See 'Meanings of Gender in Early Modern German History', p. 5.

Eunuchi Conjugium

consideration, the first of which echoes the second question posed by the Dresden High Consistory (above). In their formulation, however, Junghann's questions betray the fact that his sympathies now lay solidly behind his stepdaughter and her rather unusual husband:

> 1. Can these two people, in good, pure conscience, and without scandalising the people, be deliberately separated and divorced by the clergy, against their will and to the exclusion of the electoral decree?
> 2. Can my stepdaughter in good conscience still be denied absolution and Holy Communion, according to the Word of God, since she entered into this marriage with the foreknowledge of various eminent theologians, and that she, through the electoral taxation councillor and me, apprised her father-confessor of her intentions, and he raised no objections, and also since even though the theologians themselves are not of one mind on the subject, the execution [of her punishment] commenced immediately?[157]

The Jena faculty responded to Junghanns on 28 February 1668, less than two weeks after he had posted his letter, and their response cannot have pleased the lawyer. Like their colleagues in Strassburg and Giessen, the theologians in Jena could not lend their support to the marriage. Unlike those faculties, however, the Jena faculty responded in German, and relied solely on scriptural sources in the formulation of their argument, which, not surprisingly, echoed that of the previous opinions: the purpose of marriage is procreation, and although another goal exists, namely *'mutuum vitae consortium & adjutorium'*, this is secondary to the first.[158] If two people agree to marry in full knowledge of the fact that one party cannot beget children, their consent to the marriage is null and void.[159] The faculty saw no real problem in marriages between those who have passed their childbearing years, and who could legitimately claim to desire marriage for the secondary reason of mutual help. As far as they could see, however, the main objective of the couple in

---

[157] UAG, Theologische Fakultät Nr. 3, Junghanns to the Greifswald theology faculty: '(1) Ob mit gutem reinem gewißen, und ohne ärgernüß des Volcks, diese beÿden leuthe wieder ihren willen auß dem Churfl. *Decreto* von der Geistlichkeit können gesetzet wiederum *separir*et und zertrennet werden, (2) Ob meine Stiefftochter nach dem wortte Gottes mit gutem gewißen noch länger von der *Absolution* und heyl. Abendmahl kan abgestoßen werden, indeme Sie gleichwohl mit vorbewust unterschiedlicher vornehmer *Theologen* diese heÿrath eingegangen, und Sie ihrem eigenen Beicht Vatter durch den Churf. Sächß. StewerRath und mich solch vorhaben entdecken laßen, welcher nicht *contradicir*et, die Herren *Theologi* auch an sich selbst hierüber nicht einig seÿn, gleichwohl aber bey Ihr alßbalt mit der *Execution* der angang gemachet worden ist.' See also Delphinus, *Eunuchi conjugium*, p. 42.
[158] Delphinus, *Eunuchi conjugium*, p. 43.
[159] Ibid., pp. 44–5.

question was copulation, and they adduced Dorothea's own declaration of undying love for Sorlisi as the reason for their opinion. But, they argued, copulation belongs to the main purpose of marriage, which is the procreation of offspring, and not to the second. For this faculty, the goal of quelling sexual desire is not a goal in itself, but an accidental by-product of marriage.[160] Unlike the other faculties, however, the Jena faculty did concede that there was one scenario in which Sorlisi could have been allowed to marry without risk of scandal: if he had sought only mutual help, he could have married an 'older, sensible woman' experienced in running a household, who could tend to his (non-sexual) needs as a wife would do.[161] But the conviction that he could make no claim to intimacy with a woman still undergirds the entire argument. The Jena faculty exercised much more severe judgement on Dorothea than on Sorlisi, however, for these theologians could not fathom why a young woman in her prime childbearing years would marry a man known to be infertile. Thus they harshly condemned her decision to have marital relations with him:

> Sexual intercourse with one who is known to be unable to beget children, owing to his bodily condition, is a sin against the conscience, for intercourse is *per se* and *natura sua* for the generation of offspring, and no other intention can be given to it. A woman who is able to bear children, and who has intercourse with a man who she knows cannot beget children, does so not for the reason nature intended, and which is ordained by the law of nature, but solely for the satisfaction of the libido, which, because it knowingly goes against the light and law of nature, is of course a wanton sin against the conscience.[162]

Like the Giessen and Strassburg faculties, the Jena faculty also firmly believed that sex with a eunuch could not achieve its goal –

---

[160] *Ibid.*, pp. 43–4, 46.
[161] *Ibid.*, p. 44: 'Und wenn *Sorlisi* den andern *finem* allein *intendi*ret hätte/ so hätte er solcher ohne Aergerniß besser erlangen können/ wenn er eine betagte/ verständige und in Haushaltung erfahrne Weibs=Person zu sich genommen hätte/ derer Dienst er sich beydes in Haushaltung/ und zu seines Leibes Wartung so wohl sich gebrauchen können/ als etwan durch eine Ehe=Frau geschehen mag/ bevorab bey Versprechung seines Unterhalts/ als etwa in gegenwärtigen Fall geschehen seyn mag.'
[162] *Ibid.*, p. 45: 'Ist der Beyschlaff mit einem/ von dem bekandt ist/ daß er/ seines Leibes Beschaffenheit wegen/ nicht Kinder zeugen könne/ eine Sünde wider das Gewissen: Denn der *concubitus* ist *per se & natura sua propter generationem prolis*, und kan dessen kein ander *finis per se intentus* gegeben werden: Eine Weibes-Person aber/ die zum Kinder-Gebähren tüchtig ist/ und mit einem/den sie weiß/ daß er zum Kinder-Zeugen untüchtig sey/ *concumbi*ret/ die thut solches nicht ob *eum finem*, den die Natur *intendi*ret/ und *ipsa lex naturae praescribi*ret/ sondern bloß *ad explendam libidinem*, welches/ weil es wissentlich wider das Liecht und Gesetzt der Natur geschicht/ freylich eine muthwillige Sünde wider das Gewissen ist.'

rather than quell the woman's desire, it would only cause it to become all the more inflamed.[163] In contrast to the previous opinions, however, the Jena faculty neither declared the marriage invalid nor demanded its dissolution. Instead, the theologians focused on Dorothea's commission of sins against the conscience, the direct result of her decision to marry Sorlisi, and they placed the burden of conscience-clearing on her shoulders: 'Out of all of this it can be seen that the gentleman's stepdaughter cannot, with a good and clear conscience, have sexual relations with Sorlisi, as a eunuch.'[164]

Although doubtless disappointed by this setback, Junghanns remained undeterred in his quest to secure a positive ruling. Some time before Easter (22 March) 1668, he sent his letter and accompanying materials to the theology faculty at the University of Königsberg, and requested judgements on the same two questions put forth to the Jena faculty. The faculty in Königsberg issued its opinions on 17 April of that year.[165] In reading the letter that accompanied the decision, Junghanns quickly learned that he had finally won support for his cause, for the theologians 'wish[ed] the couple luck and happiness and God's blessing', and added that they '[stood] ready to provide additional help if needed'.[166] At forty quarto pages in print, the Königsberg opinion stands as the longest of all of those rendered, and surpasses all of the others in its erudition and marshalling of sources. It also presents the most innovative argument, and reveals a much more modern understanding of the human condition and the role of sexual relations within marriage than expressed in the other opinions.

The first significant departure that emerges from this opinion is the clear distinction that this faculty draws between Old and New Testament views of marriage, and its rejection of the former in

---

[163] *Ibid.*, pp. 46–7: 'Der *Medicorum* Meynung nach/ auch dieser *accidentarius finis*, durch solchen *Concubitum*, auf Seiten des Weibes/ nicht könte erreichet werden/ auch die bekandte *Constitutio Leonis ad Stylianum: Si vel maximè quidam Eunuchi, quibus scil. testiculi exsecti, congredi cum uxore possit, tamen commixtio illa tantum abest, ut libidinem extinguat, ut eandem potius in foemina accendat*, besaget.'

[164] *Ibid.*, p. 47: 'Aus welchen allen denn zu sehen ist/ daß des Herrn Stieff-Tochter nicht mit guten und reinen Gewissen dem *Sorlisi*, als einem *Eunucho*, beywohnen könne.'

[165] *Ibid.*, pp. 47–8 (letter from the faculty to Junghanns); the decision proper occupies pp. 49–89.

[166] *Ibid.*, p. 48: 'Wünschen den Eheleuten GOttes Gnade/ Glück und Heyl/ und alles ersprießliche Wohlergehen/ den sämptlichen Anverwandten auch viel Freude in völliger Vergnügung: Können wir unserm Hochgeehrten Herrn weiter dienen/ werden wir uns bereitwilligst erfinden lassen.'

favour of the latter. In order to argue for the validity of this necessarily childless marriage, the theologians were compelled to find a way to redefine the purpose of marriage, and most importantly, to dissociate marriage from procreation. This they achieved through a reliance on the Law/Gospel dichotomy that informs much Christian theology:

> When we consider the era of the New Testament, however, and compare it to the time of the old covenant, there is no doubt that the second goal [of marriage], namely the prevention and overcoming of fleshly desire, is now the principal goal. For under the Old Testament, the promise of the increase of the human race was incorporated into the covenant of God: 'Look towards heaven, and number the stars – can you count them? So shall your seed (descendants) be' (Gen. 15: 5). . . . But in the New Testament, the seed of Abraham is multiplied in a spiritual manner, and such a promise is not linked to the covenant made with us in Christ. In addition, the human race has sufficiently proliferated that one need not be concerned with increase itself, but much more should heed the advice of Christ on celibacy: 'He that is able to embrace it, let him embrace it' (Matt. 19: 12).[167]

After discussing the three goals of marriage at length, the Königsberg theologians moved on to an extensive discussion of the various types of eunuchs, largely taken from Aristotle, which reveals what they believed to be true concerning the castrated. Significantly, these types include 'those from whom only the testicles are removed, and the *vasa seminaria* are left undamaged; these not only have semen, although not in abundance, but also an erect member and can copulate with a woman, yea, they are more salacious and *in venerem propensiores* than the non-castrated, as Aristotle shows in chapter 4 of 'On the Generation of Animals' (*De generatione animalium*)'.[168] In the passage that follows, the faculty seeks to demonstrate beyond any reasonable doubt, through multiple citations, that the

---

[167] *Ibid.*, pp. 54–5: 'Wenn wir aber die Zeit des Neuen Testaments betrachten/ und sie gegen die Zeit des alten Bundes halten/ ist kein Zweiffel/ daß der ander *finis*, nemlich die Hintertreibung und Uberwindung der fleischlichen Lüste/ nunmehr wohl der vornehmste ist: Denn unter dem alten Testamente war die Verheissung von Mehrung des menschlichen Geschlechtes dem Bunde GOttes mit einverleibet: Siehe gen Himmel/ und zehle die Sternen/ kanstu sie zehlen? Also soll dein Saame seyn *Gen. 15. v. 5.* . . . Aber im Neuen Testament wird der Saame Abrahams geistlicher Weise vermehret/ und ist solche Verheissung dem Bunde in Christo mit uns gemacht/ nicht angehengt: Es ist auch das menschliche Geschlecht genugsam ausgebreitet/ daß man auf Vermehrung desselben nicht groß zu dencken hat/ sondern vielmehr den Rath Christi in Acht nimmt von der Einsamkeit: Wer es fassen mag/ der fasse es/ Matth. 19/12.'

[168] *Ibid.*, pp. 73–4: 'Etzlichen aber sind bloß die *testiculi* weggeschnitten/ und die *vasa seminaria* unverletzt gelassen/ dieselben haben nicht allein *semen, quamvis infoecundum*, sondern auch *erectam virgam*, und können *cum muliere coiren*; Ja, sind *salaciores & in venerem propensiores*, als die nicht verschnitten sind/ wie Aristoteles anzeigt *Lib. 1. de Generat. Animal. cap. 4*'.

Eunuchi Conjugium

castrated do have a greater propensity for sex, and that castration does not remove desire. But then, in a stunning display of reverse logic, they turn these traditional grounds for the castigation of the eunuch into support for the marriage:

> If that is so,[169] as it without a doubt is, we cannot see why such a eunuch should not avail himself of the remedy that God established against roaming desires, and placed at every man's disposal, that he should find a partner who sincerely loves him, and will gladly cohabitate with him, and who has foreknowledge about his inability to procreate, and despite that, will consent to marriage and conjugal cohabitation with him. For even if they cannot engender children, they can still offer one another mutual help, and drive off the desires of the flesh through honest conjugal cohabitation, which end is addressed chiefly in the New Testament.[170]

The definition of marriage that provides the foundation upon which the other theologians construct their opinions is thus dismissed as specious: 'what the canonists and scholastics say against the marriage of eunuchs, who can have sexual relations and exercise the act of generation, comes from the false principle that there can be no marriage without the aptitude to procreate offspring'.[171] Like the other theologians, the members of the Königsberg faculty stipulate that marriage has three purposes – the procreation of offspring, the avoidance of fornication (*evitatio scortationis*) and mutual help (*mutuum adjutorium*) – but unlike their colleagues, they reprioritise the list; as a result, the latter two goals now significantly outweigh the first in importance: 'If there is only one goal of marriage, it is mutual help; if there are two, the necessity of avoiding fleshly desire is added.'[172] Throughout the lengthy argument, the Königsberg faculty also

---

[169] I.e., that the eunuch suffers from great desire.
[170] Delphinus, *Eunuchi conjugium*, p. 76: 'Ist dem so/ wie es ausser allen Zweiffel ist/ können wir nicht sehen/ warum nicht ein solcher *Eunuchus* sich aus des *Remedii*, welches GOtt wider die *vagas libidines* geordnet/ und einem jeglichen an die Hand gegeben hat/ gebrauchen solle/ da er eine *Comparem* findet/ die ihm mit Treuen meynet/ und ihm gern *cohabitiren* will/ und sie *simpliciter, impotentia generandi probe ante cognita, eaque non obstante, in copulam & cohabitationem Conjugalem consentiren*: Denn es ob sie gleich keine Kinder zeugen können/ so können sie doch einander *mutuum auxilium praestiren*/ und die *libidines carnis per honestum conjugalem concubitum* vertreiben/ welcher *finis* vornehmlich unterm Neuen Testament *attendiret* wird.'
[171] Ibid., pp. 78–9: 'Was die *Canonistae* und *Scholastici* wider das *Conjugium Eunuchorum, qui congredi & actum generationis exercere possunt*, beybringen/ kömmt aus dem *falso principio*, daß der Ehestand nicht seyn könne ohne der *aptitudine ad procreandum Sobolem*.'
[172] Ibid., p. 64: 'So denn das *Conjugium* bestehet/ wenn nur ein *finis* ist/ nemlich das *mutuum adjutorium*, wie viel mehr/ wenn zweene sind/ und die Nohtwendigkeit/ fleischliche Lüste zu vermeiden/ dazu kommt.' See also p. 79: 'Aber es seyn mehr *fines matrimonii*, als *procreatio sobolis*, und sind nicht *subordinati, sed ultimi: Procreatio Sobolis: Evitatio scortationis; Mutuum adjutorium*, daß einer ohne den andern gar wohl seyn kan'; see also pp. 50–4. In their reprioritisation they would seem to agree with the Catholic view as expressed in the 1566 Roman catechism, but they do not invoke that text.

show great concern for what they see as a dangerous precedent – the dissolution of this marriage solely on the grounds of infertility – and argue that many other couples, unable to conceive due to a host of legitimate reasons, would be adversely affected. As a result, their views stand diametrically opposed to those of Geier: whereas the court preacher was blinded by his fears of the damage that this marriage could do to the church as a sacred institution, the Königsberg faculty instead regarded the implications of its dissolution as far more injurious to the individual members of that institution.

At the conclusion, the Königsberg faculty sum up their responses to the two questions to which Junghanns requested responses. First, they urge the couple to continue to live as man and wife, and in so doing, leave no room for doubt about their assumptions concerning Sorlisi's capability for marital relations:

Out of all of which is then sufficiently illuminated what is to be thought of the present marriage of a eunuch and a maiden, where the same is a pious and conscientious man, indeed unfit for *generationis effectum*, but not unfit for *generationis actum*, also has semen, although not prolific, and can satisfy a woman, as his wife has demonstrated from experience, all of which is revealed in the report, namely, that this marriage shall be regarded as a true marriage, and they can in good conscience live together, for the sake of true help, which marriage brings with it, and for the avoidance of fornication and indecent desires, although they cannot achieve the first goal, which by this time in the New Testament is no longer the primary goal, namely the procreation of offspring, which is also the case with many other marriages. Desire, which outside marriage would be for them a mortal sin, is a venial sin within the marriage, *propter matrimonium*, as God ordained.[173] However, because eunuchs are *propensiores in venerem* than others, they will sometimes restrain themselves, and sometimes, out of mutual agreement, as St Paul mentioned, will keep themselves from one another that they may have leisure for fasting and prayer, and also ever strive ultimately to live with one another not as husband and wife, but as brother and sister, that is, without marital relations, but only with the consent of both, towards which other married couples, from whom the years have taken desire away, must also strive.[174]

On the issue of Holy Communion, which receives far less attention in the opinion, the theologians indicate that both should be readmitted to the table:

---

[173] This reflects the teaching of Augustine: 'it is no sin to render the conjugal debt, but to exact it beyond the need for generation is a venial sin'; see Sommerville, *Sex and Subjection*, pp. 128, 138, n. 37.

[174] Delphinus, *Eunuchi conjugium*, pp. 88–9; the German text appears as Doc. 7 in the Appendix. This edition of the text includes an apparent misprint, and substitutes 'nimmermehr' for 'immermehr' (see Ortkemper, *Engel wider Willen*, p. 200, quoting the 1685 edition; the 1697 edition agrees with that of 1685).

Eunuchi Conjugium

That one now still opposes the marriage on this account, reproaches the couple on moral grounds, and desires to force the dissolution of the marriage, and also denies them Holy Communion until they are divorced, we hold for not simply unjust, but also scandalous, for nothing can be brought forward to show why this marriage should not be considered legitimate. It also cannot be proved that the married couple remain and persist in a state of mortal sin; therefore they should justly enjoy their right to be considered a married couple, and should be allowed to receive Holy Communion.[175]

In his letters to the three theology faculties, Junghanns made no mention of the fact that Martin Geier had involved himself in the case after his meeting with Sorlisi back in the late autumn of 1666. But despite the fact that his efforts to convince Johann Georg to dissolve the marriage had all come to nought, the minister did not abandon his cause, and, at some point during the spring of 1668, drafted a set of 'Theological Deliberations' pertaining to the Sorlisi–Lichtwer marriage.[176] In this lengthy opinion, Geier posed and answered a different question than that which he had previously presented to the faculties in Strassburg and Giessen, one that reveals a potentially new and significant development in the relationship between Sorlisi and his wife. According to Geier, at some point during the previous few months – well after they had begun to engage in marital relations – the two had decided to abstain from further sexual relations, and to live as brother and sister – in other words, to enter into a 'chaste marriage'.[177] But Geier's essay and the purported vow of abstinence that occasioned its writing are difficult

---

[175] Delphinus, *Eunuchi conjugium*, p. 89: 'Daß man nun derowegen noch dieser Ehe widersprechen/ denen Ehe-Leuthen Gewissens-Scrupel machen/ und auf die Trennung dringen wolte/ auch so lange vom Heiligen Abendmahl sie abhalten/ biß sie getrennet werden/ halten wir nicht allein unbillich/ sondern auch ärgerlich/ denn nichts kan beygebracht werden/ warum diese Ehe nicht für rechtmäßig zu halten/ es kan auch nicht erwiesen werden/ daß die Eh-Leute in einer Tod-Sünde stecken und verharren/ derohalben geniessen sie auch billich ihres Rechten/ daß sie für Ehe-Leuthe gehalten/ und zu dem Heiligen Abendmahl zugelassen werden.'

[176] Delphinus published the document under the title 'Theological Deliberations of D[r] G[eier] Concerning the Marriage of a Eunuch and a Young Woman' ('Theologisches Bedencken/ D. G. Uber die Ehe eines *Eunuchi* und jungen Weibes-Person'; *Eunuchi conjugium*, pp. 158–64); an undated manuscript copy, identical to the published version and signed by Geier, survives in Sächs. HStA Loc. 7445/18, fols. 10ʳ–11ᵛ. The survival of the document together with other of Geier's writings on the case suggests that his thoughts reached the eyes of the elector. Although both copies of Geier's reflections are undated, the second Leipzig consistory decision provides a *terminus post quem*, for that body stated that it had received a copy of the 'Deliberation' from Junghanns in May 1668 (*ibid*., p. 94). Geier does not mention these 'Deliberations' in his December 1667 covering letter to Johann Georg II, which suggests that this document did not accompany his submission of the Strassburg and Giessen decisions at that time.

[177] See M. McGlynn and R. J. Moll, 'Chaste Marriage in the Middle Ages', in Bullough and Brundage (eds.), *Handbook of Medieval Sexuality*, pp. 103–22. Various church fathers rejected

to date with precision. In his letter to the Greifswald faculty of 18 April 1668, Junghanns made no mention of such a vow or of Geier's 'Deliberations'; in fact, his declaration that Dorothea and Sorlisi were 'extremely content with one other *in all things*' suggests that the couple's connubial activities continued unabated. If in the late winter or early spring of 1668 the couple had already declared themselves prepared to abstain from sexual relations, it would seem that Schneider, had he been informed of it, would have had no grounds to continue to bar Dorothea from communion, which eventuality provided the impetus for Junghanns's letters to the three faculties.

Purported or not, Geier clearly believed that the couple had taken such a vow. But rather than regard this pledge as a positive development, Geier used it as an opportunity to attack the marriage again, from yet a different angle, and thus he posed the following question for a one-sided debate: 'Can two people, one of whom is unfit for marriage according to ecclesiastical and secular laws, but [who are] nevertheless publicly wed as a married couple, be further tolerated as a married couple by Christian authorities, if they declare to live with one another in the future as brother and sister only verbally and in secret?'[178] Geier's protracted answer to this question constitutes a pointed and stinging criticism of his patron and sovereign masquerading under the guise of 'theological deliberations' – a rather innocuous description of a sarcastic and often virulent screed. Whereas Junghanns and members of the Königsberg faculty granted humanity to Sorlisi, Geier either cannot or will not. He strongly advocates the dissolution of the marriage, and uses the Strassburg and Giessen opinions to buttress his case, pointing out that 'two impartial foreign Lutheran theological faculties' have 'held [the marriage] to be a loathsome abuse, mockery and profanation of that institution that God established for whole men and women for the preservation and increase of the

chaste marriage, as did Luther; see Wiesner-Hanks, *Christianity and Sexuality in the Early Modern World*, pp. 32, 63–4.

[178] Delphinus, *Eunuchi conjugium*, p. 158: 'Es fraget sich/ wenn zwo Personen/ deren eine/ vermöge Göttl. und Welt. Rechte/ zum Ehestande untüchtig/ dennoch öffentlich als Eheleute sind getrauet worden/ von Christlicher Obrigkeit also ferner beysammen also Eh-Leute können geduldet werden/ wenn sie nur in Geheim/ und Mündlich sich erklären/ einander künfftig/ als Bruder und Schwester beyzuwohnen?' (One wonders how Geier came to learn of this pledge, if made in secret.)

human race'.[179] As far as Geier is concerned, these two people had 'bound themselves together for the sake of indecent sexual desire',[180] and thus for an illegitimate reason that negates any argument that, once established, the bond of matrimony is sacred and holy and cannot be dissolved. Geier exhibits far more concern for the reputation of the church in the eyes of its confessional opponents than for the welfare of these two individuals (one of whom is not even Lutheran), and warns that, if the marriage is allowed to stand,

> even the foreign Papists and Calvinists will mock our church as dissolute, and will declare that we publicly tolerate among us as married couples those who are held as condemnable in the published writings of all of our old and new teachers, as well as unanimously by all Papists. Defamatory pamphlets will appear and will be unanswerable, as there has been no public statement against allowing this marriage. It will remain an enduring reproach even to the next generation, and a blemish that cannot be removed. In all provinces (since the matter is well known to all the world), one will say that, because the cohabitation of such people was tolerated without a single objection, one must conclude that both the ecclesiastical and temporal authorities recognised it and approved it as legitimate.[181]

Geier also took as an affront the suggestion that this new concession on the part of Sorlisi and Dorothea could in any way be seen to ameliorate the scandal that the two had caused, particularly as the wedding had taken place in public, but the declaration was made in secret and was to remain so, 'so that these two people shall not be mocked, even though both the church and highest civil authorities

---

[179] *Ibid.*, p. 159: 'Ist in dem doppelten *Responso* zwo Evangelischer/ auswärtiger/ gantz unpartheyischer *Theologi*schen *Facultä*ten/.../ daß solche Vermählung ein abscheulicher Mißbrauch/ Spott und Verunehrung sey des jenigen Standes/ welchen GOTT/ für vollständige Mannes- und Weibes-Personen/ zur Erhaltung und Vermehrung Menschliches Geschlechts eingesetzt.'

[180] *Ibid.*, p. 160: 'die doch unordentlicher Brunst halber sich also hiebevor mit einander verbunden haben'.

[181] *Ibid.*, p. 160: 'Die auswärtigen Päbstler und Calvinisten selbsten werden bey fernerer Verstattung/ unsere Kirche/ als Zucht-loß spotten und ausschreyen/ daß wir bey uns als Eheleute öffentlich duldeten/ welche doch von unsern alten und neuen Lehrern in öffentlichen Schrifften/ ja einmüthig von allen Päbstlern als verdammlich gehalten würden: Solten Schmäh-Schrifften über kurtz oder lang heraus kommen/ würde niemand solchen begegnen können/ indeme öffentlich kein Mißfallen oder Enderung über solcher Sache wäre gespüret/ noch etwas anders gesprochen worden: Bliebe also dieses ein ewiger Vorwurff/ auch bey denen Nachkommen/ und ein Flecken/ der sich nicht so bald auslöschen liesse. Ja in allen Provintzien (wie denn die Sache allbereit Welt-kündig gnug ist) würde man sagen/ weil solche Personen ohne eintzige Widerrede beysammen gedultet würden/ so müsse man ja einhellig/ Geistliche und Weltliche diß für eine rechtmäßige Ehe erkennet und gebilliget haben.' In his concern for the reputation of the church, Geier echoes the words of the Strassburg faculty; see *ibid.*, pp. 36–7.

will suffer negative consequences'.[182] And he could express only contempt for the suggestion that the couple would be able – or even willing – to abide by their recent vow of chastity:

> In such an arrangement, the woman will be in perpetual danger of the rekindling of her desire, owing to such close proximity [of Sorlisi]. Fire does not cease to burn when there is straw in the vicinity. Moreover, there is as of yet no indication from her that she feels the least bit remorseful over the previous abomination.[183]
>
> What castrati suffer for sexual desire is known to us from their own admissions and from published writings; what young women, having already slept with a man, may have for self-restraint when they remain alongside and together with their present husbands, will be scarcely believed by the modern world; yea, how much more the same will laugh out loud at those who would believe this without suspicion, out of Christian love.[184]

Just as he had done in his letter of December 1667, Geier concluded his 'deliberation' by reminding the elector of his human fallibility, but then went on to appeal to his ego, by invoking various biblical figures as models for emulation – those whose willingness to reverse their own decisions had only augmented their glory. 'Great leaders', he pointed out, 'can sometimes be taken in, or can act precipitately; these afterward retract [their decisions] with even greater fame, or, more precisely, admit to having been in error.'[185] No evidence survives to suggest that Johann Georg issued a response to Geier. He had, after all, issued a decree on the matter, and as far as he was concerned, the case was closed.

Despite the Königsberg opinion, which Junghanns presented to Schneider, Dorothea's situation vis-à-vis the sacraments remained

---

[182] *Ibid.*, p. 161: 'Diese Erklärung aber soll geheim sein/ damit beyde Personen nicht geschimpffet werden/ ob gleich hohe Obrigkeit und die Kirche übeln Nachtheil ihrenthalben haben und behalten müsse.' The wedding did not take place in public in the traditional sense, of course, but was performed before a number of witnesses.

[183] *Ibid.*, p. 160: 'Auf solche Art wird das Weib in steter Gefahr gelassen/ indem bey so naher Anwesenheit alte Brunst wieder rege wird. Feuer lässet das Brennen nicht/ wenn es Stroh in der Nähe findet: Zudem ist an ihr noch nie zu spüren gewesen/ daß sie eintzige Reue vorigen Greuel empfunden.'

[184] *Ibid.*, p. 161: 'Was für Brunst *Castrati* leiden/ ist aus ihrer eigenen Bekäntniß und öffentlichen Schrifften bekandt: Was junge Weibes-Personen/ so des Mannes allbereit gewohnet/ für *Continentz* neben und bey ihrem anwesenden Manne haben mögen/ wird von der heutigen Welt wenig gegläubet/ ja vielmehr lachet sie dieselben aus/ welche dieses aus Christlicher Liebe ohne Argwohn gläuben wolten.'

[185] *Ibid.*, p. 163: 'Hohe Häupter können mannichmahl eingenommen/ oder auch übereilet werden/ welche hernach mit grössern Ruhm *retractir*en/ oder genauer sich erbiethen/ als Irriges behaupten.' Geier's biblical models include Kings Rehoboam, Ahasuerus, Darius, Nebuchadnezzar and David, as well as the prophet Nathan (*ibid.*, pp. 163–4).

Eunuchi Conjugium

the same. Junghanns then sought redress from the Leipzig consistory, and wrote to the body in late April or early May 1668; according to the text of the consistory's opinion, the lawyer submitted thirteen enclosures with his petition, including Geier's 'theological deliberations' and a *'Frage'* – undoubtedly Sorlisi's *Urthels-Frage*.[186] In their opinion, the members of the consistory indicated that they now realised that the request for an opinion submitted by 'Johann Gericke' back in 1666, to which they had responded, actually concerned the Lichtwer–Sorlisi marriage.[187] According to the consistory's second opinion, Junghanns had informed them that a controversy had developed among the clerics in Dresden after the wedding had taken place, and that 'Frau Sorlisi's' father-confessor still refused to hear her confession and pronounce absolution, and to administer Holy Communion, despite the recent decision of the Königsberg faculty and the elector's decree on the matter. Junghanns had thus asked the consistory to rule on only one question – whether his stepdaughter could, under these circumstances, be suspended from the confessional and Holy Communion any longer. In May 1668, the consistory issued its opinion:

Although the way in which he was to comport himself towards her regarding the confessional was emphatically communicated to the Father Confessor of Frau Sorlisi by the High Consistory, through the Superintendent, and because the Sorlisi marriage is to be charitably tolerated, and both parties are to be left unassailed and undisturbed by one and all, by the power of the Saxon Elector's most gracious decree, so is it the right of Frau Sorlisi freely to petition Your Electoral Highness for an additional most gracious proclamation of the decree and repeal of the order given to her Father Confessor, by rights.[188]

[186] *Ibid.*, pp. 94–5, 'Das andere Leipzigsche Urthel': 'Als Ihr Uns Abschrifften etlicher Schreiben *sub A. B.* und *C.* wie auch *vidimirte Copiam* eines *Theologi*schen Bedenckens/ *sub D.* samt darzu gehöriger Frage und Beylagen/ *sub n. 1. 2. 3. 4. 5. 6. 7. 8.* und *9.* benebst einer Frage/ zugeschickt/ und/ euch des Rechten darüber zu belehren/ gebethen.'
[187] *Ibid.*, p. 95. The date of the first decision is erroneously given here as 1667; Junghanns gives the date as October 1666. The decision preceded the wedding, and although in its second decision the Leipzig consistory claimed to have been unaware of the author's true identity back in 1666, and to have been incognisant of the fact that the case actually concerned the Sorlisi marriage, Junghanns indicates the contrary in his letter to the Greifswald faculty: 'In regard to this it should be noted that the question was prepared under fictitious names; nevertheless, the members of the consistory knew very well that it concerned the case of Sorlisi' ('Hierbey ist zuerinnern, daß die frage *sub nominibus fictis* eingerichtet worden, alleine, es haben die Herren *Consistoriales* zu Leipzig wohl bewust, daß der *Casus* den von *Sorlisi concernire*, und angehe'). But the letter of Lange (above), a member of the Leipzig consistory, suggests otherwise.
[188] *Ibid.*, p. 95: 'Ob nun wohl dem Beicht-Vater der Frau Sorlisin von dem obern *Consistorio*, durch den *Superintendent*en/ nachdrückliche Bedeutung geschehen/ wessen er sich gegen sie/

Given the scandal that had accompanied this marriage, one to which they had lent their official imprimatur, the Leipzig consistory clearly had no desire to issue a ruling challenging the views held by some members of the High Consistory in Dresden. Once again, the decision was left to Johann Georg II. If Dorothea Sorlisi did indeed appeal to Johann Georg II for redress, no evidence survives of either her petition or his response.

Later that same month, Junghanns received another favourable decision, this time from the theological faculty at the University of Greifswald in Pomerania.[189] While these theologians also expressed reservations about the wisdom of such a marriage, they felt that they 'must justly praise [Junghanns's] circumspection, in that [he] so carefully sought first the advice and decision of the clergy, then of the consistories of Dresden and Leipzig, and then of the elector of Saxony himself'.[190] Although much more concise than the Königsberg decision, the opinion from the Greifswald faculty adduces many of the same arguments – such marriages are not expressly forbidden by the Word of God, the reasons for marriage include mutual help and the satisfaction of 'fleshly desire' (which, in Sorlisi's case, 'undoubtedly stems from an abundance of semen, although infertile'),[191] the marriages of other infertile couples are not dissolved, and so forth. Junghanns's letter convinced the faculty that Sorlisi and Dorothea truly loved one another, and that they

---

des Beicht-Stuhls halber/ zu verhalten/ demnach aber/ und weil die Sorlisische Verehligung/ krafft des Churfürstl. Sächs. gnädigsten *Decrets, sub No. III.* Christlich soll geduldet/ und beyde verheyrathete Personen von männiglichen unangefochten und unbekümmert gelassen werden/ So ist bey Ihrer Chur-Fürstl. Durchl. der Sorlisin um anderweitige gnädigste *Declaration* des *Decrets* und *Cassation* der an ihren Beicht-Vater beschehenen Verordnung gebührend anzusuchen unbenommen/ von Rechts wegen.'

[189] *Ibid.*, pp. 90–4 ('Beantwortung Der Theologischen Facultät zu Greiffswald in Pommern'), Sächs. HStA Loc. 7445/18, fols. 23^r–27^v (manuscript copy of the decision), and UAG, Theologische Fakultät Nr. 3 (draft in German of the final document; this set of materials also includes the opinions, composed in Latin, of Battus and Michaelis). The decision is dated 24 May 1668. Lüterius's covering letter is dated 5 May 1668, and the envelope is addressed to Professor Bartholomeus Battus, Pastor of St Mary's Church in Greifswald, Professor of Theology and General Superindentent. Other signatories were Professors Johann Michaelis and [??] Beringe.

[190] *Ibid.*, p. 90: 'So müssen wir wohl bekennen/ daß es sehr bedencklich gewesen/ solche Heyrath zu stifften und einzugehen/ doch haben wir billich ihre Sorgfalt zu rühmen/ daß sie so vorsichtig bald bey dem Ehrwürdigen *Ministerio*, bald bey dem Hochpreißlicher Ober-*Consistorio* zu Dreßden und Leipzig/ bald bey Ihrer Churfürstlichen Durchl. zu Sachsen selbst Rath und Entscheidung der Sachen gesucht haben.'

[191] 'wie auch des Fleisches Brunst/ *ex abundantia seminis, licet infoecundi* ohne Zweiffel entstanden/ unterzudrücken/ und also Hurerey zu meiden'; *ibid.*, p. 91.

Eunuchi Conjugium

entered into this union with honourable intentions, and thus they held that the couple 'should be left undisturbed in their continuing mutual love (wherein the true form of marriage exists) and not be troubled in their consciences'.[192] They also noted that the two 'bear their cross of infertility with all patience'.[193] The key to their argument, however, resides in the sanctity of marriage, which is sealed in the blessing that concludes the nuptial rite, 'from which they should be assured that "God has joined them together, and no man shall separate them" '. Thus to separate the couple after the marriage has taken place would, in their view, be to desecrate 'the name of God, which was invoked over them at the wedding to grant them a peaceful and good marriage'.[194] On the second question – whether Dorothea could still be denied the sacraments – the Greifswald faculty take a firmer stand than did their colleagues in Königsberg. While they agree that Dorothea should have the sacraments restored her, they do not let her off lightly, but instead admonish her for her behaviour during the engagement, 'in which she caused all manner of scandal to many eminent people'.[195] Given the determination she exhibited in her effort to wed a normally unmarriageable man, she must have possessed a strong will and lively personality; perhaps she had shown some disrespect to her elders, with whom she probably had lost all patience. With respect to the sacraments, however, the theologians recommended that she be reinstated, and that she 'recall everything told her by her father-confessor' and accept it 'with all patience'.[196]

The Greifswald opinion represents the last known document related to this saga; at this point, the trail grows much colder. While Dresden court records indicate that Sorlisi remained active there in various capacities until his death in March 1672, little additional information has surfaced concerning his marital situation. It seems quite certain, though, that Geier failed in his campaign to have the

---

[192] *Ibid.*: 'also hat man sie billich in solcher beharrlichen Liebe und Gegen-Liebe/ (darinn die rechte Form des *Conjugii* bestehet/) ungekräncket zu lassen/ und die Gewissen nicht zu verwirren.'
[193] *Ibid.*, pp. 91–2: 'und ihr Creuz der Unfruchtbarkeit mit aller Gedult ertragen'.
[194] *Ibid.*, p. 92; a longer excerpt from the German text appears as Doc. 8 in the Appendix.
[195] *Ibid.*, p. 93: 'dadurch sie allerhand Aergerniß bey vielen vornehmen Leuten verursachet'.
[196] *Ibid.*, p. 94: 'derowegen sie denn billich von ihrem Beicht-Vater mit Fleiß zu erinnern/ welches sie zugleich mit aller Gedult hat anzunehmen'.

marriage dissolved, for late in the nineteenth century, Theodor Distel discovered Sorlisi's will, which indicated that his wife, Dorothea, had inherited part of his estate.[197] According to Distel, Dorothea relocated to Rome after her husband's death, which suggests that she had either abandoned the Lutheran church and converted to Catholicism, or planned to do so. Thus, despite the melodramatic scenarios contrived by Angus Heriot and Patrick Barbier, no evidence survives to suggest either that 'all of [the couple's] endurance was in vain, and in the end Sorlisi died broken-hearted', or that 'the poor castrato did not have the strength to fight back and died of despair'.[198] Rather than abandon his goal, Sorlisi had pursued it energetically for over five years, and had met every challenge. While the stress of the decade of the 1660s must have exacted a great physical and psychological toll on the singer, his unflagging determination in the face of such adversity suggests that the protracted battle served to strengthen rather than weaken his resolve.

In the history of the castrato, the story of Bartolomeo Sorlisi and his marriage to Dorothea Lichtwer stands out as a singular chapter, one that sheds great light on the consequences of one castrato's determination to shake off the sexual shackles with which he had long been bound. His success stands as a tribute to his sheer mettle and considerable intelligence, two qualities that allowed him to develop strategies for survival in a world in which he could claim no 'natural' place. Surely one of these strategies may be seen in his effort to craft for himself a particularly 'male' self-image, and another in his candid approach to the question of his sexual capacity. As he knew that the reality of his physical circumstances would dominate any discussion of his suitability for marriage, he made it one of the driving issues in his own marriage campaign, and described his sexual capability in considerable detail. But while convincing an impartial jury of his marriageability was essential, it was not enough: Sorlisi also needed to win over such people as Moritz Junghanns and Johann Georg II, without whose support he

---

[197] Distel, 'Einiges über den Kastraten Sorlisi', p. 88. Ortkemper reports (without citation) that Sorlisi was buried in Kloster Ossegg (Osek), a Cistercian abbey in Bohemia that lies about 15 miles south of Schmiedeberg (*Engel wider Willen*, p. 202).

[198] Heriot, *The Castrati in Opera*, p. 57; Barbier, *The World of the Castrati*, p. 142. Neither author cites a source for his information.

Eunuchi Conjugium

could not hope to reach his goal. In this effort he could only rely upon the power of his personality, and the fact that he succeeded in gaining the respect and support of both men speaks volumes about his character. And although the radical nature of his objective would seem to have called for a correspondingly drastic approach, he eschewed any and all extreme measures (such as elopement to Bohemia), and instead sought to attain his goal through legitimate means. Thus, to the likely surprise and frustration of his opponents, he willingly submitted himself to each and every test. In one way or another, each of these circumstances reveals an aspect of Sorlisi's approach to life in a world not well equipped to deal with those of his type. Yet it is ultimately his struggle to establish close familial relationships through courtship and marriage that must be seen as his most fundamental survival strategy, for it represents the attempt of one who resided 'in between' in so many respects to achieve some degree of normalcy in his life – whatever that may have meant for him.

University of Notre Dame

APPENDIX

Documents

1. Betrothal agreement between Bartolomeo Sorlisi and the parents of Dorothea Lichtwer, 1 May 1664 (UAG, Theologische Fakultät Nr. 3; appears as Addendum no. 1 to the letter of Moritz Junghanns to the Theological Faculty at Greifswald, 18 April 1668).

Zu wißen sey hiermit daß wegen dieser beyden Persohnen, als Hn. *Bartholomaeo Sorlisi*, Churf. Durchl. zu S. wohlbestallten Geheimbden Cammerirer und Jungfer Dorotheen Elisabethen Lichtwern heutiges Tages dieses ist abgehandelt worden, Nemlichen, Es hat wohlgemeldter *H. Sorlisi* bey Uns als der Jungfer leibl. Mutter und deren Stiefvater vor und angebracht, wie Er nehmlichen eine Zeit her zu itztbemeldter Jungfer Lichwern eine ehrliche und redliche *Affection* getragen, darauf auch gelegenheit gesuchet mit Ihr bekand zu werden, und als Er dieses werckstellig gemachet, hatte Er ihr seine Liebesmeinung[,] nehmlichen daß Er Sie ehlichen und heyrathen wolte, entdecket, welche in weniger Zeit darauf ihme ihre Gegenliebe versprochen, auch darbey biß an den Todt zuverharren, sich mit theuren Worten herausgelaßen, Wenn denn solches Uns denen Eltern, als auch der andern freundschaft gantzl.

zuverschweigen, ihme nicht anständig seyn wolte. So hat Er Uns vor wenig tagen dieses alles eröfnet und auch umb unsern *Consens* und Willen angesuchet. Ob Uns nun schon solches Vorhaben nicht wenig befrembdlich vorgekommen, wir auch alsobalden darauf die Jungfer hierüber vorgenommen und befraget und so denn beyden theilen deutlich und weitläuffig *remonstrir*et und dargethan, daß diese heyrath nicht bestehen oder iemahls bewilliget werden könne. So haben sie doch beyderseits von einander nicht zu laßen, der Todt schiede Sie denn beständig darauf verharret, in sonderheit aber hat sich die Tochter mit nachdenckl. worten vernehmen laßen, wie Sie darvon nicht abzubringen were[,] man dürfte sich auch keine einbildung machen, daß Sie außer diesen Herrn *Sorlisi* zeit ihres lebens einen andern sich verehlichen laßen wolte; Nachdem wir nun das Werck nach viel einlauffenden Umbständen also befunden, daß diese beyde leuthe mit liebe und Gegenliebe unabläßlich bey einander zuhalten gemeinet, So haben wir nicht alleine denen andern freunden solches zuerkennen gegeben, worauf wir endlichen[,] ingesambt erheischender Nothdurft nach, und weil kein ander Mittel zuerfinden gewesen, diesen Schluß gemacht, daß wir nebenst andern aus der freundschafft[,] endlichen ihme die Tochter dergestallt wolten versprochen haben, iedoch aber mit diesen ausdrücklichen *reservat*, und *annectir*ten *conditionibus*, daß H. *Sorlisi* solches (1) im stande des Rechtens, absonderlich aber vor den geistl. Richter ausführen solle, ob ihme diese Person zu erheyrathen erlaubet werden könne. Nechst diesem (2) wenn das *matrimonium* ie verstattet würde, daß Er Sie bey der lutherischen *religion* iederzeit verbleiben laßen und in keine Wege zu seiner lehre[,] weder durch wiederwertigkeit noch in andere Wege darzu anlaß geben wolle, und denn endl. (3) auf den Todesfall Sie dergestallt zu verleibdingen[,] damit Sie[,] biß auf ihren Todt[,] Noth und gebrauch nicht leiden dürffe, Welche Ehestifftung aber vor allen dingen zu rechen, und ehe die Trauung geschiehet solle vollzogen und hierüber versicherung ausgehändiget werden. Weiln nun bemelter *H. Sorlisi* zu diesen allen sich erbotten, so seind wir auch unsers theils darmit zufrieden, und wollen, was ihn zu rechen versprochen worden, in keine wege wiederkommen, aller maßen an dem Ende dieses *in duplo mundir*et, und von denen beystände nebst den Principal *Interessen*ten und uns eigenhändig unterschrieben und besiegelt worden. Geschehen zu Dreßden den 1 Maÿ 1664.

(L.S.) *Bartholomaeo Sorlisi.* (L.S.) George Lebe (L.S.) Johann George Baumgarten. (L.S.) Anna Dorothea Junghanßen (L.S.) M. Junghannß D.

Eunuchi Conjugium

2. Excerpt from Sorlisi's petition to the Leipzig Consistory (Delphinus, *Eunuchi conjugium*, pp. 1–2).

Es ist vor etlichen Jahren bey dem auf der Insul Fühnen zwischen Ihrer Königl. Majestät von Dennemarck und Schweden vorgegangenen bekandten und harten Treffen ein Schwedischer von Adel/ vornehmen Geschlechts, so wir *Titium* nennen wollen/ durch einen sehr gefährlichen Schuß aus einer Carteßschen an beyden Schenckeln und den *Genitalibus* dermassen getroffen worden/ daß dabey daß meiste Theil des *Scroti*, sammt dem einen *Testiculo*, gäntzlich hinweg genommen/ der andere aber dergestalt gequetschet/ daß er hernach bey der Cur vollends drauf gangen/ und heraus gelanget werden müssen/ also durch dieses Unglück der *Titius*, zur Fortpflanzung des menschlichen Geschlechts/ gantz unvermögend und untüchtig worden; dieser Zufall nun ist/ durch Verschwiegenheit des damahligen *Medici* und Feld-Scherers/ gantz heimlich blieben, hat auch niemand unter der gantzen *Armee* anders gewust als daß der *Titius* nur am Schenckel *blessi*ret/ gleichwohl hat er sich nach solcher Zeit nicht wieder zu Felde brauchen lassen wollen/ sondern in Vor-Pommern häußlich niedergelassen und angekaufft; weilen er nun, solches Zufalles ungeachtet, nichts destoweniger zuweilen *erectionem membri virilis* verspüret/ auch befunden/ daß er zu denen *congressibus veneres* nicht allerdings *inhabilis*, zumahl die *mentula* nur an dem *praeputio* und *glandibus* etwas weniges *laedi*ret gewesen/ so ziemlich *restitui*ret/ im übrigen aber des einsamen Lebens/ zumahl auf seinen abgelegenen Land-Güthern/ überdrüßig/ hat er sich vorgenommen/ einen Adeliche Dame in Pommern/ *Lucretiam*, zu heyrathen.

3. Excerpt from Sorlisi's petition to the Leipzig Consistory (Delphinus, *Eunuchi conjugium*, pp. 6–7)

Zumahlen 4. des *Titii* und der *Lucretiae* Vorsatz bey diesem Werck ist/ daß/ wie sie einander von Hertzen lieben/ also dieselben Zeit ihres Lebens solche ihre Liebe gegen einander *continui*ren/ in treuer *Affection* und ehelicher Vertraulichkeit mit einander leben/ in Noth und Tod einander beystehen/ bey Kranckheit und andern Zufällen einander pflegen und warten/ wie sonst treuen und Christlichen Eheleuten eignet und gebühret: Wie nun *secundum vulgatum istud: Unius rei plures possunt esse fines:* Also ist auch nicht zu leugnen/ daß bey dem heiligen Ehestande andere End=Ursachen/ als *procreatio sobolis*, mehr mitunterlauffen/ denn ja *mutua cohabitatio vitaeque societas* nicht weniger *pro fine matrimonii*, ja fast *primario* zu halten/ indem GOtt/ nach Erschaffung menschlichen Geschlechts/ und bey Einsetzung des heiligen Ehestandes Gen. 2. zuförderst in diese Worte sich heraus gelassen: *Non est bonum, hominem esse solum, faciamus ei adjutorium, ut scil. non sit*

Mary E. Frandsen

solus, ut habeat sociam vitae, cum qua familiariter perpetuo amore & fide conversetur & cohabitet. Und wer wolte verneinen/ daß *illud adjutorium, auxilium,* nicht *in pluribus vitae officiis, quam sola procreatione & educatione liberorum* bestehen?

4. Excerpt from the Decision of the Leipzig Consistory, October 1666 (UAG, Theologische Fakultät Nr. 3; Delphinus, *Eunuchi conjugium,* 14–15).

Und dieweil die *principal Interessenten* beyderseits umb diesen Gebrechen Wißenschafft haben, und deßen ungeacht, einander zu heyrathen, eines beständigen Sinnes seind und bleiben, die Mutter der Braut auch darein gewilliget, und die Verlöbnüs darauf fortgegangen, die andern Freunde darein nichts zu reden, und der heil. Ehestand zwar von Gott, zu ehrlicher und rechtmäßiger Fortpflanzung des menschlichen Geschlechts eingesetzt, zugleich aber auch dem Manne das Weib zu Gehülffen zugesellet, und über dis nirgends verbothen worden, daß dieienigen Mannes Personen, so nicht Kinder zeugen können, deßwegen auch nicht freyen, noch ein Weib zur Ehe nehmen, und damit, wenn es zumahl ohne Betrug geschicht, und das Weib zufür deßen verständiget wird, ihrer Nahrung, Pflegung und Wartung keinen Gehülffen suchen solten, zu geschweigen, daß bey dieser Manns Person nicht eine solche *impotentia* und unvermögenheit zu befinden, *quae generationis actum,* wie die Schullehrer reden, die das Ehewerck, *sed generationis effectum,* sondern die Ehefrucht allein verhindert, und was dergleichen von euch wohl angeführte Umbstände und *Motiven* mehr seindt. So kan auch das geistl. Gerichte diese einmahl mit allem Fleiß und guten Bedacht erwogene und abgehandelte *Sponsalia* und Eheverlöbnüs wieder der Principal Personen öffentlichen Willen, mit Fug keines Weges trennen, noch weniger ihnen die Priesterliche *Copulation* und Trauung versagen: Sondern es gehet dieselbe auf ihr ferneres gebührendes Suchen, billig fort. *Von Rechts wegen.* Uhrkündl. mit unserm Insiegel Versiegelt. Die verordnete der Chur. und Fürstl. Sächß Consistorÿ zu Leipzig. Mens. Octobr: Anno 1666.

5. Copy of the electoral decree permitting Sorlisi to marry, 14 January 1667 (appears as Addendum no. 1 to the 13 February 1667 letter of the Dresden High Consistory to Elector Johann Georg II; Sächs. HStA Loc. 7445/18, fol. 5ʳ).

Des Durchlauchtigsten Churfürstens zu Sachßen vndt Burggraffens zu Magdeburg, Herzog Johann Georgens des Andern gnädigster Befehl ist hiermit, daß der Pfarrer zu Sadißdorff, Matthes Kühn, auff Deroselben Geheimden Cämmerirers, *Bartholomaei de Sorlisi,* anmelden, ihn mit seiner Verlobten, Jungfer Dorotheen Elisabethen Lichtwerin, auf seinen Hause Schmiedebergk, alsbaldt nach verlesung dieses, *privatim copuli*ren, vndt trawen, vndt sich hiervon in keine wege etwas irren oder abhalten laßen

Eunuchi Conjugium

solle; Höchstgedachte Chürfurstl. Durchl. wollen ermelten Pfarr, aller verantworttung halber, dißfals gnädigsten Schutz leisten, vndt schadtloß halten, allermaßen Sie zu dem ende das gewöhnliche Chur *Secret* hierunter drucken laßen, haben es auch eigenhändig vnterschrieben, geschehen in Dreßden den 14. Januarÿ, 1667.
Johann Georg Churfürst
L. S. Elect.

6. Letter of Moritz Junghanns to Pastor Kühn, 3 February 1667 (appears as Addendum no. 3 to the 13 February 1667 letter of the Dresden High Consistory to Elector Johann Georg II; Sächs. HStA Loc. 7445/18, fols. 5^v, 8^r).

Wohl Ehrwürdiger, Vorachtbar vndt Wohlgelahrter, insonders großgünstiger H[err] Pfarr, Demselben berichte ich, wie wir hier vor gut befinden, Daß der Herr die jüngste Trawung dem H[errn] Superintenden nacher Pirna berichte, Vndt Ihme *Copiam* von seinem gn. Befehl beÿlege, Er kan nur berichten, wie er Zwart hette wollen anstehen, alleine ich, H[err] George Metzner vndt der H[err] Verwalter hetten auf die Wortte getrungen, daß es alsobalden nach verlesung der gn[ädigsten] Anordnung geschehen, undt wie Ihre Churf. Durchl. ihm schutz leisten vndt schadtloß halten solle, Item Ihre Churf. Durchl. weren *Supremus Episcopus*, vndt hette Er macht zu befehlen wie Er wolte, Item Er solte sich keine vngnade auf den Halß Ziehen, Er kan auch berichten, Daß die Trawung in beÿseÿn der Eltern, Schwester, Nähesten Freunde vndt auch anderer Personen, geschehen, vndt were darauf gar *repetir*lich gespeiset worden, vndt solches muß schleinig geschehen, sonsten möchte er in das Ober *Consistorium citir*et werden, wann Sie aber werden seinen Befehl sehen, so gehet die sache schon schlaffen, Daß *Consilium* schicke Er durch Zeigern zurücke, ich will es Ihme hier abschreiben laßen, zu seinem Priester Rock soll schon rath werden, *Vale.* Dreßden den 3. Febr. 1667.
Des H[errn] Pfarrs
Dienstgefl.
Moritz Junghannß Dr.
Dem Wohl Ehrwürdigen Vorachtbaren vndt Wohlgelahrten Herrn Matthes Kühnen, trewfleißigen Seelsorgern der Gemeinde Zu Satißdorff, meinem grosg[ünstigen] Herr[n] dienst.

7. Excerpt from the Opinion of the Faculty at Königsberg (Delphinus, *Eunuchi conjugium*, pp. 88–9).

Aus welchen allen denn gnugsam erhellet/ was von gegenwärtiger Ehe eines *Eunuchi* und einer Jungfrauen zu halten sey/ da derselbe ein frommer und gewissenhaffter Mann/ untüchtig zwar *ad generationis effectum*, aber nicht untüchtig *ad generationis actum*; auch *semen* hat/ *licet non prolificum*, und einem Weibe eine Gnüge thun kan/ wie seine Frau nunmehr aus der Erfahrung zeuget/ welches alles der Bericht meldet; Nemlich/ das ist zu halten/ daß diß ein *verum matrimonium*, und sie mit gutem Gewissen bey einander leben können/ um der treuen Hülffe willen/ die der Ehstand mitbringet/ und um Vermeidung der Unzucht und ungeziemten Lüste/ ob sie gleich den ersten *finem*, der nunmehr unter dem Neuen Testament nicht der vornehmste ist/ nemlich die *procreationem sobolis*, nicht erlangen können/ welches bey vielen andern Eh=Ständen sich auch findet: Die Lust/ die ausser der Ehe ihnen eine Tod=Sünde wäre/ ist in dem Ehstand/ *propter matrimonium*, als *Dei ordinationem*, ihnen ein *peccatum veniale:* Nur allein werden sie/ weil die *Eunuchi propensiores in venerem* seyn/ als andere sich mäßigen/ und bißweilen aus beyder Bewilligung/ wie Paulus erwehnet/ sich von einander enthalten/ daß sie zum Fasten und Beten Musse haben mögen/ auch immermehr dahin trachten/ daß sie endlich nicht als *Maritus* und *Uxor*, sondern als *Frater* und *Soror*, das ist/ ohne Vermischung/ bey einander wohnen mögen/ doch mit beyder Bewilligung/ wie auch andere Eheleute dahin trachten müssen/ denen ja mit den Jahren die Lust abnimt.

8. Excerpt from the Opinion of the Faculty at Greifswald (Delphinus, *Eunuchi conjugium*, p. 92).

Wer wolte denn die Versehung GOttes hemmen/ und durch die Ehe-Scheidung hindern? Nachdem auch beyderseits richtiger Ehelicher *Consens*, und daraus nicht undeutlicher abgenommener gnädiger Wille Gottes/ durch die Priesterliche *copulation*, über sie bestätiget und *declari*ret/ daß sie daraus versichert seyn sollen/ GOtt habe sie zusammen gefüget/ und kein Mensch soll sie scheiden. Und denn solche Scheidung auch nicht geschehen mag ohne Entheiligung des Nahmens GOttes/ der über ihnen bey der *Copulation*, ümb eine friedsame und wohlgerathene Ehe/ ist angeruffen worden/ so sehen wir vielweniger/ wie diese Leuthe hinwiederum zur Scheidung anzuhalten seyn möchten/ denn wie die Verhütung der Entheiligung des Nahmens GOttes nicht zuläßig noch verstatten/ daß die Ehe derselben/ wiewol aus mehr wichtigen Ursachen/ billich zu trennen seyn möchte/ als da ein Theil der Eh=Leute mit gar naher Blut=Freundschafft verwandt/ der mit Aussatz/ *Epilepsia* und dergleichen unheilsamen Kranckheiten behafft/ und also ohn viel grössere Gefahr beyzuwohnen/ ungeschickt seyn/ nach der *Consistoriali*en und *Casuist*en Meynung/ nicht kan noch soll getrennet werden?

JAMES GRIER

THE MUSICAL AUTOGRAPHS OF ADÉMAR DE CHABANNES (989–1034)

Late in the year 1028, Adémar de Chabannes embarked on an ambitious and audacious project to create a new liturgy for the Feast of Saint Martial that would venerate its honoree as an apostle.[1] It is difficult to exaggerate the monstrous nature of the venture and the claim it supported. The historical Martial was well known from the works of Gregory of Tours, the sixth-century historian, as a third-century Roman missionary to Aquitaine and first bishop of Limoges.[2] There his burial place became an important pilgrimage destination and the eventual site of a Benedictine monastery founded in Martial's memory.[3] Adémar, with the full support of the

A portion of this paper was presented under the title 'Adémar de Chabannes and the Earliest Compositional Autograph' at the meeting of the American Musicological Society in Atlanta, 16 Nov. 2001. I thank my audience for a stimulating response to the paper. I am also grateful to the Principal's Development Fund and the Advisory Research Committee, both of Queen's University, the Social Sciences and Humanities Research Council of Canada, the A. Whitney Griswold Faculty Research Grant and the John F. Enders Research Assistance Grant, both of Yale University, and the Office of Research Services, University of Western Ontario, for grants that enabled me to consult manuscript sources in Paris and prepare this article for publication. I am also very grateful to M. François Avril and Mme Marie-Pierre Laffitte of the Département des Manuscrits, Bibliothèque Nationale de France, and Mme Contamine of the Section Latine, Institut de Recherche et d'Histoire des Textes, for their many kindnesses.

[1] On the date, see J. Grier, '*Scriptio interrupta*: Adémar de Chabannes and the Production of Paris, Bibliothèque Nationale de France, MS latin 909', *Scriptorium*, 51 (1997), pp. 234–50, at pp. 245–6.
[2] Gregory of Tours, *Libri octo miraculorum*, 8, *Liber in gloria confessorum* 27–8, ed. B. Krusch, in *Monumenta Germaniae historica, Scriptores rerum merouingicarum* [hereafter *MGH, SRM*], 1, pt. 2 (Hannover, 1885), pp. 764–5; on the date of his mission, see id., *Historia Francorum* 1.30, 2nd ed., ed. B. Krusch and W. Levison, in *MGH, SRM*, 1, pt. 1 (Hannover, 1937–51), p. 23.
[3] On Saint-Martial as a pilgrimage destination, see C. de Lasteyrie, *L'abbaye de Saint-Martial de Limoges: Étude historique, économique et archéologique précédée de recherches nouvelles sur la vie du saint* (Paris, 1901), pp. 31–41; B. Töpfer, 'Reliquienkult und Pilgerbewegung zur Zeit der Klosterreform im burgundisch-aquitanischen Gebiet', in H. Kretzschmar (ed.), *Vom Mittelalter zur Neuzeit: Zum 65. Geburtstag von Heinrich Sproemberg* (Forschungen zur Mittelalterlichen Geschichte, 1; Berlin, 1956), pp. 420–39, esp. 428–33; D. F. Callahan, 'The Sermons of Adémar of Chabannes and the Cult of St. Martial of Limoges', *Revue Bénédictine*, 86 (1976), pp. 251–95, at pp. 253–5, 280–95; and R. Landes, *Relics, Apocalypse, and the Deceits of History: Ademar of Chabannes, 989–1034* (Harvard Historical Studies, 117; Cambridge, Mass., 1995), pp. 50–3, 61–9. On the reform of the abbey under the Benedictine rule, see *Annales lemovicenses* ad annum 848, in *MGH, Scriptores*, 2, ed. G. H. Pertz (Hannover, 1829; repr. Stuttgart and

125

James Grier

abbot, Odolric, and monks of the abbey of Saint-Martial, and Bishop Jordan of Limoges, sought to transform the historical Martial into a first-century Jew, younger cousin of Simon Peter, an intimate of Jesus himself, whom he served at the Last Supper, Saint Peter's personal delegate to Gaul, and a saint of apostolic rank.

Adémar's new liturgy would become the most public aspect of this fraudulent, eventually scandalous, and ultimately successful programme to elevate Martial to the apostolicity. To place this claim in perspective, it overshadows by a significant margin, in terms of sheer temerity, other ecclesiastical deceptions, such as the 'discovery' of the tomb of the apostle Saint James the Greater at Santiago de Compostela in the ninth century, or the identification of Saint Denis, patron saint of the royal abbey just north of Paris, as Dionysius the Areopagite, the first-century Greek philosopher and disciple of Saint Paul.[4] The monks of Saint-Martial went beyond these deceptions to revise biblical history in order to transform their patron saint into the counterfeit first-century figure identified above. They stopped short of rewriting the Gospel accounts of the Last Supper to include Martial's presence on that occasion, but they

---

New York, 1963), p. 251; Adémar de Chabannes, *Chronicon* 3.18, ed. P. Bourgain, R. Landes and G. Pon, *Ademari Cabannensis Opera Omnia Pars I* (Corpus Christianorum Continuatio Mediaevalis, 129; Turnhout, 1999), pp. 135–6; [Adémar de Chabannes], *Commemoratio abbatum lemouicensium basilice S. Marcialis apostoli*, in *Chroniques de Saint-Martial de Limoges*, ed. H. Duplès-Agier (Paris, 1874), p. 1; Bernard Itier, *Chronique* 22, ed. J.-L. Lemaître (Les Classiques de l'Histoire de France au Moyen Age, 39; Paris, 1998), p. 5; and Geoffrey of Vigeois, *Chronica* 59, in *Novae bibliothecae manuscriptorum librorum*, ii: *Rerum aquitanicarum, praesertim bituricensium, uberrima collectio*, ed. P. Labbe (Paris, 1657), p. 312. For commentary, see Lasteyrie, *L'abbaye de Saint-Martial de Limoges*, pp. 51–3; and A. Sohn, *Der Abbatiat Ademars von Saint-Martial de Limoges (1063–1114): Ein Beitrag zur Geschichte des cluniacensischen Klösterverbandes* (Beiträge zur Geschichte des Alten Mönchtums und des Benediktinertums, 37; Münster in Westfallen, 1989), pp. 13–25.

[4] On the the tomb of Saint James the Greater, see L. Vázquez de Parga, J. M. Lacarra and J. U. Ríu, *Las peregrinaciones a Santiago de Compostela*, 3 vols. (Madrid, 1948–9; repr. Pamplona, 1992), i, pp. 27–36; J. Guerra, 'El descubrimiento del cuerpo de Santiago en Compostela, según la "Historia de España" dirigida por Menéndez Pidal', *Compostellanum*, 1 (1956), pp. 513–51; id., 'Notas críticas sobre el origen del culto sepulcral a Santiago en Compostela', *La Ciencia Tomista*, 88 (1961), pp. 417–74, 559–90; id., *Exploraciones arqueológicas entorno al sepulcro del apostel Santiago* (Santiago de Compostela, 1982), pp. 557–68; and M. C. Díaz y Díaz, M. A. G. Piñeiro and P. del Oro Trigo, *El códice calixtino de la catedral de Santiago: Estudio codicológico y de contenido* (Monografías de Compostellanum, 2; Santiago de Compostela, 1988), pp. 15–32. On Saint Denis, see D. Luscombe, 'Denis the Pseudo-Areopagite in the Middle Ages from Hilduin to Lorenzo Valla', in *Fälschungen im Mittelalter: Internationaler Kongreß der Monumenta Germaniae Historica München, 16.–19. September 1986*, i: *Kongreßdaten und Festvorträge: Literatur und Fälschung* (MGH, Schriften, 33, 1; Hannover, 1988), pp. 133–52.

The Musical Autographs of Adémar de Chabannes

overlooked few other opportunities to justify the extravagant and unprecedented claims they made for their patron saint.

Adémar's chief vehicle for the promulgation of Martial's apostolicity was a complete liturgy, Mass and Office, for the saint's feast. The liturgy, with its dramatic combination of word, sound, gesture and even fragrance, held tremendous power to shape public opinion. Adémar, as a monk from his 'tenderest youth' ('ab ipsa tenerrima pueritia'), participated in its celebration for virtually his entire life.[5] And he had just witnessed its intoxicating effect during the dedication of the new abbatial basilica at Saint-Martial on 18 November 1028. The ceremony had a profound impact on him, which he expressed in several sermons about the event, and I believe that it provided the final impetus for his decision to embrace the apostolicity of Martial.[6] He therefore resolved to take the liturgy's power into his own hands to produce a lasting monument to the abbey where he was educated, its patron saint, and ultimately himself. The public celebration of a liturgy recognising Martial as an apostle had the potential to affirm the claim in the minds of the citizens of Limoges, to make real what everyone knew to be false. Such was Adémar's goal, and he chose a powerful tool with which to achieve it.

His involvement in this blatant fraud is extraordinary because, prior to this undertaking, he was acknowledged to be the foremost historian of his generation in Aquitaine, and so he, better than anyone, would have known the utter mendacity of the apostolic claims for Martial.[7] Adémar was intimately familiar with the texts of Gregory of Tours, cited above, that documented Martial's journey

[5] Adémar de Chabannes, *Epistola de apostolatu sancti Martialis*, ed. J.-P. Migne, *Patrologia cursus completus: Series latina* (hereafter *PL*), 221 vols. (Paris, 1844–64), cxli, col. 89C.
[6] Adémar's sermons on the Dedication survive in autograph in Pa 2469, fols. 89^r–97^r, numbered 38–46 in Léopold Delisle's inventory: 'Notice sur les manuscrits originaux d'Adémar de Chabannes', *Notices et extraits des manuscrits de la Bibliothèque Nationale et autres bibliothèques*, 35 (Paris, 1896), pp. 241–358, at pp. 282–3. Editions: excerpts from nos. 38, 39, 44 and all of 46, E. Sackur, *Die Cluniacenser in ihrer kirchlichen und allgemeingeschichtlichen Wirksamkeit bis zur Mitte des elften Jahrhunderts*, 2 vols. (Halle, 1892–4), ii, pp. 479–87; no. 44, Lasteyrie, *L'abbaye de Saint-Martial de Limoges*, pièce justificative 5, pp. 422–6; and no. 45, *Sermo III*, *PL*, cxli, cols. 120–4. A complete edition of the sermons is forthcoming in Corpus Christianorum Continuatio Mediaevalis. See also Landes, *Relics, Apocalypse, and the Deceits*, pp. 199–204. On the role of the ceremony in convincing Adémar to seek affirmation of Martial's apostolicity, see Grier, '*Scriptio interrupta*', pp. 245–6.
[7] Adémar's most important historical work is his *Chronicon*, ed. Bourgain *et al.*; I am very grateful to the editors for granting me access to their edition while it was in proof. On Adémar as a historian, see Landes, *Relics, Apocalypse, and the Deceits*.

to Gaul in the middle of the third century with six other bishops, including, incidentally, Saint Denis, whose martyrdom in Paris inspired the founding of the abbey that bears his name.[8] But Adémar faced a personal and professional crisis in the years 1028–9, and attempted to solve it by promoting the apostolic status of Martial.

An oblate at the abbey of Saint-Cybard in Angoulême, Adémar had completed his advanced studies at Saint-Martial under the tutelage of his paternal uncle, Roger de Chabannes (later the abbey's cantor) around the year 1010.[9] As part of these studies, Adémar achieved professional competence as a musician, skilled in the technology of musical notation, and intimately familiar with the liturgical repertories practised at Saint-Martial. He returned to Angoulême well trained in grammar, rhetoric, computus and the liturgy, and with every expectation of a brilliant career, leading eventually to the office of abbot. All did not turn out according to plan, however. In 1027 the office fell vacant, but Count William of Angoulême chose another to fill the post; and then the count, Adémar's principal supporter in Angoulême, died under mysterious circumstances on 6 April 1028.[10] Adémar sensed that his career at Saint-Cybard was at a standstill and so he turned to the place of his youth, Saint-Martial in Limoges, for a refuge.

He arrived at Saint-Martial between 25 April and 18 November, most likely in the late spring or early summer.[11] He immediately set

---

[8] See n. 2 above.

[9] On Adémar's biography, see L. Saltet, 'Une discussion sur Saint Martial entre un Lombard et un Limousin en 1029', *Bulletin de Littérature Ecclésiastique*, 26 (1925), pp. 161–86, 279–302; 'Une prétendue lettre de Jean XIX sur Saint Martial fabriquée par Adémar de Chabannes', *ibid.*, 27 (1926), pp. 117–39; 'Les faux d'Adémar de Chabannes: Prétendues décisions sur Saint Martial au concile de Bourges du 1er novembre 1031', *ibid.*, 27 (1926), pp. 145–60; and 'Un cas de mythomanie historique bien documenté: Adémar de Chabannes (988–1034)', *ibid.*, 32 (1931), pp. 149–65; and Landes, *Relics, Apocalypse, and the Deceits*. For further bibliography, see J. Grier, '*Ecce sanctum quem deus elegit Marcialem apostolum*: Adémar de Chabannes and the Tropes for the Feast of Saint Martial', in B. Gillingham and P. Merkley (eds.), *Beyond the Moon: Festschrift Luther Dittmer* (Wissenschaftliche Abhandlungen, 53; Ottawa, 1990), pp. 28–74, at p. 2, n. 82; and the bibliography cited in Landes, *Relics, Apocalypse, and the Deceits*.

[10] On the abbacy, the death of Count William and events through 25 Apr. 1028, see Adémar, *Chronicon* 3.65–8, ed. Bourgain *et al.*, pp. 184–9. See also Landes, *Relics, Apocalypse, and the Deceits*, pp. 170–1, 179–82.

[11] On 25 Apr., Adémar was still witnessing events in Angoulême; see n. 10 above. And he attended the dedication of the abbatial basilica at Saint-Martial in Limoges on 18 Nov.; see n. 6 above. On these and the other details mentioned in this paragraph, see also Grier, '*Scriptio interrupta*', pp. 240, 245–6, 248.

The Musical Autographs of Adémar de Chabannes

to work as the music scribe for the first layer of Paris, Bibliothèque Nationale de France, MS latin (hereafter Pa) 909, originally a troper executed in the scriptorium at Saint-Martial as a commission for the neighbouring abbey of Saint-Martin. Then, after the dedication ceremony of 18 November, Adémar, in the flush of excitement for the cult of Martial generated by that event, appropriated the codex, in an advanced yet incomplete state, for the inscription of the apostolic liturgy for the saint, the composition of which he decided to undertake at this time. By the following summer, the liturgy was ready for public presentation. Bishop Jordan, whose full cooperation and support Adémar had obtained, convened a diocesan synod at Limoges in the first days of August 1029. On 3 August, at the conclusion of the synod, the liturgy was inaugurated in the city's cathedral. The date is significant, for it corresponds not only with the feast of the Invention of Saint Stephen (who was, incidentally, the patron saint of the Limoges cathedral) but also with the feast of the dedication of the cathedral itself.

Unfortunately for Adémar, the première met with disaster. A Lombard monk, Benedict of Chiusa, confronted Adémar, apparently at the urging of the cathedral canons, at the entrance to the cathedral just as the bishop was to join the procession at the beginning of the Mass.[12] Benedict, speaking in the vernacular ('barbare'), condemned the new liturgy as a heresy and an affront to God. He quickly swayed the assembled crowd, to the considerable embarrassment of Adémar, Bishop Jordan and Abbot Odolric. Although the entire liturgy was apparently celebrated, Adémar beat a hasty retreat to Angoulême the next day, 4 August, and spent the rest of his life fabricating evidence for Martial's apostolicity, including a large interpolation into the proceedings of the church council at Limoges in 1031 and a letter purportedly from Pope John XIX.[13] What Adémar could not possibly have foreseen was that his

---

[12] For Adémar's version of these events, see *Epistola de apostolatu sancti Martialis*, cols. 89–112; see also Saltet, 'Une discussion'; and Landes, *Relics, Apocalypse, and the Deceits*, pp. 214–68.

[13] On the forgeries, see Saltet, 'Une prétendue lettre'; 'Les faux d'Adémar de Chabannes'; and 'Un cas de mythomanie'. R. Landes, 'A Libellus from St. Martial of Limoges Written in the Time of Ademar of Chabannes (989–1034): "Un faux à retardement" ', *Scriptorium*, 37 (1983), pp. 178–204; and *Relics, Apocalypse, and the Deceits*, pp. 269–81. D. Callahan, 'Adémar of Chabannes, Apocalypticism and the Peace Council of Limoges of 1031', *Revue Bénédictine*, 101 (1991), pp. 32–49; and 'Ademar of Chabannes and his Insertions into Bede's *Expositio actuum apostolorum*', *Analecta Bollandiana*, 111 (1993), pp. 385–400. Further on the Council of Limoges

campaign would succeed far beyond his wildest expectations before the end of the eleventh century.[14] At that time, the monks at Saint-Martial produced a gradual, Pa 1132, that acknowledged Martial as an apostle; by the early twelfth century, the cult was firmly entrenched, and it remained so until the end of the nineteenth century. Adémar had created one of the most spectacularly successful frauds of the entire Middle Ages.

Our knowledge of the musical portion of Adémar's apostolic liturgy derives from a unique source of exceptional historical, liturgical, musical and palaeographic importance: portions of Pa 909 transmit the musical items for the full corpus of liturgical ceremonies on Martial's feast day in the autograph hand of Adémar himself.[15] Here I shall address two issues: first, the palaeographic evidence that establishes Adémar as the text and music scribe of the pertinent sections of Pa 909, as well as portions of three other music manuscripts; and second, an overview of Adémar's compositional activities as attested by these manuscripts. The combination of this evidence permits a remarkable deduction: the music manuscripts Adémar left behind, principally Pa 909, but others as well, as I show here, contain the earliest identifiable compositional autographs, I believe by several centuries. This is a conclusion I have adumbrated elsewhere, but here I present full documentation and discussion of the matter.[16]

Simultaneously, I announce here what for me was a startling discovery, and one that confirmed and amplified a suspicion formed by Richard Crocker over forty years ago in his Yale dissertation: that Adémar was the music scribe of large portions of Pa 1121. This discovery carries two important ramifications. First, it necessitates modifying Adémar's biography to provide for an extended visit by him to Limoges and the abbey of Saint-Martial sometime between the death of his paternal uncle, Roger de Chabannes, the abbey's cantor, on 26 April 1025, and his longer sojourn at Saint-Martial,

in 1031, see J. Becquet, 'Le concile de Limoges de 1031', *Bulletin de la Société Archéologique et Historique du Limousin*, 128 (2000), pp. 23–64.
[14] See Grier, '*Scriptio interrupta*', pp. 249–50.
[15] On Adémar's participation in the production of Pa 909, see Grier, '*Scriptio interrupta*'.
[16] J. Grier, *The Critical Editing of Music: History, Method, and Practice* (Cambridge, 1996), p. 185.

The Musical Autographs of Adémar de Chabannes

from mid-1028 to 4 August 1029.[17] Second, and more important, this discovery shows that Adémar was the first Aquitanian music scribe to use the vertical orientation of the notes to present firm intervallic, or relative pitch information. That is, the vertical distance between two notes fixes the musical interval between them, and notes of the same pitch appear at the same height above the literary text sung to the melody.

This was a development of enormous significance in the emerging technology of musical notation because it supplies a centrally defining feature of the Western notational system. Most of the notational dialects that appear in early music manuscripts from the medieval West use, to a greater or lesser degree, the vertical placement of signs to indicate melodic direction.[18] In most cases, heighting occurs within the context of a single neume; that is, the notes of a compound neume are written higher and lower to show the direction of the melody within that neume. The direction of the melody between neumes was either not indicated at all or shown by means other than their vertical placement; for example, by their morphology, as in the case of the *uirga* indicating a higher note, a *punctum* a lower one; or by the use of *litterae significatiuae* such as *e* (=*equaliter*, same pitch), *alt* (=*altius*, higher) and *io* (=*iusum*, lower).[19] These notations principally show which notes are to be sung to

---

[17] On Roger, see J. Grier, 'Roger de Chabannes (d. 1025), Cantor of St Martial, Limoges', *Early Music History*, 14 (1995), pp. 53–119; on Adémar's visit to Saint-Martial of 1028–9 and his musical activities then, see id., '*Scriptio interrupta*'.

[18] The best studies of notation in Western chant remain P. Wagner, *Einführung in die gregorianischen Melodien: Ein Handbuch der Choralwissenschaft*, ii: *Neumenkunde: Paläographie des liturgischen Gesanges*, 2nd edn (Leipzig, 1912); G. M. Suñol, *Introduction à la paléographie musicale grégorienne* (Paléographie Grégorienne, 708; Paris, Tournai and Rome, 1935); and S. Corbin, *Die Neumen* (Palaeographie der Musik, 1/3; Cologne, 1977).

[19] On *litterae significatiuae* in general, see Wagner, *Einführung*, ii: *Neumenkunde*, pp. 233–51; R. Van Doren, *Étude sur l'influence de l'abbaye de Saint Gall (VIIIe au XIe siècle)* (Académie Royale de Belgique, Classe des Beaux-Arts, Mémoires, 2, fasc. 3; Brussels, 1925; also published as Université de Louvain, Recueil de Travaux Publiés par les Membres des Conférences d'Histoire et de Philologie, ser. 2, no. 6 (Louvain, 1925)), pp. 94–118; R.-J. Hesbert, 'L'interprétation de l'"equaliter" dans les manuscrits sangalliens', *Revue Grégorienne*, 18 (1933), pp. 161–73; J. Smits van Waesberghe, *Muziekgeschiedenis der Middeleeuwen*, ii: *Verklaring der Letterteekens (litterae significatiuae) in het gregoriaansche Neumenschrift van Sint Gallen: Een Onderzoek naar de historische Waarde van den zoogenaamden Notker-Brief en naar den Oorsprong en de Beteekenis der Letterteekens in St. Gallen* (Nederlandsche Muziekhistorische en Muziekpaedagogische Studiën, A; Tilburg, 1939–42); J. Froger, 'L'épitre de Notker sur les "lettres significatives": Édition critique', *Études Grégoriennes*, 5 (1962), pp. 23–71; and T. J. McGee, *The Sound of Medieval Song: Ornamentation and Vocal Style according to the Treatises* (Oxford, 1998), pp. 32–3.

which syllables of the literary text, and secondarily, the direction of melodic motion.

No early notational dialect uses the vertical orientation of the notes to show direction to a greater degree than tenth- and early eleventh-century Aquitanian notation. This characteristic of Aquitanian notation derives directly from the extensive use of individual *puncta* to represent the notes of a melody, which are then grouped, rather than ligated, into neumes analogous to the conjunct neumes, or ligatures, of other contemporary notational dialects.[20] By the generation before Adémar, the principal features of Aquitanian notation were in place, most significantly, for our purposes, in the troper-proser Pa 1120, produced at Saint-Martial during the lifetime of Adémar's uncle Roger, and possibly under his direct supervision as cantor. In the next generation, and probably within a couple of years of Roger's death in 1025, the monks at Saint-Martial produced another elaborate troper-proser, Pa 1121.[21]

Over thirty years ago, Paul Evans identified this manuscript as the earliest Aquitanian source to contain reliable intervallic information in the inscription of its melodies. For that reason, he chose it as the basis for his published transcriptions of tropes.[22] By the simple device of consistently heighting notes of the same pitch, and by linking the pitch level of one line of music to the next by the *custos* (a sign written at the end of one line to show the relative pitch level of the first note of the next line), the music scribe of Pa 1121 transformed Aquitanian notation into a dialect in which the relative pitch values are fixed. I now attribute that development to Adémar de Chabannes, whom I here identify as the music scribe of Pa 1121.

---

[20] No comprehensive survey of Aquitanian notation exists. See J. Lapeyre, 'La notation aquitaine et les origines de la notation musical d'après les anciens manuscrits d'Albi', *Tribune Saint-Gervais*, 13 (1907), pp. 193–8, 226–36, 255–62, 275–86; *Le codex 903 de la Bibliothèque Nationale de Paris (XIe siècle), Graduel de Saint-Yrieix* (Paléographie Musicale, 13; Tournai, 1925–30), pp. 54–211; Suñol, *Introduction à la paléographie*, pp. 164–72, 260–81; Corbin, *Die Neumen*, pp. 94–100; R. L. Crocker, *The Early Medieval Sequence* (Berkeley, Los Angeles and London, 1977), pp. 15–26; M. Huglo, 'La tradition musicale aquitaine: Répertoire et notation', in *Liturgie et musique (IXe–XIVe s.)* (Cahiers de Fanjeaux, 17; Toulouse, 1982), pp. 253–68; and J. Mas, 'La tradition musicale en Septimanie: Répertoire et tradition musicale', *ibid.*, pp. 269–86, at pp. 280–5.

[21] On the production of Pa 1120 and 1121, see Grier, 'Roger de Chabannes', pp. 108–19.

[22] P. Evans, *The Early Trope Repertory of Saint Martial de Limoges* (Princeton Studies in Music, 2; Princeton, 1970), pp. 48, 121–5; the transcriptions, pp. 129–273. See also A. E. Planchart, 'The Transmission of Medieval Chant', in I. Fenlon (ed.), *Music in Medieval and Early Modern Europe: Patronage, Sources and Texts* (Cambridge, 1981), pp. 347–63, at p. 355.

The Musical Autographs of Adémar de Chabannes

Still, singers who used Pa 1121 needed to know the melodies before they could read them from the musical notation, just like their predecessors who had used Pa 1120 and earlier Aquitanian manuscripts. Yet this notational development permitted significantly greater and more precise information about the melodies to be preserved in writing, and constituted an essential step on the way to a notation whose pitches could be read by the musically literate without previous knowledge of the melody. That achievement would require two further innovations: the imposition of horizontal lines on the music to regulate the heighting of the notes (eventually drawn in groups of as many as five or six to form a staff), and clefs that identify the pitch values of the staff lines. The music theorist Guido d'Arezzo, Adémar's contemporary, discusses both developments, although they took some time to appear in Aquitanian sources.[23]

Adémar already draws a few horizontal lines freehand in the sequentiary (a collection of untexted and partially texted sequences for the entire liturgical year) of Pa 909 (fols. 122^r and 125^v), and Aquitanian scribes commonly begin to use a single horizontal line for heighting around AD 1050.[24] The full staff with clefs becomes customary in Aquitanian notation about a century later.[25] It is difficult to exaggerate the significance of this development, beginning with Adémar's systematic use of consistent heighting to show relative pitch, for the history of Western music. In comparison with

---

[23] Guido d'Arezzo, *Prologus in Antiphonarium* 46–76, ed. J. Smits van Waesberghe (Divitiae Musicae Artis Collectae, ser. A, no. 3; Buren, 1975), pp. 67–81 (also edited and translated by D. Pesce in *Guido d'Arezzo's Regule rithmice, Prologus in Antiphonarium, and Epistola ad Michahelem: A Critical Text and Translation* (Wissenschaftliche Abhandlungen, 73; Ottawa, 1999), pp. 418–35). See J. Smits van Waesberghe, 'The Musical Notation of Guido of Arezzo', *Musica Disciplina*, 5 (1951), pp. 15–53; id., *De musico-pedagogico et theoretico Guidone Aretino eiusque vita et moribus* (Florence, 1953), pp. 48–85; H. Oesch, *Guido von Arezzo: Biographisches und Theoretisches unter besonderer Berücksichtigung der sogenannten odonischen Traktate* (Publikationen der Schweizerischen Musikforschenden Gesellschaft, ser. 2, 4; Bern, 1954), pp. 5–11; and N. Phillips, 'Notationen und Notationslehren von Boethius bis zum 12. Jahrhundert', trans. G. Tillmann-Budde, in *Geschichte der Musiktheorie*, iv: *Die Lehre von einstimmigen liturgischen Gesang*, ed. T. Ertelet and F. Zaminer (Darmstadt, 2000), pp. 293–623, at pp. 581–5.

[24] The earliest music manuscript from Saint-Martial that uses this device is Pa 1119, probably produced after 1050. See J. Chailley, *L'école musicale de Saint Martial de Limoges jusqu'à la fin du XIe siècle* (Paris, 1960), pp. 70 and 102.

[25] S. Fuller, 'The Myth of "Saint Martial" Polyphony: A Study of the Sources', *Musica Disciplina*, 33 (1979), pp. 5–26, at pp. 19–23; and J. Grier, 'Some Codicological Observations on the Aquitanian Versaria', *ibid.*, 44 (1990), pp. 5–56, at pp. 19 and 51–2.

James Grier

musics of other cultures, Western music and its notation place higher importance on pitch than many other elements, such as rhythm and timbre. Therefore heighting, the device by which notation may precisely communicate pitch, holds a central place in the development of the musical language.

PA 1121

Prior to my discovery of Adémar's contribution to Pa 1121 as music scribe, I had believed that his hand appeared only in the sequentiary of this codex, fols. 58–72, and further that he had written this portion of the manuscript in Angoulême, after to his departure from Limoges on 4 August 1029. Therefore, I considered the sequentiary to be Adémar's 'second edition' of that repertoire, the 'first' occurring in Pa 909, fols. 110–25, continuing on fols. 198^r and 205^{r-v}.[26] Adémar did make some modifications to Pa 1121 after his return to Angoulême in 1029, and they are discussed below. The discovery that Adémar noted both the sequentiary and the rest of the first layer, however, shows, in view of other evidence for a close relationship between these parts of the codex, that they were both executed at the same time.

Codex Pa 1121 was conceived as a lavish book in comparison with the previous troper-proser produced at Saint-Martial, Pa 1120. The current size of its pages is 265 × 170 mm, as compared with that of Pa 1120, 230 × 105 mm, and it contains significantly more elaborate decoration.[27] Like Pa 1120, it is organised in libelli according to liturgical genre, which I analyse in detail below.[28] The dependency of Pa 1121 on its predecessor and model, Pa 1120, has been amply demonstrated by Jacques Chailley, Paul Evans and

[26] Grier, 'Roger de Chabannes', pp. 63–4; and *The Critical Editing of Music*, pp. 188–9.
[27] For the page size, see Bibliothèque Nationale [de France], Département des Manuscrits, *Catalogue général des manuscrits latins*, i (Paris, 1939), pp. 409–10; on the decoration, see D. Gaborit-Chopin, *La décoration des manuscrits à Saint-Martial de Limoges et en Limousin du IXe au XIIe siècle* (Mémoires et Documents Publiés par la Société de l'École des Chartes, 17; Paris and Geneva, 1969), pp. 71–5 and plates 65–8, 70–2 and 74.
[28] On the libellus structure of this type of manuscript in general, see M. Huglo, 'Les Libelli de tropes et les premiers tropaires-prosaires', in R. Jacobsson (ed.), *Pax et sapientia: Studies in Text and Music of Liturgical Tropes and Sequences in Memory of Gordon Anderson* (Acta Universitatis Stockholmiensis, Studia Latina Stockholmiensia, 29; Stockholm, 1986), pp. 13–22; id., *Les livres de chant liturgique* (Typologie des Sources du Moyen Age Occidental, 52; Turnhout, 1988), pp. 64–75; and Grier, 'Roger de Chabannes', pp. 108–9.

Alejandro Enrique Planchart.[29] Elsewhere, I have shown that Pa 1121 was extant upon Adémar's arrival in Limoges in mid-1028, when he began work as the notator of Pa 909, because the principal scribe of the first layer of Pa 909, Adémar's collaborator, drew on it as a source, alongside Pa 1120, when compiling the Proper tropes.[30] Therefore, the original layer of Pa 1121, including the tropers, Proper and Ordinary, was produced at Saint-Martial between the death of Roger de Chabannes on 26 April 1025 and Adémar's arrival in Limoges in mid-1028; and the principal scribe, who organised the codex and copied the text, was possibly the cantor who succeeded Roger on his death.[31]

Adémar de Chabannes, music scribe of Pa 1121

A more precise date depends upon the identification of Adémar as the manuscript's music scribe. Previous scholarship had attributed, with greater or lesser certainty, the sequentiary of Pa 1121 (fols. 58–72) to Adémar on the basis of the signatures it contains.[32]

---

[29] Chailley, *L'école*, pp. 81–2; Evans, *The Early Trope Repertory*, pp. 47–8; and Planchart, 'The Transmission', pp. 353–60.

[30] Grier, '*Ecce sanctum*', pp. 54–69.

[31] Grier, 'Roger de Chabannes', pp. 115–17; see also J. Chailley, 'Les anciens tropaires et séquentiaires de l'école de Saint-Martial de Limoges (x^e–xie s.)', *Études Grégoriennes*, 2 (1957), pp. 163–88, at pp. 169–71; id., *L'école*, pp. 81–3; and H. Husmann, *Tropen- und Sequenzenhandschriften* (Répertoire International des Sources Musicales, B 5^1; Munich, 1964), pp. 130–1.

[32] Léopold Delisle stated that Adémar participated in the making of the codex in some way: *Le cabinet des manuscrits de la Bibliothèque impériale*, 4 vols. (Histoire Générale de Paris; Paris, 1868–81; repr. Amsterdam, 1969 and New York, 1974), i, pp. 388–9; 'Les manuscrits de Saint-Martial de Limoges: Réimpression textuelle du Catalogue publié en 1730', *Bulletin de la Société Archéologique et Historique du Limousin*, 43 (1895), pp. 1–60, at p. 4; and 'Notice', pp. 352–3. Chailley is hesitant to attribute the sequentiary in Pa 1121 to Adémar: 'Les anciens tropaires', p. 169; and *L'école*, pp. 82–3. Husmann also suggests that Adémar contributed to the sequentiary, but more firmly asserts that the scribe of the sequentiary also produced the second layer of Pa 909: *Tropen- und Sequenzenhandschriften*, p. 130. D. Gaborit-Chopin, 'Les dessins d'Adémar de Chabannes', *Bulletin Archéologique du Comité des Travaux Historiques et Scientifiques*, new ser., 3 (1967), pp. 163–225, at p. 167, suggests that Adémar contributed only to the libellus fols. 58–72, as this is the only portion of the codex in which his name appears (but cf. *ibid.*, p. 225, where she includes this sequentiary in a list of Adémar's autographs); she is more hesitant about the attribution in *La décoration*, pp. 71, 186–7. Michel Huglo is also tentative in his attribution, 'Codicologie et musicologie', in P. Cockshaw, M.-C. Garand and P. Jodogne (eds.), *Miscellanea codicologica F. Masai dicata MCMLXXIX*, 2 vols. (Les Publications de Scriptorium, 8; Gand, 1979), i, pp. 71–82, at p. 80. Only Paul Hooreman and Robert Lee Wolff unequivocally identify Adémar's hand in the sequentiary: Hooreman, 'Saint-Martial de Limoges au temps de l'Abbé Odolric (1025–1040): Essai sur une pièce oubliée du répertoire limousin', *Revue Belge de Musicologie*, 3 (1949), pp. 5–36, at p. 21; and Wolff, 'How the News was Brought from Byzantium to Angoulême; or, The Pursuit of a Hare in an Ox Cart', *Byzantine and Modern Greek Studies*, 4 (1978), pp. 138–89, at p. 153.

James Grier

Of these, the most important is the colophon, in hexameter verse, that stands at the end of the libellus on fol. 72^v.[33]

> O Danihel monachus praelucens dogmate Christi
> in mirabilibusque bonis, tu sis Ademari,
> pertractans actis, qui hunc biblum rite notauit.

O Daniel, the monk, shining forth in Christ's doctrine and busying yourself with miraculous good deeds, may you be a friend of Adémar's, who noted this book according to religious usage.

The hand is undoubtedly Adémar's, as is evident from a comparison with the samples offered by Delisle and Landes.[34] Most distinctive are the way in which he writes the letters *re* and the slant of letters that use ascenders and descenders, like *s* and *p*. As well, the line of writing tends to vary, particularly when he does not have benefit of a rule, as in the middle line of the colophon. The identification of Adémar as scribe and therefore author of the colophon guarantees the meaning of the verb *noto*. Adémar uses it with precisely this meaning in his *Chronicon* when he describes the dispute between the Frankish cantors of Charlemagne and the papal cantors at the court

---

[33] The colophon is reproduced in Grier, '*Scriptio interrupta*', plate 17b, and has been printed in full several times: Delisle, *Le cabinet*, i, p. 389; id., 'Les manuscrits', p. 4; id., 'Notice', p. 352; *Chroniques de Saint-Martial de Limoges*, ed. Duplès-Agier, p. vi, n. 2; L. Gautier, *Histoire de la poésie liturgique au moyen âge: Les tropes* (Paris, 1886), p. 105, n. 1; Hooreman, 'Saint-Martial de Limoges', p. 21; R. L. Crocker, 'The Repertoire of Proses at Saint Martial de Limoges (Tenth and Eleventh Centuries)', 2 vols. (Ph.D. diss., Yale University, 1957), i, p. 191; Chailley, *L'école*, p. 83; Husmann, *Tropen- und Sequenzenhandschriften*, p. 130; C. Samaran and R. Marichal, *Catalogue des manuscrits en écriture latine portant des indications de date, de lieu ou de copiste*, ii: *Bibliothèque Nationale, fonds latin (nos 1 à 8.000)* (Paris, 1962), p. 57; Les Bénédictins du Bouveret, *Colophons de manuscrits occidentaux des origines au XVIe siècle*, 6 vols. (Spicilegii Friburgensis Subsidia, 2–7; Fribourg, 1965–82), nos. 256, 3267, i, pp. 33, 406; D. Escudier, 'Des notations musicales dans les manuscrits non liturgiques antérieurs au xiie siècle', *Bibliothèque de l'École des Chartes*, 129 (1971), pp. 27–48, at p. 36, n. 3; Huglo, 'Codicologie et musicologie', p. 79; id., 'On the Origins of the Troper-Proser', *Journal of the Plainsong & Mediaeval Music Society*, 2 (1979), pp. 11–18, at p. 14 (trans. of 'Aux origines du Tropaire-Prosaire', in *Nordiskt kollokvium i latinsk liturgiforskning*, iv (Oslo, 1978), pp. 53–65) (both Huglo's transcriptions contain two errors: he gives *dogmata* for *dogmate* and *actus* for *actis*); and P. Merkley, *Modal Assignments in Northern Tonaries* (Wissenschaftliche Abhandlungen, 56; Ottawa, 1992), p. 49. The translation is my own.

[34] Delisle, 'Notice', plates I–VI, between pp. 240–1; Landes, 'A Libellus', plates 21–2; and id., *Relics, Apocalypse, and the Deceits*, pp. 346–68. On his hand in general, see Delisle, 'Notice'; J. Vezin, 'Un nouveau manuscrit d'Adémar de Chabannes (Paris, Bibl. nat., lat. 7231)', *Bulletin de la Société Nationale des Antiquaires de France* (1965), pp. 44–52; J. A. Emerson, 'Two Newly Identified Offices for Saints Valeria and Austriclinianus by Adémar de Chabannes (MS Paris, Bibl. Nat., Latin 909, FOLS. 79–85v)', *Speculum*, 40 (1965), pp. 31–46, at pp. 34–5; M.-C. Garand, 'Auteurs latins et autographes des xie et xiie siècles', *Scrittura e Civiltà*, 5 (1981), pp. 77–104, at pp. 81–2; Landes, 'A Libellus', pp. 190–3, 202–4; and id., *Relics, Apocalypse, and the Deceits*, pp. 344–5.

The Musical Autographs of Adémar de Chabannes

of Pope Adrian I in 787: 'notaverat nota romana' ('he had noted with Roman notation').[35] So here, Adémar unequivocally identifies himself as the music scribe of at least the sequentiary, a conclusion already reached by Paul Hooreman and Michel Huglo.[36] Huglo goes on to infer that Daniel wrote its literary text.[37] Nowhere, however, does the colophon refer to Daniel as a text scribe. He is expert in doctrinal issues and does good deeds, but he does not appear to copy manuscripts. These verses seem rather to constitute a simple appeal to Daniel to remain kindly disposed towards Adémar, whose deep feelings for him may be revealed in another signature in the sequentiary, this one on fol. 60^r, which reads simply ADEMARVS MONACHVS DANIHEL MONACHVS.[38] (See Figure 1.) He may be the same Daniel who, along with another monk named Stephen, announced to Adémar the dissent Benedict of Chiusa was fomenting just as the Mass was to begin on 3 August 1029.[39] In fact, Adémar wrote the literary text in the rest of the sequentiary as well, as the partially texted sequentia *Celsa polorum* at the top of Pa 1121 fol. 60^r (Figure 1) shows.

Richard Crocker suggested that the main body of the manuscript was the work of Adémar, extrapolating the evidence from Adémar's signatures in the sequentiary to the surrounding manuscript context.[40] He did not specify whether Adémar wrote text, music, or both. Adémar's text hand, however, appears nowhere in the manuscript other than the sequentiary. This deduction is clear from the troped Mass for Saint Martial in Pa 1121. Here, and in the same Mass in Pa 1120, Adémar erased some of the cues for the Proper

---

[35] Adémar, *Chronicon* 2.8, ed. Bourgain *et al.*, p. 89. On the interpretation of this passage, see J. Grier, 'Adémar de Chabannes, Carolingian Musical Practices, and *Nota Romana*', *Journal of the American Musicological Society*, 56 (2003), pp. 43–98, at pp. 46–50.
[36] Hooreman, 'Saint-Martial de Limoges', p. 21; Huglo, 'Codicologie et musicologie', p. 79; and id., 'On the Origins', p. 14.
[37] Huglo, 'Codicologie et musicologie', p. 79; id., 'On the Origins', p. 14. Cf. Samaran and Marichal, *Catalogue des manuscrits*, ii, p. 57, who suggest, on palaeographic grounds, that the text was written by Adémar; and Escudier, 'Des notations musicales', p. 36, n. 3, who proposes that Adémar wrote the text, Daniel the music.
[38] Delisle, *Le cabinet*, i, p. 388; id., 'Les manuscrits', p. 4; id., 'Notice', p. 352; Gautier, *Histoire de la poésie*, p. 105, n. 1; Crocker, 'The Repertoire of Proses', i, p. 191; Chailley, 'Les anciens tropaires', p. 170, and *L'école*, p. 82; Samaran and Marichal, *Catalogue des manuscrits*, ii, p. 57; Les Bénédictins du Bouveret, *Colophons de manuscrits occidentaux*, no. 256, i, p. 33; Huglo, 'Codicologie et musicologie', p. 79; and id., 'On the Origins', p. 14.
[39] Adémar, *Epistola de apostolatu sancti Martialis*, col. 93A. See also Hooreman, 'Saint-Martial de Limoges', p. 21, n. 6; and Grier, '*Scriptio interrupta*', p. 234.
[40] Crocker, 'The Repertoire of Proses', i, pp. 190–1; ii, p. 146.

James Grier

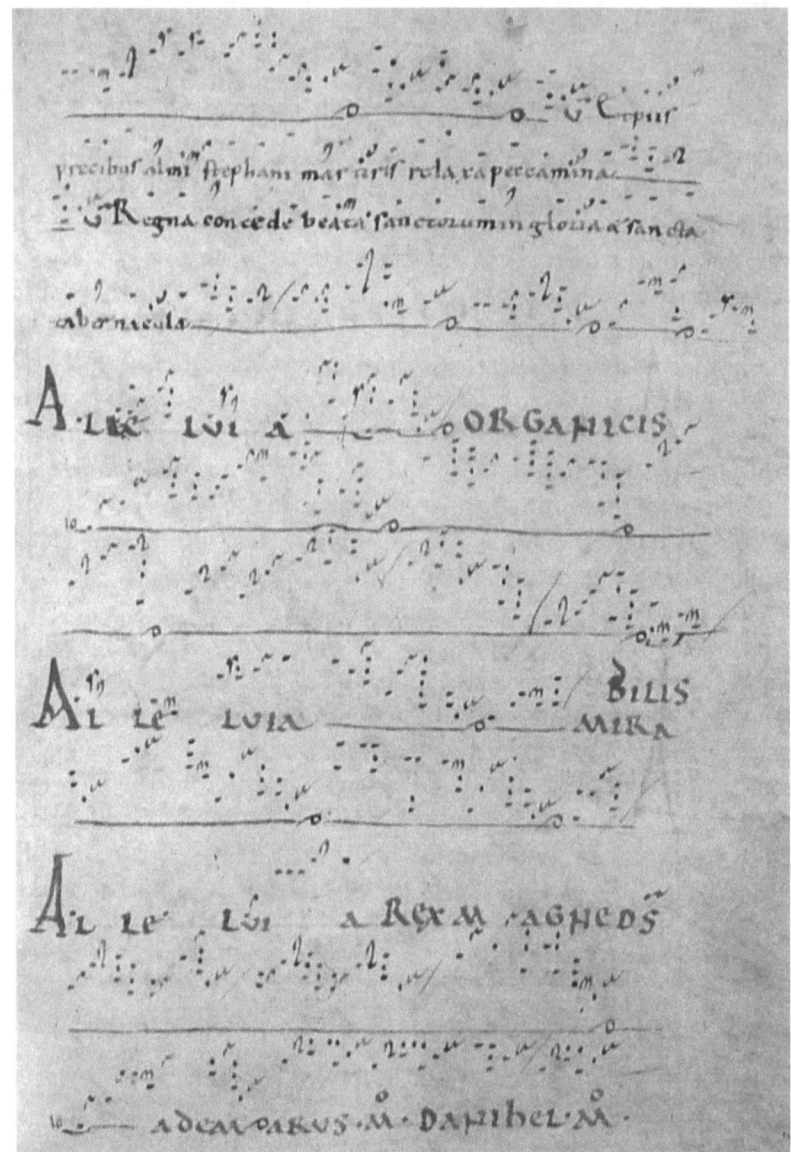

Figure 1   Paris, Bibliothèque Nationale de France, MS latin 1121, fol. 60ʳ. Cliché Bibliothèque Nationale de France

Mass chants that belong to Martial's episcopal liturgy and replaced many of them with cues to the apostolic Propers that he himself

The Musical Autographs of Adémar de Chabannes

composed. He made other changes to the trope texts with the same goal of creating the image of an apostolic liturgy.[41] The difference between Adémar's text hand and that of the principal scribe is clear, particularly in the module of writing, which is larger in Adémar's hand. Adémar also uses a small loop above a single-compartment *a*, as opposed to a single-compartment *a* without loop in the hand of the principal scribe. Therefore, the only portion of the codex in which Adémar's text hand appears, besides his alterations to the troped Mass for Saint Martial, is the sequentiary.[42]

During my extended consultation of Pa 1121 during the summer of 1999, I did detect that Adémar's music hand occurs throughout the codex.[43] The first sign I noticed was the similarity between the *cliuis* in the sequentiary and elsewhere. The *cliuis* is one of the very few ligatures in Aquitanian neumatic notation, and the form that appears in Pa 1121 is somewhat distinctive.[44] The neume represents two notes in descending melodic motion; it can indicate any interval from a second to a fifth, and greater intervals sometimes occur. *Cliues* that represent a descending second in the sequentiary are extremely compact, with markedly bowed vertical strokes, and they match the form found throughout Pa 1121. Further examination revealed that the *custos*, the symbol used to show the relative pitch of the first note of the succeeding line, and the *litterae significatiuae* also matched. I therefore attribute all of the music in Pa 1121, fols. 2–231, to Adémar's hand.[45]

---

[41] Pa 1120, fols. 46ʳ–51ᵛ; Pa 1121, fols. 28ᵛ–32ʳ. See Huglo, 'Codicologie et musicologie', pp. 79–81 and plate 10; and Grier, '*Ecce sanctum*', pp. 61–2.

[42] See also the analyses of the text hands by Chailley, 'Les anciens tropaires', pp. 169–71; id., *L'école*, pp. 81–3; Husmann, *Tropen- und Sequenzenhandschriften*, p. 130; and Merkley, *Modal Assignments*, pp. 48–9.

[43] Compare fol. 28ᵛ (reproduced at Huglo, 'Codicologie et musicologie', plate 10), from the libellus of Proper tropes, with fols. 58ʳ and 60ʳ (reproduced here as Figures 2 and 1, respectively) and 72ᵛ (reproduced at Grier, '*Scriptio interrupta*', plate 17b), from the sequentiary. I am very grateful to M. François Avril and Mme Marie-Pierre Laffitte, both of the Département des Manuscrits, Bibliothèque Nationale de France, for granting me generous access to Pa 1121.

[44] The ligated form of the neume that represents two notes in descending motion occurs only in combination with one or more preceding *puncta*; it nevertheless is called *cliuis* in Paléographie Musicale 13, p. 118.

[45] The musical notation begins on fol. 2ʳ; fol. 1 is a palimpsest used as a front cover for the manuscript, and possibly taken from the Saint-Martial Bible, Pa 5; see Gaborit-Chopin, *La décoration*, p. 42, n. 3. Fols. 207–9, at the end of the tonary, were originally left blank and were subsequently filled with a later addition that required fol. 210ʳ as well. The latter originally held the opening chants of the libellus of Alleluias with music in Adémar's hand, but it was erased to make room for the addition begun on fols. 207–9.

His contribution to the earliest stages of production is further attested by the ruling system used throughout the main body of the codex. That found in the sequentiary agrees with the ruling of the libellus of Proper tropes, with eleven rules to the page and a writing frame of 169 × 115 mm. The balance of the libelli in the first layer, beginning with the libellus of Ordinary tropes, employ thirteen rules per page on a writing frame of the same width, but a height of 185 mm to accommodate the two extra rules. Therefore, Adémar used parchment for the sequentiary that was prepared by or to the specifications of the principal scribe for the libellus of Proper tropes, and so his contribution remains precisely coincidental with that of the principal scribe.

The date of Pa 1121

Even with a firm attribution to Adémar, a more precise date for the codex is difficult to determine because we know relatively little about his whereabouts between the proposed *termini inter quos* for its production: the death of Roger de Chabannes on 26 April 1025 and Adémar's arrival at Saint-Martial in mid-1028. In another study, I suggested that Adémar's rate of production when working on Pa 909 was approximately two folios per day.[46] Of the 247 extant folios that now make up Pa 1121, Adémar entered music on 227. Furthermore, several gatherings are missing: the libelli of Proper tropes, Ordinary tropes, Alleluias, and particularly the proser, of which less than one full gathering survives, are all incomplete. The manuscript could easily have exceeded 250 folios in its original form and, if the proser was of any size, it might have reached 300. If Adémar worked on Pa 1121 at the same rate as he did on Pa 909, then he had to spend upwards of 120 working days in Limoges to complete the manuscript. Indeed the total might well have risen to 150 days or more if he did not work on the manuscript every day. Therefore, I posit a stay of approximately four to six months to allow him enough time to finish the codex.

Although we cannot ascertain where Adémar spent most of his time between 1025 and mid-1028, it is difficult to find a period of a half-year or so that he could have spent at Saint-Martial. He

---

[46] Grier, '*Scriptio interrupta*', p. 244.

The Musical Autographs of Adémar de Chabannes

narrates only two events in this period that he definitely witnessed, the return of Count William of Angoulême from a pilgrimage to Jerusalem in the third week of June 1027, and the count's death the following year on 6 April 1028.[47] He also describes William's entry into Limoges, en route back to Angoulême in the spring of 1027, but in much less detail. Nevertheless, Adémar might have been in Limoges about this time, possibly with Simeon and Cosmas, two Greek monks from Mount Sinai who met William while he was on pilgrimage, accompanied him for part of the journey home, and then went on ahead to Angoulême to await his return.[48] Landes suggested that Adémar went to Limoges with the two Greeks shortly before William's return,[49] and it is not impossible that he greeted the count there and then travelled with him back to Angoulême.

Therefore, before and after June 1027, Adémar could have enjoyed an extended stay in Limoges. Much of this time, however, from late 1026 until early 1028, Adémar spent on the first two recensions of his *Historia*, both of which were apparently composed in Angoulême.[50] He does seem to have made two trips to Limoges after Roger's death, once in 1025 and again in 1027.[51] Each visit presents problems for assigning to it the production of Pa 1121. Adémar apparently journeyed to Saint-Martial soon after his uncle's death in April 1025, possibly to attend his funeral. Under these circumstances, it strikes me as unlikely that the scriptorium would undertake an elaborate replacement (Pa 1121) for the Mass manuscript executed under the abbey's recently deceased cantor (Pa 1120).

Moreover, if Landes's reconstruction of events is accurate, Adémar's visit in 1027 could not have been long enough to

---

[47] Adémar, *Chronicon* 3.65–6, ed. Bourgain, *et al.*, pp. 184–7. On Count William's return and the possible error in the date, see Landes, *Relics, Apocalypse, and the Deceits*, pp. 167–70 and 372; on his death, *ibid.*, pp. 179–82.
[48] Eberwin, *Vita [sancti Symeonis]* 2.13–14, in *Acta sanctorum*, June, i, 3rd edn (Paris, 1867), p. 89a; and [Adémar de Chabannes], *Acta concilii lemovicensis II*, in *PL*, cxlii, col. 1363C. See Wolff, 'How the News was Brought', pp. 181–9.
[49] Landes, *Relics, Apocalypse, and the Deceits*, pp. 163–7, 370 and 372.
[50] *Ibid.*, pp. 158–61 and 172–7. Adémar, *Chronicon*, ed. Bourgain, *et al.*, pp. xiii–xxxi and cx–cxvi.
[51] Landes, *Relics, Apocalypse, and the Deceits*, pp. 122–4, 163–7 and 370. Cf. *ibid.*, pp. 138–9, where Landes suggests that Adémar also visited Limoges in 1026; this must be a misprint for 1027 because he assigns the same entries by Adémar in Pa 5239 to this sojourn as he does (*ibid.*, pp. 163–7) to the 1027 visit. Landes also suggests (*ibid.*, pp. 161 and 370), independently, another trip to Limoges in 1026, but notes that 'specific evidence for this one seems sparse' (*ibid.*, p. 161, n. 42).

complete his work on Pa 1121. Landes suggested that he took the Greeks Simeon and Cosmas to Limoges, but Adémar states that 'diu nobiscum Engolismae fuissent exspectantes principem civitatis' ('they were with me for a long time in Angoulême, awaiting the prince of the city').[52] Simeon and Cosmas travelled with William in the eastern Mediterranean before separating from the main party of pilgrims. They could not have arrived in Angoulême more than a few weeks before him. If they waited for him there 'for a long time' and then went to Limoges with Adémar (whence Adémar might have accompanied the count home), the visit would have been short, surely not adequate for Adémar to copy between 250 and 300 folios of music.

The signatures in the sequentiary of Pa 1121, however, offer a clue as to its date. At the bottom of fol. 58ʳ, Adémar wrote ADEMARVS MONACHVS SANCTI MARCIALIS.[53] (See Figure 2.) This statement is, of course, a lie, because Adémar repeatedly calls himself a monk, not of Saint-Martial, but of Saint-Cybard.[54] It may indicate, however, that he had turned his allegiance away from his home abbey to that of his ancestors, and the reason for that change is not far to seek. One of Count William's companions on pilgrimage, Richard, abbot of Saint-Cybard, died during the journey on 5 January 1027 before the pilgrims reached Constantinople.[55] Adémar had great hopes of succeeding Richard, but, shortly after William returned from pilgrimage in June of that year, the count named another of his fellow pilgrims, Amalfredus, to the office.[56]

---

[52] [Adémar], *Acta concilii lemovicensis II*, col. 1363C. See Landes, *Relics, Apocalypse, and the Deceits*, p. 372.

[53] Delisle, *Le cabinet*, i, p. 388; id., 'Les manuscrits', p. 4; id., 'Notice', p. 352; Gautier, *Histoire de la poésie*, p. 105, n. 1; Crocker, 'The Repertoire of Proses', i, p. 191; Chailley, 'Les anciens tropaires', p. 170, and *L'école*, p. 82; Samaran and Marichal, *Catalogue des manuscrits*, ii, p. 57; Husmann, *Tropen- und Sequenzenhandschriften*, p. 130; Les Bénédictins du Bouveret, *Colophons de manuscrits occidentaux*, no. 256, i, p. 33; Huglo, 'Codicologie et musicologie', p. 79, and 'On the Origins', p. 14; and Merkley, *Modal Assignments*, p. 49.

[54] 'Ademarum Engolismense monachum', *Chronicon* 3.45, ed. Bourgain, *et al.*, p. 165; 'Ademarus Egolismensis', *Epistola de apostolatu sancti Martialis*, col. 89B; 'revertens ad Egolismam civitatem, ubi ab ipsa tenerrima pueritia hactenus, aetate quadragenarius, vitam in monasterio beati Eparchii transigo', *ibid.*, col. 89C.

[55] Adémar, *Chronicon* 3.65, ed. Bourgain, *et al.*, p. 185. See Landes, *Relics, Apocalypse, and the Deceits*, pp. 157 and 162.

[56] Adémar, *Chronicon* 3.65, ed. Bourgain, *et al.*, p. 185. On the possibility of Adémar's anticipation of obtaining the office himself, see Landes, *Relics, Apocalypse, and the Deceits*, pp. 162–3; on Amalfredus, *ibid.*, pp. 170–1.

The Musical Autographs of Adémar de Chabannes

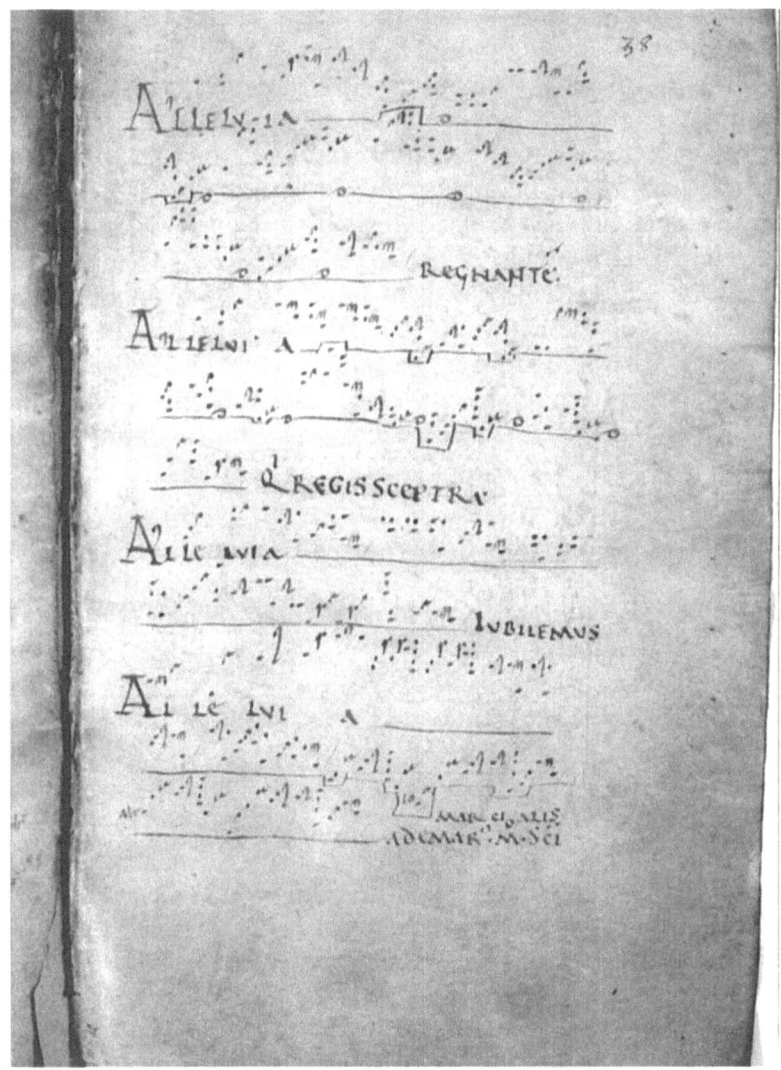

Figure 2   Paris, Bibliothèque Nationale de France, MS latin 1121, fol. 58ʳ. Cliché Bibliothèque Nationale de France

Adémar's disappointment at being overlooked and the subsequent death of Count William certainly motivated his trip to Limoges in mid-1028, where the enthusiasm for the cult of Saint Martial led him to embrace the saint's apostolicity.[57] It is possible that, between William's return to Angoulême in the summer of 1027 and his death the following April (two events that Adémar definitely witnessed), Adémar split his time between Saint-Cybard, where he produced the second recension of his *Chronicon*, and Saint-Martial, where he copied the music into Pa 1121. In any event, he could not have entered the signature on fol. 58^r before the installation of Amalfredus as abbot of Saint-Cybard, marking the effective end of his career at his home abbey. He may also at this time have made the entries in Pa 5239 that Landes attributed to his visit to Limoges with Simeon and Cosmas in May 1027.[58] I therefore propose that Pa 1121 was executed sometime between the return of Count William in mid-1027 and his death on 6 April 1028.

Adémar's shifting allegiance and the signature on Pa 1121 fol. 58^r

If Adémar's signature on fol. 58^r constitutes a subtle hint of his changing affections, its original placement in the sequentiary shows that he exercised a certain amount of caution in expressing it. The libellus originally consisted of two quaternions, from which the first folio is missing today.[59] Huglo, however, analyses the gathering structure as a ternion (fols. 58–63) followed by a single leaf (fol. 64) added to a quaternion (fols. 65–72).[60] His opinion seems to be based on the fact that fol. 64 is today glued to fol. 65, and that no stub exists, either between fols. 57 and 58 (which would show that fol. 64 was originally part of the first gathering) or between fols. 72 and 73 (which would place it in the second gathering). When the missing folio was removed, the cut was made along the fold of the bifolium. A strip of tape originally attached fol. 64 to fol. 63, and a stub of that

---

[57] For Adémar's account of William's death, see n. 47 above. See also Grier, '*Scriptio interrupta*', pp. 245–6.
[58] Landes, *Relics, Apocalypse, and the Deceits*, pp. 164–6 and 370.
[59] Crocker, 'The Repertoire of Proses', i, p. 192; and Husmann, *Tropen- und Sequenzenhandschriften*, p. 130.
[60] Huglo, 'Codicologie et musicologie', pp. 78–9, and 'On the Origins', p. 14 and n. 15 (note on p. 18).

The Musical Autographs of Adémar de Chabannes

Fols. 58–64

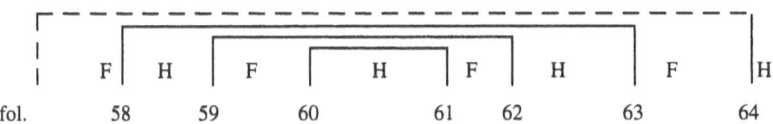

Fols. 65–72

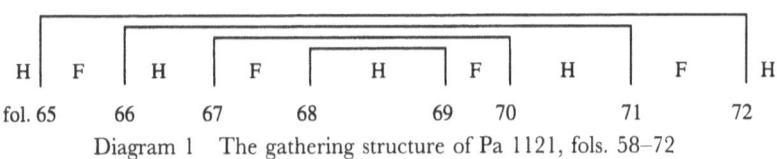

Diagram 1   The gathering structure of Pa 1121, fols. 58–72

piece is visible between fols. 57 and 58.[61] Nevertheless, the current state of the manuscript does not unequivocally indicate its original configuration.

That configuration is discernible, however, from the disposition of the hair and flesh surfaces of the parchment; this shows that fol. 64 is the last folio of the first gathering, which was originally, therefore, a quaternion. (See Diagram 1.) Quaternions in Aquitaine usually employ a regular alternation of hair and flesh sides of the parchment so that the facing surfaces of each opening are the same; the hair side is most often used for the outside surfaces of the quaternion.[62] As the diagram shows, both fols. 58^r and 64^r are flesh, making them unsuitable for the first folio of a gathering. Folios 64^v and 65^r, however, are hair, and so they could serve as the outside surfaces of their respective gatherings. Moreover, if fol. 64 is half of an original outside bifolium, the missing folio before fol. 58 would have begun the gathering with the usual hair surface.

In addition, the sequentiary in Pa 1121 lacks the first four sequentiae found in Pa 909. The first sequentia on fol. 58^r is identified as *Laetatus sum* in Pa 909, where it is assigned to the second Sunday of Advent.[63] The absence of a rubric in Pa 1121 is suggestive, as Adémar is meticulous about giving at least the titles of sequentiae in this manuscript. The title for *Laetatus sum*, therefore,

[61] See the bottom left corner of Figure 2 above.
[62] On typical gathering structure in Aquitanian manuscripts of this period, see Grier, 'Some Codicological Observations', pp. 16–18.
[63] Crocker, 'The Repertoire of Proses', i, pp. 200, 261.

could well have appeared at the bottom of a preceding folio. More compelling is the similarity in repertoire and order between the sequentiaries in Pa 909 and 1121.[64] This similarity, coupled with the absence in the main corpus of the sequentiary in Pa 1121 of any sequentia for the first Sunday of Advent, the first day of the liturgical year, indicates that the sequentiary of Pa 1121 originally opened with the same four sequentiae, all for Advent Sunday, that begin the sequentiary in Pa 909.

These four occupy one full page in Pa 909 (from the bottom of fol. 110^r to near the bottom of its verso). This reconstruction permits us to speculate on the reason for the disappearance of the sequentiary's first folio. Almost all of fol. 110^r in Pa 909 is blank. Adémar originally conceived an elaborate initial here.[65] It seems possible that such an initial might have been executed on the first page of the sequentiary in Pa 1121 (there would have been room for it, because the four sequentiae for Advent Sunday would not require the entire first folio, and it would be consistent with the level of decoration elsewhere in the codex, mentioned above), which was then excised because of its artistic value. In any event, it is clear that one folio is missing from the beginning of the sequentiary, that this folio contained the four sequentiae for the first Sunday of Advent given in Pa 909, and that Adémar's mendacious signature originally stood on the second folio of the codex.

Adémar placed it there in order to keep it hidden from all except those who actually used the libellus. The same pattern of concealment is to be found in Pa 5240, the first gathering of which was originally a separate libellus containing Easter tables for the years 1064–1594, and a letter, which purports to be from Pope John XIX, concerning the apostolic status of Martial.[66] The letter was composed by Adémar and constitutes the pivotal piece of evidence in the controversy over Martial's apostolicity: papal recognition of

---

[64] See the inventories *ibid.*, pp. 200–9, 261–9.

[65] *Ibid.*, i, p. 250; and Grier, '*Scriptio interrupta*', p. 249; Pa 909, fol. 110^r is reproduced *ibid.*, plate 27. Adémar left space for a similar initial at the beginning of the troped Mass for Saint Martial in Pa 909 (fol. 42^r); see Grier, '*Ecce sanctum*', pp. 71–2; id., 'Editing Adémar de Chabannes' Liturgy for the Feast of St Martial', *Plainsong and Medieval Music*, 6 (1997), pp. 97–118, at p. 117 (Pa 909, fol. 42^r is reproduced on p. 105); and id., '*Scriptio interrupta*', p. 249 (Pa 909, fol. 42^r is reproduced at plate 26).

[66] Landes, 'A Libellus' (text of the letter, pp. 200–1); see also id., *Relics, Apocalypse, and the Deceits*, pp. 274–6. The letter is also printed in *PL*, cxli, cols. 1149–50; and Saltet, 'Une prétendue lettre', pp. 129–30, who also provides commentary.

The Musical Autographs of Adémar de Chabannes

Martial's status. Adémar copied it, together with the Easter tables, into a kind of time capsule: the letter follows the Easter tables and ends on the penultimate folio of the gathering. No part of it, therefore, is visible on an outside surface of the gathering, and, from the inside, no one need turn to it until the Easter tables have been exhausted in 1594. By the time the letter was discovered, so Adémar hoped, all memory of the defeat of 1029 would have faded, and the letter would be taken as incontrovertible proof of Martial's apostolicity. Adémar's concealment of his signature in Pa 1121 is in no way as elaborate as his strategy in Pa 5240, but then the signature is not nearly as important to the polemic. Its purpose, I believe, is to associate Adémar with the abbey of Saint-Martial in the eyes of his companions in the scriptorium.

The libellus structure of Pa 1121

As in the case of Pa 1120 and 909, Pa 1121 consists of a series of libelli organised according to liturgical genre. Also like Pa 909, the order of the gatherings has been disrupted and some are missing.[67] Most libelli begin with a new gathering, but some overlap begins to appear later in the codex (e.g., the libellus of processional antiphons and the proser both end in the middle of a gathering). Consequently, it is difficult to ascertain precisely how many gatherings are lost. All music in the first layer of the manuscript, to the end of fol. 231^v, is in Adémar's hand.

1. Proper tropes, fols. 2–41. Begins on fol. 2^r, leaving fol. 1^r blank as an outside cover; fol. 1^v was left blank for a decoration. The libellus is incomplete at the end; fol. 41^v ends with a rubric for Saint Andrew.
2. Ordinary tropes, fols. 42–57. Begins with the Gloria trope *Omnipotens altissime* and is therefore incomplete at the beginning. The preceding gathering certainly contained Kyrie tropes and possibly an untroped version of so-called Gloria A to accord

[67] On the order of the gatherings in Pa 909 and attempts to reconstruct the original order, see Crocker, 'The Repertoire of Proses', i, pp. 255–8; Chailley, 'Les anciens tropaires', pp. 176–7; Husmann, *Tropen- und Sequenzenhandschriften*, p. 119; and Grier, '*Scriptio interrupta*', pp. 241–2. On the libellus structure of Pa 1121, see Crocker, 'The Repertoire of Proses', i, pp. 192–5; Chailley, 'Les anciens tropaires', pp. 169–71; Husmann, *Tropen- und Sequenzenhandschriften*, pp. 130–1; and Merkley, *Modal Assignments*, p. 48.

with the libellus of Ordinary tropes in Pa 1120, fols. 67^r–82^v. One or two gatherings are missing here, containing the end of the Proper tropes and beginning of Ordinary tropes. The libellus breaks off in the middle of a Gloria trope, and therefore is missing at least one gathering with the end of the Gloria tropes, as well as Sanctus and Agnus tropes. As in Pa 909, many of the Gloria tropes are introduced by rubrics that give specific liturgical assignments.[68]

3. Sequentiary, fols. 58–72. Music and text in Adémar's hand. The first folio is missing, as discussed above. The appendix breaks off with sequentiae for John the Baptist, in the middle of the liturgical year, and is therefore incomplete at the end. I treat the libellus in more detail below.

4. Tracts, fols. 73–89. Complete for the liturgical year. The libellus ends with a series of Benedictions, fols. 86^v–89^v.

5. Offertories, fols. 90–137. Complete for the liturgical year; fol. 137^v is blank.

6. Processional antiphons, fols. 138–79. Four litanies occur, fols. 161^v–165^r. The processional antiphons end on fol. 174^r with explicit. The balance of the gathering (through fol. 179^v) contains invitatories with their tones integrated (fols. 174^r–176^v), Lamentation of Jeremiah (fols. 176^v–178^r) and antiphons for the four Sundays after Epiphany (fols. 178^r–179^v). The Easter invitatory (fol. 175^{r-v}) has double notation in red and black with two different melodies; Adémar uses the same notational device in the seventy-two verses for Saint Martial, Pa 909, fols. 202^r–205^v.[69] The antiphons continue on fol. 218^r; see below.

7. Alleluias, fols. 180–86. The second gathering of the libellus of Alleluias that originally began on fol. 210^r; see below. Beginning with Assumption, it follows directly on from fol. 217^v. It ends with dominical Alleluias and is incomplete.

---

[68] For an inventory of the rubrics, see K. Rönnau, *Die Tropen zum Gloria in excelsis Deo: Unter besonderer Berücksichtigung des Repertoires der St. Martial-Handschriften* (Wiesbaden, 1967), p. 22.

[69] See M. P. Ferreira, 'Is it Polyphony?', *Revista Portuguesa de Musicologia*, 12 (2002), pp. 9–34, at pp. 31–2. On the seventy-two verses in Pa 909, see Hooreman, 'Saint-Martial de Limoges'; and Ferreira, 'Is it Polyphony?'.

The Musical Autographs of Adémar de Chabannes

8. Antiphons for gospel chants on the Sundays after Pentecost, fols. 187–95. A collection of antiphons commonly grouped together for each Sunday following Pentecost without assignment to specific gospel canticles.[70] There are several antiphons for each Sunday, typically three or four, although the first Sunday has seven. The gathering ends with a rubric for Vespers, and therefore the libellus is incomplete at the end.
9. Proser and tonary, fols. 196–209. Begins towards the end of the proser and contains mostly variable and dominical prosae. I give a more detailed analysis of its contents below. The tonary begins fol. 202^r, introduced by a rubric at the bottom of fol. 201^v, and ends on fol. 206^v.[71] Folios 207–9 were originally left blank; a piece was added much later in square notation and continues on to fol. 210^r, which was erased for the addition.
10. Alleluias, fols. 210–17. The first gathering of the libellus of Alleluias. The first folio was erased for the conclusion of the addition begun on fols. 207–9, and therefore, the chants for the first two Sundays of Advent at the beginning of the liturgical year are missing. The material on fol. 217^v carries on directly to 180^r; see above.
11. Antiphons with alleluias, Office of the Trinity, antiphons *ad ungendum infirmum* and antiphons for the three boys cast into the fire, fols. 218–31. The material on fol. 218^r continues on directly from the rubric at the bottom of fol. 179^v. The Office of the Trinity occupies fols. 223^v–229^r. The final gathering of the libellus, fols. 226–31, was originally a regular quaternion, but its outside bifolium is now missing. Consequently, the Trinity Office is lacking most of the second nocturn of Matins, which the first lost folio, originally between the current

---

[70] See R.-J. Hesbert (ed.), *Corpus antiphonalium officii*, 6 vols. (Rerum Ecclesiasticarum Documenta, Series Maior, Fontes, 7–12; Rome, 1963–79), i, no. 144, pp. 404–13; ii, no. 97^3, pp. 461–7. For Aquitanian examples, see Toledo, Biblioteca Capitular, MS 44.1, fols. 96^r–100^v; and MS 44.2, fols. 207^v–212^v; inventories of these two manuscripts are located in the CANTUS database, currently at http://publish.uwo.ca/ ∼ cantus/; that of the latter is also published as CANTUS, *An Aquitanian Antiphoner: Toledo, Biblioteca capitular, 44.2* (Wissenschaftliche Abhandlungen, 55/1; Ottawa, 1992).
[71] C. T. Russell, 'The Southern French Tonary in the Tenth and Eleventh Centuries' (Ph.D. diss., Princeton University, 1966), pp. 41, 43–6 (the tonary is transcribed *ibid.*, pp. 222–34); see also Evans, *The Early Trope Repertory*, pp. 271–3; and M. Huglo, *Les tonaires: Inventaire, analyse, comparaison* (Publications de la Société Française de Musicologie, 3rd ser. 2; Paris, 1971), pp. 155–6.

fols. 225ᵛ and 226ʳ, would have contained. The last antiphon on fol. 231ᵛ, *Lux erat in flammis*, is complete and ends several lines above the bottom of the page;[72] it therefore concludes the collection of antiphons for the three boys, and may have ended the first layer of the codex.

12. Folios 232–47 contain later additions with no trace of Adémar's handwriting in either music or text. The gathering fols. 240–7 begins with a fragmentary proser, the first piece of which is an incomplete copy of the prosa *Nobis annua* (fol. 240ʳ), composed by Adémar for the Dedication of the cathedral of Saint Stephen in Limoges.[73]

The presence of Adémar's music hand in Pa 1121 explains one aspect of his contribution to the production of Pa 909 and permits one further speculation. He was apparently invited to write the music in Pa 909 soon after his arrival at Saint-Martial in mid-1028; such an invitation marks the esteem in which the monks of the scriptorium held him. I would aver that that esteem stemmed from his innovation of accurately heighting the neumes for the representation of relative pitch and was earned through his participation in the execution of Pa 1121. Moreover, his achievement gained in value when the monks of Saint-Martial attempted to produce another music codex.

The principal portion of Pa 909 from which Adémar's hand is altogether lacking is the libellus of Offertories (fols. 206–45). The text hand is the same as the rest of the first layer of the manuscript, but Adémar did not write the music and it is not accurately heighted. I suggest that the scriptorium undertook this libellus first, as part of their commission from the abbey of Saint-Martin, but they were disappointed when their music scribe could not replicate Adémar's accuracy in heighting the music in Pa 1121. The latter, of course, reposed in the library or sacristy, where it could be compared with the scriptorium's latest production. When Adémar appeared at Saint-Martial in mid-1028, the monks of the scriptorium leapt at the opportunity to have him enter the music in Pa 909, and perhaps to learn from him the technique of heighting neumes.

[72] Hesbert (ed.), *Corpus antiphonalium officii*, iii, no. 3650, p. 321.
[73] On the fragmentary proser, see Crocker, 'The Repertoire of Proses', i, p. 199. On *Nobis annua*, see Grier, '*Scriptio interrupta*', p. 248.

The Musical Autographs of Adémar de Chabannes

The proser and sequentiary of Pa 1121

The proser and sequentiary of Pa 1121 transmit what I take to be Adémar's first essays in musical composition. Therefore, I adjudge this codex to contain the earliest identifiable compositional autographs. Five unica occur in the fragmentary proser in Pa 1121 with music in Adémar's hand (fols. 196–201).[74] The melodies of these pieces also occur, grouped together but not consecutively, in the sequentiaries of Pa 1121 (fols. 68^r–69^r) and 909 (fols. 123^r–124^v), also with music in Adémar's hand, and in no earlier sequentiary. Margot Fassler attributes one of these, *Alte uox canat*, to Adémar on the grounds that it narrates the vision of the cross that appeared to him in 1010 when he was studying at Saint-Martial under Roger de Chabannes.[75] I certainly concur with regard to the melody, not only for this prosa, but for the other four unica as well, because they appear in no earlier source than Adémar's autograph. And it is always possible that Adémar prevailed upon the principal scribe of Pa 1121 to include a few of his original compositions in this proser, but I stop short of attributing the prosa texts to Adémar.

Above, I mentioned the similarity in repertoire and arrangement between the sequentiaries in Pa 909 and 1121. Of the seventy sequentiae Adémar copied into Pa 909, all but six appear in Pa 1121, and four of these are the pieces for the first Sunday of Advent that almost certainly filled the missing first folio of the libellus. The other two are *Arce polorum* and *Apostolorum gloriosa*, both original compositions of Adémar's discussed in more detail below. Moreover, Adémar added a second series of sequentiae to Pa 1121, beginning on fol. 70^r with the rubric ALIAE SEQVENTIAE QVAE NON SVNT VALDE IN VSV.

There follow twenty-two sequentiae, arranged according to the liturgical year, none of which occurs in Pa 909.[76] As the rubric suggests, these sequentiae knew very limited circulation, and, when Adémar came to compile the sequentiary for Pa 909, he suppressed

---

[74] Crocker, 'The Repertoire of Proses', i, pp. 197–8. The unica are *Mente pura, Per saecula, Alte uox canat, Corde deuoto* and *Coaequalis*.
[75] M. Fassler, *Gothic Song: Victorine Sequences and Augustinian Reform in Twelfth-Century Paris* (Cambridge, 1993), pp. 47–56. Text of the prosa: *ibid.*, pp. 53–4; and *Analecta hymnica*, 55 vols., ed. G. M. Dreves, C. Blume and H. M. Bannister (Leipzig, 1886–1922) (hereafter *AH*), vii, no. 94, p. 107. Adémar's narrative: *Chronicon* 3.46, ed. Bourgain, *et al.*, pp. 165–6 (quoted in Itier, *Chronique* 53.2, ed. Lemaître, p. 14).
[76] See the inventory in Crocker, 'The Repertoire of Proses', i, pp. 207–9.

them. I find this slightly unusual in that I believe Adémar to be the composer of two of these sequentiae: the first bears the rubric LETATVS SVM, the Alleluia verse for the second Sunday of Advent, identifying its liturgical assignment and melodic incipit (fol. 70^r); the second occurs on the Feast of Saint John the Evangelist with the as yet unidentified rubric HODIERNA (fol. 70^v).[77] Perhaps Adémar was dissatisfied with these early attempts at composition and so excluded them from Pa 909 with the rest of the appendix.

The appendix ends abruptly at the bottom of fol. 72^v with two sequentiae for John the Baptist (24 June), about halfway through the liturgical year. A rubric at the bottom of the page introduces the next sequence as *Christo cantica*, but no sequence follows.[78] No prosa with this incipit is known to Dreves or Crocker.[79] Adémar provides the further identification 'sancte confessor'. An Alleluia with the verse *Sancte confessor* occurs in Pa 1121 with music in his hand (fol. 217^r), where it is assigned to Martial; although other sources preserve this melody, the verse is unique to Pa 1121.[80] Perhaps this is a vestige of another original composition of Adémar's, a prosa for Saint Martial. The last item on the page is the colophon mentioned above. These last texts suggest two conclusions: first that Adémar originally intended to continue the appendix, probably to complete the liturgical year; and second that, having arrived at the end of a quaternion, and needing probably one or two additional folios for the pieces that remained, he decided to abandon the sequentiary, and wrote the verse colophon that ends the gathering.

For the sequentiae in his appendix, Adémar drew on two sources that we can now place in the library at Saint-Martial by the beginning of AD 1028 at the latest: Pa 1084 and 1118. Of the twenty-two pieces that make up the appendix to Pa 1121, two, mentioned above, are elsewhere unattested in Aquitanian sources, and so might be original compositions of Adémar's, and nineteen occur in Pa 1084, five of which are unique to Pa 1084 and 1121. The remaining sequentia, neither an original composition of

---

[77] *Ibid.*, pp. 207–8.
[78] *Ibid.*, p. 209.
[79] *AH*, vii; Crocker, 'The Repertoire of Proses', ii, pp. 7–79.
[80] K.-H. Schlager, *Thematischer Katalog der ältesten Alleluia-Melodien aus Handschriften des 10. und 11. Jahrhunderts, ausgenommen das ambrosianische, alt-römische und alt-spanische Repertoire* (Erlanger Arbeiten zur Musikwissenschaft, 2; Munich, 1965), no. 38, pp. 86–7.

The Musical Autographs of Adémar de Chabannes

Table 1 *Sequentiae and prosae for the feast of Saint Martial*

Pa 1120, fols. 125ᵛ–130ᵛ	Pa 1121, fols. 64ʳ–65ᵛ	Pa 909, fols. 118ʳ–119ᵛ
Valde lumen	Valde lumen	Arce polorum
Concelebremus	Concelebremus	Apostolorum gloriosa
Alme deus	Alme deus	Valde lumen
Alle sublime	Alle sublime	Alme deus
Adest nempe	Marcialis clara	Concelebremus
	Adest nempe	

Adémar's nor found in Pa 1084, appears in the sequentiary in Pa 1118, along with fourteen of the pieces common to Pa 1084 and 1121. As I demonstrate below, Adémar knew Pa 1118, and so might have derived those fifteen sequentiae in his appendix from it, but no known source for the other five sequentiae besides Pa 1084 survives. It is possible that he had access to another witness, now lost, that contained these five sequentiae, but the troper of Pa 1084 can also be placed at Saint-Martial immediately after the events of 3 August 1029, as I discuss below. Therefore, I suggest that Adémar had access to both codices when he was compiling the sequentiary of Pa 1121 in the second half of 1027 or early 1028.

The order of the sequentiae in Pa 909 and 1121 is virtually the same, but those for the feast of Saint Martial in the former demonstrate Adémar's revision of the repertoire to support Martial's apostolic status. In Pa 909, he presents five sequentiae for this feast, as shown in Table 1, the second of which, *Apostolorum gloriosa*, is introduced by the rubric ALIA DE SANCTO MARCIALE APOSTOLO GALLIAE. Furthermore, the first two, *Arce polorum* and *Apostolorum gloriosa*, occur in no earlier source than Pa 909, and both, when texted as prosae, unequivocally endorse Martial's apostolic status.[81] For these reasons, I attribute their composition to Adémar. The sequentiary, therefore, forms a part of Adémar's apostolic programme, fully consistent with the rest of Pa 909. Moreover, he assigns two sequentiae present in Pa 1121, *Alle sublime* and *Marcialis clara*, to Alpinian and Austriclinian in Pa 909, the companions of

[81] Both prosae occur consecutively in another section of Pa 909 in Adémar's hand: *Arce polorum*, fols. 198ʳ–199ᵛ; *Apostolorum gloriosa*, fols. 199ᵛ–201ᵛ. Editions of the texts: *AH*, vii, nos. 168–9, pp. 185–8.

Martial. Finally, *Adest nempe*, which belongs to the group of sequences for Martial in both Pa 1120 and 1121, appears at the end of the sequentiary in Pa 909 (fol. 205^{r–v}), as a piece of variable assignment. This later sequentiary, then, represents the true 'second edition', created to support Martial's apostolicity.

In Pa 1121, Adémar presents six sequentiae that follow the selection and order of prosae for the feast in Pa 1120 with one exception, as Table 1 shows, *Marcialis clara*. No prosa with this incipit is known to Dreves or Crocker from the surviving Aquitanian sources.[82] The melody appears with at least three other texts, however: *Alle uox promat*, for Saint Yrieix, *Alle boans luia*, for Saint Valery, the first convert of Martial, and *Alma cohors*, for Martial himself.[83] Clearly, the sequence is closely, though not exclusively, associated with the cult of Martial, and it is possible that Adémar composed a prosa, now lost, for the melody, beginning with the phrase 'Marcialis clara'. It may have appeared in the lost portion of the proser in Pa 1121.

Revisions to Pa 1121 in Angoulême

When Adémar left Limoges on 4 August 1029, he took with him, I believe, several music manuscripts, namely Pa 909, which included his autograph of the failed apostolic liturgy, Pa 1120 and 1121, the abbey's two other troper-prosers, and Pa 1118, which I discuss below. The principal evidence for this theft is the series of erasures and revisions to the cues for the Mass Propers in the troped Mass for Saint Martial in both Pa 1120 and 1121, mentioned above; he also made changes to the prosa *Valde lumen*, for Martial, in Pa 1120 (fol. 126^v). Prior to 3 August 1029, Adémar would have had no need to effect these alterations because all his energy would have been expended on preparations for the inauguration of the apostolic liturgy, including the completion of Pa 909. The subsequent changes to Pa 1120 and 1121 constitute a retrospective falsification of the abbey's earlier liturgical manuscripts, codices that pre-date his attempt to introduce the apostolicity; and he made the changes

---

[82] See n. 79 above.
[83] Editions of the texts: *AH*, vii, nos. 126, 204 and 218, pp. 139–40, 224–6 and 238 respectively. See also Crocker, 'The Repertoire of Proses', ii, pp. 12–14.

The Musical Autographs of Adémar de Chabannes

in reaction to the failure of the apostolic liturgy. Therefore, I suspect he altered the manuscripts after 4 August, back in Angoulême.

The second piece of evidence that supports my hypothesis is the supplementary Proper troper added to Pa 1084. Opinions about the origin of this manuscript vary, but there is general agreement that it was produced around the year 1000 somewhere in southern Aquitaine.[84] The original collection of Proper tropes (fols. 53^v–90^r, termed Pa 1084b by the Corpus Troporum group of researchers, following the analysis of David Hughes)[85] contains one characteristic that seems common in tropers from southern Aquitaine, but not in those from Limoges: when an Introit is assigned several trope complexes, the first consists of a single introductory trope. Thus, after this first trope, the Introit antiphon is sung without further interruption. The supplementary troper (fols. 39^r–50^v, termed Pa 1084a) converts these single introductory tropes into full trope complexes by providing further trope elements that then introduce the subsequent phrases of the host Introit antiphon, and thereby bring this troper into line with practice at Saint-Martial.[86]

My reconstruction of the chain of events is that, first, Adémar took Pa 909, 1120 and 1121 (along with Pa 1118), but left behind Pa 1084 because it did not accord with liturgical practice at Saint-Martial and he had already consulted it when compiling the sequentiary of Pa 1121. Second, the monks at Saint-Martial, faced with the unexpected loss of all three Mass books suited to their usage, had at their disposal only Pa 1240, which was obsolete, and Pa 1084, whose usage did not accord with theirs. Consequently, they adapted for their purposes the troper of Pa 1084. If any one of Pa 1120, 1121 or 909 had remained at the abbey, its monks would not have had to follow this course. And so Adémar returned to

[84] Crocker, 'The Repertoire of Proses', i, pp. 56–64; Chailley, 'Les anciens tropaires', pp. 171–2; id., L'école, pp. 83–6; and Husmann, Tropen- und Sequenzenhandschriften, pp. 120–2.

[85] D. G. Hughes, 'Further Notes on the Grouping of the Aquitanian Tropers', Journal of the American Musicological Society, 19 (1966), pp. 3–12, at p. 3, n. 3; and G. Björkvall, G. Iversen and R. Jonsson (eds.), Corpus troporum, iii: Tropes du propre de la messe, part 2, Cycle de Pâques (Acta Universitatis Stockholmiensis, Studia Latina Stockholmiensia, 25; Stockholm, 1982), p. 38, n. 1 (note on p. 41).

[86] A. E. Planchart, 'Fragments, Palimpsests, and Marginalia', Journal of Musicology, 6 (1988), pp. 293–339, at p. 301, n. 19; id., 'On the Nature of Transmission and Change in Trope Repertories', Journal of the American Musicological Society, 41 (1988), pp. 215–49, at p. 221, n. 13; and Grier, 'Ecce sanctum', p. 72. Hughes, 'Further Notes', pp. 8–10, remarks on the close relationship between Pa 1120 and 1084a without speculating on the latter's production at Saint-Martial.

James Grier

Table 2 *Portions of Pa 909 in which the music only was copied by Adémar de Chabannes*

Folios	Inventory
9ʳ–40ᵛ, 49ʳ–59ʳ	Proper tropes
86ʳ–109ᵛ	Ordinary tropes
126ʳ–140ᵛ	Tracts
140ʳ–149ᵛ	Benedictions, litany, antiphons, miscellaneous items for Easter
150ʳ–165ᵛ	Processional antiphons
166ʳ–167ʳ	Alleluias
168ᵛ–173ᵛ	Antiphons for Easter
174ʳ–197ᵛ	Alleluias
246ʳ–251ʳ	Processional antiphons
251ʳ–257ᵛ	Tonary
258ʳ–269ᵛ	Antiphons

Pa 1121, the manuscript in which he initiated his musical activities at Saint-Martial as a scribe and perhaps as a composer as well, modifying the troped Mass for Saint Martial to make it agree with the apostolic liturgy he himself had created.

PA 909

I have described elsewhere how Pa 909 began production as a commission from the scriptorium of Saint-Martial for the neighbouring abbey of Saint-Martin in Limoges, and how Adémar participated in its preparation as music scribe from soon after his arrival in Limoges in mid-1028.[87] Table 2 shows those portions of Pa 909 for which Adémar wrote the music alone. I date these contributions to the period between his arrival at Limoges and the dedication ceremony of 18 November 1028, when he decided to embrace the apostolicity of Saint Martial and appropriated the entire production of the codex. From this deduction, and from the calculation that the production of the first layer of Pa 909 progressed at the rate of two folios per day, it is possible to propose a slightly more specific date for Adémar's arrival at Saint-Martial.[88]

---

[87] Grier, '*Scriptio interrupta*'. On Pa 909 in general, see Crocker, 'The Repertoire of Proses', i, pp. 246–58; Chailley, 'Les anciens tropaires', pp. 174–7; id., *L'école*, pp. 88–92; and Husmann, *Tropen- und Sequenzenhandschriften*, pp. 118–19.

[88] See n. 46 above.

The Musical Autographs of Adémar de Chabannes

Table 3   *Portions of Pa 909 in which music and text are in the hand of Adémar de Chabannes*

Folios	Inventory
41ʳ–48ᵛ	Proper tropes (fols. 42ʳ–46ᵛ troped Mass for Saint Martial)
59ʳ–61ᵛ	Proper tropes
61ᵛ–62ʳ	Alleluias for Saint Martial
62ᵛ–77ᵛ	Office and miscellaneous liturgical items for Saint Martial
79ʳ–85ᵛ	Offices for Saints Valery and Austriclinian
110ʳ–125ᵛ	Sequentiae (fols. 118ʳ–119ᵛ sequentiae for Saint Martial)
177ᵛ–178ʳ	Alleluias for Saint Martial
198ʳ	Sequentia
198ʳ–201ᵛ	Prosae for Saint Martial
202ʳ–205ʳ	Versus de Sancto Marciale LXXta IIo
205ʳ⁻ᵛ	Sequentia
251ʳ	Processional antiphon for Saint Martial
251ʳ–257ᵛ	Tonary: additions by Adémar

The 179 folios on which Adémar inscribed the music would have taken ninety days to produce.[89] If we assume that he did not work seven days a week, we might suggest that this copying took 120 days or four months. Therefore, he could not have arrived at Saint-Martial any later than 18 August (allowing him exactly three months to complete the copying), or, more likely, on or before 18 July. I propose that he arrived sometime in the month of June. Thus, he would have some time after 25 April (on which date he was still in Angoulême) to prepare for his departure, make the journey to Limoges, and settle into work in the scriptorium at Saint-Martial.

Table 3 lists those portions of Pa 909 in which Adémar wrote both text and music. His text hand has long been recognised in this second layer of the codex, beginning with Paul Hooreman's identification of Adémar as the scribe of the seventy-two verses about Saint Martial (Pa 909 fols. 202ʳ–205ʳ).[90] He also states that Adémar's hand occurs elsewhere in the codex, without specifying where, and, on the evidence of the colophon from Pa 1121 fol. 72ᵛ, suggests that he may have copied the music of the seventy-two verses.[91] Jacques Chailley mentions the appearance of a second

---

[89] To the 163 folios listed in Table 2, I add the lost gatherings E and H, which comprised a further sixteen folios. See Grier, '*Scriptio interrupta*', pp. 241–2.
[90] Hooreman, 'Saint-Martial de Limoges', pp. 16–30.
[91] *Ibid.*, p. 21.

hand in this codex, and makes a tentative attribution to Adémar.[92] Only John A. Emerson unequivocally attributes fols. 59–85 of Pa 909 to Adémar.[93] Emerson's conclusion is contradicted, however, by Michel Huglo, who states that the Office for the Feast of Saint Martial (fols. 62^v–77^v) is not in Adémar's hand.[94] Unfortunately, Huglo gives no substantiation for his statement, and an examination of the codex shows that he is incorrect.

A comparison of the hand in the colophon from Pa 1121 fol. 72^v with that in the second layer of Pa 909 (e.g., the troped apostolic Mass and the Office for Saint Martial) shows that Adémar is indeed the text scribe (and music scribe as well) of the apostolic Office for Saint Martial in Pa 909.[95] Particularly striking is the slant of the letters *s* and *f*, for example, in the phrase 'consortes ipsius effici' of the Magnificat antiphon *Venerandam* (fol. 62^v). His music hand is characterised by the orientation of vertically aligned *puncta*, which, in Aquitanian notation, indicate descending motion. Adémar typically writes them from the top with a slight slant back to the left.

Huglo may have been misled in his conclusion by the manuscript's format. Adémar's handwriting on fols. 59^r–64^v is more compressed than it is elsewhere in the codex, and the Office for Saint Martial begins here, on fol. 62^v. These folios were prepared for the principal scribe of the manuscript's first layer, whose handwriting is smaller than Adémar's. Each folio is ruled with fourteen lines, as in the other gatherings of the first layer. The gatherings that were prepared for Adémar are ruled with eleven lines to accommodate his larger hand.[96] Hence, while he completed the gathering fols. 57–64, he adopted a slightly smaller module of writing.[97]

---

[92] Second hand: Chailley, 'Les anciens tropaires', pp. 174–5. Tentative attribution to Adémar: id., *L'école*, pp. 88–91.
[93] Emerson, 'Two Newly Identified Offices', pp. 33–5.
[94] Huglo, 'Codicologie et musicologie', p. 80.
[95] Reproductions of Pa 1121, fol. 72^v and representative folios of the troped Mass and Office for Saint Martial (fols. 42^r and 62^v, respectively) appear in Grier, '*Scriptio interrupta*', plates 17b, 26 and 18 respectively.
[96] See e.g. fols. 62^v and 70^v, where Adémar writes on parchment with fourteen and eleven rules respectively, and fol. 57^{r-v}, where the principal scribe of the first layer writes on parchment with fourteen lines; both hands appear on fol. 59^r; reproduced in Grier, '*Scriptio interrupta*', plates 18 (fol. 62^v), 25 (fol. 70^v), 20 (fol. 57^r), 21 (fol. 57^v) and 22 (fol. 59^r).
[97] For a similar problem encountered by a new scribe assuming production of a manuscript on parchment prepared for an earlier scribe whose hand was a different size, see the early twelfth-century Aquitanian versarium Pa 1139, discussed in Grier, 'Some Codicological

The Musical Autographs of Adémar de Chabannes

Adémar produced the second layer of the manuscript between 18 November 1028, when, in the aftermath of the dedication of the abbatial basilica, he decided to undertake the composition of an apostolic liturgy for Saint Martial, and 3 August 1029, when the liturgy received its unsuccessful première. At this point, the manuscript was incomplete, lacking two initials that were clearly intended to be elaborate. They were to begin the troped Mass for Saint Martial (fol. 42ʳ) and the sequentiary (fol. 110ʳ).[98] After Adémar's debate with Benedict of Chiusa, Pa 909, with its explicitly apostolic rubrics, was useless, and so he abandoned it.

I identify a substantial number of the musical items in this second layer of Pa 909 as original compositions of Adémar's. These include the five Proper items in the apostolic Mass for Martial, several tropes and two sequences (which appear in both texted and untexted form; I attribute both text and music to Adémar); a handful of items in the apostolic Office for Martial, together with some processional items; and most of the chants in the Offices for Valery and Austriclinian.[99] This manuscript, then, preserves the bulk of Adémar's original compositions, and provides the fullest record of his compositional activity.

PA 1978 FOLS. 102–3

After his return to Angoulême, Adémar continued producing music manuscripts. The endleaves at the back of Pa 1978 consist of a

---

Observations', pp. 25–9; reproduced in B. Gillingham (ed.), *Paris Bibliothèque Nationale, fonds latin 1139* (Veröffentlichungen Mittelalterlicher Musikhandschriften, 14; Ottawa, 1987).

[98] Grier, '*Scriptio interrupta*', p. 249, and plates 26 (fol. 42ᵛ) and 27 (fol. 110ʳ).

[99] On the Mass items, see Grier, '*Ecce sanctum*', pp. 38–40, 47–54; and 'The Music is the Message: Music in the Apostolic Liturgy of Saint Martial', *Plainsong and Medieval Music*, 12 (2003), pp. 1–14. On the Office for Martial, see J. Grier, 'Liturgy and Rhetoric in the Service of Fraud: Adémar de Chabannes and the Apostolicity of Saint Martial', in *Latin Culture in the Eleventh Century: Proceedings of the Third International Conference on Medieval Latin Studies, Cambridge, September 9–12 1998*, 2 vols., ed. M. W. Herren, C. J. McDonough and R. G. Arthur (Publications of the Journal of Medieval Latin, 5; Turnhout, 2002), i, pp. 384–97, at pp. 391–7. On the Offices for Valery and Austriclinian, see Emerson, 'Two Newly Identified Offices'. The full list of nearly 100 extant musical compositions appears in J. Grier, *The Musical World of a Medieval Monk: Adémar de Chabannes in Early Eleventh-Century Aquitaine* (Cambridge, forthcoming).

bifolium with both music and text in Adémar's hand (fols. 102–3).[100] (See Figure 3.) The contents are portions of an Office for Saint Cybard (the patron saint of Adémar's home abbey in Angoulême), and of what seems to be an Office for the octave of Saint Martial.[101] The Matins responsories of the latter are written in full, but the antiphons are cued *ut supra*. Adémar thereby refers to a complete set of antiphons written above, probably in the Office for the feast itself, in a portion of the manuscript that does not survive. This agrees precisely with the arrangement of materials in the episcopal Offices for the feast and the octave of Saint Martial in Pa 1085, an antiphoner written before the Dedication of 18 November 1028, possibly under the direction of Roger de Chabannes, and perhaps in his own hand.[102]

Adémar produced this manuscript after he wrote the Office for Saint Martial in Pa 909, as a copying slip in *Venerandam*, first responsory in the first nocturn, shows. The refrain in Pa 909 gives the reading 'aquitanico', which Adémar changed in Pa 1978 to 'galliarum'. This word then occurs in the *repetendum* following the verse, and, at this point in Pa 1978, Adémar reverted to the reading of Pa 909, 'aquitanico', which shows that he was copying Pa 1978 from his own autograph exemplar in Pa 909.[103] The appearance of an Office for Saint Cybard further suggests a dating for the manuscript after Adémar's return to Angoulême following the disastrous events of 3 August 1029 in Limoges.

The folios that constitute the endleaves in Pa 1978 are conjunct but not consecutive, and so came from a gathering of at least two bifolia. The original manuscript was larger, however, and contained

---

[100] First tentatively identified in Delisle, 'Notice', pp. 350–1, who reproduces Pa 1978, fol. 102ᵛ as plate VI between pp. 240 and 241; see also J. Lair, *Études critiques sur divers textes des Xe et XIe siècles*, ii: *Historia d'Adémar de Chabannes* (Paris, 1899), p. 281; Bibliothèque Nationale [de France], Département des Manuscrits, *Catalogue général des manuscrits latins*, ii (Paris, 1940), p. 269; and Samaran and Marichal, *Catalogue des manuscrits*, ii, p. 99. Unequivocally identified as the work of Adémar in Huglo, 'Codicologie et musicologie', p. 80. But cf. Gaborit-Chopin, 'Les dessins', p. 225, who lists these folios among the autographs of Adémar without discussion.

[101] The texts of the items for Cybard are given in Delisle, 'Notice', pp. 351–2.

[102] Feast of Saint Martial, Pa 1085, fols. 76ᵛ–77ʳ; octave, fols. 77ᵛ–78ʳ. On Pa 1085, see J. Grier, 'The Divine Office at Saint-Martial in the Early Eleventh Century: Paris, BNF lat. 1085', in M. E. Fassler and R. A. Baltzer (eds.), *The Divine Office in the Latin Middle Ages: Methodology and Source Studies, Regional Developments, Hagiography, Written in Honor of Professor Ruth Steiner* (New York, 2000), pp. 179–204.

[103] *Venerandam* occurs at Pa 909, fol. 63ᵛ, and at Pa 1978, fol. 103ʳ.

The Musical Autographs of Adémar de Chabannes

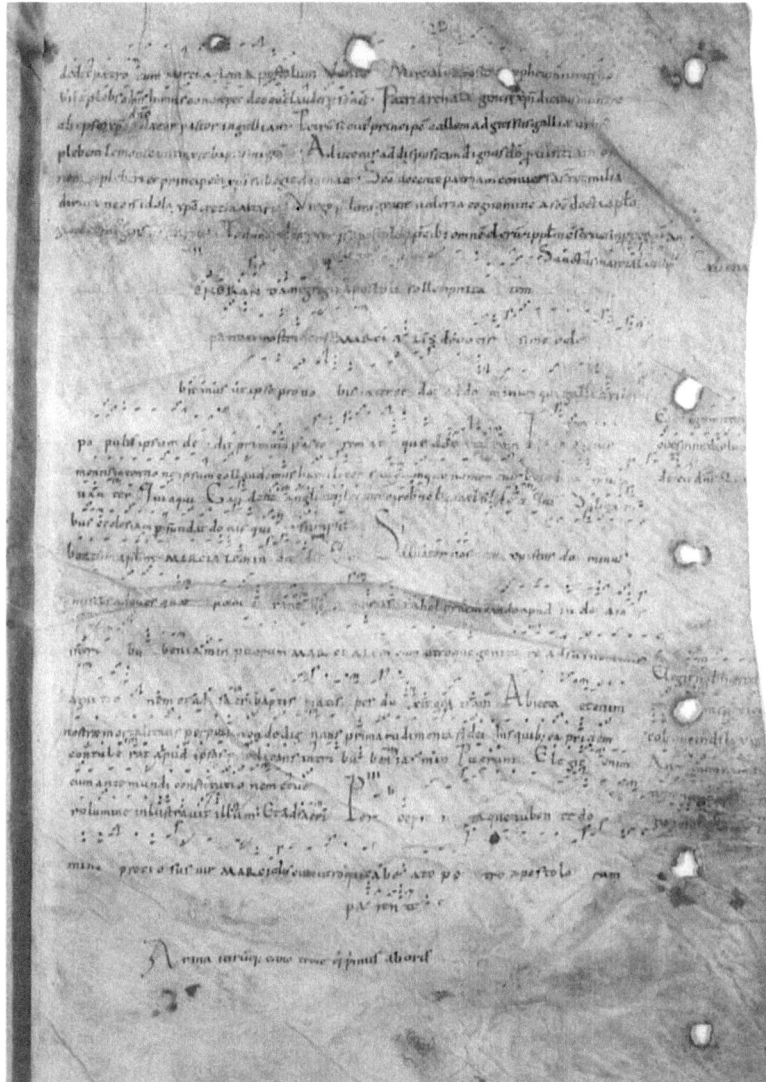

Figure 3 Paris, Bibliothèque Nationale de France, MS latin 1978, fol. 103ʳ. Cliché Bibliothèque Nationale de France

at least the following material: Offices for the feasts of Saint Martial (30 June), Saint Cybard (1 July), and the octave of Saint Martial (7 July). The last two Offices would almost fill one quaternion (the nearly universal structure for gatherings in manuscripts of this era

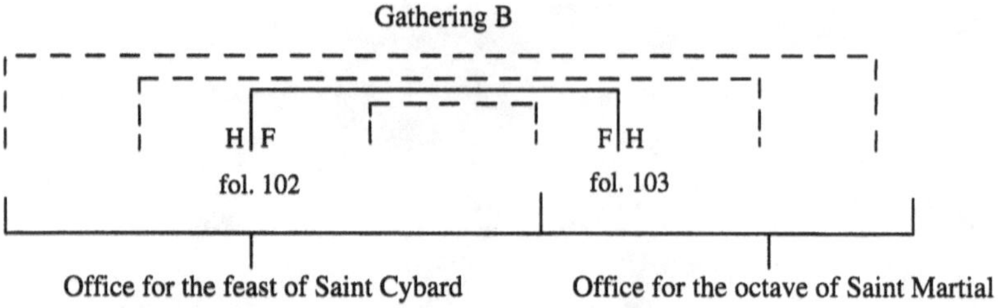

James Grier

Gathering B

```
┌─────────────────────────────────────┐
│  ┌──────────────────────────────┐   │
│  │  H│F           F│H           │   │
│  │  fol. 102      fol. 103      │   │
└──┴──────────────┴───────────────┴───┘
       │                    │
Office for the feast of Saint Cybard    Office for the octave of Saint Martial
```

Diagram 2   The putative gathering structure of Pa 1978, fols. 102–3

from Saint-Martial). With the typical arrangement of quaternions at Saint-Martial in mind, it is possible to posit the situation of the endleaves from Pa 1978 given in Diagram 2.[104]

As a hair surface, fol. 102^r could be the first of any size gathering, or the third bifolium of a quaternion, as I suggest in Diagram 2. The top of fol. 103^r opens with the invitatory for Matins of the octave of Saint Martial, and therefore the Office began, with the Magnificat antiphon for First Vespers, on the verso of the previous folio. The rest of fol. 103 contains the first nocturn of Matins plus the first two responsories from the second nocturn. Folio 103^v ends about two-thirds of the way through the respond of the second responsory. Adémar would have written, on the two folios that originally followed fol. 103, the rest of the second nocturn, the third nocturn, antiphons for Lauds, four antiphons for the little hours and the Magnificat antiphon for Second Vespers. These items would just have filled the final two folios of the quaternion I designate as gathering B.

Folio 102 contains the second nocturn of Matins for the feast of Saint Cybard, as well as most of the final responsory from the first nocturn, the antiphon ad cantica that opens the third nocturn, and the beginning of the first responsory that follows. The rest of the third nocturn and the antiphons for Lauds would fill the next folio, leaving the next recto and perhaps half of the succeeding verso for the completion of the Office; items that Adémar most likely placed here include the Benedictus antiphon for Lauds, antiphons for the little hours and the Magnificat antiphon for Second Vespers. The following items from the beginning of the Office would have preceded fol. 102, in reverse order: the first nocturn of Matins,

[104] See above, n. 62.

The Musical Autographs of Adémar de Chabannes

Table 4 *Projected contents of gathering A, Pa 1978*

Office	Musical item	Space
First Vespers	Magnificat antiphon	0.3 page
Matins	Invitatory	0.2 page
Matins, First Nocturn	six antiphons	1 page
	four responsories	1.5 pages
Matins, Second Nocturn	six antiphons	1 page
	four responsories	1.5 pages
Matins, Third Nocturn	antiphon ad cantica	0.2 page
	four responsories	1.5 pages
Lauds	five antiphons	1 page
	Benedictus antiphon	0.3 page
Little hours	four antiphons	0.7 page
Second Vespers	Magnificat antiphon	0.3 page
TOTAL		9.5 pages = 4.75 folios

preceded by its invitatory, and the Magnificat antiphon for First Vespers. The nocturn probably occupied one full folio (just what the second nocturn takes on fol. 102), and perhaps half of the preceding verso held the Invitatory and the Magnificat antiphon. These two Offices, then, would nearly fill our proposed gathering B, with the probable exception of the first recto and some, perhaps half, of the first verso.

Another gathering must have preceded gathering B, in which the Office for the feast of Saint Martial, to which the Office on fol. 103 alludes, would have been found. The makeup of gathering A, however, is somewhat less certain. Table 4 gives the proposed contents of an Office for the feast of Saint Martial, with an estimate of how much room each component would take, based on the layout of the existing fols. 102-3 from gathering B. My calculations show that nearly five folios would be required for these texts. Approximately three-quarters of the first folio of gathering B would be available before the beginning of the Office for Saint Cybard, and the remainder of the Office for the feast of Saint Martial could be accommodated in a binion, gathering A, as suggested in Diagram 3.

The problem with this analysis and hypothesis is that it would appear to be unusual for Adémar to start this libellus with a binion.

James Grier

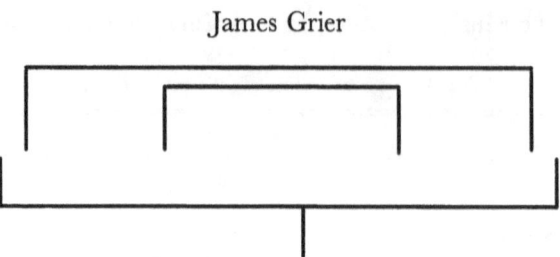

Office for the feast of Saint Martial
Diagram 3   Proposed structure of gathering A, preceding proposed gathering B of Pa 1978

He does use a binion in Pa 909, but it occurs at the end of the Offices for Saints Valery and Austriclinian, companions of Saint Martial (fols. 82–85).[105] The fact that this binion completes, rather than begins, a section or libellus distinguishes the two situations. It is certainly conceivable that gathering A, like gathering B, was a quaternion, in which case we would need to speculate on what might have filled its first four folios. The feast of Saints Peter and Paul falls on 29 June, the day before the feast of Saint Martial, and this feast may have been sufficiently important to Adémar for him to include it here because one of the abbatial basilicas at Saint-Martial in Limoges was dedicated to Saint Peter.[106]

It is always possible, of course, that the original manuscript was larger, perhaps even a full antiphoner for the entire liturgical year. The nature of the surviving texts, their relationship with Pa 909, and Adémar's copying habits in other liturgical manuscripts, particularly the second layer of Pa 909 with its devotion to Martial, however, all combine to suggest that this project was limited in scope. The original form of the manuscript most probably comprised the three Offices for Martial and Cybard, described above, possibly preceded by an Office for Saint Peter or Peter and Paul, and supplemented by an Office for the octave of Cybard, to mirror the arrangement for Martial.

In the Office for Martial, Adémar alters the distribution of material between main feast and octave. First, he retains the same group of antiphons for the main feast and the octave, as in Pa 1085.

[105] Grier, '*Scriptio interrupta*', pp. 246–7.
[106] Lasteyrie, *L'abbaye de Saint-Martial de Limoges*, pp. 321–2; see also the Dedication feast on 2 May in the kalendars of Pa 1240 (fol. 12va) and Pa 822 (fol. 4^r), and the Dedication Office on the same date in Pa 1085 (fols. 65^r–66^r).

The Musical Autographs of Adémar de Chabannes

Then he shifts the responsories for the main feast to the octave. He used a similar strategy in Lauds of the apostolic Office in Pa 909. There, he brought into the main feast the antiphons assigned in Pa 1085 to the octave, and deferred those for the main feast in Pa 1085 to an appendix in Pa 909.[107] Finally, he added verses to the responsories in Pa 1978, giving as many as five (for *Instante uero* in the second nocturn). Many of these appear in the margin and thus show Adémar revising as he produced the manuscript. Multiple responsorial verses constitute a distinguishing characteristic of the Office liturgy at Saint-Martial as attested by Pa 1085.[108] Adémar takes the practice to one extreme here. He also takes the opportunity to reaffirm his devotion to the patron saint of his home abbey in Angoulême, Cybard, by supplying an Office with a large number of original compositions. The endleaves of Pa 1978, too, constitute a compositional autograph.

PA 1118 FOL. 248

The penultimate folio of Pa 1118 contains a copy of the two pieces for the procession to Montjovis with which Adémar ends the Office for Saint Martial in Pa 909.[109] Their texts are here written in Adémar's hand also, as Richard Landes was the first to point out.[110] (See Figure 4.) Originally, no musical notation was entered, and that which is today present was inscribed later by someone other than Adémar. Subsequently, portions of both texts were erased on the top half of fol. 248ᵛ, and sequentiae written over the erasures in another hand. Circumstantial evidence strongly suggests that both processional chants are original compositions of Adémar's, and so he may have wished to make an additional copy of both pieces to help ensure their survival. Neither text carries any substantive variants from the versions in Pa 909.

The presence of Adémar's hand in this codex gives us important information about its history. The text at the top of fol. 248ʳ, the

---

[107] J. A. Emerson, *An Edition of Four Medieval Offices Dedicated to Saint Martial de Limoges: Their Literary Origins and Liturgical Development*, ed. J. Grier (Studies in Music from the University of Western Ontario, 18 (for 1999); London, Ont., 2004), p. 45.
[108] Grier, 'The Divine Office', pp. 185–6.
[109] *[A]ue pastor optime* and *O saluatoris minister*, Pa 909, fols. 73ᵛ–74ᵛ; a second copy of the latter occurs in Adémar's hand over an erasure at fol. 251ʳ.
[110] Landes, *Relics, Apocalypse, and the Deceits*, p. 342.

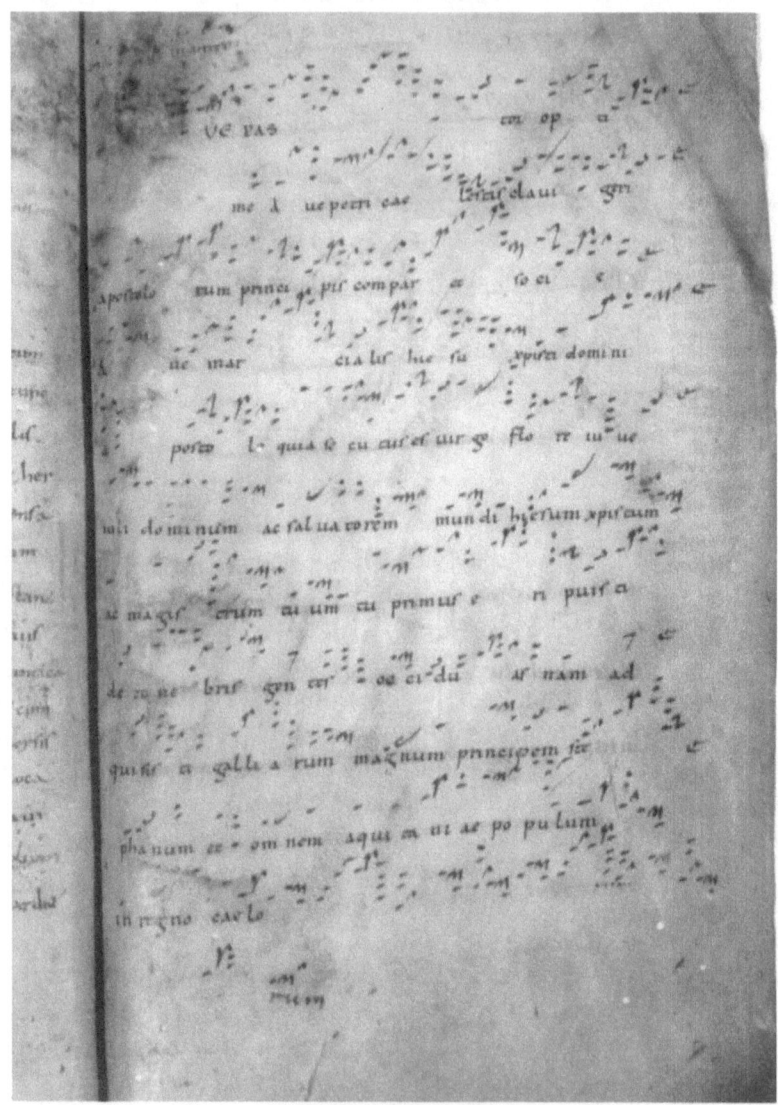

Figure 4 Paris, Bibliothèque Nationale de France, MS latin 1118, fol. 248ʳ. Cliché Bibliothèque Nationale de France

The Musical Autographs of Adémar de Chabannes

secular song *Iam dulcis amica uenito*, continues from the preceding verso, and so the bifolium fols. 248–49 already formed part of the book when Adémar came to enter his texts on fol. 248.[111] This evidence thus overturns Chailley's dates for this portion of the codex; he posited the end of the eleventh century for *Iam dulcis*, and the twelfth or thirteenth century for what are now identified as Adémar's additions.[112] I assert that the song was present in Pa 1118 by mid-1029 at the latest and that Adémar added the processional material on fol. 248 between August 1029 and his departure on pilgrimage in 1033. Therefore, Pa 1118 was present in the library at Saint-Martial before 4 August 1029, the date of Adémar's departure from the abbey, along with Pa 1084, and furthermore, he took it with him on his flight back to Angoulême. I leave aside speculation as to why the monks at Saint-Martial would collect two large troper-prosers from other houses in Aquitaine, probably within a quarter-century or so of their production, and why the houses in question relinquished them.

In summary, Adémar began his professional career as a music scribe with the production of Pa 1121 at Saint-Martial, probably in the second half of 1027 or early 1028. In this codex, he introduced the technique of accurately heighting the neumes to show precise relative pitch information. In conjunction with the *custos*, this device permitted the accurate recording of all the intervallic information for a melody. The notation does not allow a musician to read a previously unknown melody from sight, but it constitutes a centrally important step towards a fully literate musical notation. This accomplishment seems to have given him sufficient prestige in the scriptorium at Saint-Martial that its monks invited him to contribute to the execution of Pa 909, a commission for the neighbouring abbey of Saint-Martin in Limoges, soon after his arrival there in

---

[111] Editions of *Iam dulcis amica uenito*: *AH*, xi, no. 91, pp. 57–8; and *The Cambridge Songs (Carmina cantabrigensia)*, ed. and trans. J. M. Ziolkowski (Garland Library of Medieval Literature, 66 series A; New York and London, 1994), no. 27, pp. 92–5 (commentary pp. 251–60). See also P. Dronke, *Medieval Latin and the Rise of European Love-Lyric*, 2nd edn, 2 vols. (Oxford, 1968), i, pp. 271–4; and *Secular Medieval Latin Song: An Anthology*, ed. B. Gillingham (Wissenschaftliche Abhandlungen, 60/1; Ottawa, 1993), pp. 28–33 (commentary, id., *A Critical Study of Secular Medieval Latin Song* (Wissenschaftliche Abhandlungen, 60/2; Ottawa, 1995), pp. 74–5).

[112] Chailley, 'Les anciens tropaires', p. 179; and *L'école*, p. 94.

mid-1028. This codex eventually became the vehicle for Adémar's apostolic liturgy for Martial.

After the debacle of 3 August 1029, he continued working on music manuscripts, now back at Saint-Cybard. He completed one small libellus, the surviving fragment of which is now in Pa 1978, containing Offices for Saints Cybard and Martial, the patron saints of the two abbeys with which he was most closely associated; and he added two of his original compositions on an empty folio at the back of Pa 1118, one of the music manuscripts he took from the library at Saint-Martial. This material adds little to the dossier advocating Martial's apostolic status. The manuscripts are plain, without decoration or elaborate rubrics. They are the output of a man working alone, without significant resources, perhaps in despair.

Yet, these documents preserve a bold story that permits us to acknowledge and appreciate the contributions of Adémar de Chabannes to ecclesiastical and music history. They record the singular musical accomplishments of an extraordinary musician of the Central Middle Ages. Among those accomplishments stand a number of original compositions written in the composer's autograph hand. They also attest a key development in the history of Western musical notation, namely the use of the vertical axis to indicate relative pitch, a significant step towards full musical literacy. And finally, these manuscripts present us with the strategic liturgical programme devised by Adémar to secure the recognition of Martial's status as an apostle. They counteract Adémar's failure and obscure death, which might have caused us to overlook the significance of his musical autographs altogether. They speak, now louder than Adémar's own voice, of a remarkable musical career.

University of Western Ontario

Yossi Maurey

A COURTLY LOVER AND AN EARTHLY KNIGHT TURNED SOLDIERS OF CHRIST IN MACHAUT'S MOTET 5

> These words seem to sound like something carnal, but nevertheless spiritual things are described by means of them.
> Richard of St Victor, *The Twelve Patriarchs*

The tenor occupies a special role in vernacular motets of the thirteenth and fourteenth centuries: not only does it underpin the melodies of the upper voices contrapuntally, it also provides intellectual and interpretative undergirding for the texts of these pieces. The biblical or liturgical context of a tenor, drawing on well-understood exegetical and literary traditions, often facilitates an allegorical reading of the upper voices, and vice versa. Because of the foundational nature of the tenor within the Ars nova motet in particular, the identification of the exact musico-liturgical sources of this voice, where possible, is of special significance. While the origins of most of Machaut's twenty-one Latin tenors have been identified,[1] the tenor of one work, Motet 5 (*Aucune gent/Qui plus aimme/*T. *Fiat*

Large portions of this paper were written at the Center for Renaissance Studies, the Newberry Library, Chicago, while I was an Annette Kade Fellow in French Studies in the Middle Ages during 2001–2. I am particularly grateful to Professor Paul Gehl, Custodian, John M. Wing Foundation on the History of Printing at the Newberry Library, who read an earlier version; I greatly benefited from his prudent observations. I would also like to thank Professors Margaret Bent, Amnon Linder and Craig Wright, who read this paper in various stages of writing and made several invaluable comments. I also benefited from the comments of colleagues who attended readings of earlier versions of this paper at the meeting of the International Musicological Society in 2002, at a colloquium held at the Hebrew University of Jerusalem in May 2003, and also at the annual meeting of the American Musicological Society in November 2003. Finally, I am most grateful to Professor Anne Walters Robertson, who accompanied this paper from its inception, and made critical suggestions throughout its development.
  The epigraph comes from Richard of St Victor, *The Twelve Patriarchs, The Mystical Arc, Book Three of the Trinity*, trans. and ed. G. A. Zinn (The Classics of Spirituality; New York and Toronto, 1979), p. 76.
[1] For listings of Machaut's motets see L. Earp, *Guillaume de Machaut: A Guide to Research* (Garland Composer Resource Manuals, 36; Garland Reference Library of the Humanities, 996; New York and London, 1995), p. xvii, and A. W. Robertson, *Guillaume de Machaut and Reims: Context and Meaning in his Musical Works* (Cambridge, 2002), pp. 80–1. There remain two motets whose tenors have never been identified, Motets 13 and 18. On the latter, see *ibid.*, pp. 53–68.

Yossi Maurey

voluntas tua, hereafter M5), is alleged to have a most unusual source.[2] I offer new observations about the tenor of M5 that emphasise certain compositional procedures congruent with Machaut's practice in writing his motets and may tie together the various secular and sacred references in the piece.

MOTET 5: TEXTS AND TENOR

Motet 5 is a four-voice work with a Latin tenor that is paired with an untexted contratenor. Tenor and contratenor move in a rhythmic retrograde motion (see below, pp. 204–5) beneath two French-texted voices, the motetus and the triplum (see text below). These two upper lines carry texts in the masculine voice emblematic of the courtly-love idiom. The narrator of the triplum incessantly complains about the hardships inflicted on him by his lady but vows nonetheless to remain entirely hers; he concludes by alluding to Yvain and his lion, characters in a romance by Chrétien de Troyes. The narrator of the motetus, who is somewhat less optimistic than the speaker in the triplum, believes that those who love most suffer most. The text of the tenor, *Fiat voluntas tua* (Thy will be done), underscores the frame of mind depicted in both voices: the will of the speakers is subsumed in that of their ladies.

Text and translation

Triplum
Aucune gent m'ont demandé que j'ay
Que je ne chant et que je n'ay cuer gay,
Si com je sueil chanter de lié corage;
Et je leur di, certes, que je ne sçay.
Mais j'ay menti, car dedens le cuer ay
Un trop grief dueil qui onques n'assouage.
Car sans sejour ay mise ma pensée
A bonne Amour faire ce qui agrée,
Ne à nul fuer n'i pensasse folage;
Et je sçay bien que ma dame honnourée,
Que je tant criem, si m'a ma mort jurée
Par crueus cuer et par simple visage.
Car, quant je voy son gracieus viaire,
D'un dous ottroy me moustre un exemplaire

Motetus
Qui plus aimme plus endure
Et plus mainne dure vie,
– Qu'Amours qui est sans mesure
Assés plus le contralie, –
Que il mauvais qui n'a cure
De li, einsois met sa cure
En mal et en villonnie.
Hé! Diex, que n'ont signourie
Les dames de leur droiture,
Que ciaulz qui ont la pointure
D'amours au cuer atachie
Choisissent sans mespresure!
S'einsi fust, je m'asseüre,
Tels est amés qui ne le seroit mie

[2] M5 is edited in *Polyphonic Music of the Fourteenth Century*, ed. L. Schrade (Monaco, 1956), ii, pp. 123–6. More recently, a new transcription of M5 has been provided in J. Boogaart, 'Encompassing Past and Present: Quotations and their Function in Machaut's Motets', *Early Music History*, 20 (2001), pp. 1–86, at pp. 81–6.

A Courtly Lover and an Earthly Knight

Et si me vuet tenir en son hommage,
Ce m'est avis; mais aus doleurs retraire,
J'ay cent tant pis qu'on ne me porroit faire,
Car nuls ne puet penser si grief damage
Com le refus que ses durs cuers m'envoie;
Et si l'aim plus, se Diex m'en envoit joie,
Que riens qui soit. Dont n'est ce droite
  rage?
Certes, oïl; mais, pour riens que je voie,
De ce peril issir je ne voudroie,
Car tous siens sui sans changement de gage,
Quant esperer me fait ma garison;
Et c'est tout cler que monsignour Yvon
Par bien servir, non pas par vasselage,
Conquist l'amour dou grant lion sauvage.

Et telz haïs qui tost aroit amie.

Tenor FIAT VOLUNTAS TUA

FIAT VOLUNTAS TUA

Triplum
Some people have asked me what is wrong, why I do not sing and my heart is not merry, for I am wont to sing with a happy heart; and I say to them, 'Truly, I do not know'. But I have lied, for in my heart I have a very great sorrow which is never eased. For I have ceaselessly turned my thoughts both to doing that which is pleasing to good Love and to avoiding all thought of folly; and yet I know well that my honoured lady, whom I so fear, has sworn to cause my death through her cruel heart and sweet face. For when I see her gracious countenance she seems to me a very example of sweet acceptance, and I believe that she wishes me to pay her homage; but, to speak of my sorrows, I have a hundred times worse than anyone might do to me, for none could think so great a harm as the refusal that comes to me from her hard heart; and – may God send me joy of it! – I love her more than anything in the world. Am I not then on the road to madness? Truly, I am; but for nothing I might see would I wish to be free from this danger, for I am entirely hers, with no exchange of pledge, for she causes me to hope for relief; and it is quite clear that my lord Yvain won the love of the great wild lion through true service and not through his knightly valour.

Motetus
He who loves most endures most and lives the hardest life, because Love, who lacks measure, most opposes him, for the wicked fellow cares nothing for him, but rather puts his effort into doing him harm and playing him base tricks. Dear God, why do not ladies exercise such sovereignty over their favours so as to choose unerringly those who have the arrow of love fixed in their hearts! I am certain that, if this were so, many who are now loved would not be, and many a one who is hated would soon have his lady's love.

Tenor
THY WILL BE DONE.[3]

---

[3] Slightly adapted from the translation of C. Donagher, in Robertson, *Guillaume de Machaut and Reims*, pp. 301–2.

Example 1   The tenor of M5: Leech-Wilkinson's pastiche hypothesis (adapted from *Compositional Techniques*, ii, example 19)

Two important attempts have been made to elucidate the musical source of the tenor of M5. The first is an ingenious hypothesis by Daniel Leech-Wilkinson, who offers a pastiche theory, suggesting that the tenor is based (1) partly on the melody set to the words *Fiat voluntas tua sicut in coelo et in terra* (Thy will be done in earth as it is in heaven), as extracted from a certain *Pater noster* melody, and (2) partly on the tenor of Philippe de Vitry's Motet 6, *Douce playsence/ Garison*/T. *Neuma quinti toni* (see Example 1).[4]

More recently, another theory has been advanced, albeit more cursorily, by Jacques Boogaart, who suggested that the tenor of M5 is based on the melody that sets the words *Fiat voluntas tua* found in the Maundy Thursday responsory *In monte Oliveti*, and since the matching is based primarily on textual, not musical criteria (as the author himself recognises), this melody is perhaps conflated in part with the tenor of Vitry's Motet 6, similar to Leech-Wilkinson's suggestion (see Example 2).[5]

The common element in both theories is the supposition that the tenor of M5 combines two different chants. Yet the use of a double

---

[4] D. Leech-Wilkinson, *Compositional Techniques in the Four-Part Isorhythmic Motets of Philippe de Vitry and his Contemporaries* (Outstanding Dissertations in Music from British Universities; New York, 1989), i, pp. 88–104. Vitry's Motet 6 is edited by Schrade in *Polyphonic Music of the Fourteenth Century*, i, pp. 72–5.

[5] 'Encompassing Past and Present', pp. 70–1.

A Courtly Lover and an Earthly Knight

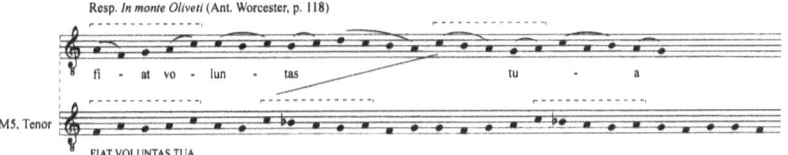

Example 2 The tenor of M5 and the responsory *In monte Oliveti* (Boogaart, 'Encompassing Past and Present', p. 71)

tenor source is highly unusual in thirteenth- and fourteenth-century motet composition and would represent a radical departure from Machaut's compositional norm.[6] In fact, Boogaart evokes a pastiche hypothesis only as an afterthought, indicating that 'maybe the chant was conflated with Vitry's tenor, the *Neuma quinti toni*?'[7] His melodic comparison, in addition, leaves much to be explained: the responsory segment has a different final than that of Machaut's tenor, it opens with a descending third while the tenor of M5 opens with an ascending one, and a substantial part of the tenor's melody cannot be accounted for in the suggested chant segment.[8] In short, the melody set to the words *Fiat voluntas tua* in the responsory *In monte Oliveti* is not a convincing source for the tenor of M5. Let us now examine Leech-Wilkinson's pastiche theory, which relies on somewhat different lines of reasoning that deserve to be explored in depth.

Although in his complete-works manuscripts Machaut clearly indicates that the tenor tag of M5 is *Fiat voluntas tua*, Leech-Wilkinson cites melodic material that accompanies a much longer text. Machaut occasionally did construct his tenors using more

---

[6] Indeed, I know of only one motet whose tenor is a combination of two chants: Vitry's *Heu fortuna subdola/Aman novi*/T. *Heu me, tristis est anima mea*, found in the *Roman de Fauvel* (I thank Margaret Bent for drawing my attention to this unique example). As Susan Rankin notes, Vitry explicitly identifies his tenor as having a double source: the first four notes of the tenor correspond to the opening of the antiphon *Heu me, quia incolatus meus prolongatus est* from the Office of the Dead, while most of the remainder corresponds to the opening of the responsory *Tristis est anima mea usque ad mortem* for Maundy Thursday. See Rankin, 'The Divine Truth of Scripture: Chant in the *Roman de Fauvel*', *Journal of the American Musicological Society*, 47 (1994), pp. 203–43, at pp. 241–2. In Vitry's motet, then, the two chant sources combined into a single tenor are clearly identified both textually and musically. In M5, by contrast, Machaut alludes to the text of a single chant alone, and there is no reference to *Neuma*, for instance. As we will see below, in all probability Machaut was referring to a single musical source as well.

[7] 'Encompassing Past and Present', p. 71.

[8] Significantly, even Boogaart's pastiche proposition cannot provide a convincing solution, for it too would result in an unsatisfactory match, leaving several notes unaccounted for.

melodic material than the tag would suggest, but it is nevertheless possible, as we will see, to locate a substantial portion of the tenor of M5 in a melody that is set to exactly the same words that Machaut used. This modus operandi conforms to his practice in the majority of his other Latin-tenor motets.

In order to understand the challenges that M5 poses, it is essential to situate it within the broader context of Machaut's other motets. Machaut's motet repertoire is somewhat atypical for the fourteenth century, for he took great care to name his tenors by designating their precise liturgical or secular source. While, for most composers, the possibility exists that discrepancies between their intentions and the scribe's actions within a particular manuscript may occur, Machaut is unique in that he was not only a poet and composer, but also a supervisor of scribes, a trio of activities with significant implications.[9] Not only did he choose a certain melody for the tenor of M5, but he also made it known in his manuscripts that this melody comes from a chant segment set to the words *Fiat voluntas tua*. Indeed, the majority of Machaut's tenors take exactly the melody that lies above the words named in the tenor tag, and this melody always hails from a single chant.[10] This implies that Machaut himself regarded the tenor source as significant, and it suggests that the tenor melody and its text are important factors in the inception and reception of the motet.

Given Machaut's well-known precision in these matters, it is therefore unlikely that the tenor source for M5 is a pastiche, especially since the tenor's text, *Fiat voluntas tua*, gives no hint that he was diverging from his usual method of selecting a chant source. The words *Fiat voluntas tua* are primarily associated with the *Pater noster*, one of the fundamental and most commonly used prayers in Christianity. Yet no extant *Pater noster* melody that Machaut might have known is even close to the one he seems to have used in composing M5, as will be discussed below – hence the peculiarity of the solution that Leech-Wilkinson proposes.

---

[9] L. Earp, 'Machaut's Role in the Production of Manuscripts of his Works', *Journal of the American Musicological Society*, 42 (1989), pp. 461–503, at p. 461.

[10] A. V. Clark, '*Concordare cum Materia*: The Tenor in the Fourteenth-Century Motet' (Ph.D. diss., Princeton University, 1996), p. 48. The tenors of only four motets (M2, M7, M15 and M23) use more melodic material that their tenor tags would suggest (*ibid.*, p. 47).

A Courtly Lover and an Earthly Knight

According to Leech-Wilkinson (see Example 1) musical phrases 1 and 3 of Machaut's tenor 'are taken from one of the *Pater noster* chants at the words *Fiat voluntas tua sicut in coelo et in terra*', while phrases 2 and 4 share 'essential structural features' with the tenor of Vitry's Motet 6.[11] Let us first consider the latter part of Leech-Wilkinson's hypothesis and examine the relationship between the tenor of Vitry's Motet 6 and that of M5. Noting that M5 may well have been Machaut's first attempt in writing a four-part isorhythmic motet, Leech-Wilkinson attributes the composer's modifications of Vitry's model and the resulting dissonances to his inexperience, stating that Machaut was 'clearly not equipped to overcome' such problems of construction at this early stage of his career as a motet composer.[12]

Even a cursory examination confirms that indeed phrases 2 and 4 of Machaut's tenor are almost identical to the tenor of Vitry's Motet 6. This may not be a coincidence, Leech-Wilkinson asserts, for it is possible that Machaut learnt the technique of isorhythm from the works of Vitry, and perhaps even from Vitry himself.[13] Leech-Wilkinson proposes that the words *Fiat voluntas tua* function as a homage of sorts, since the sentiment expressed in the words *Thy will be done* would be particularly appropriate in a master–disciple relationship.[14] Emulating Vitry, Machaut would have accomplished a major pedagogical objective, namely, learning the technique of four-voice isorhythm. And music was apparently not the only field in which Machaut sought to emulate Vitry; Lawrence Earp notes

---

[11] *Compositional Techniques*, i, pp. 89 and 92. Musical phrases are indicated by roman numerals. For example, M5 and Vitry's Motet 6 have the same isorhythmic scheme (7 notes × 4 *taleae*). See also Leech-Wilkinson, 'Related Motets from Fourteenth-Century France', *Proceedings of the Royal Musical Association*, 109 (1982–3), pp. 1–22, at p. 5.

[12] Leech-Wilkinson, *Compositional Techniques*, i, p. 104.

[13] He could have been introduced to the genre, however, during his tenure at the court of John of Luxembourg. As Earp states, the isorhythmic motet was 'a primary vehicle for the projection of courtly love poetry at the court of John of Luxembourg in the 1330s', where Machaut was in service between *c.* 1320 and 1346. See Earp, *Guillaume de Machaut*, p. 276. Earp surmises that Machaut and Vitry had at least one occasion to meet 'near the end of the extended excursion of 1323 to 1324 that brought together members of the French court . . . with the entourage of John of Luxembourg, which probably included the young clerk Guillaume de Machaut'. *Ibid.*, pp. 10–11.

[14] 'it is extremely unlikely that Machaut should have learnt these techniques [thorough-going isorhythmic motets] . . . from the works of anyone other than Vitry, perhaps even from anyone but Vitry himself. Perhaps this is the meaning of the text incipit of Machaut's Tenor, "Fiat voluntas tua", Thy Will be done.' Leech-Wilkinson, *Compositional Techniques*, i, p. 104. See also his 'Related Motets', p. 20.

Yossi Maurey

that 'Vitry's influence on Machaut's poetic efforts, particularly in the field of lyrical poetry, was also probably decisive'.[15] Despite the lack of records documenting possible contacts between Machaut and Vitry,[16] the silence of the sources is overshadowed by what seems to be cogent musical and circumstantial evidence. The latter is provided by Anne Walters Robertson, who offers reasons why Machaut and Vitry, although coming from different regions in northern France, may in fact have known each other in Paris, perhaps during the time the *Roman de Fauvel* was put together (*c.* 1317).[17]

If Machaut based his motet on a model by Vitry, why did he insist that the tenor be associated with the words *Fiat voluntas tua*? Let us now turn back to the first part of Leech-Wilkinson's pastiche hypothesis. He states that in phrases 1 and 3 of M5, Machaut uses a chant segment taken from a *Pater noster* melody,[18] which he identifies as one cited by Bruno Stäblein in his 1962 article 'Pater noster' in *MGG*. As its title suggests, Stäblein's article is indeed devoted solely to *Pater noster* melodies, but not necessarily to assessing the applicability of those melodies to particular polyphonic works. The latter task was undertaken more than a decade later, in 1973, by Ernest Sanders, who examined one of Stäblein's *Pater noster* melodies and suggested that it was a probable source for the tenor of M5.[19] Like Vitry's motet tenor, 'Stäblein's' *Pater noster* melody is

---

[15] Earp, *Guillaume de Machaut*, p. 10.
[16] One wonders of what such records might consist. Few medieval documents record meetings between two composers, notwithstanding their roles within their respective patrons' entourages. Moreover, if the years 1323–4 are indeed the *locus* of a possible meeting between the two, as Earp suggests (see n. 13 above), Machaut would then have been a simple clerk in the service of John of Luxembourg (he became secretary only in 1333), reducing even further the probability that a meeting with Vitry might be documented. See *ibid.*, p. 9.
[17] Both Vitry and Machaut may have come to Paris to study at the university and to live in the Collège d'Arras, the former in the early years of the fourteenth century, the latter perhaps a decade later. See Robertson, *Guillaume de Machaut and Reims*, pp. 36–7. In a recent article, moreover, R. Bowers suggests that Hugues of Chastillon, hailing from a prominent seigneurie that exercised manorial lordship over the village of Machaut's birth, 'had been in a position to serve as an early personal link between Vitry and Machaut'. See his 'Guillaume de Machaut and his Canonry of Reims, 1338–1377', *Early Music History*, 23 (2004), pp. 1–48 at p. 23, n. 63.
[18] *Compositional Techniques*, i, p. 92, and ii, p. 13.
[19] 'The cantus firmus seems to be an elaborate version of the appropriate phrases from [that] '*Pater noster*'. E. Sanders, 'The Medieval Motet', in W. Arlt *et al.* (eds.) *Gattungen der Musik in Einzeldarstellungen: Gedenkschrift Leo Schrade* (Bern, 1973), pp. 497–573, at pp. 563–4, n. 287. Demonstrating the extent to which Sanders's hypothesis has been accepted as fact, S. Huot, citing the latter article, plainly states that 'The tenor [of M5 is] adapted from the musical

equally attractive: it fits Machaut's tenor almost perfectly, although the two chants begin on different notes.

The *Pater noster* melody in question, however, comes from a late fourteenth-century missal housed in Milan, whose provenance is reportedly Utrecht.[20] While in the service of John of Luxembourg (*c.* 1320–46), Machaut travelled extensively, particularly in eastern Europe during the 1320s and 1330s.[21] There is no evidence to suggest that he ever visited Utrecht for any length of time, short or long. Nor is there any reason to believe that Machaut's education was acquired outside France. In brief, if Machaut used a melodic segment of a chant as fundamental as the *Pater noster*, it is more likely that he would have had recourse to a melody taken not from Utrecht, far removed from the orbit of his existence, but rather from a *Pater noster* that he learnt as a child and adolescent in northern France, or from one that he performed daily as part of his liturgical duties as a canon at Reims Cathedral.[22] His memorisation of the tune might have been accomplished almost instinctively, for the prayer would have been on his lips virtually every day. In addition, selecting a chant from Utrecht would contradict Machaut's usual practice in choosing tenors: as Alice Clark concludes in a study of all of Machaut's tenors, the composer typically 'used chants from his native tradition rather than that in which he worked'.[23] This pattern, in and of itself, does not rule out the possibility that he departed from his usual practice in M5. But, as the discussion below shows, this was probably not the case.

---

setting of the *Paternoster*'; see her 'Patience in Adversity: The Courtly Lover and Job in Machaut's Motets 2 and 3', *Medium Ævum*, 63 (1994), pp. 222–38, at p. 223.

[20] See T. Gnoli, D. Bassi and P. Nalli, *Catalogo descrittivo della mostra bibliografica: Manoscritti e libri miniati, libri a stampa rari e figurati dei secc. XV–XVI, legature artistiche, autografi* (Milan, 1929), p. 10. The missal in question has the siglum Milan, Brera, A. E., XIV 12. The *Catalogo descrittivo* states that 'se ne ignora la provenienza'. Stäblein does not explain why he believes that the missal originated in Utrecht, but his conclusion was perhaps based on the *Catalogo descrittivo*, which notes that the missal is characterised by 'carattere gotico tedesco grande', a palaeographical detail that might support an Utrecht provenance. See *Catalogo*, p. 10. It seems that Stäblein erroneously states that this manuscript was copied in the twelfth century, although this may simply be a misprint. See Stäblein, 'Pater noster', *MGG*, x, p. 947; the *MGG*[2] 'Pater noster' article omits the Utrecht *Pater noster* melody.

[21] Earp, *Guillaume de Machaut*, p. 8.

[22] He was born in Champagne, perhaps in Machault or Reims, and received his canonry at Reims in the late 1330s. See *ibid.*, p. 3. Bowers suggests that the composer may have been born in Cauroy de les Machaut, a village situated some twenty-five miles east of Reims. For his reasoning see 'Machaut and his Canonry of Reims', pp. 22–3.

[23] Clark, '*Concordare cum Materia*', p. 32.

Yossi Maurey

What *Pater noster* melody would Machaut have been likely to know? Would it have been similar to the one from Utrecht? A comparison of extant northern French *Pater noster* melodies clarifies the issue. Example 3 aligns the predominant melodic traditions of the *Pater noster* at the words *Fiat voluntas tua*. Compared is only the melodic segment set to those words, rather than the entire chant. Machaut worked similarly: in the majority of his motet corpus the tenors employ only the portion of the melody set to the words he so carefully noted below the tenor line.[24] This precision is best illustrated in Motets 8 and 21.[25] Both tenors are drawn from a single Psalm verse taken from the liturgy of Passion Sunday (Ps. 21: 12): 'Tribulatio proxima est et non est qui adiuvet.' As seen in Example 4, the tenor of M8 employs only the melody set to the latter part of the verse (*et non est qui adiuvet*), while the tenor of M21 is based on the music encompassing the entire textual excerpt. The respective tenor tags of the two motets clearly illustrate this difference.[26] Regardless of the presence, in this instance, of a shared source, the tenor of M8 uses only the melodic material that its tag suggests, while the tenor of M21 does likewise.

Returning to Example 3, there are essentially two melodic traditions of the *Pater noster* in medieval manuscripts:[27] (1) a single northern tradition with multiple, but similar, variants, and (2) two south Italian traditions, one ferial and one festal. Example 3 lists several melodic variants of the *Fiat voluntas tua* segment, representing both major traditions; more variants of the northern melodic traditions are given for their potential relevance to Machaut.[28] Of the seven northern variants, the first three are particularly popular in manuscripts from all over France beginning in the

---

[24] But see n. 10 above.
[25] As Clark demonstrates, the single liturgical source closest to the tenors of both M8 and M21 is found in the Lucca Antiphoner (*LA*), and is reproduced in Example 4. See '*Concordare cum Materia*', pp. 192 and 199. Note that the Lucca version is a fourth lower than Machaut's tenor.
[26] The author of the text of this responsory is using the Gallican version of the Psalter (Jerome's revision of the Old Latin Psalter), where Psalm 21: 12 is translated as 'Ne discesseris a me quoniam tribulatio proxima est non est qui adiuvet.' In the Vulgate, the same excerpt is translated slightly differently: 'Ne longe fias a me quoniam tribulatio proxima est quoniam non est adiutor.'
[27] J. Boe, 'Pater noster', *New Grove II*, xix, p. 231.
[28] Nos. 1, 4, 7, 8 and 9 of Example 3 are taken from Boe, 'The Frankish *Pater noster* Chant: Tradition and Anaphoral Context', in B. Gillingham and P. Merkley (eds.), *Chant and its Peripheries: Essays in Honour of Terence Bailey* (Ottawa, 1998), pp. 179–203, at pp. 189–203. I have collected the remainder.

A Courtly Lover and an Earthly Knight

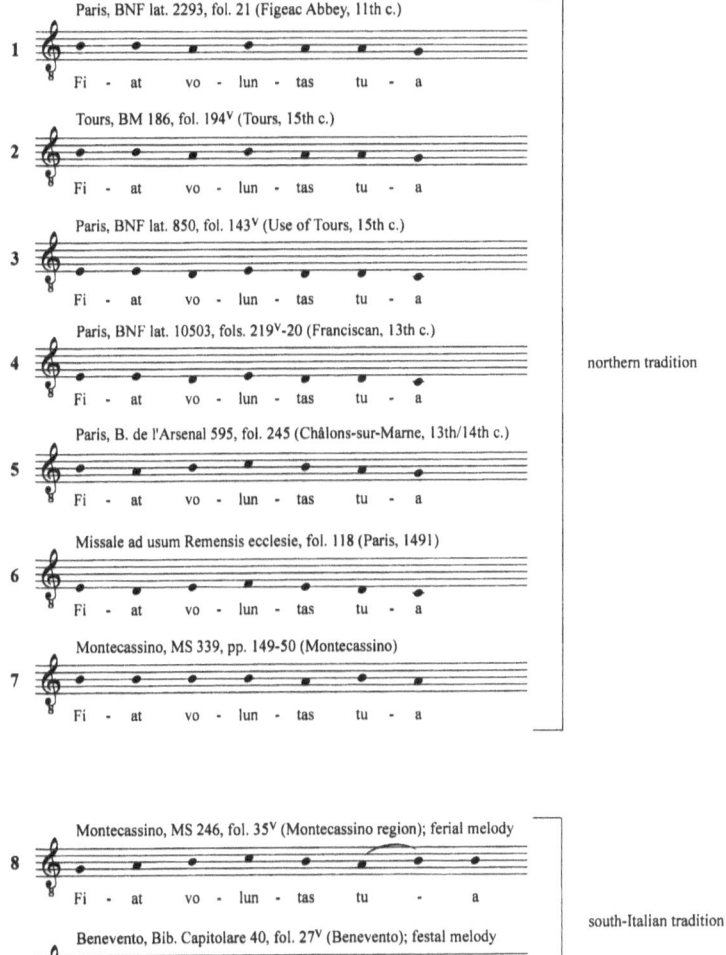

Example 3   Melodic traditions of the *Pater noster*: the *fiat voluntas tua* segment

eleventh century.[29] As John Boe notes, the northern melody and its variants appear occasionally in southern Italy as well (as can be seen

---

[29] The number of such instances is too large to be listed here. For a more comprehensive list, refer to the examples given in Boe, 'Pater noster', *New Grove II*, xix, *passim*, and Boe, 'The Frankish *Pater noster* Chant', pp. 189–203. For an additional list of manuscripts and select transcriptions of *Pater noster* melodies, see Dom F. Cabrol, 'Le chant du Pater à la messe', *Revue Grégorienne*, 14 (1929), pp. 1–17, at pp. 12–14.

Example 4   The tenors of M21 and M8 compared with their liturgical source

in Example 3, no. 7), where it is given the rubric 'francisca' ('Frankish').[30]

Judging from the selected examples at the words *Fiat voluntas tua*, it is clear that none of the melodic traditions presented in Example 3 could have served as a model for the tenor of M5, nor could they have provided the kernel from which a longer tenor might have been constructed.[31] Moreover, the Utrecht *Pater noster* version (the one Leech-Wilkinson uses), which resembles Machaut's tenor, was not, in all likelihood, Machaut's model, because of what may be called 'liturgical distance' in both geographical and musical senses.

The question remains, however, whether there are other possible musical inspirations for Machaut's tenor, taken entirely from a chant which he had reason to know, and that can explain in a more compelling way the inscription written painstakingly below the tenor of M5 in six of Machaut's manuscripts of complete works, most of which transmit the tenor tag *Fiat voluntas tua*.[32] One has to

---

[30] Boe, 'Pater noster', *New Grove II*, xix, p. 233.

[31] An important caveat pertains to every comparison of motet tenors with chants, such as the one presented here and further below. Such comparisons may pose a methodological problem because of the need to accommodate the upper voices supported by the tenor, which often entails structural and modal changes in the borrowed chant segment. For a more detailed discussion of this and other related caveats, see Robertson, 'Local Chant Readings and the *Roman de Fauvel*', in M. Bent and A. Wathey (eds.), *Fauvel Studies: Allegory, Chronicle, Music, and Image in Paris, Bibliothèque Nationale de France, MS français 146* (Oxford, 1998), pp. 495–524, at p. 512, n. 23. See also S. Fuller, 'Modal Tenors and Tonal Orientation in Motets of Guillaume de Machaut', *Current Musicology*, 45–7 (1990), pp. 199–245, at p. 215.

[32] Except for MS **G** (Paris, Bibliothèque Nationale de France [hereafter BNF], fr. 22546, fol. 107ʳ), where the tenor tag lacks the final word *tua*, all other 'complete works' manuscripts

A Courtly Lover and an Earthly Knight

wonder why, if Machaut was indeed so keen on dedicating M5 to Vitry, he did not do so in a more explicit way.[33] He could have named his tenor 'Neuma quinti toni', for example, a clear reference to the tenor of Vitry's Motet 6. But Machaut wrote under his tenor melody only these three words, which, despite their popularity, have so far failed to point to a musical source for the tenor of M5.

FIAT VOLUNTAS TUA IN NEW TESTAMENT SOURCES

For all of Christendom in the Middle Ages, the words *Fiat voluntas tua* would have had a familiar ring. Most would recognise these words as coming from the *Pater noster*, a text first set forth in Matthew 6: 9–13. Used on various occasions during Mass and Office, the *Pater noster* was sung by a single priest, by the entire congregation, and sometimes antiphonally, between the two. The custom of a priest reciting the *Pater noster* alone goes back to at least the end of the sixth century. A letter written by Pope Gregory the Great (r. 590–604) in 598 advocates exactly this, adding that the *Pater noster* comes right after the Canon of the Mass.[34] In addition, following the singing of psalms and antiphons during the daily Offices, a versicle and a response were commonly followed by a *Pater noster*, with all but the last two verses sung *in secreto*. In both monastic and secular uses, the *Pater noster*, together with *Ave Maria* and *Credo*, were silently intoned before Matins began. The Rule of St Benedict, moreover, states that 'the celebration of Lauds and Vespers must never pass by without

transmit the tenor tag *Fiat voluntas tua*: MS **C** (BNF fr. 1586, fol. 210ʳ); MS **E** (BNF fr. 9221, fol. 136ʳ); MS **B** (BNF fr. 1585, fol. 263ʳ); and MS **A** (BNF fr. 1584, fol. 419ʳ). MS **Vg** (New York, Wildenstein Collection, MS without shelf mark) is normally not available to scholars. On the provenance and date of these sources see Earp, *Guillaume de Machaut*, ch. 3.

[33] Boogaart speculates that M5 might in fact have been dedicated to Machaut's Maecenas, King John of Bohemia. In support of his hypothesis he cites stylistic features pertinent to the texts of the triplum and the motetus: their respective opening lines are apparently borrowed from two poems by Thibaut de Champagne (1201–53), and 'all five chansons quoted in M5 belong to the aristocratic *grand chant*', a poetic genre that, according to Grocheio, is normally 'sung in the presence of kings and princes'. See 'Encompassing Past and Present', pp. 63 and 69.

[34] Letter of Gregory the Great to John, bishop of Syracuse (Oct. 598). Edited by D. Norberg in Corpus Christianorum, Series Latina 140A (Turnholt: Brepols, 1982), p. 587. But even before the sixth century the *Pater noster* belonged to the Roman Mass: the *Libera nos* cited in the so-called *Sacramentarium Leonianum* or *Veronense* (Verona, Biblioteca Capitolare, LXXXV (early seventh century), which contains material of the fifth and sixth centuries, presupposes the presence of the *Pater noster*. See J. A. Jungmann, *The Early Liturgy to the Time of Gregory the Great*, trans. F. A. Brunner (Notre Dame, Ind., 1959), pp. 300–1. See also his 'Das *Pater noster* im Kommunionritus', *Zeitschrift für katholische Theologie*, 58 (1934), pp. 552–71.

Example 5 *Fiat voluntas tua* from the communion *Pater, si non potest* (*Graduale Romanum*, 149)

the superior's reciting the entire Lord's Prayer at the end for all to hear'.[35] That the *Pater noster* was also sung *in secreto* testifies to the widespread knowledge of the prayer, which, like the Lesser Doxology, must have been so internalised through frequent singing that one forgot the moment at which it was ever memorised.

Another New Testament passage, Matthew 26: 42, incorporates the words *Fiat voluntas tua*.[36] This verse is the source for the text of the short communion *Pater, si non potest* which follows the offertory *Improperium expectavit*, sung during the solemn Mass of Palm Sunday. The melody at the words *Fiat voluntas tua*, which conclude this communion (see Example 5), does not shed light on the model for M5.[37] But there is yet a third, unexplored source.

THE VITA OF ST MARTIN OF TOURS

The phrase *Fiat voluntas tua* is also found in a chant for the liturgy of St Martin of Tours, a ritual that Machaut had reason to know. Martin was one of the first Christians to be canonised not because of the way he died but because of the way he lived. The prominence of Martin in the ecclesiastical sphere, moreover, was a product of his accomplishments in the episcopal and monastic realms: in the 360s he founded in Ligugé (in the Poitou) a hermitage, the first monastery in Gaul, and from *c*. 371 he served as the third bishop of Tours until his death in 397. During his residence in Tours, he brought into being one other establishment, Marmoutier, a monastery located just outside the city, where he also served as abbot; during the three

---

[35] *The Rule of St. Benedict in Latin and English with Notes*, ed. T. Fry (Collegeville, Minn., 1981), p. 209.

[36] A somewhat different form of the *Pater noster* is found in Luke 11: 2–4, but it does not include the phrase *Fiat voluntas tua*. For a discussion of the *Pater noster* in general and *Fiat voluntas tua* in particular, see V. Gillespie, 'Thy Will Be Done: Piers Plowman and the Paternoster', in A. J. Minnis (ed.) *Late-Medieval Religious Texts and their Transmission: Essays in Honour of A. I. Doyle* (Woodbridge and Rochester, NY, 1994), pp. 95–119. See especially pp. 95–101 and the informative footnotes.

[37] There are some general similarities with Machaut's tenor, to be sure (the leap of a third, although in reverse direction, among other things), but little more than that.

A Courtly Lover and an Earthly Knight

final decades of his life, then, he served in the double capacity of monk as well as the bishop of Tours. As unblemished as his aura was, the posthumous image of Martin could not have been propagated as effectively as it did were it not for the literary oeuvre of Sulpicius Severus (c. 360–420), a Gallo-Roman lawyer and supporter who befriended him, became his admirer, and set out to write his biography while Martin was still living. Indeed, owing to him and to Gregory of Tours (the sixth-century historian and bishop of Tours from c. 573 to 594), the cult of St Martin is 'the best-documented ... in the late-antique West'.[38] It was owing to the engaging *vita* by Severus, made popular among clerics and the general public throughout the Christian world, that the cult of Martin spread and prospered.

The *vita*, the first biography of its kind of a Christian saint,[39] was published just months before the death of its protagonist. It was complemented by three additional letters, and finally by the author's *Dialogues* in c. 404.[40] The ensemble of works by Severus inspired and informed virtually all subsequent forms of Martinian veneration, whether they were devotional, literary, anecdotal, iconographic, or musical in nature. As Raymond Van Dam has argued, it was Severus who 'transformed bishop Martin into St Martin'.[41] Already in the fifth century a versified *vita* of Martin was written by Paulinus of Périgueux, and a century later, between 573 and 590, Venantius Fortunatus penned one as well.[42] Gregory of Tours too dedicated an entire work to Martin: his *Miracles of the Bishop St Martin* consists of four *libri* (completed in the 580s) and

---

[38] R. Van Dam, *Saints and their Miracles in Late Antique Gaul* (Princeton, 1993), p. 5. The most recent edition and translation of Severus's *vita* of St Martin is *Sulpice Sévère: Vie de Saint Martin*, ed. J. Fontaine, 3 vols. (Sources Chrétiennes, Série des Textes Monastiques d'Occident, nos. 22–4; Paris, 1967). For an English translation, see B. M. Peebles, 'Sulpicius Severus: Writings', in *The Fathers of the Church*, ed. R. J. Deferrari, 7 (New York, 1949), pp. 79–140.
[39] B. Abou-El-Haj, *The Medieval Cult of Saints: Formations and Transformations* (Cambridge, 1994), pp. 8–9.
[40] On the history of these writings, see C. Stancliffe, *St. Martin and his Hagiographer: History and Miracle in Sulpicius Severus* (Oxford, 1983), pp. 71–85.
[41] Van Dam, *Saints and their Miracles*, p. 13.
[42] On the two versified *vitae* of Martin, and especially on the shift in the image of the saint that they underline, see the discussion in S. Labarre, *Le manteau partagé: Deux métamorphoses poétiques de la vie de Saint-Martin chez Paulin de Périgueux (V S.) et Venance Fortunat (VI S.)* (Collections des Études Augustiniennes, Série Antiquité, 158; Paris, 1998), pp. 203–20.

records more than 200 miracles performed by Martin, by and large posthumously.[43]

The writings of Severus were the main source of knowledge concerning Martin in the medieval world; not surprisingly, large selections of his oeuvre were incorporated into the saint's liturgy. Since Severus disseminated Martin's *vita* while the saint was still alive, the biography naturally left out the events leading to his passing, episodes that were to be recounted in a separate appendix. Martin's death provided Severus with the grounds for writing three documents in letter form, one of which holds special importance for the tenor source of M5. In what is commonly known as the author's 'third letter', Severus addresses Bassula, his mother-in-law. There he meticulously recounts the final days of the saint, namely, his mission to resolve a dispute between the clergy in the church of Candes (a city situated along the Loire River, downstream from Tours), his death there due to illness, his funeral procession and burial in Tours:[44]

> There was a dispute among the clergy of that church [in Candes] and he wished to restore peace ... When peace was restored among the clergy, he thought about returning to the monastery [in Tours]. But he suddenly began to lose his strength. He called his brothers and said he was going to die ... 'why, father, do you abandon us', they all lamented, '... to whom do you leave us? ... who will defend us ... Have pity on us whom you abandon ...' [and then Martin] addressed himself to the Lord and only in this way replied to those who were weeping: 'Lord, if I am still needed by your people, I do not decline the task, *thy will be done*' ['*Domine, si adhuc populo tuo sum necessarius, non recuso laborem, fiat voluntas tua*'].[45]

The words *Fiat voluntas tua*, then, form part of Martin's valediction.

Enjoying wide circulation in medieval Europe, at least two copies of Severus's *vita* of St Martin were found in Reims at the time when Machaut was likely to be in residence in the city as a canon of the cathedral (*c.* 1337–77), along with other accounts of miracles and legends pertaining to St Martin.[46] Significantly, a condensed version

---

[43] Gregory of Tours, *Libri de Virtutibus Sancti Martini Episcopi*, ed. B. Krusch (Monumenta Germanica Historica, Scriptores Rerum Merovingicarum, 1; Berlin, Hannover and Leipzig, 1885), pp. 584–661. For an English translation, see Van Dam, *Saints and their Miracles*, pp. 199–303.
[44] Peebles, 'Sulpicius Severus: Writings', pp. 153–9.
[45] *Ibid.*, pp. 155–6.
[46] It is certainly possible, even likely, that Reims Cathedral had a copy of St Martin's *vita*. As far as can be judged from modern catalogues, however, the city of Reims had only two copies of the *vita*, both housed in the church of St Thierry (Reims, Bibliothèque Municipale, MS 1405 and MS 1409, dating from the tenth and twelfth centuries respectively). Some of the Reims

A Courtly Lover and an Earthly Knight

of St Martin's *vita* containing his prayer ending with *Fiat voluntas tua* appears in the widely read *Golden Legend*, written before 1267 by Jacobus de Voragine.[47] Although it is highly probable that medieval clerics would have been familiar with the text of St Martin's *vita*, it is more likely that their knowledge of Severus's biography of St Martin came first and foremost from their intimate familiarity with the liturgy that it spawned: the feast of St Martin on 11 November.

THE TENOR OF M5 AND THE LITURGY FOR THE FEAST OF ST MARTIN (11 NOVEMBER)

Owing no doubt to a composer's need to make minor changes for contrapuntal or structural reasons, the tenors of fourteenth-century motets rarely match perfectly the chants from which they come, as they are transmitted in extant medieval sources. Clark has shown that the tenors of M9 and M14, for instance, find melodic matches in a notated missal-breviary from Châlons-sur-Marne, a city just south-east of Reims.[48] She also notes that several of Machaut's other tenors closely correspond to chant readings from this manuscript, more so on occasion than to melodies found in extant manuscripts from Reims.[49] Machaut's mass provides a further link between the liturgies of Reims and Châlons-sur-Marne: Robertson has shown that sources from both cities offer identical readings for the openings of the tenors of the Kyrie and Sanctus.[50] Whereas no surviving manuscripts from Reims contain the Office music for St Martin's feast, the text of this Office is extant in an eleventh-century breviary from the cathedral.[51] Moreover, the melody set to the words *Fiat voluntas tua* in the liturgy of St Martin appears in two manuscripts

---

manuscripts containing legends and miracles of St Martin include Reims, Bibliothèque Municipale, MS 1400 (thirteenth century) and MS 1395 (ninth century).

[47] This ubiquitous work survives in about 900 manuscripts. For an English translation see *The Golden Legend: Readings on the Saints*, trans. William Granger Ryan (Princeton, 1993).

[48] Clark, 'Concordare cum Materia', pp. 25–7. The manuscript in question is Paris, Bibliothèque de l'Arsenal, MS 595 (late thirteenth/early fourteenth century).

[49] *Ibid.*, pp. 31–2.

[50] Robertson, *Guillaume de Machaut and Reims*, pp. 261–9.

[51] There are only two extant breviaries from medieval Reims: Meaux, Bibliothèque Municipale, MS 5 (St Nicasius, Reims, 2nd half of the thirteenth century), and BNF lat. 17991 (eleventh century, emanating from the cathedral). The former manuscript provides only the text of St Martin's Office (fols. 368ᵛ–370ᵛ), while in the latter space was left for the music to be inserted, but for unknown reasons it was never supplied (fols. 226ᵛ–228ᵛ).

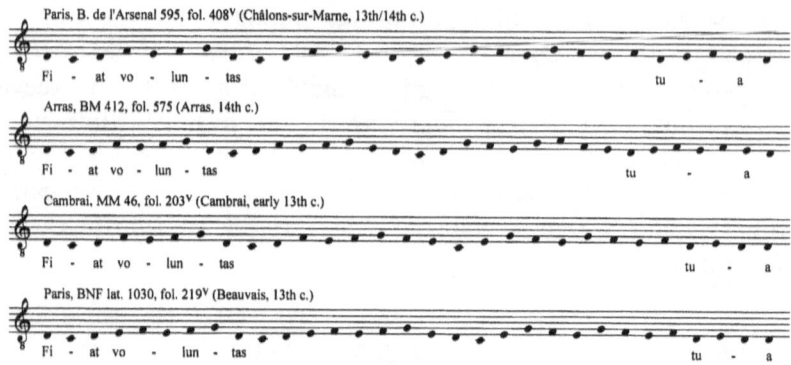

Example 6 Music set to *Fiat voluntas tua* in the responsory *Domine, si adhuc*

from Châlons: a thirteenth-century notated breviary (summer), as well as the notated missal-breviary mentioned above.[52] The melody transmitted in these and other sources from northern France offers insight into the source of Machaut's tenor.

The words of the moribund St Martin, as recounted by Severus, were incorporated into the saint's liturgy of 11 November in two guises: they appear in the Matins responsory *Domine, si adhuc*, where *volunTAS* contains a long melisma. This form, for which four instances are offered in Example 6, was clearly not Machaut's model in M5, although responsory and tenor share some features, notably the first five notes (with the exclusion of the example from BNF lat. 1030). In addition, the phrase *Fiat voluntas tua* is found in the antiphon *Domine, si adhuc* from Lauds, sung immediately following Matins.

In both the responsory and the antiphon, the common words *Fiat voluntas tua* clearly evoke the imagery of Matthew 26: 42, namely, the notion that the believer's will is always subsumed in God's:

Matthew 26: 42	St Martin's feast (11 November)
Pater mi, si non potest hic calix transire nisi bibam illum, *fiat voluntas tua*.	Domine, si adhuc populo tuo sum necessarius, non recuso laborem, *fiat voluntas tua*.
My Father, if this chalice cannot pass away, unless I drink it, then let *thy will be done*.	Lord, if I am still needed by your people, I do not decline the task, *thy will be done*.

[52] BNF lat. 802, fol. 257ᵛ.

A Courtly Lover and an Earthly Knight

Example 7 Music set to *Fiat voluntas tua* in the antiphon *Domine, si adhuc*: main tradition (first four); and variant tradition (last two)

It is the melody of the antiphon that offers an interesting alternative, one within Machaut's reach, for the *Pater noster* melody that Leech-Wilkinson proposes and that comes from Utrecht.[53] As can be gleaned from Example 7, the most common version of this antiphon has a leap of a third (A–C) between its third and fourth notes, contrasting with the less frequently found reading exemplified in the last two sources reproduced in Example 7. Note that none of the *Pater noster* melodies belonging to the two major traditions (French and Hispanic), and more importantly, none of the northern French melodies for the prayer (see Example 3) can claim a similar leap of a third, the interval so characteristic of the first and third *taleae* in the tenor of M5.

Significantly, the antiphon *Domine, si adhuc* was sung in Reims Cathedral on St Martin's feast, as the only extant medieval breviary

---

[53] Interestingly, the antiphon's melody resembles the opening notes of the Kyrie Machaut uses in his mass.

from that church clearly indicates.⁵⁴ The unequivocal presence of this antiphon in Reims indicates that Machaut would most likely have known it. Thus it is conceivable that the melody for *Fiat voluntas tua* that Machaut used in M5 was more likely drawn from this antiphon, taken from an Office that he would have sung regularly at Reims, than from the combination of the *Neuma* melisma with a *Pater noster* from Utrecht, the latter especially being a melody he had little reason to know.

Although the veneration of St Martin in Reims was similar to that found elsewhere in northern France, there was a church dedicated to St Martin (from as early as 627) that was one of the stations on processions of the canons of Notre Dame of Reims (including Guillaume de Machaut), one of them occurring on St Martin's feast.⁵⁵ Similarly, on the Wednesday preceding Ascension (that is, the third day of the Lesser Rogations), one ordinal prescribes a procession from the cathedral to the abbey of St Remigius, requiring a stop in the church of St Martin along the way.⁵⁶ Machaut, then, could also have become familiar with St Martin's liturgy, including the antiphon *Domine, si adhuc*, through his participation in such processions.

Before aligning the tenor of M5 with the newly considered chant segment, let us first take a closer look at Machaut's melody. Example 8 shows the repetitions within this line, which resemble those found in a long *Jubilus*, in ABB' structure. Indeed, the sheer quantity of repeated material suggests that the entire tenor is made

---

⁵⁴ BNF lat. 17991, fol. 228ʳ.
⁵⁵ P. Desportes, *Reims et les rémois aux XIIIᵉ et XIVᵉ siècles* (Paris, 1977), p. 51 n.14, and *Sacramentaire et martyrologe de l'abbaye de Saint-Rémy: Martyrologe, calendrier, ordinaires et prosaires de la métropole de Reims (VIIIᵉ–XIIIᵉ siècles), publiés d'après les manuscrits de Paris, Londres, Reims et Assise*, ed. U. Chevalier (Bibliothèque Liturgique, 7; Paris, 1900), pp. 218–19.
⁵⁶ *Ibid.*, p. 221. The ordinal is found in Reims, Bibliothèque Municipale, MS 329. The most straightforward itinerary from the cathedral to the abbey entails marching south of the cathedral to the abbey of St Denis, and then proceeding in an almost straight line eastward directly to the final destination, the abbey of St Remigius. But processions are hardly ever economical in this sense, and marching from one place to the other is rarely a matter of saving time, or finding the shortest way between two points. The ordinal in question prescribes an itinerary that is, however, quite practical, with only a slight deviation from the most direct possible way between the cathedral and the abbey of St Remigius. The only additional station mentioned in the ordinal for this day involves the parish church of St Martin. This station presented to the marchers the only departure from the cathedral–St Remigius axis, for it was located north-west of St Remigius, in the same horizontal line as the cathedral. See the seventeenth-century engraving of Reims reproduced in Robertson, *Guillaume de Machaut and Reims*, p. 13, figure 2.

A Courtly Lover and an Earthly Knight

Example 8 Internal repetitions in the tenor of M5

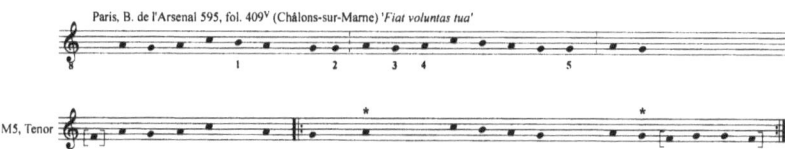

Example 9 The tenor of M5 aligned with *Fiat voluntas tua* (pitches marked * occur only in the repeat)

up of a much shorter melodic kernel, which is then extended through tenor repetition, a common feature of thirteenth-century motet tenors.[57]

Example 9 aligns Machaut's tenor with the *Fiat voluntas tua* melody from the antiphon *Domine, si adhuc*, drawn from one of the chant segments in Example 7. In order to make the degree of correspondence between tenor and chant segment clearer visually, I notate the tenor melody in Example 9 in abbreviated form, with repeat signs, a procedure prompted by Example 8, and I duplicate the eight-note chant melody (the vertical dotted lines denote the opening of a complete and a partial repetition respectively).[58] The two asterisks above A and G in the tenor denote pitches that appear only the second time, and the vertical dotted lines in the chant segment denote iterations of melodic material. In addition, I have square-bracketed the opening F and the concluding cadence on F in the tenor; the reason for this will be discussed in detail below. Arabic numerals under certain notes of the chant segment signal pitches that find no correspondence in the tenor melody. The latter can easily be accounted for: all such instances are either the filling of a third found in the chant segment (1), simple repetitions of the same

[57] Norman Smith traces the origin of tenor repetition as early as the Notre-Dame organa, beginning with the musical activity of Leoninus (that is, probably in the middle of the twelfth century). For example, in the ninety-seven organa copied in MS F, the overwhelming majority of clausulae (79) have two statements of the tenor. See his 'Tenor Repetition in the Notre Dame Organa', *Journal of the American Musicological Society*, 19 (1966), pp. 329–51, at pp. 334–5.
[58] Needless to say, the melodic integrity of the tenor remains intact.

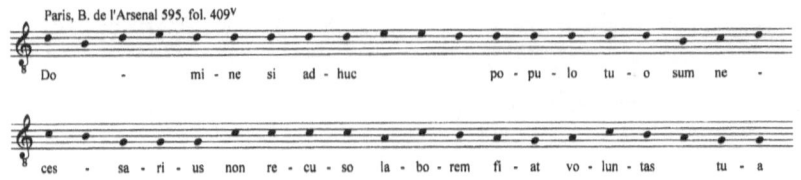

Example 10   The antiphon *Domine, si adhuc*

pitch (2 and 5), or a consequence of a lower auxiliary figure (3 and 4).

In Example 9 all occurrences of F in Machaut's tenor are square-bracketed in order to align the two melodies better. Explicit in this approach is the notion that in M5 Machaut did not adopt the final of the original chant segment he chose as his tenor.[59] Indeed, F is nowhere to be seen in the antiphon, reproduced in Example 10. If this was, perhaps, the first time that Machaut did not allow his selected melody to determine the concluding sonority of his motet, it was certainly not the last: he returned to this practice in one of his last motets, likewise written for four voices. In M22 (*Tu qui gregem/ Plange, Regni respublica!/*T. *Apprehende arma et scutum et exurge*) the tenor ends on F, whereas the final of the chant source is D.[60] The circumstances in which the tenor of M22 eschews the final of the original chant segment are quite distinct from those of M5: the third and final *color* of M22 is incomplete, hence the tenor ends *in medias res*, on F (see Example 11). While the compositional procedures in both motets differ, the end result is nonetheless similar: both tenors end on a different final than that of their respective chant segments.

In altering the final of an original chant segment in M5, Machaut did not set a precedent; he might have followed the practice of Vitry who, in his Motet 9 (*Colla jugo subdere/Bona condit cetera/*T. *Libera me [de sanguinibus]*) used a line ending on C, but chose nevertheless to

---

[59] This observation also holds for any analysis asserting that the tenor of M5 is (partially) based on a *Pater noster* chant, for, except for the Hispanic traditions, most chants do have G as their final, not F. This observation is less crucial for Leech-Wilkinson's analysis, since, according to him, the concluding *talea* of the tenor of M5 is derived from a certain portion of the tenor of Vitry's Motet 6 which ends on F.

[60] See Clark, '*Concordare cum Materia*', pp. 45–6, and Fuller, 'Modal Tenors and Tonal Orientation', p. 214, n. 35. One other motet by Machaut ends on a sonority other than that of the original chant segment: the tenor of M23 ends on A while the chant ends on D. In this case, however, the motet as a whole does end on a D sonority, because the 'final word' is given to the contratenor, sounding D below the Tenor's A. See Fuller, *ibid*.

A Courtly Lover and an Earthly Knight

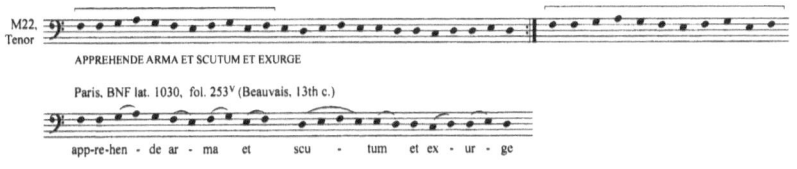

Example 11   Partial repetition in the tenor of M22, compared with its chant source

end the tenor on F, the result of a partial *color* repetition.[61] As suggested above, there are good reasons to regard all occurrences of F in the tenor of M5 as a reflection of Machaut's penchant for F finals and concluding sonorities.[62] Moreover, that F functions as the final in M5 should not necessarily be taken as a positive attestation to the modality of the original tenor source, as the case of M22 instructs us. Jehoash Hirshberg determined that 'The selection of *finales* in Machaut's repertoire is genre sensitive':[63] while F is the final of almost 50 per cent of Machaut's motets, it is the final of only about 6 per cent of his chansons. The antiphon *Domine, si adhuc* is invariably transmitted in mode 7, that is, with G as its final.[64] For reasons that can only be hypothesised, Machaut apparently altered this final G to F, a procedure he then repeated years later in M22.

Some aspects of compositional practice of medieval composers have been gleaned by modern scholars from medieval manuals and treatises. For the Ars nova isorhythmic motet, however, information is scarce. Only two treatises address this genre, Johannes Boen's *Ars [Musicae]* of *c.* 1355, and Egidius de Murino's *De modo componendi*

---

[61] The tenor is comprised of four *taleae*: the first and third contain exactly the melodic material the tag suggests and end on C (for the chant source, see BNF lat. 10482, fol. 163ᵛ, a fourteenth-century breviary from Paris), but the second and fourth *taleae* conclude with a reiteration of the tenor's three opening notes. The motet, therefore, ends on F, the third pitch in the selected chant source. See also Clark, '*Concordare cum Materia*'.
[62] Perhaps he acquired this penchant from Vitry, whose preference for F finals is even greater. See Fuller, 'Modal Tenors and Tonal Orientation', p. 213, n. 32.
[63] J. Hirshberg, 'The Exceptional as an Indicator of the Norm', in U. Günther, L. Finscher and J. Dean (eds.), *Modality in the Music of the Fourteenth and Fifteenth Centuries / Modalität in der Musik des 14. und 15. Jahrhunderts* (Neuhausen-Stuttgart, 1996), pp. 53–64, at p. 55.
[64] See for example the following manuscripts from northern France, indexed in the CANTUS website http://publish.uwo.ca/~cantus/): Arras, Bibliothèque Municipale, MS 465 (fourteenth century), fol. 480ᵛ; Cambrai, Médiathèque Municipale, MS 38 (thirteenth century), fol. 363ᵛ; BNF lat. 12044 (twelfth century), as well as the following examples that I have examined on microfilm: Verdun, Bibliothèque Municipale, MS 107 (fourteenth century), fol. 371ᵛ; BNF lat. 1255 (thirteenth and fifteenth centuries), fol. 346ᵛ; and Cambrai, Médiathèque Municipale, MS 46 (thirteenth century), fol. 204ʳ.

tenores motetorum of c. 1400.[65] Although both authors pay close attention to matters ranging from the segmentation of the chosen chant to the rhythmic layout of the motet as a whole, issues of modality and by extension the notion that a final might govern both *musica plana* and polyphony (to the extent that the modal system was applied to polyphony at all), are not treated.[66] Indeed, as Sarah Fuller concludes, 'However individuals came to terms with tonal orientation in polyphony, determination of mode was hardly a burning public issue in Machaut's century.'[67]

Fuller further elucidates some of the most salient issues pertaining to Ars nova motets from the point of view of modern listeners, including how one might understand and discuss the role and centrality of modality in polyphonic works of the fourteenth century. In order to achieve this, she relies on the music and what can be learnt from it. Pertinent to understanding Machaut's possible motivation for modifying the original melody set to *Fiat voluntas tua* is the following consideration, which deserves to be quoted in full:

> It is crucial, however, to distinguish between tonal characteristics of a chant phrase in its original plainsong state, sung as a continuous melody, and the characteristics of the same phrase when segmented, subjected to distinctive rhythmic patterning, greatly slowed in tempo, and absorbed into a polyphonic texture. Characteristics of the plainsong may be reaffirmed, but can also be reinterpreted or rejected in the polyphony. Because it is not a fixed artifact but raw material, the tenor provides an apt point of departure from which to investigate tonal structure in Machaut motets.[68]

Following Fuller's reasoning, I suggest that the melodic and, consequently, modal differences between the tenor of M5 and the antiphon *Domine, si adhuc* may be a result of compositional alterations and variants needed to accommodate the chant segment to Machaut's preferred overall modal plan of the piece (F), or possibly to fashion more convenient *colores*, as Leech-Wilkinson has hypothesised with regard to the motet repertory of Vitry.[69] Furthermore, taking into account the compositional challenge for the young Machaut of writing a four-voice isorhythmic motet, perhaps he wished to work within a modal framework in which he felt more

---

[65] For Boen's treatise, see *Johannes Boen: Ars*, ed. F. A. Gallo (Corpus Scriptorum de Musica, 19; [Rome], 1972). For Murino's, see Leech-Wilkinson, *Compositional Techniques*, i, pp. 18–23.
[66] On this issue, see the excellent discussion in Fuller, 'Modal Tenors and Tonal Orientation', pp. 199–201.
[67] *Ibid.*, p. 209.
[68] *Ibid.*, p. 214.
[69] Leech-Wilkinson, *Compositional Techniques*, i, p. 35.

A Courtly Lover and an Earthly Knight

comfortable. Significantly, three out of his four motets for four voices have F as a final (M5, M21, M22), and one of these, M22, as stated above, also has an altered tenor.[70]

Returning to Example 9, the bracketing of the Fs in M5 does not by any means suggest that these are non-essential notes in Machaut's tenor. But they do have relatively little structural harmonic weight – they are not the main source of F sonorities in this motet. Throughout M5, F sonorities are more often a result of the contratenor sounding below the tenor than of the tenor per se. In the *integer valor* section alone, for example, this is the case in twelve out of a total of fifteen F sonorities.[71] Surprisingly, F appears only once in each of the first three *taleae* of the tenor, and twice in the final *talea*, a further testimony to the minor role it occupies within the tenor line. The distance between each of the five occurrences of F in the four *taleae* further substantiates the view that F might have been imposed on a chant segment that originally had G as a final. The first F is inserted before the opening A of the chant segment *Fiat voluntas tua*, perhaps in order to establish F as the tonal centre of the motet from the outset.[72] Machaut then composed the motetus line above one of the longest-sustained and transparent F sonorities in the entire motet, lasting virtually for the six opening breves.[73] Apart from the opening sonority, F always appears in the tenor either immediately before or after the pitch G, or squeezed in between two Gs.

A *contrapunctus* reduction of the *integer valor* section (see Example 12) allows a glimpse into the kinds of terminations that Machaut employs, shedding further light on the issue at hand. As Fuller suggests, 'Terminations produce diverse effects and affective reactions according to the manner in which they are approached as well as according to the nature of the sonority held . . .'.[74] Let us examine

[70] On the compositional procedures characteristic of some of Machaut's other four-voice works, see K. N. Moll, 'Paradigms of Four-Voice Composition in the Machaut Era', *Journal of Musicological Research*, 22 (2003), pp. 364–72.
[71] I include in the number of F sonority prolongations (as in breves 1–6, and 61–6, for example), as well as places such as breves 39 and 61, where the contexts suggest F rather than A.
[72] In Machaut's motet corpus, however, the opening sonority is not always that of the concluding one, although the latter is true for almost half his motets (M4, 5, 10, 13, 16, 17, 19–23).
[73] The F sonority is sustained by the tenor melody first, then by the contratenor sounding below the tenor.
[74] S. Fuller, 'On Sonority in Fourteenth-Century Polyphony: Some Preliminary Reflections', *Journal of Music Theory*, 30 (1986), pp. 35–70, at p. 56.

Example 12 *Contrapunctus* reduction of the *integer valor* section of M5 (tenor line in square notes)

the first cadence in M5 in the light of the distinction Fuller makes between an 'arrival' and a 'hold': the former resolves a 'dissonant agglomerate ... and captures a sense of anticipation and progress to a settled destination', the latter 'is by no means the anticipated goal ... [conveying] no more than the action of sustaining'.[75] Although the prominent sonority in the first eighteen breves is F, the D sonority in breve 22 effectively becomes the main goal when the directed progression of two leading notes (the triplum G♯, and the motetus C♯) takes place in breves 20–1. Thus the termination point in breve 22 seems to resist such designations as 'arrival' and 'hold', since it is not the anticipated harmonic goal (F in *talea* I), but at the same time it does convey a sense of a directed progression and resolution of the immediately preceding dissonances. There is only one other double leading-note cadence in the *integer valor* section of

[75] *Ibid.*

A Courtly Lover and an Earthly Knight

M5, and it is also on D, not F (end of *talea* II, breves 43–7).[76] There, however, the arrival on D sounds less imposed since *talea* II effectively establishes D as a possible harmonic goal, witnessed in the frequent D–F pitch relations. In brief, Machaut uses prolongation, rather than strong, conclusive cadences as his main means of emphasising the centrality of F in M5.

The foregoing analysis suggests that F has a somewhat nominal role in the tenor of M5, and that it might have been imposed in order to mask, quite ingeniously, the modal underpinnings of the original chant segment.[77] Although Machaut would not have altered the tenor indiscriminately, since a melodic relation to the original melody needed to be preserved, his use of the added fourth voice, the contratenor, enabled him to scatter F sonorities throughout M5 without ever producing a convincing cadence on F.[78]

If the melody of the St Martin antiphon does not match the tenor of M5 in all respects, the general shape is certainly similar. This may be partially due to the following reasons. We do not, after all, have the exact music from Reims. It is possible that a Reims reading of the melody was even closer to the tenor of M5 than the reading from Châlons-sur-Marne. Secondly, the phrase *Fiat voluntas tua* appears in at least four different liturgical contexts, and has more than that number of melodic variants associated with each and every occasion. Notwithstanding their marked differences, the transmission of the melodies set to these three words in the antiphon and responsory *Domine, si adhuc*, as well as in the northern French *Pater noster*, may point to the existence of a core melodic cell which had slightly different versions as it wandered from region to region.[79] An expression such as *Fiat voluntas tua* may have been

[76] The diminution section likewise has only two double leading-note cadences on D.
[77] See also other unusual harmonic procedures in M5, discussed by Leech-Wilkinson, *Compositional Techniques*, i, pp. 99–102.
[78] Leech-Wilkinson concludes that in composing M5 Machaut encountered 'problems of construction which ... [he] was clearly not equipped to overcome', probably a consequence both of his inexperience as a four-voice motet composer and of his self-imposed restrictions, brought on by the rigid rhythmic scheme and limited range of the contratenor. See *ibid.*, i, pp. 99 and 104.
[79] It is futile to speculate on the identity of such a *Grundgestalt*, however, nor is it necessary, or indeed feasible, for the present argument. As Leo Treitler has noted, such a *Grundgestalt* 'will always elude us' if it is narrowly applied. For this and other important insights relevant to the use of 'formulas' and 'formulaic systems' in oral transmission of chant, see L. Treitler, 'Homer

195

associated commonly and orally with a generic type of chant, which, not unlike the medieval *Laudes regiae*, was sung all over Europe and had a varying melody from one place to another.[80] Machaut, therefore, might have resorted to one of these 'wandering' tunes commonly associated with *Fiat voluntas tua*, two of which derive from the liturgy of St Martin.

Machaut chose a chant segment comprised of only eight notes (see Example 7 above) and used it, albeit with minor changes, as a basis for all four *taleae*. His strategy was perhaps to highlight the words *Fiat voluntas tua*, even though this meant that he had only these eight notes at his disposal. Had he used the melody set to the same words in the responsory *Domine, si adhuc*, he would have had a longer melisma of either twenty-eight or thirty-two notes, which he could then conveniently have divided among four *taleae*.[81] Perhaps he concluded that the syllabic version found in the antiphon *Domine, si adhuc* had a more perceptible and distinct melodic association with the words he wished to single out, although this idea must remain pure conjecture. The composer, then, took a brief line and repeated it four times, whereas normally he chose a relatively long chant segment and divided it into a number of *taleae* (usually three or four).[82] Such normative considerations may have been outweighed for a rhetorical purpose: by repeating the melody set to the well-known words *Thy will be done* in each *talea*, Machaut emphatically affirms the centrality of these words as the fundamental concept of M5.

If the pitches of the St Martin antiphon helped inspire Machaut's tenor in M5, what might an adumbrated presence of St Martin himself in this motet mean? In what follows, I offer some speculative thoughts on this question, addressing (1) the possibility that M5 is a

---

and Gregory: The Transmission of Epic Poetry and Plainchant', *Musical Quarterly*, 60 (1974), pp. 333–71, at pp. 346 and 347–53.

[80] Craig Wright, pers. comm. Although the melodic versions of the *Laudes regiae* show a common origin, they vary in regard to melodic style and place of origin. Comparing the three families of melodic versions of the *Laudes* (syllabic, neumatic and highly neumatic), Bukofzer found a fundamental structure at the basis of these three versions. See M. F. Bukofzer's essay in E. H. Kantorowicz, *Laudes Regiae: A Study in Liturgical Acclamations and Mediaeval Ruler Worship*, 2nd edn (University of California Publications in History, 33; Berkeley and Los Angeles, 1958), p. 201.

[81] As in Paris, Bibliothèque de l'Arsenal, MS 595, and Arras, Bibliothèque Municipale, MS 412 respectively (see Example 6 above).

[82] When choosing tenors from responsories, Machaut evidently preferred interior portions, such as the beginning or end of the verse. See Clark, '*Concordare cum Materia*', p. 55.

A Courtly Lover and an Earthly Knight

dedicatory motet, (2) the figure of Yvain in the triplum, and the presence of retrograde in the tenor and contratenor and (3) the particular relevance of St Martin in the fourteenth century. Although the melody from the antiphon *Domine, si adhuc* provides a close counterpart to the essential characteristics of the tenor of M5, it cannot qualify as an 'exact match'. As mentioned above, however, most of Machaut's motets do not find precise matches, at least not in extant liturgical manuscripts. Still, now that a new source for the tenor of M5 has been advanced, the question arises why Machaut might have chosen a tenor hailing from the liturgy of St Martin. The centrality of this figure in the Middle Ages is hardly in doubt, but Machaut composed only one motet whose tenor is taken from the Sanctorale, M19 (*Martyrum gemma latria/Diligenter inquiramus*/T. *A Christo honoratus*).[83] Like M19, does M5 have an honorific function, or might the allusion to St Martin have another purpose?

M5, A DEDICATORY MOTET?

Along with other rituals in medieval France, the feast of St Martin (11 November) was accorded a high rank in the calendar of Notre-Dame in Reims. A late thirteenth-century ordinal from the cathedral calls for nine lessons and seven candles,[84] and in the fourteenth century St Martin's octave was added to the ritual of the church.[85] Judging from a sample of fourteenth-century liturgical sources from Reims, the feast of St Martin enjoyed the same level of solemnity throughout the city, where it was regularly celebrated with nine lessons.[86]

Although it might be tempting to try to make a case for M5 as some sort of a dedicatory motet, there is effectively no evidence to sanction such a hypothesis. Machaut seems to have had no

[83] The tenor of M19 comes from the liturgy of St Quintinus. Machaut became a canon of St Quintinus between 1333 and 1335. Three additional motets, however, have their tenor's source in the Marian liturgy (M14, 17 and 23). Robertson speculates that M19 was not only a motet dedicated to St Quintinus, but also that it 'served as a sort of anthem for the canons [of the collegiate church of St Quintinus]' during their annual meetings. See *Guillaume de Machaut and Reims*, p. 74.
[84] *Sacramentaire et martyrologe de l'abbaye de Saint-Rémy*, ed. Chevalier, p. 88.
[85] Robertson, *Machaut and Reims*, p. 41.
[86] See, e.g., the following fourteenth-century manuscripts: Reims, Bibliothèque Municipale, MS 217 (*olim* C. 202), fol. 6ʳ, a missal from St-Denis of Reims, and two ordinals from the Notre-Dame Cathedral in Reims, Bibliothèque Municipale, MS 329, fol. F, and MS 330, fol. 13ʳ.

exceptional connection with the cult of St Martin, and he was not affiliated with a church dedicated to the saint (cf. M19). However, if the tenor of M5 is indeed to be linked convincingly with St Martin's liturgy, a fundamental issue needs to be addressed: since in the Middle Ages the words *Fiat voluntas tua* had, and still have, a clear and immediate association with the *Pater noster*, why choose those same words from a different, and admittedly lesser known, context?[87] In other words, what does St Martin have to do with M5?

I have thus far concentrated solely on the tenor voice of M5, purposely ignoring one of the most important distinguishing features of Machaut's motets, namely, his use of French in the upper voices of most of his motets, despite the tendency in the fourteenth century towards the composition of entirely Latin motets or of *formes fixes*, sung in French and eschewing a tenor altogether.[88] An examination of the intertextuality between Machaut's sacred Latin tenor and the two secular (French) upper voices might help explain his decision to base M5 on a tenor perhaps taken from the antiphon *Domine, si adhuc* from the feast of St Martin. The point of departure for the following discussion is the concluding phrase of the triplum: 'and it is clear that my lord Yvain won the love of the great lion through true service and not through his knightly valour'.

Yvain, or the knight with the lion

Decontextualised from its existence as a Latin phrase taken from an antiphon, the tenor abstracts the mood of both motetus and triplum. The narrator of the triplum is the more explicit: although he admits his fear of the lady who threatens to kill him and causes him countless sorrows, he does not intend to leave her. On the contrary, he is 'entirely hers', and does not 'wish to be free of this danger'. The tenor thus underlines the narrator's submission to the lady: her *voluntas* (will) be done. The concluding words of the triplum, however, present the listener with a semantic problem; in more than one way, the last phrase seems detached from the general context

---

[87] Paul Gehl suggested a possible reason for this preference: Christ's words in Gethsemane are expressions of individual sufferings; those of the *Pater noster* are the collective words of the church community (pers. comm.).

[88] Except for motets 9, 18, 19 and 21–3, composed entirely in Latin, and motets 11, 16 and 20, that have French in all voices.

A Courtly Lover and an Earthly Knight

presented in the triplum. It marks a sudden shift from the first person 'je' to the third person – it does not seem to relate in any way to the preceding phrases. How can we reconcile the sudden and late appearance of two new figures, Yvain and the lion? And what do they have to do with the rest of the triplum, the motet as a whole, and St Martin?

Yvain and the lion are leading characters in a romance of the second half of the twelfth century, Chrétien de Troyes's *Yvain, ou le chevalier au lion* (c. 1176–1181).[89] *Yvain* is the story of a knight who wins the hand of Laudine after killing her husband in a bitter fight. Promising to return after one year, he sets out on a journey during which he gains fame and glory in numerous tournaments. However, he neglects to come home on time to Laudine, who now asks him to stay away from her. Yvain goes mad but through a series of adventurous and heroic deeds ultimately regains the love of his wife.

The episode relevant to our discussion begins in line 3341, when the lion is first mentioned.[90] Wandering through the forest, Yvain suddenly hears a piercing scream. Approaching the scene, he sees a serpent with flames coming out of its mouth, biting the lion's tail. Instinctively, Yvain decides to help the lion. Before doing this, however, he contemplates his reasons for doing so. He first realises that he should not help the serpent 'because such a venomous and treacherous creature deserves nothing but maltreatment' (ll. 3359–61).[91] Yvain then rationalises his desire to protect the lion despite the possibility that the beast might eventually kill him. He regards the lion as a noble beast ('[un] animal noble par excellence') and cannot bear the idea that the treacherous serpent will kill him. After Yvain slays the serpent, the lion stands rampant, crying and thanking him for saving his life. Having won his love, Yvain is thereafter served and helped by the lion.

In the Hebrew Bible, animals constitute the summit of the non-human creation. The existence of all animals is considered a

---

[89] For the original middle French, I have used the edition of P. Walter in *Chrétien de Troyes, Œuvres complètes*, ed. D. Poirion (Paris, 1994), pp. 340–503. Line numbers correspond to this French edition. I have also consulted the following English edition, from which all English translations in this article are taken: *Yvain, The Knight of the Lion*, trans. B. Raffel (New Haven and London, 1987).
[90] The figure of the lion disappears from the romance in line 6727, very near the end.
[91] 'Car une créature venimeuse et félonne ne mérite que d'être maltraitée.'

fundamental good, with the biblical lion emblematic of magnanimity and courage.[92] In Genesis 49: 9, Jacob refers to his son Judah as a lion's whelp: 'Judah is a lion's whelp: from the prey, my son, thou art gone up: he stooped down, he couched as a lion, and as an old lion; who shall rouse him up?' One of the most famous Hebrew Bible descendants of this 'lion's whelp' is King David.[93] The prophecy of Amos, moreover, is rich with animal images; chapter 3: 8 reads: 'The lion hath roared, who will not fear? The Lord God hath spoken, who can but prophesy?'[94]

The serpent in the Bible, however, represents the other pole; whereas the lion is majestic and noble, the serpent embodies everything evil. In Genesis 3: 14, God informs the serpent: 'Because thou hast done this, thou art cursed above all cattle, and above every beast of the field; upon thy belly shalt thou go, and dust shalt thou eat all the days of thy life.' In Revelation 12: 7–9 the dragon (serpent) is portrayed as the Devil: 'And there was war in heaven: Michael and his angels fought against the dragon; and the dragon fought and his angels, and prevailed not; . . . And the great dragon was cast out, that old serpent, called the devil, and Satan, which deceiveth the whole world: he was cast out into the earth . . .'.[95]

Throughout medieval Europe, the dichotomy between lion and serpent flourished: the serpent was seen as the incarnation of evil, while the lion was usually the epitome of good. This view was primarily transmitted through the *Physiologus*, written in Alexandria in the second century AD. In the twelfth century the *Physiologus* regained currency, and, together with Isidore's *Etymologiae*, was transformed into the literary genre known as the bestiary.[96] The

---

[92] Genesis 1: 21: 'And God created great whales, and every living creature that moveth, which the waters brought forth abundantly, after their kind, and every winged fowl after his kind: and God saw that it was good.' English translations of the Bible follow the Authorised Version. As J. Voisenet notes, more than any other beast, the biblical lion is viewed with some ambivalence: it is seen as majestic on the one hand, but demonic on the other. See his *Bestiaire chrétien: L'imagerie animale des auteurs du Haut Moyen Âge (V^e–XIe S.)* (Toulouse, 1994), p. 313.

[93] See also Revelation 5: 5: 'Weep not: behold, the Lion of the tribe of Juda, the Root of David, hath prevailed.'

[94] In Proverbs 19: 12 we find the following imagery: 'The king's wrath is as the roaring of a lion.'

[95] In his *Etymologiae*, Isidore of Seville refers to *Draco* as a kind of serpent: 'draco maior cunctorum serpentium, sive omnium animantium super terram . . . Unde et derivatum est in latinum ut diceretur draco'). See *Isidori Hispalensis Episcopi Etymologiarum sive Originum*, ed. W. M. Lindsay (London and New York, 1911), Liber XII (*De animalibus*), iii.

[96] M. Hoogvliet, 'De ignotis quarumdam bestiarum naturis', in L. A. J. R. Houwen (ed.), *Animals and the Symbolic in Medieval Art and Literature* (Groningen, 1997), pp. 189–208, at p. 199. See also

A Courtly Lover and an Earthly Knight

Physiologus is structured allegorically, with every animal used to teach a moral lesson. Characteristically, medieval bestiaries are not scientific works, but rather moralised treatises used by priests to deliver moral lessons to their congregations.[97] In the *Physiologus* and consequently in medieval bestiaries in general, the lion is invariably the symbol of Christ, or God.[98] Like all medieval bestiaries, the first chapter of Philippe de Thaün's *Bestiaire*, for example, is devoted to the lion. Here, we find numerous references to Christ and God. Verses 47–9 carry the following symbolism: 'The lion signifies the son of St. Mary; He is king of all people.'[99] In the third chapter, devoted to the panther, there is a further reference to God as lion: 'When God assembles us, he resembles a Panther, and a lion he resembles when he resurrects.'[100]

Yet another link between the lion and God/Christ is provided in Isidore's *Etymologiae*: 'but *leo* is Greek, in Latin it is interpreted "king", the one who rules all animals ... when they [the lion and the lioness] sleep, the[ir] eyes are watching [guarding]'.[101] In *Yvain*, the lion likewise stands guard at night while Yvain is sleeping. The image of the lion as Christ in the Middle Ages thus seems to resonate strongly with Yvain's lion. Nevertheless, merely suggesting

---

D. Hassig, 'Marginal Bestiaries', *ibid.*, p. 171. For the popularity and influence Isidore's *Etymologiae* enjoyed during the Middle Ages, see Voisenet, *Bestiaire chrétien*, pp. 16–17. Although no exemplar of the *Physiologus* survives in the Reims Cathedral library, a copy of Isidore of Seville's *Etymologiae* is extant. It is reasonable to assume a direct or secondary knowledge of this literature by educated persons in the Middle Ages; there exist over 250 manuscripts of the *Physiologus* in Latin and other Romance languages, copied between 1100 and 1400. See F. Carmody, 'Physiologus Latinus Versio Y', *University of California Publications in Classical Philology*, 12 (1941), p. 95.

[97] G. R. Merimier, *A Medieval Book of Beasts: Pierre de Beauvais' Bestiary* (Lampeter: The Edwin Mellen Press, Ltd., 1992), pp. iv–vi.

[98] A. G. Brodeur, 'The Grateful Lion', *Publications of the Modern Languages Association of America*, 39 (1924), pp. 485–524, at p. 510. See also *Physiologus*, trans. M. J. Curely (Austin, Tex., 1979), pp. 3–4, and T. H. White, *The Book of Beasts, Being a Translation from a Latin Bestiary of the Twelfth Century* (London, 1954), pp. 7–9.

[99] 'Le Leüns signifie Le fiz Sainte Marie; Reis est de tute gent.' Philippe de Thaün's *Bestiaire*, composed in England, is the first to be written in French, in the first third of the twelfth century. Much of the imagery he uses is derived from Isidore of Seville's *Etymologiae*. References to Thaün's *Bestiaire* are based on the following edition: *Le bestiaire de Philippe de Thaün*, ed. E. Walberg (Lund, 1900).

[100] 'Quant Deus nus asemblat Pantere resemblat, E leün resemblat Quant il resuscitat' (ll. 523–26). In ancient legends one often reads that lions are born dead but come to life three days after their birth. Thus the lion has become associated with the Resurrection, a symbol of Christ. See G. Ferguson, *Signs and Symbols in Christian Art* (New York, 1954), p. 20.

[101] 'Leo autem Graece, Latine rex interpretatur, eo quod princeps sit omnium bestiarum ... Cum dormierint [leo et leaena], vigilant oculi'. See Isidore, *Etymologiae*, ed. Lindsay, XII, ii.

that Yvain's lion symbolises God/Christ still does not explain why Machaut chose to allude to Yvain and the lion at the end of the triplum of M5.

Let us return to Chrétien's romance. In more than one way, the lion not only represents Christ symbolically, but also functions as Christ. Julian Harris has suggested that the moment in the story where Yvain meets the lion marks a turning point. Until this time Yvain has been motivated by his sense of pride: he is more interested in taking part in various tournaments and fights than in acting like a noble knight. His fame and success have made him forget the promise he made to his wife Laudine to return home after his mission had been completed. After the lion incident, however, Harris points out that Chrétien 'make[s] it a point to say that the hero is moved by *pitié* before resolving to fight'.[102] Something in Yvain has changed. Indeed, as the triplum asserts, 'he has won the love of the great lion'. Yvain is now left to win back the love of his bitter wife. Having attained the love of the lion, he performs his knightly duties in a way that underlines not his 'knightly valour', but his 'true service'. Whereas his actions prior to meeting the lion are mere feats of arms motivated by pride and revenge, thereafter his behaviour has a clear moral impetus: he overcomes the giant to save an innocent girl accused of treason and about to be burned at the stake, and he successfully fights the three knights to save Lunete, Laudine's maid, from an unjust trial (ll. 4323–4579). Through these deeds, the lion helps Yvain achieve his victories, and Chrétien makes it clear that without the lion, Yvain would have failed in his mission.

The notion of the lion as a guardian, or Christ-like figure, is further enhanced in lines 3479–83: 'Yvain rested his head on his shield all night; he rested as best as he could. The lion had enough sense to remain awake and watch over the horse.'[103] These lines resonate with a familiar theme in Scripture, one that affirms God's role as a watchman over his people. Most famously, perhaps, this

---

[102] J. Harris, 'The Rôle of the Lion in Chrétien de Troyes' *Yvain*', *Publications of the Modern Languages Association of America*, 64 (1949), pp. 1143–63, at p. 1147. See, e.g., Yvain's pity before fighting for Lunete (ll. 4357–9): 'And an immense pity seized him, hearing and seeing and understanding the poor ladies of that court.'

[103] 'Tote la nuit sor son escu, A tel repos come ce fu; Et li lyons ot tant de sens Qu'il veilla et fu an aspens Del cheval garder ...'. This point is suggested in Brodeur, 'The Grateful Lion', p. 497.

A Courtly Lover and an Earthly Knight

idea is encapsulated in the spirit of Psalm 121: 4–5: 'Behold, he that keepth Israel shall neither slumber nor sleep. The Lord is thy keeper: the Lord is thy shade upon thy right hand.' In both the triplum of M5 and the romance, the appearance of the lion marks a turning point as well as a climax. In the romance, Yvain's meeting with the lion underscores a moment of metamorphosis: he has 'seen the Lord [lion]' and won back the love of his wife. Similarly, in M5, the concluding allusion to Yvain in the triplum serves to highlight a moment of transformation that has just been stated by the narrator: after expressing the grievances towards his lady, he finally admits that 'for nothing [he] might see would [he] wish to be free from this danger [a reference to his lady], for [he] is entirely hers, with no exchange of pledge . . .'.

Chrétien's romance seems to supply M5 with more than just a pretext for winning the love of God. In a more general sense, it is possible to situate the upper voices of the motet within the context of the romance. Yvain's earliest adventure leads him to the castle of Escaldos the Red, whom he eventually kills in a bitter fight. Upon seeing Escaldos's wife, Laudine (whom he later marries himself), he immediately falls in love with her, and is subsequently 'tortured with grief' (ll. 1508–9) over the thought of the poor lady. Although he is 'mightily afraid' (l. 1951) and 'half overcome with fear' (l. 1955) of her, he still hopes that she will marry him. Yvain's meeting with the lady clearly evokes the content and style of Machaut's triplum, a trope found in other courtly love settings, to be sure: although Yvain fears that she will kill him (ll. 1230–1), he will do whatever she wishes.[104] Like the narrator of Machaut's triplum, Yvain fears his lady although he 'did nothing wrong' (ll. 1993–4); he is entirely hers and will consent to her will 'completely and in every regard' (l. 1989).

St Martin: a *miles christi*

In all probability, Machaut chose to include an explicit reference to Yvain and the lion because they symbolise Yvain's metamorphosis from a brutish warrior to a veritable noble knight – or, in the light of the allegorical reading offered above, from a violent knight to a

---

[104] The original French reads: 'Dame, la vostre grant merci, que ja ne m'an orroiz dire el'.

Christian one now solely motivated by the wish to perform good deeds under the protective eyes of God. The situation is strikingly similar to that of St Martin, whose *vita* may provide a context not only for the tenor of M5, as I have argued above, but also for the motet's upper voices.

As Severus recounts in Martin's *vita*, and as was later incorporated into the saint's liturgy, Martin was born in Pannonia (now in Hungary) to pagan parents. His father was a military tribune, and Martin soon followed in his footsteps, serving under Emperor Constantine, and later under Emperor Julian.[105] But as Severus makes clear, Martin did not serve voluntarily, 'for, from almost his first years, he aspired rather to the service of God'.[106] Chapter 4 in the *vita* revolves around Martin's military duty under Emperor Julian. Here Martin reportedly articulates the concept of *miles Christi*.[107] Assembled alongside other soldiers by Emperor Julian in the city of Worms, Martin declares: 'I have fought for you [Julian] up to this point ... now let me fight for God.'[108] Unlike Yvain, therefore, and very much in keeping with the hagiographic genre, Martin never yields to empty displays of bravery, nor is he the careless warrior in the service of women, as Yvain is reported to have been. Rather, he is apparently charitable, kind and humble, even while still in the army. Although the narratives of Yvain and Martin show these differences, both underline a process of change whereby each is transformed into a knight/soldier of God.

The transformations of St Martin and Yvain may well be mirrored in Machaut's musical structure in M5. As noted earlier, the tenor and contratenor together form a retrograde rhythmic relationship (see Example 13), featuring the kind of symmetry that fascinated Machaut in numerous other works.[109] The *talea* of the

---

[105] Peebles, 'Sulpicius Severus, Writings', p. 105.
[106] *Ibid.* A military vocation was not compatible with Christian sainthood. Apparently, Severus reduced the number of years that the historical Martin served in the army from twenty-five to just five. See Labarre, *Le manteau partagé*, pp. 207–11, and B. Rosenwein, *Rhinoceros Bound: Cluny in the Tenth Century* (Philadelphia, 1982), p. 64.
[107] See also J. Fontaine, 'Sulpice Sévère a-t-il travesti Saint Martin de Tours en martyre militaire?', *Analecta Bollandiana*, 81 (1963), pp. 31–58, and Fontaine, trans. and ed., *Sulpice Sévère: Vie de St Martin*, trans. and ed. J. Fontaine (Paris, 1968), ii, pp. 428–538.
[108] Peebles, 'Sulpicius Severus, Writings', pp. 108–9.
[109] See, for example, the various canons at the unison (e.g., L16 (*Le Lay de Confort*), B17), and the famous example of the retrograde canon, R14 (*Ma fin est mon commencement*). See the discussion in Wright, *The Maze and the Warrior: Symbols in Architecture, Theology and Music* (Cambridge, Mass.

A Courtly Lover and an Earthly Knight

Example 13   Retrograde rhythmic relationship of the tenor and contratenor in M5 (Robertson, *Guillaume de Machaut and Reims*, p. 171)

tenor turned around thus becomes the contratenor *talea*. Just as Yvain and St Martin changed directions and sought to adopt humility and devotion in their respective capacities as knight and solider, so the retrograding of the tenor in the contratenor offers a graphic metaphor for their conversions.[110] Admittedly, the St Martin imagery is allusive and abstracted, evident only in the tenor melody, while the reference to Yvain is incontestable and found in the words of the triplum. In the context of M5, St Martin is perhaps an aural, Christianised echo of the Yvain story.

In her monograph on Machaut's motets, Anne Walters Robertson identified Machaut's first seventeen motets as a self-contained series. Reading these works in the light of medieval mystical treatises suggested that they were ordered as steps in a spiritual journey, influenced by the pilgrimage-of-life literary genre (cf. Dante's *Divine Comedy* and Chaucer's *Canterbury Tales*). The tenors of M1–17 encapsulate themes elaborated in the motets' upper voices, guiding the interpretation of the motets as a whole.[111] These pieces mark the mileposts of the journey through their ordering according to steps traditionally found in mystical works. The tenors, she believes, reveal the gist of the story of M1–17. As mentioned above, M5 is the first and only four-voice motet in this series. Within this self-contained series of seventeen motets, the four-voice layout of M5 is meaningful, as is the retrograde motion between the tenor and contratenor. It is possible that Machaut deliberately chose to symbolise retrograde motion at this point in the series, where, according to Robertson, the lover/pilgrim's first submission (or

---

and London, 2001), pp. 111–14. Robertson discusses the question of musical symmetry in Machaut's motets 1–17 in *Guillaume de Machaut and Reims*, pp. 168–71.

[110] The Latin verb *convertere* means to turn back, to reverse (meanings which are infrequent in modern English use), but also to change direction and 'convert' in a religious sense.

[111] Robertson, *Guillaume de Machaut and Reims*, chs. 3–6.

turning around) occurs (*Fiat voluntas tua*).[112] In symbolising this relationship, the fourth, slow-moving retrograde voice is graphically striking.[113]

The portrait of Martin as *miles Christi* clearly emerges through the proper chants and readings for Matins on 11 November, and, as we shall see below, also through his numerous iconographic representations. One of the opening lessons in Martin's Office regularly treats his early history as a pagan soldier, where 'he fought under Emperor Constantine, later under Emperor Julian' ('sub rege constantio, deinde sub iuliano cesare militavit'), as the eleventh-century breviary from Reims Cathedral has it.[114] This Office offers but scant impression of the central position that the military trope would assume in later centuries, dedicating only a single *lectio* to Martin's career as a soldier. By the fourteenth century, however, the military vocation of St Martin came to occupy a more dominant position among the readings at the 11 November feast. In a breviary from Châlons-sur-Marne, for example, four out of nine *lectiones* relate to Martin's military career.[115] In addition, one of the proper antiphons sung in Matins, already present in the eleventh-century breviary mentioned above,[116] offers particularly evocative imagery: 'With the sign of the cross, protected by neither shield nor helmet, I shall break through the lines of the enemy in safety' ('Ego signo crucis, non clipeo protectus aut galea hostium cuneos

---

[112] *Ibid.*, p. 120. In and of itself, the idea that Machaut's first seventeen motets constitute a well-defined series does not diminish the likelihood of Leech-Wilkinson's pastiche hypothesis. It is possible that Machaut paid tribute to Vitry in passing while composing his series of motets 1–17. However, Robertson's study of M5 does cast doubt on Leech-Wilkinson's hypothesis, for she shows that the four-voice layout of M5 is purposeful, and that it carries significant symbolic weight given its relative place within the seventeen-motet series as a whole, as mentioned above.

[113] In Thomas Mann's *Doctor Faustus*, the narrator, Serenus Zeitblom, reports his impressions of one of Kretschmar's lectures, entitled 'Music and the Eye'. Discussing the pleasure that the mere sight of a musical score might afford, Kretschmar quotes the following from a Shakespeare sonnet: 'To hear with eyes belongs to love's fine wit.' Referring to the Dutch masters of polyphony, he alludes to musical devices 'that could not be perceived by the way they actually sounded . . . for it was intended rather for the eye of the guild'. Given Machaut's personal supervision of his complete-works manuscripts, and his well-documented fascination with symmetry, it may well be possible that the retrograde relation between contratenor and tenor also owes something to an *Augenmusik* fascination. The foregoing analysis, however, suggests that Machaut had a far more solemn objective.

[114] BNF lat. 17991, fol. 227^r.

[115] Lessons 1–3 and 5. See Paris, Bibliothèque de l'Arsenal, MS 595 (fourteenth century), fol. 408^{r-v}.

[116] BNF lat. 17991, fol. 226^v.

A Courtly Lover and an Earthly Knight

penetrabo securus').[117] The suggestive reference to the triumphal Constantinian *signum* is a characteristic military allusion, not only to Constantine as the Warrior of God, but to countless generations of crusaders as well – by definition Warriors of God – who counted on the protection of this *signum* against *hostium cuneos*.

The medieval iconography of St Martin centres not around the militaristic episode of the saint's life, but rather on his charity and humility. As a saint who ceased to be a soldier for Rome in favour of becoming a soldier of Christ, he was not expected to fight earthly battles in the name of Christ; rather, he simply did not fight.[118] Although one of the most popular medieval images of St Martin depicts him as a soldier mounted on a horse and holding a sword, he is rarely portrayed in the context of warfare. Drawing on an episode narrated in Severus's *vita*, the most popular scene portrays Martin at the gate of the city of Amiens (in northern France), where he meets a naked beggar on a particularly cold day. Feeling pity for the beggar, he cut his military cloak into two pieces with his sword, clothing the poor man with one portion. In a dream the beggar revealed himself as Christ. As Jacques Fontaine remarks, this iconography expresses in concrete manner Martin's 'love of God to the degree of self-contempt'.[119] As such, the scene represents the epitome of Martin's humility, concisely expressed in his own words *Fiat voluntas tua*.

Even the occasional portrayal of Martin in actual battlefield shows the saint's disdain of war. The painter Simone Martini (1280/5–1344) devoted to Martin a series of frescoes in the church dedicated to St Francis in Assisi. On the lower level of the San Martino chapel we see Martin as an officer in the Roman army face to face with the enemy, announcing his decision to cease fighting. Although Martin is clearly a knight, he does not hold a sword in his hand, nor is he mounted on a horse, two prominent themes in his

---

[117] *Ibid*. Contrary to lesson texts, which vary in length and contents from manuscript to manuscript, the transmission of antiphon texts such as *Ego signo crucis* is quite stable; it appears in fourteenth-century breviaries from Châlons-sur-Marne (for example, in Paris, Bibliothèque de l'Arsenal, MS 595, fol. 408ᵛ).

[118] A. J. Frantzen, 'Tears for Abraham: The Chester Play of Abraham and Isaac and Antisacrifice in Works by Wilfred Owen, Benjamin Britten, and Derek Jarman', *Journal of Medieval and Early Modern Studies*, 31 (2001), pp. 445–76, at p. 450. I thank Allan Frantzen for kindly sharing with me a copy of his article prior to publication, as well as for the conversation we had on St Martin.

[119] *Sulpice Sévère: Vie de Saint Martin*, trans. Fontaine, ii, p. 475.

iconography. Although the threat of war is imminent (we see the barbarians approaching from over the hills with their weapons), Martin is looking towards the emperor but walks towards the enemy. Holding only a cross in his left hand, and making a sign of blessing in his right, we can imagine him saying to the emperor: 'With the sign of the cross, protected by neither shield nor helmet, I shall break through the lines of the enemy in safety.'

The pictorial image of St Martin in soldier's garb thus eschews the violence often associated with soldiers' duties; the sword that accompanies him in numerous depictions, though the unmistakable companion of the Christian warrior, is now but a vestige of Martin's former life as a worldly warrior.[120] To be sure, this particular reception and understanding of Martin's military career, although dominant, was not common to all strata of society. Not surprisingly, those belonging to military orders and to the monarchy preferred to see in Martin a saint who never ceased to fight earthly battles. Indeed, the French monarchs evoked Martin the military saint rather than the ex-soldier exemplary for his 'charity and humility'. After Clovis's conquest of the Loire Valley in 507, Martin was adopted by the Merovingians as their patron saint, and his cape (*cappa*) steered the armies into battle in times of war. Echoing Clovis's supplication to Martin in the sixth century, Charles VII appealed in 1433 for Martin's intervention in securing 'the recovery of the kingdom and its other concerns'.[121] But it was especially between the 1340s and 1360s, during the time that Machaut was composing M5, that the image of St Martin became particularly pertinent, and with growing urgency.

---

[120] By the time the sword had become a fixture in his iconography, from as early as 1000, Martin's transformation from soldier to soldier of Christ had already inspired the lives of other saints, such as St Edmund (d. 869) and St Gerald of Aurillac (d. 909). See Frantzen, 'Tears for Abraham', p. 451. Having examined the identity of the Armed Man (l'Homme armé), the theme of a tune bearing the same name that inspired more than thirty-five cantus firmus masses composed in the fifteenth and sixteenth centuries, Craig Wright concluded that 'depending on the context, [the Armed Man] is Christ, St Michael, and ... every Christian soldier'. See *The Maze and the Warrior*, p. 164. Further research will clarify the extent to which St Martin also served as an exemplary Christian soldier for Renaissance composers. On St Martin as *miles dei*, see also A. Magro, 'Jean de Ockeghem et Saint-Martin de Tours (1454–1497): Une étude documentaire' (Ph.D. diss., Université François-Rabelais, Tours, 1998), pp. 96–7. He speculates that as an emblematic *miles dei* and as protector of knights, St Martin might have been associated with the figure of 'l'Homme armé'. See *ibid.*, p. 97.

[121] *Ordonnances des rois de France de la troisième race*, ed. E. de Laurière et al. (Paris, 1723–1849), xiii, p. 192; quoted in C. Beaune, *The Birth of an Ideology*, trans. Susan Ross Huston (Berkeley, 1991), p. 135.

A Courtly Lover and an Earthly Knight

Intermittently at war with England from 1337 to 1453, France saw many of its cities occupied and pillaged, its population devastated by natural and man-made disasters, one of its kings captive, and many of its sanctuaries increasingly under English, and later on also under Anglo-Burgundian rule. Especially in the second and third quarters of the fourteenth century, the areas to suffer the most were those found in north-eastern France, located on the invasion route taken by the English: Artois, Picardy, Champagne and the Île-de-France.[122] The first decades of the Hundred Years War witnessed a series of English victories both on land and at sea: the naval battle of Sluys (1340), the defeat at Crécy (1346), the siege and fall of Calais (1347), the Black Prince's *chevauchée* through Languedoc (1355) and his capture of John II in Poitiers (1356), and, finally, the treaty of Brétigny, in which the captive John II renounced about one-third of his kingdom. In addition to the changing geo-political boundaries of certain French territories controlled by various dynastic families (the Plantagenets, the Valois and the Burgundy branch of the Valois), prolonged internal unrest impinged on the French monarchy and on ordinary people as well, notably the peasant uprising of the Jacquerie in 1358, and the taking over of Paris by Charles II, king of Navarre, a move that effectively challenged the French monarchy. Adding to this grim picture were periods of famine, and notably the deadly consequences of the Black Death epidemic of 1348.[123]

Against this backdrop of a daily reality satiated with images of horror and vulnerability (personal and public, religious and intellectual, economic and social), we may understand the increasing reliance on and supplication to patron saints such as St Martin, who had a militaristic vocation and who enjoyed national recognition as well. Although national saints such as Louis IX and Denis never lost their radiance, they did not possess the military pedigree that made St Martin such an attractive figure during the fourteenth century.[124]

---

[122] M. C. Jones, 'War and Fourteenth-Century France', in Clifford J. Rogers (ed.), *The Wars of Edward III: Sources and Interpretations* (Woodbridge, 1999), pp. 343–64, at p. 345.
[123] Although it cannot be listed in the catalogue of English victories, one should also mention the prolonged siege of Reims in 1359/60, which ultimately failed.
[124] Regions south of the Loire have generally been spared the massive warfare experienced in the north-eastern and south-western parts of France. Given the association of St Martin with the city of Tours, it is likely that a connection between his increasing popularity and relevance to the French in this tumultuous period might have something to do with the relative peace that

It is perhaps owing to the renewed appeal of this saintly figure that Guillaume de Machaut, a composer whose personal and professional life were deeply influenced by the turmoil of the fourteenth century, might have alluded to Martin in one of his early motets.

> First take the Tenor from some antiphon or responsory or another chant from the antiphonal, and the words should concord with the matter you wish to make the motet.[125]

When Machaut composed M5, he must have found the tenor *Fiat voluntas tua* particularly appropriate for 'the matter [from which he wished] to make the motet'. Although he might have chosen the more familiar chant segment from the setting of these same words in the *Pater noster*, he found he had at his disposal an even more precise context, with respect to his plans for the motet. True, the words *Fiat voluntas tua* convey the same message in both settings, that is, obedience and surrender to someone else's will. However, in the antiphon *Domine, si adhuc*, these words also encapsulate the theme of conversion and humility, evidenced in both the music and subject matter of M5.

Following Murino, Alice Clark reminds us that although the selection of the tenor precedes the motet's *materia*, the motet should concord with the matter (*concordare cum materia*), and the tenor is ultimately chosen on the basis of that *materia*.[126] *Materia* thus has conceptual priority over the tenor, while the tenor possesses functional priority with respect to harmony, rhythm, and melody. If Machaut wanted a tenor match for the *materia* he had in mind for M5, then the snippet from St Martin's antiphon, carrying with it the connotation of the saint's conversion, was superior to that from the *Pater noster* prayer. The concept of transformation is particularly

---

the city and its sanctuaries experienced. I discuss this aspect of the city's history in my forthcoming Ph.D. dissertation, 'Music and Ceremony in Saint-Martin of Tours, 1205–1500' (University of Chicago, 2005), chs. 1 and 4. Despite the crusading activities of St Louis, his posthumous reputation did not include military fame. For the French nobility, for instance, St Louis 'stood for coinage, fiscal privilege, and a sound judicial system' and between 1350 and 1500 he 'became the patron saint of individual confraternities'. See Beaune, *The Birth of an Ideology*, pp. 116, 120–1. As for St Denis, he was, after all, a martyr, hardly a promising image for a nation under siege. For the French kings, moreover, Denis was a personal saint, looking after their well-being. Well into the fifteenth century, prayers for the king's health would be intoned in the abbey of St-Denis. See *ibid.*, 35–6.

[125] Egidius de Murino, *De modo componendi tenores motetorum*, quoted in Leech-Wilkinson, *Compositional Techniques*, i, p. 21.

[126] Clark, '*Concordare cum Materia*', p. 6.

A Courtly Lover and an Earthly Knight

prominent in the triplum as well: the lover first complains that he cannot understand why his Lady does not return his love ('Truly, I do not know'), but then quickly contradicts himself, admitting that he in fact does know, and that he has lied.

The life of St Martin, therefore, may offer more than simply an allusive image for M5. The antiphon *Domine, si adhuc* from the saint's Office, a chant that Machaut must have known, possibly opens a window into his choice or method of composition of a tenor for this work. This was the saint whose spiritual aura gave rise to the most important and popular pilgrimage site in medieval France (the basilica dedicated to him in Tours), and whose iconography and *vita* propagated his image as a newly committed soldier of Christ. In Martin, Machaut no doubt found an inspiring image. As a composer of vernacular poetry and sacred music, Machaut was uniquely qualified to mediate between the secular and sacred domains. The confluence of these can be clearly seen in M5, whose tenor's words, as Egidius recommends, do 'concord with the matter' of this French motet with its Latin tenor, and whose tenor perhaps does hail, at least in part, 'from some antiphon'.

University of Chicago

Early Music History (2005) Volume 24. © Cambridge University Press

LAURIE STRAS

'AL GIOCO SI CONOSCE IL GALANTUOMO': ARTIFICE, HUMOUR AND PLAY IN THE *ENIGMI MUSICALI* OF DON LODOVICO AGOSTINI

In 1571 and 1581, the Ferrarese cleric-musician Don Lodovico Agostini published two books each containing, amongst other pieces, a group of madrigals cryptically notated as musical puzzles, advertised as *enigmi musicali* on their title pages. The *enigmi* are aptly named; no doubt the composer would have delighted in the *doppio senso*, or double entendre, inherent in the term, for they are musical riddles in both a formal and a metaphorical sense. Their content and their very existence in print pose an intriguing array of questions beyond the obvious enquiries regarding the identifying characteristics of the genre and the identity of their composer. Certainly, the *enigmi musicali* invite speculation about the nature of music as a pastime in late sixteenth-century courtly Italy. Agostini's *enigmi musicali* are secular, polyphonic vocal works, but they cannot be classed simply as madrigals, nor are they representative of so-called lighter genres of *villanelle* or *canzonette*. They exist somewhere on the fringe of the repertoire, with a specific character that reaches in towards the (to us) more familiar forms of Italian secular music, but that also reaches out to and overlaps with other spheres

Portions of this article were presented at the Conference for Medieval and Renaissance Music, Bristol, July 2002, and the Sixty-Eighth Annual Meeting of the American Musicological Society, Columbus, Ohio, November 2002. I am grateful to a host of generous scholars who have read and commented upon earlier versions, or who have shared their knowledge with me: Bonnie Blackburn, Cees de Bondt, Jeanice Brooks, Tim Carter, Andrew Dell'Antonio, Flora Dennis, James Haar, Matthew Head, Leofranc Holford-Strevens, Donna Cardamone Jackson, Melanie Marshall, Anthony Newcomb, Patrick Macey, Massimo Ossi, Richard Wistreich, my anonymous readers and the community of the Ficino e-discussion list. I am particularly indebted to Andrew Dell'Antonio and Leofranc Holford-Strevens for their translation assistance; however, any vagaries or errors in the translations I must claim for myself. I am grateful to Dr Ernesto Milano, Director of the Biblioteca Estense, Modena; Prof. Domenico Carboni, Director of the Biblioteca del Conservatorio di Musica 'Santa Cecilia', Rome; and the Staatsund Stadtbibliothek, Augsburg, for permission to reproduce photographs of books in their collections. Financial assistance for the completion of this research was given by the Arts and Humanities Research Board of Great Britain.

213

of play and philosophical engagement. So where may the *enigmi* be placed within the wider compass of early modern social recreation, and what factors might have motivated their composition and their use? Furthermore, if we accept them as evidence of some sort of collective diversion, how are they intended to amuse – are they humorous or cerebral, or both? How does their composer's vocation affect our interpretations of their content and their function? Do they have precedents or correspondences that might help locate them more accurately in a cultural context? And finally, what may the study of these unusual works reveal of their equally enigmatic author?

GAMES OF REVELATION AND CONCEALMENT: PERFORMANCE AND ARTIFICE IN MUSICAL GAMES

Italian patrician society, which provides the backdrop for an assessment of both Agostini and his puzzles, was steeped in a centuries-old tradition of recreation and play. Story-telling, jokes, debate, physical activity and games, organised and impromptu contests, music and dance were part of the everyday diversions of the Italian nobility.[1] These activities may be divided into several broad, though overlapping categories: those that involved physical skill, such as dancing, fencing and hunting; those devised primarily for the promotion of laughter, including the playing of practical jokes; board-based contests, such as chess; gambling, either with cards or dice, or on the outcome of a contest; parlour games; 'conversation', the almost ritualistic display of knowledge, wit and rhetorical skill which included the posing and answering of riddles and *dubbi* (philosophical or rhetorical questions); and the practice and display of acquired accomplishments, such as musical or poetic/dramatic performances. For the courtier, activities that relied upon social interaction – where the individual could play and

---

[1] Accounts of games and debates are central to many sixteenth-century civility books, including the two most widely read and translated volumes, B. Castiglione, *Il libro del cortegiano* (Venice, 1528) and S. Guazzo, *La civil conversatione* (Brescia, 1574). The classic twentieth-century reference work (in English) which charts the recreational activities of the Italian courts, containing synopses and translations of literary documents from four centuries, is T. F. Crane, *Italian Social Customs of the Sixteenth Century* (New Haven, 1920). A more recent and specific source study of the medical and moral imperatives for recreation is presented by A. Archangeli, *Recreation in the Renaissance: Attitudes towards Leisure and Pastimes in European Culture, c. 1425–1675* (Basingstoke and New York, 2003), pp. 23–4.

'Al gioco si conosce il galantuomo'

yet remain part of a group – were extremely useful in securing admiration and status, and even gaining access to his or her ruler, through a sanctioned display of ability. Participation in games or other organised pastimes allowed the courtier to excel without winning, or at least to have permission to win from the group; thus he or she could be seen to be clever or witty without making unsolicited demonstrations.

More important even than revelation of skill was the concealment of the fact of the skill itself; in *Il libro del cortegiano*, Castiglione coined a new word, *sprezzatura*, to describe the art of concealing art ('un certa sprezzatura, che nasconde l'arte ... quella esser vera arte che non pare esser arte').[2] The concept of sprezzatura was particularly relevant for the performance of music, which necessitated long hours of study to develop both knowledge and fluency.[3] Dissimulation (*inganno*), in its various permutations of trickery, cheating and disguise, had its own place in a great variety of games. Torquato Tasso, ventriloquising through the Ferrarese noblewoman Margherita Bentivoglio in his dialogue *Il Gonzaga secondo, over Del giuoco*, expresses the essential and paradoxical nature of inganno in relation to games: 'Nor do I believe that in this game deceit is blameworthy, provided it is a game' ('né credo ch'in questo giuoco sia biasimevole l'ingannare, s'egli è pur giuoco').[4] The practice of games was thus inextricably linked with the practice of artifice, in both its senses of accumulated skill and accomplished deception.

Girolamo Bargagli's *Dialogo de' giuochi* of 1572 defines games as 'merry action[s] of a joyful and amiable company, in which upon a pleasing or ingenious proposition made by one as author and guide of such action, all the others do or say something different from each

---

[2] B. Castiglione, *Il libro del cortegiano*, ed. G. Preti (Turin, 1965), Book 1, ch. 26. *Sprezzatura* as a principle of Renaissance courtly self-fashioning is discussed by H. Berger, Jr. in *The Absence of Grace: Sprezzatura and Suspicion in Two Renaissance Courtesy Books* (Stanford, Calif., 2000).
[3] See J. Haar, 'The Courtier as Musician: Castiglione's View of the Science and Art of Music', in P. Corneilson (ed.), *The Science and Art of Renaissance Music* (Princeton, 1998), pp. 20–37, at p. 23. R. Wistreich, 'Giulio Cesare Brancaccio and Solo Bass Singing in Sixteenth-Century Italy' (Ph.D. thesis, University of London, 2002), also examines the phenomenon; his presentation at the 17th International Congress of the International Musicological Society, Leuven, 2002, 'Real Basses, Real Men: Virtù and Virtuosity in the Construction of Male Noble Identity in Late 16th-Century Italy', dealt with the issue in respect of musicians in some detail.
[4] T. Tasso, *Il Gonzaga secondo: overo Del giuoco, Dialogo*, 1582, in *Opere*, ed. B. Maier, 5 vols. (Milan, 1964), iv, p. 860.

other, and this for the purpose of pleasure and entertainment'.[5] He further divides games into two types: *piacevole*, or pleasing games of jest to make one laugh; and *grave*, or serious games of wit to make one think. The social performance of music, typified by the performance of madrigals from partbooks, fits rather well into Bargagli's definition; the 'pleasing or ingenious proposition' being the musical composition, with the individual action provided by the different voices or instruments needed for the performance. A courtier who took either the role of the originator or the participant of a musical game, as composer, player or singer, would have a way of demonstrating his or her talents whilst avoiding criticism for making overt displays of technical skill, absolved by the mutual nature of the agreement to sing.[6]

Although Bargagli's manual makes no specific reference to music as a game, a passage from Agostino Mosti's memoir of life in mid-sixteenth-century Ferrara, written in 1584, directly links the concept of games with social singing:

as was said these modest gentlemen and citizens amused themselves very decently, with as little or as much as they had, and in several of the most favoured houses there were games throughout the day, mostly for fun and to pass the time, rather than for vice or avarice, because at that time there was not the pastime of music, which came afterwards, in the playing of various instruments, in which the princes themselves delighted, and played: but now again they have turned to the older game, in which only the singing of French songs is used, but in such perfection that it is an admirable thing, and to this singing is joined various sounds [of instruments], and they play together, so that truly it is almost a wicked thing, but nevertheless most virtuous, if it is done vigorously and richly, and where there were ten there are now a hundred and even more, and these various pastimes I can say I have seen them two or three times in my younger days, and now newly revived . . .[7]

---

[5] Il Materiale intronato [G. Bargagli], *Dialogo de' giuochi che nelle vegghi sanesi si usono di fare* (Siena, 1572). This definition is quoted in Crane, *Italian Social Customs*, pp. 268–9, and in J. Haar, 'On Musical Games in the 16th Century', *Journal of the American Musicological Society*, 15 (1962), pp. 22–34, at p. 22. While Bargagli's dialogue is situated squarely in academic, rather than courtly circles, the practices it and manuals like it discuss are more or less common to the whole of privileged society in late sixteenth-century Italy. The issue is handled comprehensively by Crane; for a more specifically musical examination, see D. Fabris, 'Giochi musicali e veglie "alla senese" nelle città non toscane dell'Italia rinascimentale', in I. Alm, A. McLamore and C. Reardon (eds.), *Musica Franca: Essays in Honor of Frank A. D'Accone* (Stuyvesant, NY, 1996), pp. 213–29.

[6] On music as a spontaneous group activity, see S. Lorenzetti, *Musica e identità nobiliare nell'Italia del Rinascimento* (Florence, 2003), p. 164.

[7] A. Solerti, 'La vita ferrarese nella prima metà del secolo decimosesto, descritta da Agostini Mosti', *Atti e memorie della R. deputazione di stori patri per le provincie di Romagna*, 3rd ser., 10 (1892), pp. 164–203, at p. 194. 'ma come si è detto quei mediocri Gentilhuomini e Cittadini si trattenevano molto onestamente, e quel poco o molto che aveano, ed in alcune Case de' più

'Al gioco si conosce il galantuomo'

Mosti's account has intriguing implications for the understanding of how music was used locally in Ferrara, Agostini's birthplace and eventual permanent residence, and especially of how attitudes towards music-making may have changed over the course of the century. He describes a situation in which 'the old game' of social singing (by which we may understand the singing of polyphony) and musical performance appear to have fallen out of favour as pastimes, only gradually to have been rehabilitated.[8] But even within the circumscription of playful activity a tension remained, and Mosti expresses the perhaps uneasy relationship between the making of music and the retention of *virtù*.

Music-making is sited even more specifically within the sphere of games by the Ferrarese poet and secretary to Duke Ercole II d'Este, Giovanbattista Giraldi Cinzio, in his advice to young noblemen on conduct befitting those in service to a ruler, *L'uomo di corte. Discorso intorno a quello che si conviene a giovane e nobile e ben creato nel servire un gran principe*.[9] Giraldi includes music in his chapter on 'giuochi onesti' (decent games), putting singing and the playing of stringed instruments on an equal level with chess as pastimes which are 'most worthy of gentlemen'; however, he too warns of the dangers of over-assiduousness or excesses of display: 'But all must be done in such a way that virtue does not turn into vice' ('Ma il tutto si dee fare con tal modo che non riesca la virtù vizio').[10]

Whilst simply the act of performing music within a social context can be and was construed as a participatory game, Agostini's enigmas have an added dimension of puzzlecraft, placing them

---

favoriti era qualche trattenimento il giorno di giuoco, la più parte da spasso, e passatempo, che per vizio, nè per avarizia, perchè non vi era a quei tempi lo spasso delle musiche, che sono dapoi venute, e soni di varii strumenti, de' quali i Prencipi stessi se ne dilettavano, e sonavano: ma ecco che un'altra volta si è tornato al giuoco antico, che solo il canto delle voci Francesi è in uso, anzi in tanta perfezione, che è cosa mirabile, ed a questo aggiungono ancora parecchi suoni, e fanno concerti, che veramente è cosa quasi viziosa, non che virtuosissima, e se si giuoca la fanno cosi gagliarda e grossamente, che dove andavano li 10. vanno li 100. ed anco migliaja, e questi varj spassi posso dire de avergli veduto due o tre volte ai miei giorni disposti, e di nuovo riassunti ...'. The phrase 'il canto delle voci Francesi', particularly qualified by the adjective 'antico', appears in this instance to refer to the polyphonic chanson. One of Mosti's generation – he was born in 1505 – might view all polyphonic secular music as stemming from or related to this repertoire.

[8] Evidence exists that singing was not just considered a pastime, but a physical exercise with medical benefits; see Archangeli, *Recreation in the Renaissance*, pp. 23–4.

[9] Published in 1565. Ed. A. Guidorzi, Biblioteca Italiana Telematica (CiBit) (http://icon.di.unipi.it/ricerca/html/Giraldi-Uomo.html), accessed 2 Sept. 2003.

[10] *Ibid.*, ch. 5, para. 3 (p. 44).

more conspicuously within a more distinct tradition, albeit one which is ostensibly attenuated from the courtly environment.[11] The majority of early musical works that we might readily identify as musical games employ a sort of musical cryptography by which the successful performance of the piece relies upon the accurate realisation or appreciation of a notational puzzle; canons are obvious examples. Renaissance canons range from simple monophonic phrases that produce relatively straightforward *fugato* imitation to those that require special formatting. Geometric figures, such as circles, triangles and rectangles, were favoured, although phrases could be deployed to form more complicated patterns, and could also be enhanced by pictorial additions. Needless to say, the more advanced or complicated the cryptography, the less likely its successful realisation in moveable type; this is perhaps one reason for the relative scarcity in print of the more elaborate puzzles. As tempting as it might be for a publisher to exhibit artifice of his own in producing an intricate and complex musical puzzle, the process would be expensive and the market for the finished product somewhat restricted. However, at the other end of the scale, simple notational *doppi sensi* are plentiful in sixteenth-century printed music – 'eye-music' could be considered a very mild form of the phenomenon, visual representations of textual conceits that, whilst easy to recognise and to effect, provide an extra frisson to the entertainment. Solmisation puns are another manifestation of the same urge to create layered or multiple meanings, though in this case the realisation is both visual and performative. Neither of these playful gestures is necessarily apparent to the listener; they are specifically intended to be appreciated by the performer during the act of performance.

Although during the sixteenth century the term 'canon' came to signify that most artificial of compositional techniques, the strict *fugato* imitation, it originally referred only to the instructions for solving a piece of musical shorthand, not to the piece itself. In 1495, Johannes Tinctoris defined canon as 'a rule showing the purpose of the composer behind a certain obscurity'; thirteen years earlier, Bartolomeus Ramis de Pareja had used a similar phrase, but

---

[11] From this point, I will use the English word 'enigma' and its anglicised plural 'enigmas' to avoid both excessive italicisation and the confusion threatened by the use of the arcane, if correct, 'enigmata'.

'Al gioco si conosce il galantuomo'

specifically invoked the concept of 'enigma': 'a rule suggesting the composer's intention under the veil of some ambiguity, obscurely, and in enigmatic form'.[12] The rise and continued engagement with canon as a musical technique must to some degree have relied on the appeal of both creating and solving puzzles, although some theorists stressed the didactic function of canons, useful as novel teaching aids for solmisation and compositional rules.[13]

Yet canons also served to demonstrate the ingenuity of their creators and to flatter the intellect of those who were able to find the solutions, feeding into what Harry Berger has called 'a sprezzatura of elite enclosure[,] founded on the complicity of a coded performance in which the actor and his peers reaffirm their superiority to those incapable of deciphering the code'.[14] Throughout the sixteenth century and beyond, the most obscure puzzles were circulated among a musical elite.[15] Sergio Durante has argued that the practice of *artificioso* composition in Rome in the first half of the seventeenth century, which encompassed the creation of enigmatic canons, was a manifestation of an 'aristocratic model of behaviour' developed in the musical community, separating the most learned

---

[12] E. E. Lowinsky, 'Music in Titian's *The Bacchanal of the Andrians*: Origins and History of the *Canon per tonos*', in *Music in the Culture of the Renaissance*, ed. B. J. Blackburn, 2 vols. (Chicago, 1989), i, pp. 289–350, at p. 301; J. Tinctoris, *Dictionary of Musical Terms*, ed. and trans. C. Parrish (London, 1963), pp. 12–13: 'Canon est regula voluntatem compositoris sub obscuritate quadam ostendens.' The Ramis translation is after *A Correspondence of Renaissance Musicians*, ed. B. J. Blackburn, E. E. Lowinsky and C. A. Miller (Oxford, 1991), pp. 226–7, 'regula voluntatem componentis sub quadam amibiguitate obscure et in enigmate insinuans'; B. Ramis de Pareja, *Musica practica* (Bologna, 1482; facs. repr. Bologna, 1969), p. 90.

[13] D. B. Collins, 'Canon in Music Theory from c.1550 to c.1800' (Ph.D. diss., Stanford University, 1992); the seventh chapter of this dissertation is devoted to the discussion of canons in music pedagogy. Leeman Perkins advances a theory regarding Ockeghem's hexachordal canon *Prenez sur moi*, postulating that its initial and primary function was didactic; L. Perkins, 'Ockeghem's *Prenez sur moi*: Reflections on Canons, Catholica and Solmization', *Musica Disciplina*, 44 (1990), pp. 119–84. The use of puzzles to teach solmisation and proportions seems also to have been popular elsewhere in Europe. Contemporary examples may be found in the exercises to develop both skills composed by the Master of the Boys at the Chapel Royal, Nathaniel Giles, possibly showing a connection with the boys' education; the pieces are copied in John Baldwin's Commonplace Book. See R. Bray, 'British Museum MS Royal 24.d.2 (John Baldwin's Commonplace Book): An Index and Commentary', *RMA Research Chronicle*, 12 (1974), pp. 137–51.

[14] Berger, *The Absence of Grace*, p. 10.

[15] For instance, the explication of enigmatic canons is one of the areas frequently touched on in the correspondence between Giovanni Spataro, Marcantonio Cavazzoni, Giovanni del Lago and Pietro Aaron, documented in *Correspondence of Renaissance Musicians*, ed. Blackburn, Lowinsky and Miller. The social use of enigmatic canons among musicians is also dealt with in Lowinsky, 'Music in Titian's *The Bacchanal of the Andrians*'.

musicians from those considered 'ordinary'.[16] Nonetheless, the relationship of this academic practice with the culture of games is evident. In a letter written in 1520 to Pietro Aaron, Giovanni Spataro complained that Giovanni del Lago had infringed etiquette (or indeed, the rules of engagement) by submitting to him an enigmatic tenor without supplying the other parts – an action that was 'unheard-of'; over one hundred years later, Giovanni Briccio closed the preface to his *Canoni enigmatici musicali* by admitting that his work 'in the end is nothing but a musical joke'.[17]

The hierarchy of musical games, ranging from notational teasers to academic conundrums, and the relative skill required to appreciate them, is also reflected in the subtle differentiation between levels of artistry inherent in the terminology proposed by the Accademia della Crusca's *Vocabolario*. Published in 1612, the *Vocabolario*'s definition of *enigma* echoes Tinctoris' definition of canon: 'an obscure saying, which under the veil of words hides an allegorical sense'. It goes on: 'One also says "riddle" [*indovinello*]; but really "riddle" is an obscure proposal, made to someone else, so that he must sharpen his wits in order to extract the true meaning, for instance: [What is] that which one has, but cannot give away, but that can be given by one who has it not – the answer is death.'[18] Riddles are one-liners; enigmas are less rigidly defined, encompassing more artful or elaborate obscurities. Although Spataro's correspondence and Briccio's title show the word 'enigma' and its forms were commonly used to describe cryptographic musical works, Agostini seems to use the word generically, perhaps to indicate a correspondence with an existing literary genre. Modelled on examples from antiquity, such as those by Symphosius and Athenaeus, the Renaissance literary enigma was a cryptic poetic stanza.[19] Established as a genre in its own right, it also was

---

[16] S. Durante, 'On *Artificioso* Compositions at the Time of Frescobaldi', in A. Silbiger (ed.), *Frescobaldi Studies* (Durham, NC, 1987), pp. 195–217, at p. 200, n. 10.

[17] *Correspondence of Renaissance Musicians*, ed. Blackburn, Lowinsky, and Miller, pp. 694, 704; Durante, 'On *Artificioso* Compositions', p. 200, n. 13.

[18] *Vocabolario degli Accademici della Crusca* (1612; facs. repr. Florence, 1974), p. 315: 'ENIGMA. detto oscuro, che sotto'l velame delle parole, nasconde senso allegorico ... dicesi anche INDOVINELLO: ma propriamente INDOVINELLO è una proposta oscura, fatta ad altrui, accioch'gli abbia ad assottigliar lo'ngegno, per cavarne il vero senso, come. Quel, che l'ha non la può dare può ben darla, chi non l'ha: che è la morte.'

[19] Symposius's enigmas were published in Paris in 1533, and an Italian print followed in 1581: Caelius Symposius, *Symphosii veteris poet elegantissimi erudita iuxta ac arguta et festiua Aenigmata* (Paris,

'Al gioco si conosce il galantuomo'

circulated in collections that were published with solutions, which presumably could be used in company or alone. Examples of its use as part of social interaction are found in most civility books, and more explicitly in games manuals like Bargagli's.[20]

Agostini's musical enigmas combine the appreciation of artifice with various strands of play – mutual display, problem-solving and cryptography – in single works that look to have been designed as an entertainment for a party of a minimum of six people. Unlike the parlour games published in Bargagli's manual, Agostini's enigmas require a high degree of specialist skill and knowledge from the players; the vocal parts are not easy to sing, and the riddles' solutions frequently rely on an understanding of musical terminology and notation beyond the level needed to read the average sixteenth-century partbook. All the players, therefore, would have participated with the understanding that everyone playing could have licence to exhibit their learning. The books Agostini's enigmas appear in also contain a variety of other musical entertainments or specialities, apparently selected for novelty value: dialogues, *madrigali cromatici* (so designated, but in the harmonic, rather than the notational, sense), parodies, *concerti* (i.e., works intended for performance with instruments), echoes, canons and elaborate hexachordal jokes. The enigmas thus appear to have been conceived as recreational material for a musical elite, based on more common courtly and academic pastimes but reflecting and flattering the sophistication and ability of their dedicatees and practitioners.

THE MUSICAL CHARACTER OF AGOSTINI'S *ENIGMI MUSICALI*

With a single exception that will be discussed later, Agostini's enigmas all share a central musical characteristic, inasmuch as they are polyphonic works with textures and texts indistinguishable from ordinary madrigals; however, not all the voices are fully notated. One voice must be deciphered from a notational cryptogram and a

---

1533); Caelius Symposius, *Ænigmata Symposii. cum scholiis Iosephi Castalionis Anconitani* (Rome, 1581). An Aldine print of Athenaeus' *Deipnosophistae*, in Greek, appeared in 1514 (Venice, 1514); in 1556, a Latin translation by Natale Conti was issued simultaneously in France, Germany and Italy: *Atheni Dipnosophistarum siue cænæ sapientum libri XV. Natale de Comitibus . . . nunc primum e græca in latinam linguam uertente* (Paris, 1556; Basle, 1556; and Venice, 1556).

[20] Crane, *Italian Social Customs*, pp. 291–4. He cites numerous collections and studies of sixteenth- and seventeenth-century enigmas and riddles.

short cryptic poem (usually closely related to the madrigal's text) that gives further instructions for its realisation (see Figure 1, the sesto part of *Un mal è che mi rende afflitto e mesto*). The voice that carries the solution to the riddle (the *risolutione*) moves independently of the rest, textually and melodically, for most of the piece. The solution is derived from a single melodic unit – the *soggetto*, or subject phrase around which the outer counterpoint is worked – in a technique called 'con obbligo' by Gioseffo Zarlino:

> Musicians occasionally force themselves to keep using one passage, varying the harmony. This is called making counterpoint 'with a set condition' (*con obbligo*), and the repetitions are called *pertinacie*. One who wishes to constrain himself in this way need only to select a theme or passage and begin to write counterpoints upon this subject. Because this style of counterpoint is very difficult, certain liberties are permitted. One may at times write lines not easy to sing which would not be written in ordinary circumstances. Provided the harmony is varied, whatever note-values are most suitable may be used: now breves, then semibreves or minims, or other values. These may be syncopated or not, whichever best satisfies the pre-established condition. Of course it is always necessary to avoid the errors that have been discussed and illustrated, or the result will be condemned rather than praised. The difficult done well is far more to be praised than what is easily done well.[21]

Fully realised, the *risolutione* repeats the phrase several times, sometimes with variations of starting pitch or basic rhythmic unit (i.e., augmentation or diminution). As with a cantus firmus, the progress of the *risolutione* determines the harmonic content of the work; the way the phrase is deployed can also influence the metrical divisions with the piece, and the shape of its individual episodes of imitation, or *inventioni*. A large proportion of the subject phrases are simply stepwise movements through a fourth, fifth or sixth, either

---

[21] G. Zarlino, *Le istitutioni harmoniche* (1558; facs. repr. New York, 1965), p. 288: 'Et perche alle uolte li Musici si sogliono obligare di fare il contrapunto, usando sempre un passaggio, uariando però il concento; il qual modo è detto Far contrapunto con obligo; et tali repliche, o passaggi si chiamano Pertinacie; però quando alcuno si uorrà obligare ad una cosa simile, piglierà un Thema, o passaggio, et incomincierà a fare il contrapunto sopra il proposto Soggetto. Ma perche questa maniera di far contrapunto è molto difficile; però il Contrapuntista potrà prendere alcune licenze; come sarebbe di usare alle uolte alcune modulationi, che non fussero cosi ageuoli al cantare, si come vorebbe il douere, che fussero, quando il contrapunto si ponesse in iscritto, et fusse senza obligo alcuno. Et potrà vsar quelle figure, che più gli torneranno commode, variando il concento, vsando hora le Breui, hora le Semibreui, hora le Minime, et le altre figure; Le quali potrà porre hora sincopate, et hora senza la sincopa; a ciò possa satisfare all'obligo. Debbe nondimeno sempre hauer l'occhio alla osseruanza di quello, che è stato detto di sopra, et mostrato; et di schiuare quanto potrà gli errori; accioche il suo contrapunto non sia piu tosto biasimato, che lodato: Percioche quella cosa, che si fa bene nel difficile, è molto più da lodare, che non è quella, che è fatta bene senza alcuna difficultà.' Translation from G. Zarlino, *The Art of Counterpoint: Part Three of* Le Istitutioni harmoniche, *1588*, trans. G. A. Marco and C. V. Palisca (New York, 1968), pp. 154–8.

'Al gioco si conosce il galantuomo'

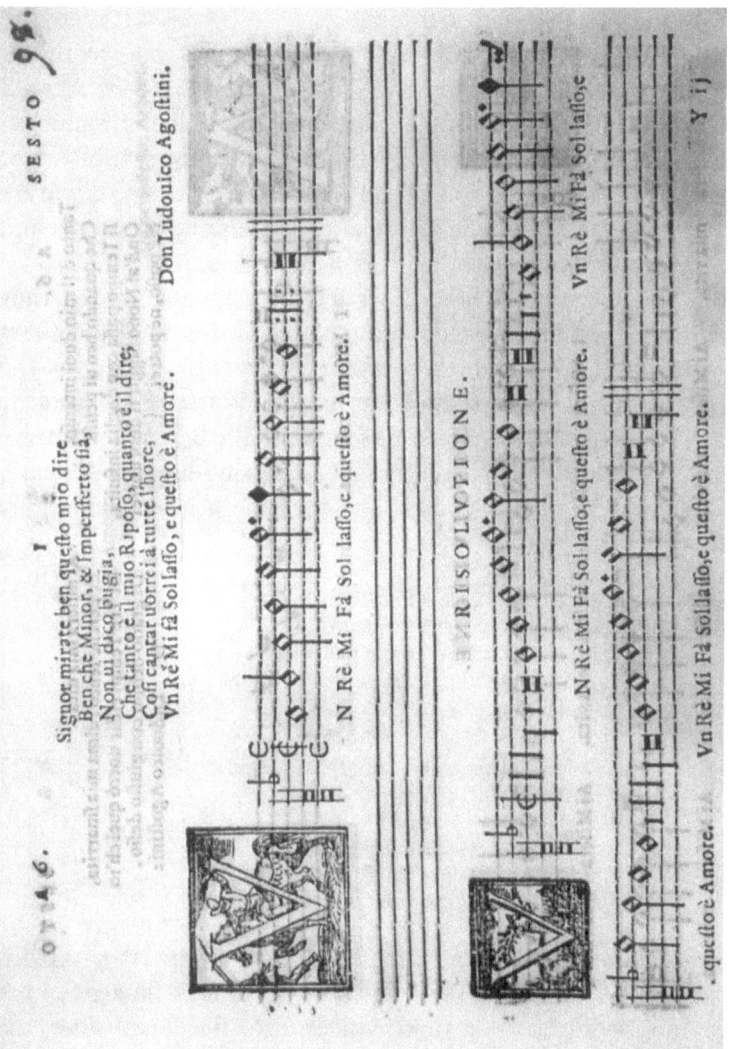

Figure 1   Sesto part of *Un mal è che mi rende afflitto e mesto* (*Enigmi musicali*, 1571)

ascending and descending, or simply descending; a variation on this is the use of ascending and descending triads. Frequently, the phrase forms the basis for the madrigal's opening or closing imitations, and its text is usually either taken from or related to the epigrammatic couplet that closes the madrigal text.

Although each enigma is uniquely intriguing in its concept and its solution, the opening enigma of the first book, *Un mal è che mi rende afflitto e mesto*, is perhaps one of the most ingenious, blending musical and textual *doppi sensi*, cryptography and contrapuntal virtuosity (see Appendix 1 for a transcription of the work). It is based on a phrase that rises and falls through the soft hexachord, ending on the second degree; the text of the *risolutione* – 'Un Re mi fa sol lasso, e questo è Amore' – states the hexachordal syllables outright, although they are given fuller meaning within the context of the madrigal's text (see Figure 1). This is an elaborate and extensive pun on the hexachord in which the syllables are gradually assembled, line by line. As the progression is initially obscured by the lack of separation between 're-' and the rest of the text in the second line ('re-medio'), it is not until the third or fourth line that the *doppio senso* is fully established.

> Un mal è che mi rende afflitto, e mesto,
> un remedio può sol farmi contento,
> un Re mi tien oppresso, et m'è molesto,
> un Re mi fa gir fuori di tormento,
> un Re mi fa sol lieto a tutte l'hore,
> un Re mi fa sol lasso, e quest'è Amore.

> One sickness is what makes me afflicted and sad,
> one remedy only can make me content,
> one King holds me oppressed and is vexatious to me,
> one King banishes me from torment,
> one King only makes me happy all the time,
> one King only makes me wretched, and this is Love.

The musical setting takes advantage of and supports the ambiguous opening by restricting the reflection of the syllables in the melodic line to only two or three voices until the fourth line, the mid-point of the madrigal, when all voices state 'un Re mi fa' to a rising tetrachord (Appendix 1, bars 16–18). Even after the hexachordal pun is firmly established, Agostini indulges in some further wrong-footing of the singers by 'mis-setting' the syllables; for instance, in the Canto 'un' is set to $f\sharp'$ (bar 16) and 'fa' is set to $b\natural'$

'Al gioco si conosce il galantuomo'

(or *b-mi'*) (Canto, bars 26, 28). However, the hexachordal games are not confined to straightforward puns and pratfalls; the more complex and erudite practice of hexachordal inganno is introduced from bar 19, in which new imitative points are created by substituting some of the subject's original pitches with others in different hexachords (e.g. Alto, bar 19; Canto, bar 20; Tenore, bars 19–20; see also Basso, bars 25–6; Tenore, bars 27–8; Basso, bar 29).

Un mal è che mi rende afflitto e mesto also provides an example of how the *risolutione* can influence the structure and progression of the madrigal as a whole. The work opens with a statement of the phrase in the Canto moving primarily in minims, in accordance with *tempo maggiore imperfetto*. The *risolutione* in the Sesto then provides the phrase at two metrical levels, first in semibreves, then in minims. As one might expect, when the *risolutione* moves in semibreves, the harmonic rate of change tends to be slower than when it occurs in minims. The outer parts imitate the rising hexachord in a variety of rhythms, gradually increasing the rate of declamation; near the end of the piece, four different rhythmic permutations of the rising scale occur, moving in semibreves, crotchets, quavers and additionally in a dotted-crotchet/quaver permutation (bars 27–31). The rapid and varied declamation rate in the outer parts highlights the slower-moving *risolutione*, again recalling cantus firmus composition and conforming to Zarlino's description of 'con obbligo' counterpoint.

The subject phrase, at least in the *risolutione*, does not change its starting pitch; this might suggest that Agostini's harmonic choices are limited by the phrase always closing on G. However, he uses the stepwise movement of the phrase to dovetail with a variety of cadential formulations, all evaded or vitiated in some way, most of which suggest a tonal focus on F and a cadential hierarchy based on pitches appropriate to the *tritus* modes in the eight-mode system (Table 1; only cadences which involve simultaneous textual closure with the use of cadential formulae in two or more voices are included). This tonal world is doubly unstable, for non-cadential F♯s and B♮s are introduced (and nearly always immediately cancelled) throughout, creating fleeting but disorienting false relations. The true 'mode' of the piece is not revealed until the final cadence, the first on G and the only full terminating cadence in the piece; this final sleight of hand shows all previous cadences to be transitory within a transposed *protus* hierarchy.

Table 1 *Cadence plan of* Un mal è che mi rende afflitto e mesto *(Enigmi musicali, 1571)*

	Cadence pitch	Cadence voices	Bar
Un mal è che mi rende afflitto, e mesto, un remedio può sol farmi contento,	f	Q and B	4
un Re mi tien oppresso, et m'è molesto, un Re mi fa gir fuori di tormento,	d	Q and T	16
un Re mi fa sol lieto à tutte l'hore,	c	C, A and B	22
un Re mi fa sol lieto à tutte l'hore,	f	A and T	25
un Re mi fa sol lasso, e quest'è Amore,	f	C and B	28
un Re mi fa sol lasso, e quest'è Amore.	G	all voices	35

The cryptogram has three mensuration signs stacked together at the opening – one for *tempo minore imperfetto* (₵) sandwiched between two for *tempo maggiore imperfetto* (C). This signifies that the phrase should be performed three times, the second time at twice the speed of the first and third, as the tactus of *minore* accounts for double the note values of *maggiore*. Solving the cryptogram, however, is only half the solution, for the phrase is given without any musical indication of how its tactus relates to the rest of the madrigal, nor of when it should begin in relation to the other parts. For this information, the singer(s) must turn to the accompanying riddle:

> Signor, mirate ben questo mio dire
> Ben che Minor, et Imperffetto [sic] sia,
> Non vi dico bugia,
> Che tanto è il mio Riposo, quanto è il dire;
> Così cantar vorrei a tutte l'hore,
> Un Re Mi fa Sol lasso, e questo è Amore.

> Sir, look well at what I say
> Even though it is Small and Imperfect,
> I'm not telling you lies,
> That my Rest is as much as my speech;
> Thus I would like to sing all the time,
> 'Un Re mi fa sol lasso, e questo è Amore.'

The riddle confirms that the mensuration of the entire piece is *tempo minore imperfetto* ('Ben che Minor, et Imperffetto sia'), and 'My rest is as much as my speech' indicates that the singer should count the full value of the phrase in rests before singing – this applies for each statement of the phrase.

'Al gioco si conosce il galantuomo'

While the solution is obvious to the owner of the printed volume (the *risolutione* is always given on the same page as the enigma), perhaps in order to play the game, the enigma would have been copied out and distributed to the company along with the other partbooks. There are several possible ways of conducting the game. One person in the company may have been charged with solving the enigma, or perhaps it was presented to the group as a whole, or perhaps each person attempted the problem in turn and tried their solution out with all the other voices; if it failed, the next person would attempt a solution, and so on. One could imagine the puzzle would provide substantial amusement for the players, who would be able to rehearse the other parts whilst trying various solutions.

AGOSTINI AND THE PUBLICATION OF THE ENIGMAS

Lodovico Agostini was born in Ferrara in 1534, the illegitimate son of the Ferrarese cleric-musician Agostino Agostini, a *mansionario* at the Cattedrale di San Giorgio in Ferrara.[22] Where he was educated and when he entered minor orders are as yet unknown; however, he seems to have spent at least part of his early career in Rome. His first musical work to be published, the four-voice *Occhi soavi e belli*, appears in Antonio Barré's 1562 Roman collection *Il terzo libro delle muse a quattro voci*, suggesting that he had at some point either studied or held a minor post in the city.[23] By the following year, 1563, Agostini may have returned to Ferrara to seek employment there, for he was granted a dispensation by Pope Paul IV allowing him to hold benefices and to join the canons regular at the cathedral – a necessity as illegitimate children of clerics were not allowed to hold

---

[22] Several biographies of Agostini exist, but the most recent and the most complete (in terms of inclusion of source material and its analysis) is in E. Durante and A. Martellotti, *Madrigali segreti per le dame di Ferrara: Il manoscritto musicale F. 1358 della Biblioteca Estense di Modena*, 2 vols. (Archivium Musicum, Collana di studi vol. II; Florence, 2000), i, pp. 86–94. A contemporary reference to his father's musical ability is reported in E. Peverada, 'Pratica musicale del clero della cattedrale e in cura d'anime a Ferrara nel Cinquecento', *Analecta Pomposiana*, 9 (1984), pp. 271–90, at p. 276. In the dedication of his *Canones, et Echo sex vocibus* (Venice, 1572), Agostini refers to himself as the fourth member of the family to offer musical services to the Ferrara cathedral.

[23] J. Haar, 'The "Madrigale Arioso": A Mid-Century Development in the Cinquecento Madrigal', in *The Science and Art of Renaissance Music*, pp. 222–38, at p. 223, suggests that Barré's *Muse* volumes draw primarily on a local repertoire compiled from composers who were either Roman or who had worked in or visited Rome, but not necessarily contemporaneously with the publication of the collections.

any office in the churches to which their fathers had been attached. The validity of the dispensation, however, was short-lived; in December of the same year, it was revoked as a result of the Council of Trent ruling for a re-enforcement of the original ban. After this disappointment, Agostini may have remained in northern Italy, possibly travelling to Venice and perhaps ending up in Milan. His first single-author print, the *Musica di Lodovico Agostini ferrarese, sopra le rime bizzarre di M. Andrea Calmo* [*Libro primo*] of 1567, was published by a Milanese printing house, Cesare Pozzo. The dedication to the *poligrafo* Andrea Calmo, 'fradel caro, dolce amigo, e amorevole', is written in Venetian dialect, but signed in Milan.[24] In 1570, Agostini dedicated his *Musica di don Lodovico Agostini ferrarese il Primo Libro de madrigali a cinque voci* to the Ferrarese ambassador to Milan;[25] the change in his mode of address ('Don') indicates that at some point in the intervening three years he had been ordained. A complete list of Agostini's single-author prints is given in Table 2.

The first book of musical enigmas, 1571

That Agostini did, in fact, spend time in Rome is confirmed by the dedication of his first book of *Enigmi musicali*, published in 1571 and directed to the brothers Giovanni Piero and Tiberio Cerasi. It speaks of the 'strong bond of friendship between us that was born in Rome through the sympathy for this most beautiful science'.[26] It seems unlikely, however, that Agostini had returned to Rome in 1571, for the following year he published two volumes dedicated to Ferrarese patrons (see below). The book is larger than the average madrigal collection, containing twenty-four pieces in total: ten enigmas, four madrigals and ten dialogues. The table of contents at the back of the book is carefully laid out in groups under headings:

---

[24] This is the only one of Agostini's publications in which he does not reveal his clerical status. Calmo's humorous poetry, some of which parodies Petrarchan texts, is all in Venetian dialect.

[25] Tomaso Zerbinati, 'Ambasciatore dell'illustriss. Duca di Ferrara in Milano'.

[26] 'per la simpathia di questa bellissima scienza nacque in Roma tra noi tanta strettezza d'amicitia'; Lodovico Agostini to Giovanni Piero and Tiberio Cerasi; dedication of L. Agostini, *Enigmi musicali di Don Lodovico Agostini ferrarese Il primo libro . . . a sei voci* (Venice, 1571). Both brothers were Roman *cavalieri*, Giovanni Piero a surgeon like his father, Tiberio a cleric. Tiberio was a noted social benefactor who was later made a cardinal. He became patron to the painters Annibale Carracci and Michaelangelo da Caravaggio, who both contributed decorations to the Cappella Cerasi in S. Maria del Popolo in Rome in the early 1600s; see F. Petrucci, 'Tiberio Cerasi', *Dizionario biografico degli italiani*, 23 (1979), pp. 655–7.

'Al gioco si conosce il galantuomo'

Table 2 *Lodovico Agostini's surviving single-author prints*

Title	Publisher	Dedicatee
Musica di Lodovico Agostini Ferrarese, sopra le rime bizzarre di M. Andrea Calmo	Milan: Cesare Pozzo, 1567	Andrea Calmo
Musica di don Lodovico Agostini ferrarese il Primo Libro de madrigali a cinque voci	Venice: Figliuoli di A. Gardano, 1570	Tomaso Zerbinati, 'Ambasciatore dell'illustriss. Duca di Ferrara in Milano'
Enigmi musicali di don Lodovico Agostini ferrarese, Il Primo Libro a sei con dialogi a sette otto e dieci. A sei voci	Venice: Figliuoli di A. Gardano, 1571	Giovanni Piero and Tiberio Cerasi, 'Dottori, et Cavalieri Romani'
Canones, et Echo sex vocibus. D. Ludovici Augustinii ferrarie: eiusdem dialogi. Liber primus	Venice: Filios Antonij Gardanus, 1572	canons of Ferrara cathedral
Musica di don Lodovico Agostini ferrarese Libro secondo de madrigali a quatro voci	Venice: Figliuoli di A. Gardano, 1572	Conte Girolamo Roverelli and Conte Enea Montecucculi
Canzoni alla napolitana a cinque voci, libro primo	Venice: Figliuoli di A. Gardano, 1574	Ottavio Morani, 'gentil'huomo di Modona'
L'Echo, et Enigmi musicali a sei voci, libro secondo	Venice: Alessandro Gardano, 1581	Guglielmo Gonzaga, Duke of Mantua
Madrigali ... Libro Terzo. A sei voci	Ferrara: Rossi e Tortorino, 1582	Alfonso d'Este, Duke of Ferrara
Il Nuovo Echo a cinque voci ... Libro Terzo. Opera Decima	Ferrara: Baldini, 1583	Alfonso d'Este, Duke of Ferrara
Le lagrime del peccatore a sei voci ... . Libro Quarto. Opera XII	Venice: Vincenzi and Amadino, 1586	Guglielmo Gonzaga, Duke of Mantua

'Enigmi a 6', 'Madrigali a 6', 'Dialoghi a 7', 'a 8' and 'a 10', presumably for quick reference by the owner. Later books do not exhibit quite this level of meticulous planning, perhaps indicating that this first book was either more consciously prepared for commercial distribution, or the materials from which it was typeset were themselves highly organised.

Despite its Roman destination, the contents of the 1571 book have clearer connections with northern Italy, supporting the suggestion that Agostini was not in Rome at the time of its publication, and that his relationship with the Cerasi brothers had been formed some years before. The text of the enigma *Va limpido ruscel* is attributed to Vincenzo Morello e Bevilacqua, and it closes with a pun on the Bevilacqua name ('Ai arsi spongia che mi bevi l'acqua'). Of Veneto origins, the Bevilacqua family had important branches in both Ferrara and Verona.[27] One of the book's ordinary madrigals, *Amor m'ha vinto hor vuol tormi la vita*, is directed to a lady named Vittoria ('Giusta Vittoria e pia'); both adjectives pun on the names of established families in the region, the Giusti of Verona and the Pii di Savoia of Sassuolo, near Modena. Perhaps even more striking, half of the enigmas are based on madrigal texts by Luigi Cassola, one of the leading poets of madrigal literature at mid-century, who died in Piacenza in 1570, but who had also served at the Ferrarese court in the mid-century.[28]

The enigmas of the first book vary not only in their complexity and difficulty, but in the way they are conceived as musical conundrums. *Un mal è che mi rende afflitto e mesto* is the only mensuration puzzle, but four other puzzle types occur, based on:

1. the subject phrase transposed to varying pitches at a regular temporal interval;
2. the subject phrase at the same pitch at decreasing temporal intervals;
3. the subject phrase at unchanging pitch and temporal intervals (the puzzle lies in working out when the phrase should start); and
4. the subject phrase transposed to set pitches at regular temporal intervals.

---

[27] Another enigma, *Laura soave vita di mia vita*, on a text by Petrarch, may constitute an early reference to the singer Laura Peverara, who was active in these years in Mantua, and possibly Verona.

[28] See W. Prizer, 'Games of Venus: Secular Vocal Music in the Late Quattrocento and Early Cinquecento', *Journal of Musicology*, 9 (1991), pp. 3–56, at p. 36. Attributions to Cassola are not found in the prints; all of his texts were previously published in L. Cassola, *Madrigali* (Venice, 1544). Cassola's importance to Piacentine cultural life is touched upon in J. Haar, 'Notes on the *Dialogo della Musica* of Antonfrancesco Doni', in *The Science and Art of Renaissance Music*, pp. 271–99, at p. 274.

'Al gioco si conosce il galantuomo'

Table 3 *Enigma types in the* Enigmi musicali, *1571*

Page	Madrigal	Type	Remarks
1	Un mal è che mi rendi afflitto e mesto	mensuration puzzle	
2	Tant'è il mio duol intenso	type 1	
3	Sia benedetto amore (*a 6*)	type 2	
4	Laura soave, vita di mia vita	type 3	
5	Madonna si un pensiero	type 4	Subject phrase restated at fourth below, then octave below, repeating pattern.
6	Quando mi doglio di quelli occhi belli	type 1	
7	Ben mi prendesti amore	type 2	
8	Va limpido ruscel Castalio humile	type 3	Puzzle resolves only the starting point.
9	Sia benedetto amore (*a 5*)	type 3	Additionally a canon at the fifth (alto/quinto); page 9 in the Sesto partbook contains the *risolutione* of *Va limpido ruscel*.
10	Io vo fra me pensando almo mio sole	type 4	Subject phrase restated at fourth below, repeating pattern; additionally a unison canon at the breve (*risolutione* is two voices rather than one).

Type 1: transposition at a regular temporal interval
Type 2: repetition at same pitch at decreasing temporal intervals
Type 3: unchanging pitch and temporal intervals
Type 4: transposition to set pitches at regular temporal intervals

There is one five-voice enigma of the third type, *Sia benedetto Amore*; the eight remaining six-voice enigmas are evenly distributed, two of each type. Additionally, the subject phrases of the last two enigmas form *fugato* canons. The order in which they appear, given in Table 3, is further evidence that the book was carefully planned for printing, as no two six-voice enigmas of similar type are placed next to each other.[29]

---

[29] The sesto partbook is printed without a table of contents, although its page numbers correspond to the table of contents given in the other partbooks. The insertion of the five-voice enigma on page 9 seems to be for expedience – in the sesto partbook it is substituted with the *risolutione* of the previous enigma, so that the puzzle and its solution are still viewed together on opposing pages. Were the five-voice enigma printed after the six-voice works (i.e., on p. 10), the printer would have had either to alter the page numbering sequence in the sesto book or to split the solution of *Va limpido ruscel* from the enigma and its accompanying text over the turn of a page.

Laurie Stras

Quando signor mi doglio
　Di que' begl'occhi, ch'in cor si
　profondo
Piagomi fer, e poi penso di dire,
Prima SEI Tempi mi convien tacere
Anzi ch'io dica con voce gioconda,
O che dolce morire?

Poi tre Tempi in silentio osservar voglio,
　Scendendo a grado a grado per
　piacere,
E dirò sin al fin senza martire;
O che dolce morire?

O　che　dol - ce　mo - ri - re?

Example 1　Cryptogram for *Quando mi doglio di quelli occhi belli*, from *Enigmi musicali* (1571)

The cryptograms for each type use a similar approach to notational shorthand to represent the *risolutione*. Type 1 uses a custos to indicate at which pitch each reiteration of the subject phrase should start, as in the cryptogram from *Quando mi doglio di quelli occhi belli* (Example 1). Type 2 normally uses no shorthand at all, but simply states the phrase; type 3 may use repeat signs, and type 4 uses a *segno* to indicate beginnings and/or endings within the pattern. By their nature, the type 4 puzzles could accommodate further encryption to make the problem even more difficult. For instance, the enigma *Madonna si un pensiero* has a cryptogram that notates the subject phrase in both its transpositions, on d' and a (Example 2(a)). However, by using the shorthand from type 1, the cryptogram could have been considerably condensed (Example 2(b)). The imprecision of the ending, however (does the repeat include the final crotchet, or not?) may have led Agostini to write the phrase out longhand, at least for publication, so that the puzzle would not be too difficult.

The first book of enigmas is a virtuosic publication, not just in terms of the variety of forms and puzzles it contains, but also in terms of its printing. The cryptograms combine poetic texts, engraved initial letters (sometimes two to a page), staves, standard musical notation and special symbols. The partbooks have a special page-numbering system that allows the same table of contents plate to be used regardless of the number of pages in each book – which differ from fascicle to fascicle due to the number of seven-, eight- and ten-voice dialogues with extra voices that need to be distributed among the six books. The Gardano firm's ownership of the technical skill necessary to create the set is proudly emphasised by

'Al gioco si conosce il galantuomo'

Madonna il mio pensiero
Scoprir vorrei, poi che tacer nol posso;
Sei Tempi taccio, questo è il spatio intiero
Del mio gentil riposo,
E dopò ancor di dirlo apena il oso

E se ben ciò desio
Isfogarmi cantando,
Pur dirò sospirando,
Intendami chi può, che m'intend'io,
Fin che giongo a quel segno ove desio.

(a)

(b)

Example 2 Cryptogram for *Madonna si un pensiero*, from *Enigmi musicali*: (a) as written; (b) conjectural condensed version

the large *impresa* found on the last page of each book. Agostini's enigmas are not unique examples of printed musical puzzles, even from the sixteenth century (as will be discussed later), but they are possibly the earliest such works to be set in moveable type by Italian printers and advertised in the title as a primary descriptor of the book's content.

The second book of four-voice madrigals and the canons, 1572

The two books from 1572 establish Agostini both as a composer of novelties and as a man rooted in the Ferrarese environment. The *Libro secondo de madrigali a quatro voci*, like the *Enigmi musicali*, was also directed to a pair of relations, this time the Counts Girolamo Roverelli and Enea Montecucculi, cousins and members of the Ferrarese court.[30] The setting of Petronio Barbati's seven-part

---

[30] *Musica di don Lodovico Agostini ferrarese Libro secondo de madrigali à quatro voci* (Venice, 1572). Enea Montecucculi was master of Duke Alfonso II d'Este's cavalry, and eventually financed the memorial to Agostini in the Franciscan church of Santo Spirito; see A. Solerti, *Ferrara e la corte*

canzona *Porgetemi la lira*, which opens the book, describes an entertainment on the banks of the Taro river near Piacenza, and as such may be a further indication of Agostini's presence in the Po valley in the late 1560s and early 1570s. However, the allusion in the text is the only specific reference besides its dedication that helps place the book into a more precise context. This volume, far less ambitious than the *Enigmi musicali*, nonetheless contains a piece specifically designated 'enigma', *Nel bel terreno della donna mia*. It is not immediately obvious how this four-voice work relates to Agostini's five- and six-voice puzzles; it has neither the musical features of its larger counterparts, nor the ludic features of the riddle and cryptogram, nor does it appear to require a solution. Its special nature will be discussed later in this essay.

The other book published in 1572, the *Canones, et Echo sex vocibus*, exhibits many of the same characteristics as the *Enigmi musicali*, and it may in some ways represent a companion volume.[31] Dedicated to the canons of Ferrara cathedral (and one assumes the double meaning of the word canon was intentional), it contains Latin-texted works for five, six, seven and eight voices. Five cryptographic canons – some with printed resolutions, some without – echoes, five *fugato* or imitative canons, the dialogues and a miscellany of other pieces are arranged more or less by genre, although the index is less specific than its secular counterpart, designating only 'Canones, et Echo sex vocum', 'Quinque vocum' and 'Octo vocum'. Two of the pieces are by his father, Agostino Agostini. The texts in this book hint tantalisingly at the career that Agostini (and indeed his father) might have followed to this point: they include a Marian devotion and a Marian sequence (*Ave mundi spes Maria*); a text dedicated to Saint Barbara; two motets celebrating the victory at Lepanto against the Turks; three Latin echoes and an 'epigramma' that are suspiciously secular, even (homo)erotic, in tone; two moral dialogues; segments of liturgy and a 'prosa di Sancto Francisco'. The Barbara motet, one of the cryptographic canons, may have been composed in honour of the Duchess of Ferrara Barbara d'Austria, who died in 1572, or

---

estense nella seconda metà del secolo XVI. I discorsi di Annibale Romei . . . Seconda edizione corretta e accresciuta con la pianta di Ferrara nel 1597 dell'ing. F. Borgatti (Città di Castello, 1900), p. 237, and Durante and Martellotti, *Madrigali segreta*, i, p. 87.

[31] *Canones, et Echo sex vocibus. D. Ludovici Augustinii ferrarie: eiusdem dialogi. Liber primus* (Venice, 1572).

'Al gioco si conosce il galantuomo'

originally intended for a Mantuan environment (Barbara being the patron saint of the Gonzagas). However, the 'prosa', taken together with several other texts, suggests a Franciscan, and perhaps even Clarissan, origin for at least some of the works in this book. Two settings of *Veni sponsa Christi*, one each by Lodovico and his father, appear in the book; the antiphon was traditionally used to accompany the ceremony of profession and marriage to Christ, signalling a woman's full entry into convent life. Agostino Agostini's other contribution to the book is a setting of the antiphon to the Benedictus for the feast of Corpus Christi, *Ego sum panis vivus*. In the second half of the sixteenth century there were four Clarissan houses in Ferrara, two of which were intimately connected with the Este and received many young women from the Ferrarese nobility: the Monastero di Corpus Domini (also known as Corpus Christi) and the smaller Monastero di San Bernardino da Siena.[32] Perhaps either or both of the Agostinis had derived income through a relationship with these houses. All convents relied on male priests for the sacraments of penance and communion, as well as sermons; furthermore, the practice of priests providing musical tuition to Ferrara's nuns was widespread and visible enough to incur an episcopal ban in 1584.[33] As tenuous as the connection with the order suggested by these settings may be, it is nonetheless strengthened by Agostini's burial in a Franciscan monastery church.[34]

---

[32] Corpus Domini received patronage from the Este from the time of Ercole I. Lucrezia Borgia took her vows as a lay sister of the Franciscan Third Order at the convent; she and many other Este princes and princesses (including Alfonso II and his sister Lucrezia) are buried there. The Ferrarese singer Laura Peverara left around 7,000 scudi to Corpus Domini in her will; see P. T. Lombardi, *I francescani a Ferrara*, 5 vols. (Bologna, 1974), iii, pp. 158–80; 199–208. San Bernardino was founded by Lucrezia Borgia for her niece Camilla, and was initially inhabited by sisters from Corpus Domini. The sisters of San Bernardino were required from 1580 to apply for a licence to sing *canto figurato*, and any failure to do so was punished in the public refectory; *ibid.*, pp. 279–86.

[33] Peverada, 'Practica musicale', p. 274, n. 4.

[34] An Agostinus da Ferrara took minor orders at the Convento di Santo Spirito in 1533; this may have been Lodovico's father, Agostino; see Lombardi, *I francescani a Ferrara*, ii, p.112. However, it is difficult to establish ultimately whether Lodovico himself professed as a Franciscan. It seems unlikely, given that he never styled himself as 'Fra', the appropriate form of address for a member of a mendicant order; however, he could have been both a priest and a Franciscan tertiary. Alternatively, he may have taken simple vows as a Franciscan in his youth, but passed to the regular clergy before ordination; such alterations to vows – especially if passing from religious to canons regular – are allowed for in the *Summa Theologica* of St Thomas Aquinas. He would have had to been granted a dispensation for this, however, and it could be that the 1563

Visually, the cryptographic canons are similar to the enigmas, and require similar musical sleuthing skills for their resolution, but they lack the poetic instruction; instead, like the more familiar *fugato* canons, they have simple, short rubrics – some are so obvious they need no printed resolution. Their lack of an enigmatic poem and their quasi-liturgical texts also suggest a different function from that of their secular counterparts. The opening work in the book, *Alma dei genetrix*, is a mensuration puzzle like *Un mal è che me rende afflitto* (see Figure 2), giving signs for both *tempo minore imperfetto* and *tempo maggiore imperfetto*. The piece is designated 'canon' rather than 'enigma', perhaps suggesting that, to Agostini, the cryptic verse is the defining criterion for an enigma. Its canonic rubric, which instructs the singer to precede the subject phrase with the same value in rests, is to the point: 'Tacendum est, quantum vis canere'; and the mirror form of the phrase is singled out by the double inscription 'Alpha, et O' placed at its beginning and end.

The printing of the *Canones, et Echo sex vocibus* is scarcely less impressive than that of the *Enigmi musicali*, for although the cryptographic canons have no poetic instructions, the texts for the echo dialogues are given in full in the Sextus partbook – presumably so the singer of the echo (and/or the owner of the book) could follow along. As with the *Enigmi musicali*, the layout of the index and the pagination of the books have been given careful consideration. A three-part, five-voice setting is placed after all but one of the six-voice works, on pages 15, 16 and 17; these pages are missing in the Sextus book, which jumps to page 18 for the final six-voice work, the secular epigram *Odi te (mihi crede)*. This piece is grouped with the other six-voice works on the index page.

Apart from the pair of publications in 1572 and a single book of *canzonette* in 1574, there is little record of Agostini's activities in the middle of the decade, but his circumstances must have changed substantially during this period.[35] By the beginning of 1578 he had become a Protonotary Apostolic (a high-ranking, but non-stipendary, title bestowed personally by Pope Gregory XIII), and

---

dispensation allowing him to hold benefices and canonic office had a dual purpose in releasing him from his simple vows and bypassing his illegitimacy.

[35] In the report of the Visitor Apostolic to Ferrara in 1574, Agostini is listed as 'musicus'; Peverada, 'Pratica musicale', p. 273, n. 3.

'Al gioco si conosce il galantuomo'

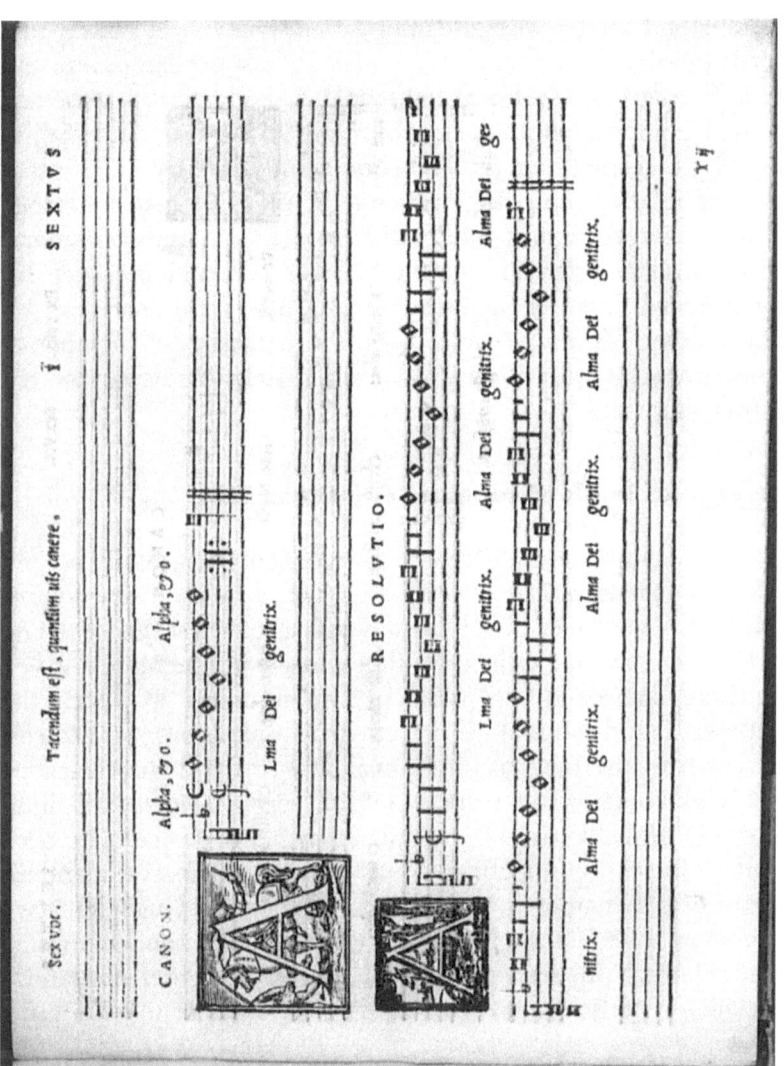

Figure 2 Sextus part of *Alma dei genetrix* (*Canones, et Echo sex vocibus*, 1572)

from this point his title is always included on the front page of his publications and appended to his signature. Notwithstanding this honour, Alfonso II d'Este's attempts to secure him a benefice, by way of compensation for a renewed refusal by the Vatican to reinstate the 1563 dispensation, met with intimations of simony that forced Agostini to decline the stipend.[36] By this time, too, Agostini was a *cappellano* of the ducal household at Ferrara and sometime informal composition tutor to the duke of Mantua, Guglielmo Gonzaga; a single letter to Guglielmo from February 1575 establishes the relationship between the cleric and the Duke.[37] Despite the monetary accretions one might expect from these positions, Agostini's polite letter refusing the benefice nonetheless reveals his poor financial situation, aggravated by his obligation to support his ailing mother. By no means was he the highest-paid member of Alfonso's *cappella*, with a salary at approximately three-quarters that of other musicians.[38]

The second book of musical enigmas, 1581

Duke Guglielmo Gonzaga became the recipient of Agostini's second book of enigmas, *L'Echo, et enigmi musicali a sei voci, libro secondo*, published in Venice in 1581. The differences between this book and the 1571 *Enigmi* may reflect the different environments for which they were composed, the different circumstances in which the composer found himself during their composition, or at least differences in the musical forces available to the dedicatees. The 1581 book contains one work specifically designated *concerto*, indicating the probable use of instruments in performance. The texts are more focused on identifiable individuals, with several mentioning courtiers by name; there is a dedicatory text for Guglielmo, two encomia of a female singer named Vittoria and a sonnet praising Agostini himself (the setting is by the Ferrarese composer Alessandro Milleville). The book also contains two parodies of the Mantuan

---

[36] Durante and Martellotti, *Madrigali segreti*, i, p. 91.
[37] *Ibid.*, p. 89.
[38] For Agostini's salary, see A. Newcomb, *The Madrigal at Ferrara, 1579–1597*, 2 vols. (Princeton, 1981), i, p. 160; compare Agostini's 15 lire with Ippolito Fiorini's 21 lire. This difference may not be an indication of Alfonso's estimation, however. Had Agostini taken simple vows as a Franciscan, he may still have felt bound by his vow of poverty; Aquinas makes the honouring of a simple vow of one order (once professed in another) a matter of conscience.

'Al gioco si conosce il galantuomo'

composer Alessandro Striggio's well-known six-voice madrigal *Nasce la pena mia*. Apart from these local features, the recreational intention of the pieces seems largely to be the same as those in the first volume of enigmas, although their arrangement in the book is less tidy. The piece for Guglielmo opens the book and several five- and seven-voice pieces are placed at the end, but between them the six-voice pieces – enigmas, parodies, the *concerto* and a number of echo dialogues – come in no particular order, nor are they differentiated by type in the table at the back. Another feature that makes its first appearance in a publication by Agostini is the inclusion of encomiastic sonnets in praise of the composer as prefatory material in the book.

L'Echo, et enigmi musicali contains fewer enigmas than the 1571 *Enigmi* – six as opposed to ten – and only one canon, but the complexity of the puzzles requires the same virtuosity of the printer. Each enigma is based on a different premise (with types 1, 3 and 4 from the previous book represented), and there are two mensuration puzzles (see Table 4). In a new type of enigma, *Una sì chiara luce*, the cryptogram appears as a mirror image, an amusing variation on the traditional looking-glass canon technique. As well as demonstrating a pleasing visual symmetry, this is also one of the more obviously playful puzzles (see Figure 3). The hapless singer chosen to solve the puzzle would initially try to sing the pitches given, but very soon would find that they are utterly wrong. The next move might be to try the part holding the book upside down (one method for solving a puzzle canon), but as the phrase is already its own retrograde inversion this, too, results in the wrong notes being sung. Only when a mirror is placed against the stave (following the instruction 'poi splende una luce', which can also mean 'hold up a mirror'), either at the end or at the top, are the true notes revealed – a simple retrograde of the cryptogram's phrase.

Despite the obvious care needed to set this puzzle in print, there are signs that the book was less meticulously prepared than its predecessors: as with the *Enigmi musicali*, the contents page is common to all the books, but it refers to two five-voice pieces that do not appear in the Sesto book and its page numbers are incorrect. Moreover, the five-voice enigma, *Ne la beata vespa*, appears to have a mistake in the cryptogram and the six-voice *S'ivi è d'Amor lo strale* is printed with a riddle and a solution, but without a cryptogram.

Laurie Stras

Table 4 *Enigma types in* L'Echo, et Enigmi musicali, *1581*

Page	Madrigal	Type[a]	Remarks
5	Scendete Muse del sacrato monte	type 3	
6	S'ivi è d'Amor lo strale	type 4	Lacks cryptogram.
7	Vagho augelin, che si soave piagni	type 1	
10	Vieni soave e dilettoso Maggio	mensuration puzzle	
11	Una sì Chiara luce	mirror puzzle (type 3)	
19	Ne la Beata vespa	mensuration puzzle	For five voices; error in cryptogram.
22	Queste care viole	unison canon	For five voices; *fugato* canon at the fifth (basso/quinto).

[a] See Table 3.

Although the errors in the book may simply indicate the condition of the materials from which it was set, it is perhaps significant that the book was printed by Alessandro Gardano, in the last years before his move from Venice to Rome. Alessandro had fewer musical commissions than his brother Andrea, and his work was generally of a lower standard.[39] One wonders how much Alessandro himself had invested in the volume, professionally or financially. The book also contains an entire page of poetic tributes to the composer, perhaps indicating the print was fully funded by either the composer or its noble recipient, Guglielmo Gonzaga, in which case Alessandro may not have felt the need to make the book into a pristine, commercially viable edition.

The new Echo, 1583

If Agostini's book for Guglielmo smacks of either the vanity press or the gift economy – or both – his third book of five-voice madrigals, *Il nuovo Echo a cinque voci . . . libro terzo*, published by Baldini in 1583 and dedicated to Alfonso II d'Este, Duke of Ferrara, is certainly even further removed from the marketplace (and the change from a commercial printing house in Venice to the ducal press in Ferrara serves to underline the shift).[40] Even more than *L'Echo, et enigmi*, this

---

[39] R. J. Agee, *The Gardano Music Printing Firms, 1569–1611* (Rochester, NY, 1998), pp. 134, 146.
[40] L. Agostini, *Il nuovo Echo a cinque voci . . . libro terzo. Opera Decima* (Ferrara, 1583). Agostini's second volume for five voices is no longer extant. A book of 'Enigmi (a5)' listed in Gardano

'Al gioco si conosce il galantuomo'

Figure 3 Sesto part of *Una sì chiara luce* (*L'Echo, et Enigmi musicali*, 1581)

booklist of 1591 could represent the lost book, although Richard Agee assumes it is one of the extant six-voice books; Agee, *The Gardano Printing Firms*, p. 381.

unusual volume, printed on thick, blue paper and elaborately decorated and bound, looks very much as if it is more a celebratory compendium of courtly music-making than a simple collection of madrigals. Its elaborate printing and varied contents make it appear to be a memento – or even a brochure – of Ferrarese music-making, a presentation volume, or the sixteenth-century equivalent of a coffee-table book. It contains many different types of pieces – echo dialogues, madrigals, encomia of various Ferrarese courtiers and singers, *concerti* with related instrumental pieces, parodies of works by Striggio and Giaches de Wert, a three-part *proposta, riposta e contrariposta* and a single enigma, the last of Agostini's enigmas to be published. Whilst perhaps not wholly haphazard, the order in which the pieces appear does not rely upon text or type.

The enigma in this book, *De l'odorate spoglie*, seems to be a token or representative sample of one aspect of Ferrarese musical activity. It does not appear to have been intended to provide a challenge to the reader/performer but would have, if performed, the same aural effect on the listener/participant as a true enigma. It is designated 'enigma' and it supplies both cryptogram and *risolutione*; but it has no riddle and the cryptogram includes appropriate rests to show how the subject phrase fits within the outer parts. Therefore, there is no real puzzle to solve. The subject phrase is taken from the opening of Giaches de Wert's madrigal *Cara la vita mia*; typically for Agostini's enigmas, this phrase moves through a descending fifth.[41] The madrigal text, by the Ferrarese Orsina Cavaletta, honours the singer Laura Peverara and urges her to perform Wert's madrigal, ending with the words 'Fateci udir: cara la vita mia' ('make us hear *Cara la vita mia*'). The piece it follows in the book is an 'imitation' of Wert's madrigal which also uses the subject phrase in its closing statement. These two pieces together are strongly evocative of the social, musical and literary environment of 1580s Ferrara, commemorating not only its activities, including the game of musical enigmas, but also one of its most favoured musicians (Wert), its most celebrated performer (Peverara) and one of its most cultivated noblewomen (Cavaletta).

---

[41] G. de Wert, *Primo libro de madrigali a cinque voci* (Venice, 1561).

'Al gioco si conosce il galantuomo'

PLAY AND HUMOUR IN THE ENIGMAS

Agostini published only one other piece with the designation 'enigma', the four-voice *Nel bel terreno della donna mia*, in his *Libro secondo de madrigali a quatro voci* of 1572. This work has no separate riddle text, no cryptogram and no solution, but there are clear reasons why Agostini might have chosen to advertise it as a puzzle. Its text is unrelentingly metaphorical and its setting attempts to wrong-foot the performer by relying upon his or her familiarity with another playful convention. The use of *doppi sensi* in this work seems to extract the fullest potential from the *Crusca*'s definition of 'enigma' ('an obscure saying, which under the veil of words hides an allegorical sense'). The veil in this case is at once diaphanous and layered, for although there are many thinly disguised and obvious metaphors to catch, they work in different spheres and on different levels, so that the experience is cumulative and can only fully be appreciated by the performers, or players. It also corresponds, in its lascivious tone at least, to contemporary literary enigmas, such as those published by the Paduan Girolamo Musici in his *Rime ingegnose* of 1566, which were described by an eighteenth-century critic as being in 'the worst taste'.[42]

The text of *Nel bel terreno* is an extended metaphor describing a woman's genitalia as a beautiful landscape, and the lover expresses his physical desire within the metaphor as a wish to work her earth again with his plough. This reading, however metaphorical it may be, is straightforward enough:

> Nel bel terreno della donna mia
> s'erge fra altiere sponde un vago colle
> qual cinge con mirabil leggiadria
> verde boschetto, delicato e molle;
> a dentro è dolce tal fonte natia
> che mai non satia et ogni sete tolle.
> Quivi col vomer mio pur fess'io un solco –
> oimè vorrei poi sempr'esser bifolco.

---

[42] G. Musici, *Rime ingegnose* (Padua, 1566). The reference to its criticism is taken from G. A. Rossi, *Enigmistica: il gioco degli enigmi dagli albori ai giorni nostri* (Milan, 2001), p. 80, quoting F. S. Quadrio, *Della storia e della ragione di ogni poesia* (Milan, 1744). Musici's enigmas contain several lascivious texts, including one whose solution is 'sodomito'. The volume is a curious compendium, for along with the humorous enigmas, Musici publishes devotional texts, encomia of Paduan dignitaries and a long lament on the death of his wife. Crane also comments on the lascivious nature of many Cinquecento riddle collections; see Crane, *Italian Social Customs*, pp. 291–2.

Laurie Stras

> In my lady's lovely terrain
> rises amidst proud banks a beautiful hill
> which is surrounded, with miraculous grace,
> by a lush forest, delicate and soft;
> inside there is such a sweet natural fountain
> that never sates, yet takes every thirst away.
> There with my plough I opened a furrow –
> ah me, I'd like always to be a ploughman.

The overall conceit is not unique; it occurs in several Florentine texts from preceding generations, including one by Lorenzo de' Medici, 'In mezzo d'una valle è un boschetto, con una fonte piena di diletto'.[43] Moreover, there are several words within the text that have not only double but multiple meanings. *Fonte natia* might also be loosely translated as 'birth canal'; *fare un solco* can also mean to deflower a woman. *Vomere* is not only a plough – and from classical times a metaphor for the penis – but it also refers to the nasal septum, suggesting the possibility that the lover's preferred sexual activity might be something other than normal intercourse. *Bifolco*, the ploughman, is also used to describe a simpleton, a peasant or an uneducated person. *Molle* may mean both 'humid' and 'soft', but it also has moral connotations, as in 'lax' or 'loose'; and as any sixteenth-century person with the most basic music education would have understood, *molle* also refers to the soft hexachord, which rises from F to D through B♭.

It is in the last two definitions that the game of this piece really resides. The first full cadence (in all four voices, followed by a rest) of the work occurs at the word 'molle' (Example 3, bar 12). Four carefully notated b♮s occur in the preceding phrase in both the Alto and Canto, but the b' in the Canto's cadential figure is unmarked. The dilemma for the Canto singer is whether or not to introduce *musica ficta* at the cadence. At first, it might seem unquestionable that the b♭ should be altered, but the astute singer would notice the word 'molle', a word frequently reflected in a setting by a flat; and, in a brief moment of doubt or confusion might therefore waver on the pitch (or even mistake it completely). Such a cultivated approach, of

---

[43] Lorenzo de' Medici, *Canzoni*, 21/1, quoted in V. Boggione and G. Casalegno, *Dizionario storico del lessico erotico italiano* (Milan, 1996), p. 421. It is also strongly reminiscent of Boccaccio's description of the 'valle delle donne', the charming location where the ladies of his company take refreshment at the end of the sixth day; see G. Boccaccio, *Decameron*, trans. G. H. McWilliam (London, 1995). I am grateful to Massimo Ossi for reminding me of this association.

'Al gioco si conosce il galantuomo'

Example 3 *Nel bel terreno della donna mia*, bars 7–12, from *Libro secondo libro di madrigali à quatro voci* (1572)

attempting to second-guess the composer's intention by reading *doppi sensi* into the work, is likely to be that taken by one concerned with modest displays of ability and knowledge. Nevertheless it would result in error and embarrassment, such that the perpetrator became the 'bifolco' of the evening.[44]

Nel bel terreno fits into another category of Renaissance 'game', the *beffa* or *burla*, a practical joke the intent of which could reside anywhere on the spectrum between harmless or malicious, especially during the earlier years of the Renaissance. By the beginning of the 1500s, however, in polite society the *burla* was practised as 'a friendly deception in things that do not offend, or that offend very little'.[45] This definition comes from Castiglione, who further subdivides the *burla* into two types: those that 'deceive a person in a discreet and amusing manner', and those in which 'we spread a net, as it were, and put out a little bait so that our man actually tricks himself'. *Nel bel terreno* would fit into the latter category, for the amusement would come if and when the singer took the bait of the word 'molle' and sang the wrong notes. In fact many of Agostini's enigmas, and indeed other pieces published in his books, are enhanced by humour, so adding a further aspect to their appreciation as acts of ingenuity and musical skill.

While it may be clear that Agostini's works are intended to amuse, and some even to cause hilarity, in order to assess their full impact or meaning one must have a basic understanding of what an Italian audience, towards the end of the sixteenth century, would consider funny. In practice, the concepts of humour and ingenuity appear to be inextricably linked in the Renaissance mind, and often what provokes most laughter – at least in elite and courtly circles – is also admired as deeply witty. The abundant examples of jokes and pleasantries quoted by Castiglione bear witness to this, as do the

---

[44] Another of Agostini's madrigals, *Sol mi fa sol*, published in the 1571 *Enigmi musicali*, uses a similar hexachordal 'joke' to wrong-foot the singers at the outset of the piece: four voices sing the syllables in turn, but in the first three voices the interval between the notes setting *mi* and *fa* is a tone (thereby thwarting the expected correlation). It is only with the final entry that the syllables match the notes.

[45] Castiglione, *Il libro del cortegiano*, Book 2; translation from C. Speroni, *Wit and Wisdom of the Italian Renaissance* (Berkeley and Los Angeles, 1964), p. 296. A fuller account of the *beffa/burla* and the way it changed over the course of the Renaissance may be found in P. Burke, 'Frontiers of the Comic in Early Modern Italy, c. 1350–1750', in J. Bremmer and H. Roodenburg (eds.), *A Cultural History of Humor: From Antiquity to the Present Day* (Cambridge, 1997), pp. 61–72.

'Al gioco si conosce il galantuomo'

countless *facezie* which circulated during the fifteenth and sixteenth centuries. Nonetheless, commentators have remarked about the 'otherness' of Renaissance Italian humour that makes it difficult to understand.[46] Many of the jokes and anecdotes in Castiglione barely seem worth relating to modern audiences; some are brutal, some dull, some distasteful, some wholly incomprehensible. To further hinder our understanding, the boundaries between the acceptable and the unacceptable, or the points at which humour tips into cruelty, obscenity or blasphemy, shift during the course of the century, although this movement can be fairly clearly mapped by comparison of editions of civility books and *facezie* from either end of the period.[47] Castiglione, Girolamo Della Casa in his *Galateo*, and later Stefano Guazzo in *La civil conversazione* are expansive on the place and the use of humour in conversation, and in many ways their writings (and the ways they were edited for Counter-Reformation consumption) constitute both a moral code and an aesthetics of humour, in that they present guidelines as to what may be considered 'good', or pleasing, humour and 'bad', or improper, humour.[48] Nevertheless, they provide no easy summary of what precisely it is that made people laugh.

To find a contemporary, concise theory of humour one must turn to writings on poetics and performance, which provide both the means of and a justification for moving an audience to laughter or to tears. The growing concern regarding propriety in all things made classical antecedents important for the justification of all matter or behaviour that might attract censorious attention. Reverence for and familiarity with Cicero's *De oratore* made it an important source for the conversationalist, and its analytical approach to both wit and humour ensured that the humanists' anecdotes had a classical appeal.[49] For the artist, the composer and the poet, however, classical writings on drama and narrative had more to offer. Plautus and Terence provided practical models, but appeals to theory were directed to the works of Aristotle. From

[46] See Speroni, *Wit and Wisdom*, p. 12; Burke, 'Frontiers of the Comic', p. 67.
[47] Burke, 'Frontiers of the Comic', pp. 69–70.
[48] On the censorship of Castiglione and Della Casa in the latter half of the sixteenth century see Speroni, *Wit and Wisdom*, p. 11, and Burke, 'Frontiers of the Comic', pp. 68–9.
[49] The influence of Cicero and other classical models on Renaissance comic theory is discussed in M. T. Herrick, *Comic Theory in the Sixteenth Century* (Urbana, Ill., 1950), throughout but especially pp. 36–57.

around the mid-century, when Robertello produced a translation and critique of Aristotle's *Poetics*, comedy became the stuff of philosophy, and thus of the educated elite.[50] The *Poetics* contains little or no reference to comedy, therefore in an effort to provide a more complete theory of drama, Robertello's book extrapolates from Aristotle's writings on tragedy what he might have thought of comedy. In 1570, the comic playwright and academician Lodovico Castelvetro produced his own glossed translation of Aristotle, his *Poetica d'Aristotele vulgarizzata, et sposta*. Castelvetro, too, found it necessary to provide a short chapter on comedy entirely from his own pen. Here we find an analysis of four basic types of laughter from which all humour springs, and these in turn may provide a broad framework for understanding the comic element of late Renaissance artworks in general, and Agostini's musical diversions in particular. Castelvetro's theory of comedy bases all humour on concealment or deception and recognition or revelation, so that laughter 'is provoked by pleasurable things apprehended by the senses or the imagination', that is, either at the point of revelation or in anticipation of revelation.[51] The four types of laughter are:

1. that which arises from affection, recognition and acquisition;
2. that which arises from deception;
3. that which arises from (disguised) wickedness or physical defect;
4. that which arises from indecencies, again presented covertly.

The first type is that which occurs spontaneously, for instance, when a child sees his mother, when the attention is suddenly focused upon something or someone that one knows well and loves or likes, or something that one has sought has been acquired or recovered. This type of laughter is an intimate reaction, not based on situation. Nevertheless, the idea of recognising with affection something already valued is central to the Renaissance audience's appreciation of *imitatio* and parody, techniques that inform a large proportion of Agostini's work. The imitation and enigma based on Wert's *Cara la vita mia* would have been calculated to engender this sort of

[50] L. G. Clubb, 'Italian Renaissance Comedy', in Paul G. Ruggiers (ed.), *Versions of Medieval Comedy* (Norman, Okla., 1977), pp. 191–210, at p. 202.
[51] 'Il riso si muone [*sic*] in noi per cose piacentici comprese per gli sentimenti, o per l'imaginatio'; L. Castelvetro, *Poetica d'Aristotele vulgarizzata, et sposta* (1570; facs. repr. Munich, 1968), fol. 51ʳ. Translation from A. Bongiorno, *Castelvetro on the Art of Poetry* (Binghamton, NY, 1984), p. 214.

'Al gioco si conosce il galantuomo'

agreeable response. Furthermore, the laughter that comes from acquisition and recognition is also the laughter that arises from wordplay and riddles, so it is an important category for understanding of the Renaissance delight in the *doppio senso*. In terms of Agostini's enigmas, the solving of the riddle and the eventual 'correct' performance of the work constitutes the acquisition of the solution and the recognition of consonant and delightful music.

The second type, that which arises from the deception of others and the deception of the audience, is entirely situational. Properly, this is the humour of the *burla*, in which the witnessing of another's discomfiture or the confounding of one's own expectations is the source of laughter. It would perhaps be stretching the point to claim that the fundamental deception of the enigma is representative of this type. However, the humour of *Nel bel terreno* certainly fits within this category, as does that of *Una sì chiara luce*, which only appears to provide its own solution in the mirrored cryptogram. The *burla* was one of the forms of humour that could most easily provoke censorship and condemnation, precisely because of the possibilities of shame, violence and injury that might befall the recipient.[52] Castelvetro's stern qualification, that one should not laugh at a person who by 'force, necessity or chance' must do something against his will, rules out gratuitous violence in favour of trickery and cunning – even though these also can have serious and unpleasant consequences for the target. But unlike the victims of the true *burla*, the players of Agostini's enigmas, and presumably anyone who consented to play games in a social situation, were complicit in their own deception and probable humiliation – although this may not always have been the case with *Nel bel terreno*. To all intents and purposes it looks just like an ordinary musical setting and could be used to trick a new member of an established musical gathering.

The third type of laughter is provoked by 'wickedness of soul and physical deformities, together with the actions of which they are the cause', but they must be presented in a way that makes it possible to attribute the laughter to something else, 'for no one wishes to be known as taking pleasure ... in the wickedness or deformity of others'.[53] Castelvetro's examples include the story of a miser who

---

[52] Burke, 'Frontiers of the Comic', pp. 66–7.
[53] Bongiorno, *Castelvetro on the Art of Poetry*, pp. 217–18.

asks that something that he had never seen before be described to him, so that he might have it painted; the answer he is given is 'generosity', for although generosity is invisible (and therefore could not have been seen), it also mocks the man's wicked avarice. This type of humour, satire, can be difficult to translate outside its immediate context. It may be that the enigmas contain texts in which individuals or institutions are satirised, but without specific terms of reference the humour they contain is lost. Nonetheless, Agostini clearly knew and understood satire as part of his spectrum of diversions, as is demonstrated by the text of a work in his *Libro terzo a sei voci* (1583), the *Sonnetto sopra la Corte*:

> Ho inteso sempre dir, che nell'Inferno
> così si sta come si vive in Corte;
> perche la vita di chi vive in Corte
> è come de' dannati dello Inferno,
> et che le pene grandi dell'Inferno
> son come i dispiaceri della Corte.
> Ond'un huom, che gran tempo è stato in corte,
> si può dir che sia stato nello Inferno.
> Così l'Inferno è simile à la Corte,
> che non ha Amor la Corte, nè l'Inferno
> nè carità l'Inferno, nè la Corte:
> ma s'alla Corte io penso, et a l'Inferno
> son differenti, perche i buoni in Corte
> si tormentano, ei tristi nello Inferno.[54]

> I have always heard said, that in Hell
> one lives just as one lives at Court;
> because the life of one who lives at Court
> is like that of the damned in Hell,
> and that the great pains of Hell
> are just like the displeasures of the Court.
> So a man who's been a long time at Court
> could say that he's been in Hell.
> Thus Hell is similar to the Court,
> because the Court does not have Love, nor does Hell,
> nor is Charity in Hell, nor at Court:
> but if I think about Court and about Hell
> they are different, because it is the good at Court
> who are tormented, and the wicked in Hell.

This artful text can allow its audience to laugh openly and without fear at the vicissitudes of courtly life, for its ingenuity provides an alternative explanation for the laughter (that is, one enjoys the

[54] L. Agostini, *Madrigali ... Libro Terzo a sei voci* (Ferrara, 1582).

'Al gioco si conosce il galantuomo'

artifice of the poem rather than the opinion it speaks) that cannot elicit condemnation from the court establishment.[55]

The final type of laughter, that which arises from indecencies, also bears the qualification of concealment and revelation to bring it within the boundaries of humour. Castelvetro insists that graphic obscenity cannot be laughed at in the company of others, so it must be clothed, so to speak, in order for it to be publicly acknowledged to be funny. Concealment might come in the form of situation, gesture or language, and the more clever or virtuosic the disguise, the more valued the experience. As the art historian Bette Talvacchia says, describing the deployment of visual *doppi sensi*, 'The skill of the artist, whose manipulation of form allows the viewer to see two things at once, is another stratum of sanctioning cover: virtuosity becomes one of the meanings of the image, an overlay of form that provides justification for the sexual content.'[56] Musical works are the perfect clothes for erotic content; only the contorted language of sexual metaphor, such as that in *Nel bel terreno*, is left to be unravelled by modern scholars. The vast lexicon of sexual vocabulary used in the Renaissance is like an iceberg, its tip being those metaphors that have survived into current or near-current usage, but the great unrealised mass being that ' "equivocal code" that refers to transgressive sexual practices whose obfuscation relies, then and now, on "the inventive, protean nature of its vocabulary (based on neologisms, dialect words, jargon, macaronic constructions and borrowings from other languages)" '.[57] Whilst the basic symbolism of *morte* and *bacio* to indicate orgasm and intercourse is, and would have been, understood by a broad audience with only a passing familiarity with the vocabulary, sixteenth-century texts – theatrical, poetic and musical – contain many more *doppi sensi* and allusions to sexual behaviour, 'normal' or transgressive, than we now recognise.

---

[55] The conceit of the court as a manifestation of Hell is not uncommon; in the dedication of T. Garzoni, *Piazza universale di tutte le professioni del mondo* (Venice, 1585), addressed to Alfonso II d'Este, the author calls courts 'the realm of wicked foxes and the most abject spongers, schools of corruptions and dens of evil'. The metaphor may have had further significance for Este courtiers and rulers, as they would have been familiar with the place of Obizzo d'Este in the seventh circle of Hell, as described by Dante in *L'Inferno*, Canto XII.

[56] B. Talvacchia, *Taking Positions: On the Erotic in Renaissance Culture* (Princeton, 1999), p. 105.

[57] A. K. Smith, 'Fraudomy: Sexuality and Politics in Burchiello', in J. Goldberg (ed.), *Queering the Renaissance* (Durham, NC and London, 1994), 89. Smith quotes from J. Toscan, *Le carneval du langage: Le lexique érotique de Burchiello à Marino, XVe–XVIIe siècles*, 4 vols. (Lille, 1981).

Castelvetro's four types of laughter are not mutually exclusive. Many written accounts of extended and complex *burle* show that two or three types can arise in a single, well-crafted situation. Agostini's enigmas, too, can fall within several categories; we have already seen that *Nel bel terreno* has multi-faceted appeal. Even more than *Nel bel terreno*, however, *Un mal è che mi rende afflitto e mesto* exploits the full range of Castelvetro's humorous possibilities in ingenious ways. The gradual revelation of the hexachordal syllables supplies the affectionate recognition; the hexachordal wrong-footing of individual singers would be witnessed by the others as a deception; the final twist in the harmonic language is the punch line of a *burla* played on the entire company; and the hexachordal syllables themselves have multiple salacious meanings, both in combination with each other and as an overall conceit. For instance, in equivocal literature the groans emitted during sexual acts are sometimes compared with solmisation.[58] Furthermore, the three syllables 'sol-la-sol' have a homonymic relationship with the noun *sollazzo* and the verb *sollazzarsi*, which loosely translate as 'relief' and 'to fool around', both in a sexual sense; 'sollazzo di preti' was a common euphemism for sodomy.[59] The multiple meanings inherent in the word-syllable *re* are the most powerful source of humour in the text. Meaning both 'the second degree of the hexachord' and 'king', 're' is also used in equivocal texts to denote 'a male sodomite'.[60] Hence, the punch line of the text (and the text of the subject phrase) 'Un re mi fa sol lasso [sollazzo], e questo è Amore' could mean 'one sodomite gives me sexual relief, and that's Love'. Although the 'king' could simply be Love himself, for its author and its original audience the text may have also satirised a particular ruler or cleric infamous for his sexual predilections.[61]

---

[58] P. Aretino, *Sei giornate (Ragionamento della Nanna et della Antonia)*, ed. G. Aquilecchia (Bari, 1969), p. 21: 'Alla fine ... s'accordano di fare ad una voce come s'accordano i cantori o vero i fabbri martellando ... e chi con sommessa voce e chi con alta smiagolando, pareano quelli dalla sol, fa, mi rene'; 'In the end ... they tuned themselves together in one voice, as do choristers or hammering blacksmiths ... and with hushed voice, and with high moaning, it sounded as if they were practising solmisation'. Aretino himself was accused of sodomitical practices in much the same terms; see Talvacchia, *Taking Positions*, p. 88.
[59] Boggione and Casalegno, *Dizionario storico*, p. 608.
[60] Toscan, *Le carneval du langage*, i, p. 97.
[61] Sodomists were frequently the subject of Roman satirical poetry; see V. Marucci, A. Marzo, A. Romano and G. Aquilecchia (eds.), *Pasquinate romane del Cinquecento* (Salerno and Rome, 1983), p. 914, for a contemporary example relating to Cardinal Carlo Carafa (1517–66).

'Al gioco si conosce il galantuomo'

Looking at Agostini's enigmas as courtly games or pastimes, particularly in the light of the lascivious content of some of them, raises the question of the participation of women, whether as singers or audience. High voices are needed for the performance of all of the five- and six-voice enigmas, but none are composed in *chiavette* or high clefs, and are therefore not beyond the range of an all-male group with a competent falsettist (or castrato) and a true bass. The four-voice *Nel bel terreno* is different; it is scored for $g_2c_1c_2F_3$. An all-male performance is perfectly feasible, and masculine attempts at the high tessitura might well make its performance all the more funny.[62] The enigmas, however, contain little or nothing that would exclude them from being experienced by ladies. Women are known to have appreciated and performed sexually suggestive material – some owned copies of Giulio Romano's explicit *I modi* prints, and there is documentary evidence that the 'paragon of Renaissance purity' Isabella d'Este sang scurrilous *villotte* in private.[63] The Accademia degli Intronati of Siena, whose activities provided the source for Bargagli's *Dialoghi*, included women in their games, during which they would have been unavoidably and continuously exposed to the running joke of the academy's device – the *mestola* (a pestle), which was yet another common euphemism for the penis.[64] The academy used the ceremonial pestle as a symbol of authority, using it to deliver blows as penalties or to indicate that a player should act. Although some women may not have been inculcated with the privileged subculture of the equivocal language, many must have been at least partially aware of the significance of the sexual metaphors that infuse so much of Renaissance high culture.[65]

---

[62] The pitch at which *chiavette* pieces are intended to be performed is still a matter of scholarly debate. Although much evidence has been produced for local practices which entail downwards transposition, the comparison of pieces that would be related in performance (such as Luzzasco Luzzaschi's *chiavette* setting of Cavaletta's poem *De l'odorate spoglie*, discussed above, and the low-clef madrigal it introduces, Wert's *Cara la vita mia*) show that, in 1580s Ferrara at least, *chiavette* pieces were probably sung 'at pitch'.
[63] For contemporary comments on female ownership of *I modi* and its consequences, see Talvacchia, *Taking Positions*, p. 54; for Isabella's performance of *Tolle in mane* see Prizer, 'Games of Venus', pp. 36–7.
[64] Crane, *Italian Social Customs*, p. 270. On *mestola* as a euphemism, see E. Scerbo, *Il nome della cosa: Nomi e nomignoli degli organi sessuali* (Milan, 1991), pp. 31–2; Boggione and Casalegno, *Dizionario storico*, p. 221.
[65] See the discussion in C. Fuhrmann, 'Gossip, *Erotica*, and the Male Spy in Alessandro Striggio's *Il Cicalamento delle donne al bucato* (1567)', in Todd Borgerding (ed.), *Gender and Sexuality in Early Music* (New York and London, 2002), pp. 167–97, at p. 181.

Nonetheless, those women who did understand the language could and should have reacted at their own discretion. Returning to Castelvetro's, and Talvacchia's, critiques, the very fact that two things may be seen at once allows a woman publicly to see only one, even if she privately understands all too well the significance of a *doppio senso*.

EDIFICATION THROUGH PLAY

Agostini's status as a composer of musical novelties, designed to entertain his secular masters, may seem at odds with his vocation. He was certainly not the first cleric to publish secular music, and his entertainments provide an important precedent for the madrigal comedies of the Olivetan monk Adriano Banchieri, some thirty years later. But viewed within the context of the increasingly feverish activity of the Counter-Reformation, and taking into account Agostini's own brushes with its powers (the revocation of his papal dispensation, the narrowly avoided accusations of simony), his activities might appear slightly incongruous. This is not to say that he was not a publicly spiritual man. His single literary publication of a set of sermons was highly enough regarded to go into several editions.[66] He also published a complete volume of *madrigali spirituali*, his *Lagrime del peccatore* of 1586 – this, too, is peppered with literary and musical 'imitations', recalling verse by Petrarch and Tansillo, and madrigals by Alessandro Striggio and Guglielmo Gonzaga.[67] It seems that, regardless of whether his subject is serious or humorous, there is always an element of play intrinsic to his music.

Why then, might a man of the cloth devote his time and his intellect so consistently to the production of games and pleasantries? The involvement of the Renaissance priesthood in the production, dissemination and reception of recreational material, including humour and erotica, has received a good deal of scholarly attention, but it remains something of an enigma itself – at least to the twenty-first-century observer.[68] Any explanation requires an

---

[66] L. Agostini, *Sermoni devotissimi sopra il Santissimo Sacramento dell'Altare* (Ferrara, 1589).
[67] L. Agostini, *Le Lagrime del peccatore a sei voci* (Venice, 1586).
[68] The studies by Talvacchia, Speroni and Burke previously cited all touch on this apparent conundrum. Three papers, comprising a condensed version of the present article and contributions by D. Cardamone Jackson, 'Erotic Jest and Gesture in Roman Anthologies of Canzoni Villanesche', and M. Marshall, 'Power, Pornography and Entertainment in a

'Al gioco si conosce il galantuomo'

understanding of how Renaissance society conveyed licence and disapprobation with regard to sexual discourse and, more broadly, morality itself. Generally, people, actions and objects are described as either *onesto* or *disonesto*, referring to their acceptability in society or the appropriateness of their ends. Subjects we now might place on one side of the divide – practical jokes, violence, prostitutes or representations of sexual acts – could then be in either camp, depending on origin and intent, among many other mitigating factors. Furthermore, the parameters for judging *onestà* seem to change, and narrow, throughout the sixteenth century. The need for all play and humour, erotic or otherwise, to demonstrate relative *onestà* increased as both the Church's control, partly through the *Index librorum prohibitorum*, grew. Nevertheless, priests at the end of the century seemed to be just as active in the use and production of secular pastimes as they were at its beginning, since the effect of the Counter-Reformation was not so much to eradicate play but to transform it. In musical circles, madrigals and villanelle written by and/or dedicated to members of the Church, with highly metaphorical but distinctly lascivious texts, continued to circulate, seemingly unhindered by the hand of the censor.[69]

It could be argued that the involvement of clerics and priests in the production of humour and erotica was the most effective way the Church could find of taking and retaining control of dangerous material. As diversions created by a cleric but cast in a secular form, Agostini's enigmas belong to a body of works and a tradition that stretches back centuries. The *exempla*, moral but entertaining anecdotes that grace sermons from the Middle Ages on, are the

---

Cinquecento Academy', examined this phenomenon with specific reference to the mid-century Italian repertoire at the Annual Meeting of the American Musicological Society at Columbus, Ohio, November 2002. I am grateful to Professor Jackson and Dr Marshall for their generous sharing of material with me.

[69] Musical books both dedicated to priests and with explicit erotic content include, among many, O. di Lasso, *Villanelle d'Orlando di Lassus e d'altri eccellenti musici libro secondo* (Rome, 1555); [F. Azzaiolo], *Primo libro di villotte alla padoana intitolate Villotte del fiore* (Venice, 1557); and G. B. Moscaglia, *Il secondo libro de madrigali a quattro voci* (Venice, 1585). These books are discussed in the papers by Jackson and Marshall cited above, in Marshall's 'Cultural Codes and Hierarchies in the Mid-Century Villotta' (Ph.D. thesis, University of Southampton, 2004) and in V. Rowcroft, 'The Secular Vocal Music of Giovanni Battista Moscaglia' (Ph.D. thesis, University of Southampton, 2002). An interesting case of censorship by a publisher involving the alteration of poetic texts is discussed in I. Fenlon, 'Music and Civic Piety in Counter-Reformation Milan', in *Music and Culture of Late Renaissance Italy* (Oxford and New York, 2002), pp. 67-85, at pp. 83-4.

mildest manifestation of the phenomenon. However, in the fifteenth century, perhaps as a result of the popularity of Boccaccio's *Decameron*, licentious content became commonplace in printed pleasantries, and the short story sometimes lost its explicitly moral or didactic tone. Among the most famous purveyors of bawdy *facezie* are the fifteenth-century priests Poggio Bracciolini and Piovano Arlotto (whose stories were beloved of the sixteenth-century Jesuit saint Filippo Neri); and the sixteenth century produced ecclesiastical raconteurs no more averse to pornographic content, for instance, Pietro Aretino, Giovanni Della Casa and Antonfrancesco Doni.[70] It is clear that the discourse that informs the works of these men was intrinsic to, rather than an aberration of, the ecclesiastical environment. Bracciolini himself gives a justification of his stories, situating them firmly in the Curia: 'This was our *Bugiale*, a sort of workshop of lies, which was founded by the secretaries in order that they might have an occasional laugh. Since the days of Pope Martin [1417–31] we had the custom of choosing an out-of-the-way place where we exchanged news, and where we would talk of various things, both in earnest and to distract our minds.'[71]

Distraction, or honest leisure (*ozio onesto*), is a common theme in Renaissance justifications of both humour and erotica – what is good for the mind is good for the soul.[72] The erotic paintings that adorned the Mantuan palaces of Guglielmo Gonzaga, Agostini's pupil and patron, were commissioned by his forebears in the spirit of repose through play; indeed the walls of the Camera di Psiche in the Palazzo del Te are inscribed with the motto 'for honest leisure after work to restore strength in quiet'.[73] Classical authority could be invoked by those who feared leisure would lead to (sexual) wickedness, as shown by Ovid's words 'Eradicate leisure and Cupid's bow is broken', inscribed by Mantegna on one of his paintings for Isabella d'Este. But the spiritual dimension to play

---

[70] B. K. Otto, *Fools Are Everywhere: The Court Jester around the World* (Chicago and London, 2001), pp. 169–70.
[71] P. Bracciolini, *Liber facetiarum* (1470), translated in Speroni, *Wit and Wisdom*, pp. 4–5.
[72] B. Vickers, 'Leisure and Idleness: The Ambivalence of *Otium*', *Renaissance Studies*, 4 (1990), pp. 1–37 and 107–54, at pp. 129–30, describes the justification of leisure time as 'a preoccupation of more concern to the leisured than to the working classes'. However, Guazzo, *La civile conversatione*, fol. 113r, describes 'otio honesto' as leisure time taken by a man after the working day, firmly placing concerns regarding idleness in a broader context than just courtly society.
[73] Talvacchia, *Taking Positions*, pp. 108–10.

'Al gioco si conosce il galantuomo'

could be supported by appealing to the works of Cicero and Seneca, who permitted study, leisurely conversation and the transmission of knowledge on the basis that they had social benefits.[74] Furthermore, scholars of Plato could argue that play was an essential element of holiness, and that playful activities bring men closer to God: 'God alone is worthy of supreme seriousness, but man is made God's plaything, and that is the best part of him. Therefore every man and woman should live life accordingly, and play the noblest games and be of another mind from what they are at present . . . Life must be lived as play, playing certain games, making sacrifices, singing and dancing, and then a man will be able to propitiate the gods, and defend himself against his enemies, and win in the contest.'[75] Honest or decent play was clearly the focus of Giraldi Cinzio's 'giuochi onesti' which, as noted above, included music. He appealed to Plato both for his justification of play and for his admission of music to his (brief) list of acceptable pastimes.[76] Not only did he prescribe decent games for the revitalisation of the soul, but he also recommended games that sharpen the wits and 'depend completely on the industry of the mind'.

Throughout the second half of the sixteenth century Ferrara and its court became a focal point for a growing interest in the teachings of Plato. The University of Ferrara, which was under ducal authority, was one of the first Italian universities to establish a chair of Platonic philosophy, a position created for Francesco Patrizi in 1577. Patrizi was already well known in Ferrara, and his appointment may have been intended to satisfy both progressive and conservative factions. Platonic philosophy provided an alternative to medieval (and to some, outmoded) Aristotelianism; however, Patrizi, following Ficino, also claimed that Plato's writings supported Christian doctrine better than Aristotle's, and that their study could 'purify Catholic theology and put an end to the Protestant schism'.[77] Patrizi's own writings extended the Ficinian combination of Platonic and Hermetic traditions, and during his

[74] Vickers, 'Leisure and Idleness', pp. 10–12 and 31–2.
[75] J. Huizinga, *Homo Ludens* (London, 1970), p. 37, quoting Plato, *Laws*, 7.
[76] Giraldi Cinzio, *L'uomo di corte*, ch. 5, paras. 1–3 (pp. 43–4).
[77] J. Hankins, 'Renaissance Platonism', in E. Craig (ed.), *The Routledge Encyclopedia of Philosophy* (London and New York, 1998), pp. 439–47. Alfonso's enthusiasm for Patrizi and his Platonic teachings may have partially been an attempt to eradicate the Protestant stain of his mother's heresy (Renée of France, Alfonso's mother, was a noted, and unrepentant, Calvinist).

tenure at Ferrara he produced several of his most important tracts, including the *Nova de universis philosophia* (*A new philosophy of everything*), published in Ferrara in 1591.

The ideas expounded in the *Nova de universis philosophia* have implications for the composition and appreciation of enigmas at Ferrara, through their enactment of the revelation of hidden truths. Patrizi's agenda in his new philosophy was to not only to systematise the knowledge of the ancient sages, who once could work miracles through their sayings, but also to interpret and to explain their mysteries through Platonist philosophy, so that they were fit for the rational world.[78] Patrizi was welcome at court, and his participation in court life at the highest level shows the importance of his position. He and his ideas feature strongly in one of the most detailed portraits of the Ferrarese court from the 1580s, the *Discorsi* of Count Annibale Romei, in which he propounds Plato's views on (in particular) beauty, love and honour.[79] Duke Alfonso's patronage of Patrizi was an enthusiastic embrace of the most current Platonistic teachings; the court – as amply illustrated in Romei's *Discorsi* – simply followed his lead.

Agostini's musical enigmas, therefore, could have come into being – or at least could have found their justification – as part of a moral imperative, however immoral some of their content may appear. That Agostini chose the enigma as an important vehicle for his musical invention fits into the concept of edification through play. His contemporary at the courts of Ferrara and Mantua, Torquato Tasso, also expresses the higher purpose of the enigma, not just to entertain but also to enrich:

> whence if Aristotle spoke of enigma, he spoke of allegory, but with a different name. However, if enigma is a question of joking and playfulness, as it is said by Athenaeus, it does not seem that it can be the same thing. But if the enigmas or symbols of Pythagoras are not proposed as a game, but for the precepts for life, enigma and allegory can easily be of the same species, or at least of the same genus. The poets avail themselves of both.[80]

---

[78] C. Leijenhorst, 'Francesco Patrizi's Hermetic Philosophy', in R. van den Broek and W. J. Hanegraaff (eds.), *Gnosis and Hermetism from Antiquity to Modern Times* (Albany, NY, 1998), pp. 125–46, at p. 140.

[79] A. Romei, *Discorsi divisi in sette giornate . . . di Annibale Romei Gentiluomo Ferrarese* (1582), in Angelo Solerti, *Ferrara e la corte estense*. Romei's work is digested in Crane, *Italian Social Customs*, pp. 219–39.

[80] 'Iaonde s'Aristotele parlò de l'enigma, parlò de l'allegoria, ma con altro nome. Nondimeno se l'enigma è una questione da scherzo e giocosa, come si legge appresso Ateneo, non pare che

'Al gioco si conosce il galantuomo'

Tasso makes his comments in the context of a defence of allegory and enigma, citing Homer and Dante. However, he also quotes from Plato's *Phaedrus*, confirming that the interpretation of allegories (and the solving of puzzles) can be considered a leisure pursuit:[81]

'Now I, o Phaedrus, admit these allegories are pleasing enough, but to a man too curious, and troubled, and unlucky [Plato's source text has: 'not very fortunate']; for no other reason than he will have to interpret the form of centaurs and chimeras; on him will converge a multitude of gorgons, Pegasuses and other monstrous images: and if any of those things suggests an opinion other than the one he is trying to narrate, and he wishes to reduce them each to a more realistic sense, relying on common sense [*rustica sapienza*], he will need an excess of leisure [*ozio*].' But if he calls 'common sense' that of those who live in the country, where Socrates never wanted to live, I believe he is speaking the truth without a doubt, because the investigation of such things suits a man with little to do [*uomo poco occupato*].

In another dialogue, *Il Gonzaga secondo, over Del giuoco*, Tasso expands on the idea of how the composition of poetry (and hence the use of allegory) may be regarded as study when part of the daily activities of one seeking the life of an 'uomo occupato'. Nevertheless, he cites the example of Virgil, who 'in praising his lord, who granted him the leisure [*ozio*] of poetising, said that he had permission to joke of what he pleased'. He goes on to say that Virgil was not alone in saying this, and that many pleasing poems were called 'giuochi'. He concludes the discussion with another *doppio senso*: poetry – along with other arts – can be both study and play.[82]

For Tasso, the arts of poetry and music are intimately connected, so his remarks provide a contemporary philosophical context for the combination of serious study and light-hearted enjoyment. Agostini more than once refers to his relationship with his dedicatees as one formed and strengthened through the mutual study of

---

sia una cosa medesima. Ma se gli enigmi o simboli di Pitagora non sono proposti per giuoco, ma per ammaestramento de la vita, potrebbe facilmente l'enigma e l'allegoria essere l'istesso di spezie, o di genere almeno. De l'una e de l'altro si vagliono i poeti'; T. Tasso, *Discorso del poema eroico*, 1594, *Scritti sull'arte poetica*, ed. E. Mazzali, 2 vols. (Turin, 1997), ii, p. 327.

[81] Tasso quotes Plato, *Phaedrus*, 229 C–E, finishing: ' "Ma io, o Fedro, stimo questo cose assai piacevoli, ma d'uomo troppo curioso ed affannato e non aventuroso; non per altra cagione se non perché gli sarebbe necessario interpretar la forma de' Centauri e de le Chimere; vi concorre ancora una moltitudine di Gorgoni e di Pegasi e d'altre imagini mostruose: onde s'alcuno di queste cose porterà altra opinione di quella che si narra, e vorrà ridurre ciascuna d'esse a senso conveniente, fidandosi d'una rustica sapienza averà bisogno d'ozio soverchio." Ma s'egli chiama *rustica sapienza* quella di coloro ch'abitano in villa, dove Socrate non volle mai abitare, dice, per mio avviso, il vero senza alcun dubbio, perché l'investigazione di sì fatte cose conviene ad uomo poco occupato'; *ibid.*, ii, pp. 325–6.

[82] T. Tasso, *Il Gonzaga secondo*, p. 870.

music (almost certainly with Agostini as the tutor); he also repeatedly refers to music as a 'professione', in the sense of a vocation, not just an accomplishment. The musical enigma could have been regarded by Agostini and his patrons as an honourable pastime, one that required serious consideration and substantial ability to counterbalance (or excuse) its evident hilarity.

The dedication of Agostini's *Libro secondo de madrigali a quattro voci* perhaps provides the most precise context for the provenance and intention of his music, and the milieu and purpose for which it was composed:

Onde sapendo certo quanto diletto prendino le Ill. S.S. V.V. della nobile, gioconda, et grave professione della Musica, et quanto sia conforme alla Natura, et genio di quelle; hò preso per ispediente dedicarle questa mia operetta di Musica, tenendo per fermo, che debba esser da esse vista, cantata, et ascoltata con viso allegro, con cor sincero, et orecchie benignissime, et io con questa buona occasione farò sapere ad ogn'uno quanto io stimi l'esser caro à così compiuti gentilhuomini, et Signori.

So, knowing for certain what delight your Illustrious Lordships take in the noble, joyful and serious profession of Music, and how it conforms to your nature and intellect, I have taken it as expedient to dedicate to you this my little work of Music, being convinced that it must be seen, sung and heard by you with a happy countenance, with a sincere heart and with the kindest ears, and I, on this good occasion, will make known to everyone how much I esteem being dear to such complete gentlemen and Lords.

Key words and phrases in this passage point to a typical humanist agenda, one that places the compositions within humanism's goal of self-improvement through education and experience. The opposition of 'gioconda' and 'grave' invokes the classically inspired antitheses of Bemboist literary criticism, *piacevolezza* and *gravità* (the same oppositions used by Bargagli in his classification of games).[83] The following dualism, between 'Natura' and 'genio', also reflects a common humanist trope. These 'complete gentlemen', therefore, can appreciate the music with both body and mind, gaining the fullest and most rewarding experience on both levels. Most revealing, however, is that Agostini clearly intends the pieces to be used, 'seen, sung and heard', by their recipients, not just admired; in other words, the dedicatees are practitioners, not just patrons. That this book and the first book of enigmas are each dedicated to a pair of relations then becomes significant. The familial connection between

---

[83] The significance of Bembo's oppositions for madrigalists is examined in D. T. Mace, 'Pietro Bembo and the Literary Origins of the Italian Madrigal', *Musical Quarterly*, 55 (1969), pp. 65–86.

'Al gioco si conosce il galantuomo'
the dedicatees seems to imply a social – if not domestic – use for the music, which could be enjoyed when members of the household came together.

FURTHER CONTEXTS FOR AGOSTINI'S ENIGMAS

A musical context

Agostini's enigmas fulfil many objectives for the courtier who is looking for diversion, complete entertainments for complete gentlemen. They have no exact parallels in the printed repertoire of the Italian madrigal, but there are some works that are at least partially related to them in concept. The playful side of the madrigal has had some limited recognition in current scholarship, and the madrigal comedies – and comic madrigals – of Orazio Vecchi, Adriano Banchieri and Giovanni Croce are clearly connected to the games and activities of elite circles in Renaissance northern Italy.[84] The history of musical puzzles is long and distinguished, from Machaut's *Ma fin est mon commencement* to Willaert's *Quid non ebrietas* and beyond, but the playfulness of notation must also have been exploited in other ways more frequently than we are currently aware. For instance, Hippolito Chamaterò's *Secondo libro de madrigali a quattro voci* of 1569 contains a madrigal, *Vita del viver mio*, that is notated with two clef systems – $c_1c_3c_4F_4$ and $g_2c_2c_3F_3$ – so that it may be sung either in a 'minor' mode with a tonal focus on D, or a 'major' mode with a tonal focus on F.[85] This fairly simple device, achieved without creating problems for the printer, nonetheless adds an extra dimension to the madrigal, and no doubt was intended to trigger discussion, thoughtful or frivolous, among its readers or performers.

The discussion of canon (meaning primarily *fugato* composition) as a compositional technique was endemic to sixteenth-century

---

[84] Studies that examine evidence from individual sources include Haar, 'Notes on the *Dialogo*' and C. A. Elias, 'Musical Performance in 16th-Century Italian Literature: Straparola's *Le piacevoli notti*', *Early Music*, 18 (1989), pp. 161–74. Laura Macy's studies, 'The Italian Madrigal and Renaissance Games' (paper presented at the Annual Meeting of the American Musicological Society, New York, 1995), and 'Speaking of Sex: Metaphor and Performance in the Italian Madrigal', *Journal of Musicology*, 14 (1996), pp. 1–34, provide further insight.

[85] H. Chamaterò, *Il secondo libro de madrigali a quattro voci* (Venice, 1569). The book is dedicated to Barbara Sanseverina, Contessa di Sala, the Piacentine beauty who from the 1560s to the 1590s maintained a strong influence on the courts of Parma, Mantua and Ferrara, as well as on Roman society.

theorists, yet few were expansive in print on the process of creating musical puzzles. Hermann Finck alone gives the subject more than passing treatment; the entire third book of his *Practica musica* is devoted to the composition of canons, and he treats the issue of developing appropriate mottoes.[86] Gioseffo Zarlino describes looking-glass canons, including those of Willaert, and gives examples, although his remarks are made in the context of a discussion of double and invertible counterpoint.[87] Nicola Vicentino is critical of puzzle canons that cannot, by their nature, take account of the meaning of the text, suggesting that their 'fanciful' composition creates unpleasant sounds, which is contrary to the purpose of music.[88] Adriano Banchieri, who includes some examples of enigmatic canons in his *Cartella musicale*, echoes Tasso's Socrates in his assessment of enigmas, yet he provides a further insight into the presentation of Agostini's pieces, and perhaps another alternative for their use:

> If anyone is pleased to compose such canons, I do indeed praise those who wish that much time be lost in solving them, but I praise more those who provide explanations, since not all will understand the obscure ones and everyone appreciates explanations, nor does one lose time in searching, as the proverb 'the sea at Ravenna' says.[89]

By printing the solution on the same page as the enigma, the singer presented with the Sesto partbook of one of Agostini's books, together with the rest of the company, could take her/his delight in the ingenuity of the puzzle's construction without having to spend much time working it out.

---

[86] H. Finck, *Practica musica* (Wittenberg, 1556). Finck's mottoes are discussed in Lowinsky, 'Music in Titian's *The Bacchanal of the Andrians*', pp. 301–2. See now B. J. Blackburn and L. Holford-Strevens, 'Juno's Four Grievances: The Taste for the Antique in Canonic Inscriptions', in Ulrich Konrad, Jürgen Heidrich and Hans Joachim Marx (eds.), *Musikalischen Quellen – Quellen zur Musikgeschichte: Festschrift für Martin Staehelin zum 65. Geburtstag* (Göttingen, 2003), 159–74.

[87] Zarlino, *Le istitutioni harmoniche*, pp. 266–7. A fuller discussion of theorists' writings on the subject may be found in Collins, 'Canon in Music Theory', pp. 288–337.

[88] N. Vicentino, *L'antica musica ridotta alla moderna practica* (1555), facs., ed. E. E. Lowinsky (Kassel, 1959), fol. 93^v.

[89] 'A chi piace componere simili Canoni, lodo sì quelli, che vogliono si perdi molto tempo a rivenirli, mà piu lodo quelli, che danno le loro Dichiarationi, atteso che gli oscuri non tutti gli capiscono, et gli dichiarati ognuno ne gode, ne si perde il tempo a ricercare come dice il proverbio il Mare per Ravenna'; A. Banchieri, *Cartella musicale nel canto figurato, fermo, et contrapunto* (1614; facs. repr. Bologna, 1968), p. 160. On the proverb, which means that it is either very easy or very hard to find something, see www.racine.ra.it/argaza/bollettini/19febbraio00.pdf.

'Al gioco si conosce il galantuomo'

Although Agostini's enigmas are unique in the madrigal repertoire, there is one other substantial source of printed musical enigmas from the second half of the sixteenth century, the final chapter of Pedro Cerone's monolithic treatise, *El melopeo y maestro*, published in 1613, but written in the 1590s.[90] Cerone's forty-six enigmas differ from Agostini's in several ways: some are infinitely more elaborate, with cryptograms in the form of a cross, or a checkerboard, or with engraved pictures significant to the riddle; most are *fugato* canons of various types; some are incomplete; very few are texted, and several are credited to other composers.[91] None of them take the very stylised form of Agostini's pieces with the repeated statement of a subject phrase in *contrapunto con obbligo*. A significant proportion of the attributed puzzles come from the sacred repertoire: for instance, Josquin's mensuration canon from the second Agnus Dei of the four-voice *Missa L'homme armé super voces musicales* opens the collection.[92] One of Cerone's few enigmas to appear with a riddle in the vernacular is attributed to Cipriano de Rore.[93] This 'enigma de la hermana' (enigma of the sister) consists of a single untexted line of music, the custos for a four-voice *fugato* canon, and a difficult riddle in Italian built around hexachordal puns, from which both the quinto and the sesto parts may be extracted. The piece could have originated in a courtly environment, if the courtiers were well enough educated in mensuration, eventually finding its way into Cerone's hands. Nonetheless, the vast preponderance of Latin riddle texts, especially those with sacred significance, and the use of fragments of chant and liturgy point to a chapel or ecclesiastical environment as the source of many of his puzzles.

---

[90] P. Cerone, *El melopeo y maestro* (1613; facs. repr., 2 vols., ed. Alberto Gallo, Bologna, 1969).
[91] The only dedicated study of Cerone's enigmas, E. A. Arias, 'Cerone and his Enigmas', *Anuario Musical*, 44 (1989), pp. 85–114, is slightly misleading in this respect. He states (p. 92) that the ninth to the forty-second enigmas are all by Cerone, although Cerone is careful to credit not only the composer, but frequently the source, of each enigma he did not himself compose.
[92] Cerone, *El melopeo*, ii, pp. 1075–6. This canon is one of the few for which Petrucci does not give a resolution; its enigmatic form is preserved in his print. See B. J. Blackburn, 'Canonic Conundrums: The Singer's Petrucci', *Basler Jahrbuch für Historische Musikpraxis*, 25 (2001), pp. 53–69, at p. 58.
[93] Cerone, *El melopeo*, ii, p. 1118. A facsimile of Cerone's explanation of the enigma is also printed in C. de Rore, *Opera omnia*, ed. B. Meier (Corpus Mensurabilis Musicae, 14; Neuhausen-Stuttgart, 1997), viii, pp. xv–xvi.

Both Agostini and Cerone had taken holy orders; perhaps their familiarity and interest in musical puzzles arose during vocational and musical training. Zarlino's comment that musicians (in an ecclesiastical context) were not beyond subjecting the singers to a *burla* shows that choirs were not always the most serious of spaces.[94] The version of Josquin's *Déploration sur la mort d'Ockeghem* copied in the Medici Codex has the cantus firmus notated a half-step too high, with a motto instructing the singers how to correct the pitch.[95] Furthermore, recalling Spataro's complaint mentioned above, puzzle canons may have had a place in chapel competitions of honour. It has been suggested that Willaert's *Quid non ebrietas* was constructed as a musical revenge on the papal choir for an insult directed at the composer near the beginning of his career, and Vicentino gives his advice for solving puzzle canons on the basis that although it is 'an annoying and tiresome task, man is not excused from hard work where honour is at stake'.[96]

Cerone appears to have collected his puzzles for his own amusement and possibly as teaching aids, for the title of the chapter, 'En el qual se ponen unos enigmas musicales, para sutilizar el ingenio de los estudiosos' ('In which are placed certain musical enigmas, to sharpen the wit of the studious'), suggests that he considered them worthwhile and edifying pastimes for students of music. The conclusion to the chapter suggests an even higher purpose: 'The perfect and true musician has not only to use diligence and much vigilance in composing and ordering the numeric music of his motets and masses; but also he must order and compose the spiritual music of his person.'[97] Cerone goes on to claim that the practice of developing and solving musical enigmas is

---

[94] 'Ma perche alle volte li Musici, non gia per necessità: ma più presto per burla, et per capriccio, o forse per volere intricare il cervello (dirò cosi) alli Cantanti, sogliono trasportare li Modi più verso l'acuto, overo verso il grave per un Tuono, o per altro intervallo'; Zarlino, *Le istitutioni harmoniche*, p. 319.

[95] Lowinsky, 'Music in Titian's *The Bacchanal of the Andrians*', p. 305.

[96] D. Keyser, 'The Character of Exploration: Adrian Willaert's "Quid non ebrietas" ', in C. E. Robertson (ed.), *Musical Repercussions of 1492: Encounters in Text and Performance* (Washington, DC and London, 1992), pp. 185–207; Vicentino, *L'antica musica*, fol. 93ᵛ; translation from N. Vicentino, *Ancient Music Adapted to Modern Practice*, trans. Maria Rika Maniates, ed. C.V. Palisca (New Haven and London, 1996), p. 298.

[97] Cerone, *El melopeo*, ii, p. 1142 (quoting Martín de Tapia): 'el perfecto y verdadero Musico, no solamente ha de usar diligencia y mucha vigilancia en componer y ordenar la Musica numeral de sus Motetes y Missas; pero tambien, deve ordenar y componer la Musica espiritual de su persona'.

'Al gioco si conosce il galantuomo'

part of the true musician's spiritual enrichment. Although formed in an entirely different social ambience, the rhetoric with which Cerone frames his treatise on the musical enigma resonates strongly with Cinzio's recommendation that play should test and enlarge the wit of the player the better to equip him for his work, and further with Tasso's visions of the enigma as a source of life enhancement, and of play as a kind of study.

Cerone's enigmas are intricate and impressive, and they must have been hugely expensive to produce. The many engravings, colouring, and even the folio format needed to present the complicated layouts of the puzzles make them a very specialised publication venture, much more so than Agostini's. Surprisingly, however, included in Cerone's book are several examples of canons from the broader repertoire which when published (or disseminated) as works in their own right appeared written out in full, with no indication that they may once have existed in a cryptic, shorthand form. For instance, Marcantonio Ingegneri's four-voice canonic motet *Noe, Noe, psallite Noe* is cited, showing the beginning of its double invertible canon in shorthand; Jacob Vaet's motet *Qui operatus est Petro* is given as an enigma, complete with pictures of the key of St Peter and the sword of St Paul as integral parts of the cryptogram.[98] The proliferation of 'normal' works digested in Cerone's book suggests that there are more works, at least among the sophisticated and virtuosic canons of the sacred repertoire, that could have begun as games in the choir rooms of many a chapel or cathedral.

A tantalising hint that such transformed puzzles also exist in the secular repertoire comes in Luzzasco Luzzaschi's *Primo libro de madrigali a cinque voci*. Luzzaschi's book was dedicated to Princess Lucrezia d'Este upon her marriage to the Prince of Urbino in 1571, the same year that Agostini's first book of enigmas was published. Two of the five partbooks, the Canto and the Basso, are lost, but much of the character of the pieces may be judged by the remaining

---

[98] *Ibid.*, ii, pp. 1086, 1103–4. Ingegneri's motet was published in his *Sacrarum cantionum cum quatuor vocibus* (Venice, 1586). Vaet's motet is included in his *Modulationes quinque et sex vocum . . . liber secundus* (Venice, 1562), although the enigma version (and presumably Cerone's source) was published as a broadside sheet by Hofhalter in Vienna in 1560; see M. Steinhardt, *Jacobus Vaet and his Motets* (East Lansing, Mich., 1951), pp. 34–5. The enigma version is in three parts; one may assume that a fourth part was added to the motet before its 1562 publication.

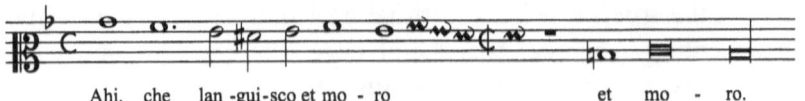

Ahi, che lan-gui-sco et mo - ro   et mo - ro.

Example 4 Conjectural cryptogram for the alto part of *S'all'hor che dolce parla et dolce ride*; Luzzasco Luzzaschi, *Il primo libro de madrigali a cinque voci* (1571)

voices. One of the madrigals, *S'all'hor che dolce parla et dolce ride*, is almost undoubtedly an enigma in which the *risolutione* is carried in the alto (Appendix 2 contains a transcription of the extant parts). The alto line can be condensed into a cryptogram similar to Agostini's (Example 4), but its riddle text would have had to explain the halving of the rests preceding each statement. It could further account for the final halving of note values and the 'coda' at the end; for instance 'Eight *tempi* I must wait before I cry "Ahi che languisco et moro", but my languishing is halved each time I die; my injury is major, but becomes minor – my final death is long and perfect, I rest but once before I speak my last.'

A Ferrarese context

The vernacular enigma attributed to Rore, Luzzaschi's 'solved' enigma and Agostini's collections have a common geographical link in that all their composers were for substantial periods of their lives employed at Ferrara. The Este court had an abiding fascination with games – indoor tennis and tarot cards are among its contributions to Renaissance pastimes.[99] There also appears to have been a familial predilection for merry-making: Borso d'Este was a renowned devotee of the *burla*, and both Alfonso I and Alfonso II earned reputations for youthful and/or childish pranks.[100] During

---

[99] Borso d'Este is said to have had an indoor tennis court in the palazzo at Belriguardo, *c.* 1457; see G. Lubkin, *A Renaissance Court: Milan under Galeazzo Maria Sforza* (Berkeley, 1994). Over one hundred years later, Antonio Scaino published the first written account of the rules of tennis, dedicated to Duke Alfonso II d'Este, in which he draws an extended analogy between the rules of tennis and the rules of musical composition; see A. Scaino, *Trattato del giuoco della palla* (1555), ed. and trans. P. A. Negretti, with facs. repr. (London, 1984), pp. 89–91. Tennis and music spectacle also shared performance conventions and spaces at the Ferrarese court; I am grateful to Cees de Bondt for alerting me to Scaino's treatise and for sharing with me the unpublished manuscript of his article, 'Tennis Entertainment and Tennis Court Theatres'. The Ferrarese origins of *tarocchi* are discussed in M. Dummett, *The Game of Tarot, from Ferrara to Salt Lake City* (London, 1980), pp. 39–50.

[100] On Alfonso I, see A. Bayer, 'Dosso's Public: The Este Court at Ferrara', in P. Humfrey and M. Lucco, *Dosso Dossi: Court Painter in Renaissance Ferrara*, ed. Andrea Bayer (New York, 1998),

'Al gioco si conosce il galantuomo'

Alfonso II's rule, academic games such as those described by Bargagli were particularly fashionable; their practice is reported in Romei's *Discorsi* in its partially fictionalised account of the summer recess of Alfonso's court in 1584.[101] In common with many Renaissance patrons, the Este took great delight in the use of symbolism and double meaning, filtering through to all art forms they patronised: visual, written and musical. The visual symbolism of the Sala dei Mesi in the palace of Schifanoia, commissioned by Borso, is an early manifestation; the thinly disguised portraits of courtiers that populate Torquato Tasso's fable *Aminta* are another.[102] Musical works dedicated to and associated with generations of Este rulers provide dozens of examples.[103] Perhaps the most visible and instantly recognisable to modern scholars are those pieces composed on a *soggetto cavato dalle vocali*; the technique seems to have been admired and fostered at Ferrara. Josquin's *Missa Hercules dux Ferrariae* for Ercole I, and Rore's two similar masses for Ercole II, the *Missa Vivat felix Hercules* and the *Missa Praeter rerum seriem*, rely on subjects based on the hexachordal

---

pp. 27–54. On Alfonso II's Venetian escapades with the future Henri III of France, see P. de Nolhac and A. Solerti, *Il viaggio in Italia di Enrico III, re di Francia* (Turin, 1890), pp. 90–3. Romei's *Discorsi* also gives accounts of numerous practical jokes played by the Duke and the Duchess on their hapless (female) guests.

[101] Alessandro Arcangeli has suggested that the encouragement and visibility of play at the court of Alfonso II had a more serious political and social purpose: 'the successful reinstatement of order and harmony after a cataclysm', referring to the restoration, both physical and metaphysical, of Ferrara after the earthquake of 1570. Commenting on the redecoration of Appartamento dello Specchio in the Castello Estense, which was divided into a 'Saletta dei giuochi' and a 'Salone dei giuochi', Arcangeli notes 'the decoration of the apartment was meant to display and embody a complex project of renewal, where play and a specific Renaissance philosophy of time, with human life interpreted in the light of a cosmic cycle, kept central ground'. Music is among the games depicted on the ceiling of the 'Saletta'. Arcangeli, *Recreation in the Renaissance*, pp. 25–7.

[102] *Aminta*, written in 1573 and first published in 1580/1 in Venice by Aldo Manuzio, contains characters intended to represent certain courtiers – those that can still be identified include Licori (Lucrezia Bendidio), Elpino (Giovanni Battista Pigna), Batto (Giovanni Battista Guarini), Mopso (Speron Speroni) and Tirsi and Aminta (both Tasso himself); T. Tasso, *Aminta*, ed. and trans. C. E. J. Griffiths (Manchester, 1972).

[103] A thorough examination of the hexachordal puzzles fostered at Ferrara is in P. Macey, 'Frescobaldi's Musical Tributes to Ferrara', in K. J. Snyder (ed.), *The Organist as Scholar: Essays in Memory of Russell Saunders* (Stuyvesant, NY, 1994). Another indication of a local appreciation of musical puzzles may be found in Spataro's correspondence regarding his enigmatic motet *Ubi opus est facto*, an explanation of 'which I once made for a friar, prior in Ferrara [*frate prior in Ferara*]', a colleague of fra Benedetto Bellabusta; see *Correspondence of Renaissance Musicians*, ed. Blackburn, Lowinsky and Miller, p. 204. Filippo Nicoletti, a Ferrarese composer who settled in Rome in the early seventeeth century, was also known as an accomplished composer of enigmatic canons; see I. Fenlon, 'Filippo Nicoletti', in *The New Grove Dictionary of Music Online*, ed. L. Macy (http://www.grovemusic.com), accessed 20 Feb. 2003.

realisations of the vowel sounds contained in their textual salutations (e.g., 'Vivat felix Hercules' becomes 'mi fa re mi re ut re').[104] These works also appear to be part of a broader appreciation of hexachordally inspired works. When scrutinising his suitability for the post of *maestro di cappella* in 1502, the abilities of Heinrich Isaac were expressed to Ercole I in terms of the quality and the speed of composition (two days) of his motet *Rogamus te, piisima virgo*, based on the subject 'la mi la sol la sol la mi'.[105] In the following year, Petrucci published a mass on the hexachord, the *Missa ut re mi fa sol la* by Antoine Brumel; in 1505, Alfonso I d'Este recruited Brumel to his *cappella* at Ferrara.[106] Over two generations later, in the 1550s and 1560s, another Este employee, Jacques Brunel, developed further the *inganno* technique of hexachordal transposition and mutation. The technique characterised his keyboard works, and its influence may be seen not only in Agostini's enigmas, but also in many works produced in Ferrara in the last decade of the century, specifically those of Carlo Gesualdo and Luzzaschi's most eminent pupil, Girolamo Frescobaldi.[107]

The musical canon and its potential for multiple meanings were particularly favoured in the visual arts commissioned by members of the Este family. Famously, Ockeghem's canon *Prenez sur moi* appears in the marquetry that adorns Isabella d'Este's *studiolo* in Mantua; another, attributed to Willaert, features in Titian's *The Bacchanal of the Andrians*, which was commissioned by Alfonso I for his *camerino*.[108] A canon which sets the words 'Vivet in aeternum' appears on the title page of Vittorio Orfino's *Musica nova, lamentationi a cinque voci*, printed in Ferrara in 1589 and dedicated to Alfonso II; the canon

---

[104] A. H. Johnson, 'A Musical Offering to Hercules II, Duke of Ferrara', in J. La Rue *et al.* (eds.), *Aspects of Medieval and Renaissance Music: A Birthday Offering to Gustave Reese* (New York, 1966), pp. 448–94.
[105] Macey, 'Frescobaldi's Musical Tributes', p. 213, citing L. Lockwood, 'Josquin at Ferrara: New Documents and Letters', in E. E. Lowinsky and B. J. Blackburn (eds.), *Josquin des Prez: Proceedings of the International Josquin Festival-Conference* (London, 1976), p. 132.
[106] Macey, 'Frescobaldi's Musical Tributes', p. 208.
[107] A. Newcomb, 'The Anonymous Ricercars of the Bourdeney Codex', in A. Silbiger (ed.), *Frescobaldi Studies* (Durham, NC, 1987), pp. 97–123. Fourteen of Brunel's ricercars are edited in *The Ricercars of the Bourdeney Codex*; ed. A. Newcomb (Recent Researches in the Music of the Renaissance, 89; Madison, 1991).
[108] On Isabella d'Este, see I. Fenlon, 'Music and Learning in Isabella d'Este's *Studioli*', in C. Mozzarelli, R. Oresko and L. Ventura (eds.), *The Court of the Gonzaga in the Age of Mantegna: 1450–1550* (Rome, 1997), pp. 353–68; on the Titian painting, see Lowinsky, 'Music in Titian's *The Bacchanal of the Andrians*'.

'Al gioco si conosce il galantuomo'

served as a hopeful symbol of the perpetuity of the Este family (Alfonso was, and remained, childless).[109] One artwork epitomises the Este fascination with musical symbolism: the *Allegory of Music* of Dosso Dossi, which dates from around 1522. The picture shows a male figure hammering notes on an anvil together with two female figures, each supporting a tablet upon which has been inscribed a canon, one circular and one triangular. The male figure has been interpreted variously as Tubalcain or Vulcan; the women as Zillah and Naamah, a dual representation of Venus, the embodiments of sacred and secular music, or even instrumental and vocal music. While the circular canon remains unattributed, the triangular canon is the Agnus Dei canon from Josquin's *Missa L'homme armé super voces musicales*.[110] Although the painting's precise provenance is unknown, it certainly hung in the ducal palace in 1598, and it is likely to have been a commission by Alfonso I who, owing at least in part to his interest in the art of metalwork and foundry, was frequently identified with and represented by Vulcan. Both Tubalcain and Vulcan were blacksmiths: in the Christian tradition, Tubalcain and his half-brother Jubal were the inventors of music; in the classical tradition, Pythagoras came to understand the science of acoustics and harmony through listening to the hammering of smiths.

Ferrara's passion for musical allegories encouraged the production of numerous works of art whose multiple meanings invited careful and inventive consideration. Agostini's enigmas may be another legacy of this culture, but since they were primarily published in the early 1570s, and his formal employment at the court did not begin until later in the decade, this may be impossible to prove.[111] Nevertheless, the evidence of his dedications shows that

[109] The significance of this canon, and others placed on title pages, is discussed in F. Dennis, 'Music and Print: Book Production and Consumption in Ferrara, 1534–1597' (Ph.D. thesis, University of Cambridge, 2002), pp. 150–2.
[110] Numerous studies of this painting exist. Of interest to musicologists are particularly F. Camiz, 'Due quadri "musicali" del Dosso', in A. Cavicchi (ed.), *Frescobaldi e il suo tempo* (Venice, 1983), pp. 85–91; H. C. Slim, 'Dosso Dossi's Allegory at Florence about Music', *Journal of the American Musicological Society*, 43 (1990), pp. 43–98; and J. Haar, 'Music as Visual Language', in I. Lavin (ed.), *Meaning in the Visual Arts: Views from the Outside. A Centennial Commemoration of Erwin Panofsky (1892–1968)* (Princeton, 1995), pp. 265–84.
[111] We cannot discount the possibility that Agostini was more closely involved with the court and/or the cathedral than records show. One contemporary commentator on the legislation that prevented Agostini from holding office at the cathedral suggests that musicians and

he was at the periphery of Ferrarese society from as early as 1570, and certainly by the time the second book of enigmas appeared in 1581, Agostini was firmly established in a court position. Luzzaschi's *S'all'hor che dolce parla et dolce ride* shows that secular madrigal enigmas were known in Ferrara in 1571; it seems highly likely that both his and Agostini's puzzles belong to the same courtly practice.

Agostini's enigmas have resonances with the works of another Ferrarese composer, Girolamo Frescobaldi, and in the correspondences between the two repertoires we may clearly see the musical legacy of the Este fascination with symbolism, riddles and *soggetti*. Frescobaldi's *Capricci* of 1624, dedicated to Don Alfonso d'Este, Prince of Modena, and his *Fiori musicali* of 1635 demonstrate the younger composer's fascination with the *contrapunto con obbligo* and the hexachordal techniques so favoured by his forebears.[112] The *Capricci* are largely based on *obblighi* stemming from works composed at Ferrara, and they include several on hexachordal subjects, making them instrumental counterparts to Agostini's enigmas. But a more striking correspondence is found in the *Fiori musicali*. The subject of the second ricercar is given in perfect breves before the full four-part counterpoint, with the instruction 'Quinta parte si placet'. The subject phrase is intended to be sung as an obbligato, but no clues are given as to how or when it should be inserted. Its hexachordal syllables (re re fa mi la re), with their consonant sounds rearranged, translate to 'Ferrara lì m[i]a fè' (Ferrara, there is my faith). A cryptic comment, 'Intendami chi può, che m'intend'io' ('Understand me who can, for I understand myself') is added underneath the canto part. The phrase comes from Canzone 105 (the *canzone-frottolata*) of Petrarch's *Rime*, 'Mai non vo' più cantar com'io soleva'.[113] Patrick Macey suggests that key passages from the canzone provide a context for Frescobaldi's unhappiness in Rome, and perhaps further express his loyalty to Ferrarese/Este patronage (note the reference to the Po river):

---

singers were exempted, leading to the possibilities that as a child Agostini may have been educated at the *duomo* and as an adult he may have been able to find casual employment that did not have to be explicitly recorded. See Durante and Martellotti, *Madrigali segreti*, i, p. 90.

[112] The contents of both books are discussed in Macey, 'Frescobaldi's Musical Tributes'.

[113] F. Petrarca, *Canzoniere*, ed. Alberto Chiari (Rome, 1992), pp. 199–204. 'Fio' may be variously translated as 'son', 'fief', 'end', 'vassal' or 'tribute'. A multiplicity of interpretations undoubtedly was intended.

'Al gioco si conosce il galantuomo'

[lines 1–3]
Mai non vo' più cantar com'io soleva
ch'altri no m'intenda, ond'ebbi scorno,
et puossi in bel soggiorno esser molesto.
[lines 16–21]
I' die' in guarda a san Pietro; or non più, no.
Intendami chi pò, ch'i' m'intend'io.
Grave soma è un mal fio a mantenerlo;
quanto posso, mi spetro, et sol mi sto.
Fetonte odo che 'n Po cadde, et morìo;
et già di là dal rio passato è 'l merlo.

I no longer wish to sing again as I used to,
since no one understands me, hence I was scorned,
and one can be vexed in a beautiful place . . .
I trusted Saint Peter, now, no more, no,
understand me who can, for I understand myself;
an evil tribute is a heavy load to bear.
As much as I can, I free [un-petrify] myself and stand alone;
I hear that Phaethon fell in the Po and died;
and already the blackbird has gone from the brook.

The entire canzone is obscure, full of double meanings and oblique references. It may have had a particular value in Ferrarese circles for these qualities. Tasso both praises and decries it; while he appreciates its more subtle use of metaphor and aphorism, he condemns its 'too obscure metaphors, those that resemble enigma[s]' ('metafore troppo oscure, le quali paiono enigma').[114] But more significantly, the line Frescobaldi quotes, 'Intendami chi può, chi m'intend'io', is also the text of the subject phrase of Agostini's enigma *Madonna un mio pensiero*, published in the *Enigmi musicali* of 1571. The canzone may have had special significance for Agostini in the years leading up to the publication of the book; at that time he also had reason to mistrust Rome, perhaps under the cloud of the revocation of his dispensation to work at Ferrara cathedral. Frescobaldi was scarcely seven years old when Agostini died, but his appropriation of the Petrarchan phrase, along with his use of *contrapunto con obbligo* in works so specifically linked with Ferrara, could indicate that he knew Luzzaschi's and Agostini's enigmas, and understood their importance as expressions of Ferrarese culture.

[114] Tasso, *Discorso del poema eroico*, Book 6, ii, p. 350: '[Grazia] Nasce ancora dalla traslazione o dalla metafora, la quale s'accommoda ancora in questa forma, come in que' versi del Petrarca: Una chiusa bellezza . . . E dalle parole basse e volgari suol nascere alcuna volta il grazioso, e da' proverbi più che dall'altre, comme nella istessa canzone del Petrarca'; and Book 4, ii, p. 293.

Laurie Stras

CONCLUSION

Agostini's *enigmi musicali* are ultimately difficult, if not impossible, to categorise. They are neither just games, nor just musical compositions; they lie on the fringes of both categories. In composing and promulgating the genre, Agostini drew on and catered for a wide range of practices and traditions. As an entertainment, a musical enigma could provide a medium for technical and intellectual display; a source of laughter or the basis of a practical joke; a springboard for philosophical discussion; or a cover for titillation. As a musical work, it could provide a diverting method for teaching and testing notation; a demonstration of its creator's expertise; or a means of developing the musician's spiritual self. With all these multiple uses and potential ways of valuing musical enigmas, it is perhaps surprising that more are not found in print. However, it should be remembered that the skills necessary for the playing of the game – whether it be finding the solution or simply appreciating the puzzle's novelty and ingenuity – were not necessarily within the grasp of a wide audience. Agostini's enigmas are specialist toys, and their publication may well have been meant to signify not only their composer's abilities but their dedicatees' as well.

One should also consider that Agostini's enigmas, unlike many other musical puzzles circulating at the time, were clearly performative material. Sergio Durante comments that the Roman school of *artificioso* composition that developed soon after Agostini's death produced a repertoire that was 'almost without precedent', in that it was produced by composers, for composers, and not intended primarily for performance.[115] The suggestion that a composer might intentionally give the outcome in performance a lesser priority in composition *con obbligo* occurs also in Zarlino:

> I do not suggest that such writing be a norm but that it should be used when suitable, as when a composer wishes to demonstrate his ingenuity and quickness of thought to those who look only for such qualities and are devoid of other interests. These methods are indeed ingenious, even though they may lead on occasion to some strange effects.[116]

Nonetheless, it could be said that not only were Agostini's enigmas intended to be savoured in performance, but also the very

---

[115] Durante, 'On *Artificioso* Compositions', p. 200.
[116] Zarlino, *The Art of Counterpoint*, p. 220.

'Al gioco si conosce il galantuomo'

act of savouring them was intrinsic to the participating courtier's performance of his or her sprezzatura, and essential to the game. Agostini's secular enigmas also initiated their players into an otherwise esoteric world, giving them a new or different sphere in which to adopt Berger's 'sprezzatura of the enclosure'. Agostini both enabled and extended the arena for the expression of sprezzatura on behalf of his dedicatees; but by bringing the musical enigma out of the realm of the esoteric into the realm of the amateur, he also found an ideal conduit for his own sprezzatura. Instead of retaining his puzzles for private consumption, or presenting them to his dedicatees in singular, manuscript form – which seems to have been by far the more common way for puzzles to circulate – he published them through commercial printing houses, thereby giving ample demonstration to both his ingenuity and his willingness to broadcast his works as public commodities.

Agostini's enigmatic self – the priest's bastard, the Pope's anointed, one duke's tutor, another's *cappellano* – is present in his works, yet his position, both as a member of Alfonso's court and as a composer of vocal music in the late sixteenth century, is still difficult to define. Certainly, one may 'recognise the gentleman in the game', as the proverb dictates, and it could be that his rise from being a nomad cleric seeking tutorial positions in houses of the minor nobility (as is suggested by the dedications of the *Enigmi musicali* and the *Secondo libro a quattro voci*) to Protonotary Apostolic and member of the Ferrarese musical elite was entirely due to how well he played the courtier's game of self-advancement. However, several aspects of his history suggest a more specialised role, one that combined the activities of cleric, scholar, musician and jester. The phenomenon of the priest-fool, the non-fictional Friar Tuck, was common at Italian Renaissance courts, and the Este family were patrons of several, including a Fra Stephano and one of the most celebrated jesters of the Renaissance, Fra Serafino.[117] Many jesters were employed specifically for the job, and their duties frequently included musical performance. However, others came by a reputation as a jester through fulfilling other duties at court, while providing material for court entertainments or initiating comical situations, as did the Englishman John Skelton at the court of Henry

[117] Burke, 'Frontiers of the Comic', p. 62; Otto, *Fools Are Everywhere*, pp. 55, 94, 172.

VIII, and the Scot George Buchanan at the court of James VI. Both these academic men were initially tutors to their rulers, and became court poets; Skelton was additionally a cleric, Buchanan a counsellor.[118] Seen in the light of one who could be simultaneously learned, pious and humorous, Agostini's possible connections with the Franciscan community are provocative; humorists who were also Minorites could be seen to be simply carrying out the wishes of Saint Francis, who desired that all preachers should be 'God's jesters'.[119]

Perhaps this was the background to Agostini's role in the various social circles to which he belonged, as a sort of arbiter of 'honest' entertainment whose works provided sanctioned and enriching games, offensive to no one because of their source. The way he is presented (or presents himself) as a composer in his books accepts, if not openly advertises, the duality inherent in his being a man who has devoted himself to both divine and earthly pleasures. Four encomia of Agostini preface his second book of enigmas, embracing both sacred and profane aspects of his work, and honouring them equally. They draw on classical mythology, and even Plato's *Phaedo*, for their imagery, but they are also careful to reference his clerical status.[120] The first of the sonnets is in general praise of Agostini, attesting to his music's restorative powers:[121]

> Maraviglia non è se Primavera
> Si scorge nel tuo dolce, e grave aspetto
> Piena di gioia, e colma di diletto,
> Di fiori adorna, ed a ragione altera.
> Nè se per dolce invidia a schiera a schiera
> Volan gl'augeli al tuo cantar eletto
> Soave garreggiando, e con effetto
> Tua gran virtù scoprendo unica, e vera.
> Tu del sangue AGOSTINI ò LODOVICO
> Co 'l bel compor dell'Armonia celeste
> L'affanno scemi, e s'ode l'E[c]ho in Cielo,
> Ne testimonio sol di quanto io dico

---

[118] Otto, *ibid.*, pp. 7, 179–80.
[119] *Ibid.*, p. 169. The Franciscan San Bernardino of Siena, who was venerated at the Ferrarese convent of Corpus Domini by Caterina Vegri (later S. Caterina of Bologna) and to whom its daughter house was dedicated, was celebrated for his humour and practical jokes.
[120] The authors are identifed, but the names are suspiciously quasi-academic, as they are all toponymic – 'l'Albanese', 'l'Alatrini', 'il Nolano' – although curiously none of the locations are northern Italian. Perhaps this suggests a community drawn from a wider pool than local gentry – an ecclesiastical community, a scholastic, or a musical one?
[121] Agostini, *L'Echo, et enigmi*, [iii]. The sonnet is credited to 'l'Albanese'.

> 'Al gioco si conosce il galantuomo'
>
> È l'human stuol, ma perciò solo meste[122]
> Le Muse insieme, co 'l signor di Delo.
>
> It is not a marvel if Spring
> is perceived in your sweet and serious face
> full of joy, and brimming with delight,
> adorned with flowers, and with lofty reason.
> Nor if, out of sweet envy, in flock upon flock
> the birds take flight at your choice song,
> sweetly competing, and with effect
> revealing your great virtue, unique and true.
> You, of the Agostini blood, o Lodovico,
> with [your] beautiful composition of heavenly harmony
> lessen weariness, and an echo is heard in heaven.
> Nor is the only witness of that of which I speak
> the human race; but for that reason alone sad [are]
> the muses, together with the lord of Delos.

Another sonnet by the same author invokes the image of Vulcan, who was also the cuckolded husband of Venus, forging Love's arrows and singing 'ut, re, mi, fa, sol, la', as a comparison to Agostini. The language of this poem is clearly equivocal; within the first eight lines *martello*, *saetta* and *penello* all are common euphemisms for penis, and the implications of the hexachordal syllables would not have been lost on Agostini's friends. The comparison to Vulcan no doubt had resonances for the Ferrarese, seemingly equating Agostini with his ruler's grandfather, Alfonso I, and recalling Dosso's painting. Yet the poet also accentuates his lowly birthright, and by calling him 'debile et humile', he provides further resonance with his clerical position and possible connections to the Franciscans.[123]

> Percotendo Vulcan co 'l suo martello
> Le saette d'Amor, lieto cantava
> UT, RE, MI, FA, SOL, LA; poi ritornava
> LA, SOL, FA, MI, RE, UT; hor questo hor quello.
> Indi tutto gioioso co 'l penello
> Della sua dolce lingua disegnava
> Il vero oggetto suo; ond'ei sperava
> Trarne gloria maggior, preggio più bello.
> Cosi mirando in te spirto gentile,
> Sublime fra gli ingegni pelegrini,
> Dissi cotai, o simili parole:
> Porgi al Principio tu debile, e humile
> Il colmo di splendor, poiche sei il sole

---

[122] Original has 'N'è testimonio sol di quanto io dico / E l'human stuol . . .'.
[123] Agostini, *L'Echo, et enigmi*, [iii].

Dell'Armonia, e honor degli AGOSTINI.
Vulcan, forging with his hammer
Love's arrows, gaily sang
'ut, re, mi, fa, sol, la'; then returned,
'la, sol, fal, mi, re, ut'; now this, now that.
Then all joyfully with the brush
of his beautiful voice [tongue] drew
his true object; from which he hoped
to draw greater glory, a more beautiful prize.
Thus, seeing in you, gentle spirit
sublime among searching intellects,
I said these, or similar words:
'Give to your meek, humble beginning
the summit of splendour, because you are the sun
of Harmony, and the honour of the Agostini.'

Another claims that Agostini's music surpasses the discoveries of Pythagoras or the music of Socrates (as imagined by Plato), and says that he possesses the 'most dear and precious styles ... of human, divine and mixed song' (by mixed we may suppose a fusion of human and divine).[124]

Non Pitagora più dè gloriarsi
Coi martelli fabrili haver trovato
Gli Armonici concenti. Non più Plato
Di Socrate prigion deve vantarsi,
Che sognando ripreso, ad accostarsi,
Al Musical negotio; onde beato
Fora; più notti al Ciel l'occhio hebbe alzato
E à l'Armonia celeste in tutto darsi,
Poscia, che i più preggiati stili, e cari
MONSIGNOR AGOSINI [sic] hoggi tenete
Del Human, del Divin, del misto Canto.
Voi sacro, e Dotto; voi portate il vanto
Di conoscer questa arte; anzi splendete
Qual sol, fra più fam[os]i autori, e gravi.

No more should Pythagoras glorify himself
for having discovered, with blacksmiths' hammers,
the consonances of harmony. No more can Plato
boast of Socrates in prison,
who, having been admonished in his sleep
to set about the labour of music whereby he should be blessed,
many a night kept his eye raised to heaven and
gave himself entirely to heavenly harmony.
Since, that the most precious and dear styles,
Monsignor Agostini, today you possess,

---

[124] *Ibid.* The sonnet is credited to 'Il Nolano'. The reference to Socrates composing music in prison is from Plato, *Phaedo*, 60 D–61 B.

'Al gioco si conosce il galantuomo'

> of human, divine and mixed song;
> you sacred, and learned, you can boast
> of understanding this art; you shine,
> as a sun, amongst the most famous and serious authors.

The last describes Apollo revisiting the spot where Phaethon fell out of the carriage into the River Po, i.e., at Ferrara, being struck by Agostini's music; Agostini then usurps Apollo as the God of music and the giver of light:[125]

> Fermato 'l Carro havea 'l Gran sir de Delo
> Ne la Riva amenissima del Fiume,
> In cui l'audace, e mal rettor del lume
> Cadde, percosso dal irato Telo.
> Intento all'Armonia ch'infonde 'l Cielo
> Nel caro albergo d'ogni bel costume
> Ne 'l Musico AGOSTIN celeste nume,
> Al cui dolce cantar s'infiamma il Gelo.
> Onde Giove che 'l Ciel di luce privo
> Vedea, gridò, ch'il nostro lum' confonde?
> Ch'ardisce d'Ecelissar il mio bel sole?
> Un huom, che per virtù s'è fatto divo
> Fa questo effetto (il nuntio gli risponde),
> Monsignor LODOVICO così vuole.

> The great lord of Delos, having stopped the carriage
> at the most pleasant bank of the river,
> in which the audacious and bad ruler of the light
> fell, struck by the irate God.
> Intent upon the harmony that infused the sky
> in the sweet resting-place of all beautiful manners
> in the musician Agostini, heavenly being,
> at whose sweet song ice ignites.
> Thus Jove, who saw that Heaven was deprived of
> light, cried, 'Who has confounded our light?
> Who dares to eclipse my beautiful sun?'
> 'A man, who by virtue has made himself divine,
> makes this effect', the messenger responded,
> 'Monsignor LODOVICO wills it so.'

These four sonnets present Agostini as a gifted master, worthy of praise by men who knew their classics and who, presumably, knew their music, but they also reveal more about the way he was viewed by their society. The circumstances of his parentage were no secret, but the first sonnet shows that his musical expertise was perceived as a way in which he had redressed the social balance, providing, as he could, something of value to the culture. Furthermore, the writers

---

[125] Agostini, *L'Echo, et enigmi*, [iii]. The sonnet is credited to 'l'Alatrini'.

intentionally underscore his vocation by referring to him as 'Monsignor', perhaps showing that this quality also earned him and his music greater esteem. The many oppositions and multiplicities that pervade Agostini's works seem also to infiltrate his social position. If we try to understand him and his music as the embodiment of the *piacevole/grave* oxymoron, as the performance of equivocation, concealment and revelation, then we may begin to understand and appreciate his works in the spirit in which they were intended.

University of Southampton

'Al gioco si conosce il galantuomo'

APPENDIX 1
Un mal è che mi rende afflitto e mesto

Lodovico Agostini, *Enigmi musicali* (1571)

Laurie Stras

'Al gioco si conosce il galantuomo'

'Al gioco si conosce il galantuomo'

Laurie Stras

APPENDIX 2
S'all'hor che dolce parla et dolce ride (extant voices only)

Luzzasco Luzzaschi, *Il primo libro de madrigali a cinque voci* (1571)

'Al gioco si conosce il galantuomo'

For EU product safety concerns, contact us at Calle de José Abascal, 56–1º,
28003 Madrid, Spain or eugpsr@cambridge.org.

www.ingramcontent.com/pod-product-compliance
Lightning Source LLC
LaVergne TN
LVHW091532060526
838200LV00036B/581